THE
AMERICAN ALPINE
JOURNAL

This page: David Gottlieb on the first ascent of Beyul,
in Nepal's Rolwaling Valley [p. 49]. *Joe Puryear*
Cover: On the first pitch of Seagull's Garden, Red Wall, not far from
Upernavik, West Greenland [p. 24]. *Bob Shepton Collection*

On the first ascent of the Northeast Pillar of
Augusta, Yukon, Canada [p. 125]. *Manu Pelliss*
GMHM

2011   Volume 53   Issue 85

CONTENTS

16 I-TO, by Katsutaka "Jumbo" Yokoyama

The first ascent of the immense south face of Mt. Logan, Canada.

24 DoDo's Delight, by Bob Shepton

The Wild Bunch slays one virgin wall after another on the Greenland 2010 – Tilman International expedition.

34 The Rose of No-Man's Land, by Bruce Normand

Eight days under threat on the east face of Mt. Edgar, in Sichuan, yields a route almost too dangerous to be proud of.

43 Season Finale, by Alex Honnold

In today's Yosemite, a good half-day is an ascent of Half Dome and El Cap, both solo. But climbing three El Cap routes still takes a full day.

49 Takargo, Joe Puryear

Nepal's Rolwaling Valley delivers a paradise of unclimbed waterfall ice and a 6,771-meter virgin summit.

58 The Serpent King, by Malcolm Bass

The first ascent of the west face of Vasuki Parbat, India.

70 Dracula, by Bjørn-Eivind Aartun

Seventy-one sleepless hours during a first ascent on the southeast face of Mt. Foraker, in the Alaska Range.

77 Journeys to Western Sichuan, by Tamotsu Nakamura

A return visit to the Shaluli Shan reveals troublesome changes in the mostly unclimbed peaks of the Litang Plateau, China.

CLIMBS AND EXPEDITIONS

88 Contiguous United States
106 Alaska
125 Canada
140 Greenland
158 Venezuela, Guyana, Brazil
164 Peru, Bolivia
171 Argentina, Chile
189 Antarctica
204 Middle East (Turkey, Oman)
212 Africa (Canary Islands, Mali, Chad)
219 Norway
226 CIS (Russia, Georgia, Tajikistan, Kazakhstan)
234 Kyrgyzstan
256 Afghanistan
269 Pakistan
285 India
312 Nepal
340 China
354 Tibet
359 Laos
362 AAC Grants

364 **Book Reviews, edited by David Stevenson**

New books by Steve "Crusher" Bartlett, Ron Fawcett, Frederic Hartemann & Robert Hauptman, Jennifer Jordan, Royal Robbins, Jane Sievert & Jennifer Ridgeway, Norman Schaefer, Stephen E. Schmid, Joseph E. Taylor III, and Freddie Wilkinson.

377 **In Memoriam, edited by Cameron M. Burns**

Remembering Ross Bronson, Rich Jack, Christian Pruchnic, Joseph Puryear, Lorna Ream, and Douglas Zimmerman.

384 **Club Activities, edited by Frederick O. Johnson**

390 **Index**

400 **International Grade Comparison Chart**

Submission guidelines, expanded reports, additional photos, topos, and comments are available at aaj.americanalpineclub.org.

Yasushi Okada during the first day on the south face of Mt. Logan, Canada [p. 16]. *Katsutaka Yokoyama*

James Pearson and Mark Synnott prepare for the final pillar during their first ascent of the Wine Bottle in Chad's Ennedi Desert [p. 215]. *Jimmy Chin*

Industry Partners

of the

AMERICAN ALPINE
JOURNAL

*We thank the following for their generous
financial support:*

SUMMIT PARTNER

BENEFACTOR

PATRONS

ARC'TERYX

Black Diamond

MOUNTAIN GEAR

Friends
of the
AMERICAN ALPINE JOURNAL

*We thank the following for their generous
financial support:*

BENEFACTORS
Yvon Chouinard
H. Adams Carter American Alpine Journal Fund

PATRONS
Gordon A. Benner, M.D.
William A. Burd
Ann Carter
Richard E. Hoffman, M.D.
John R. Kascenska, II
Edith Overly
Glenn E. Porzak
Mark A. Richey

SUPPORTERS
R. J. Campbell
Jim Edwards
Z. Wayne Griffin
William R. Kilpatrick, M.D.
Verne and Marion Read
Steve Schwartz

SPECIAL THANKS
Samuel C. Silverstein, M.D.

Kate Rutherford during a bivy on the summit of Fitz Roy after a new route [p. 182]. Mikey Schaefer

The American Alpine Journal, 710 Tenth St. Suite 100, Golden, Colorado 80401
Telephone: (303) 384-0110 Fax: (303) 384-0111 E-mail: aaj@americanalpineclub.org
www.americanalpineclub.org

ISSN: 0065-6925   ISBN: 978-1-933056-71-5   ISBN: (e-book) 978-1-933056-72-2

The American Alpine Journal

John Harlin III, *Editor*

Senior Editor
Kelly Cordes

Associate Editor
Lindsay Griffin

Art Director
Daniel Gambino

Contributing Editors
Cameron M. Burns, *In Memoriam*
Frederick O. Johnson, *Club Activities*
David Stevenson, *Book Reviews*

Copy Editors
Joe Kelsey, *Climbs & Expeditions Asia*
Katy Klutznick, *Climbs & Expeditions Americas*
Erik Lambert, *Climbs & Expeditions Various*

Translators
Luca Calvi
Peter Jensen-Choi
Todd Miller
Tamotsu Nakamura
Ekaterina Vorotnikova

Indexers
Ralph Ferrara, Eve Tallman

Regional Contacts
Mark Westman and Steve Gruhn, *Alaska*; Matt Perkins,
Washington Cascades; Drew Brayshaw and Don Serl,
Coast Mountains, BC; Raphael Slawinski, *Canadian
Rockies*; Cheo García, *Venezuela*; Sergio Ramírez
Carrascal, Peru; Rolando Garibotti, *Patagonia*; Damien
Gildea, *Antarctica*; Marten Blixt, *Norway*; Harish
Kapadia, *India*; Elizabeth Hawley and Richard Salisbury,
Nepal; Tamotsu Nakamura, *Japanese expeditions*; Peter
Jensen-Choi, *Korean expeditions*; Anna Piunova, *CIS
expeditions*; Lindsay Griffin, *Earth*

With additional thanks to
Dr. Tom Hackett, Dr. Tom Clanton, Tommy & Becca
Caldwell, Suzy Newlon Cordes, Pedro Detjan, Yang
Dongdong, Tony Higgins, Sean Isaac, Dave Nettle, Bruce
Normand, Christine Pae, Marc Piche, Mikey Schaefer

MIX
Paper from
responsible sources
FSC® C004191
www.fsc.org

THE AMERICAN ALPINE CLUB

OFFICIALS FOR THE YEAR 2011
*Directors ex-officio

EXECUTIVE COMMITTEE

HONORARY PRESIDENT
William Lowell Putnam

PRESIDENT
Steven J. Swenson*

VICE PRESIDENT
Charles B. Franks*

HONORARY TREASURER
Theodore (Sam) Streibert

SECRETARY
Paul Gagner*

TREASURER
Jack Tackle*

DIRECTORS

TERMS ENDING 2012
Ellen Lapham
John R. Kascenska
Eric Simonson
Doug Colwell
Roanne Miller
Rob BonDurant

TERMS ENDING 2013
Cody J Smith
A. Travis Spitzer
Pete Takeda
Mark Kroese
George Lowe III

TERMS ENDING 2014
Doug Walker
Dave Riggs
Clark Gerhardt
Jim Logan

SECTION CHAIRS

Alaska
Harry Hunt & James Brady
Blue Ridge
Simon Carr
Cascade
Roger Strong
Deep South
Chadwick Hagan
Great Lakes
Bill Thompson
Heartland
Jeremy Collins

New England
Nancy Savickas & Rick Merritt
New York
Philip Erard
North Central
Mark Jobman
Northern Rockies
Brian Cabe
Oregon
John Connor & Graham Williams
Sierra Nevada
Tom Burch

**Southern
Appalachian**
David Thoenen
Southwest
James Pinter-Lucke
Tetons
Brenton Reagan
Western Slope
Jim Donini
Wyoming
Don Foote

EDITORS

THE AMERICAN ALPINE JOURNAL
John Harlin III

**ACCIDENTS IN NORTH AMERICAN
MOUNTAINEERING**
John E. (Jed) Williamson

STAFF

Executive Director – Phil Powers
Director of Operations/CFO – Penn Burris
**Information/
Marketing Director** – Erik Lambert
Community Programs Director – Deanne Buck
Development Director - Keegan Young
Development Officer – Sarah Blair
IT Director – Craig Hoffman
**Membership Manager &
Grants Administrator** – Janet Miller

Membership Coordinator – Lauren Shockey
Content & Marketing Manager – Luke Bauer
Bookkeeper – Carol Kotchck
Library Director – Beth Heller
Assistant Librarian – Alex Depta
Ranch Manager – Robert Montague
**Pacific Northwest Regional
Coordinator** - Eddie Espinosa
Museum Director – Shelby Arnold

Leo Houlding on the crux pitch of The Prophet, his and Jason Pickles's new free line on El Capitan, Yosemite [p. 90].
Tom Evans

PREFACE

Here come the helicopters

Last summer I was 10 days into a 100-day circumnavigation of the borders of Switzerland when a body-sized block of rock slid off its perch and took me down with it. My fall was stopped after 50 feet when the rope fortuitously caught on a flake, but by then I'd fractured both feet. Out came the cell phone. An hour later a helicopter circled in with my rescuers; an hour after that a long-line cable whisked me off to the hospital, then came back to pick up my partner. It felt wonderfully civilized, at least until the bill arrived.

Helicopter rescues in the Alps are a marvel of efficiency. If you're properly insured (as most Europeans are) you take them for granted. If you survive your fall, weather permitting, you'll be in the hospital that afternoon. Of course this leads to abuse; I've seen people lifted off the north face of the Eiger because they were tired and the weather looked discouraging. While there are style and ethical issues about when it's acceptable to call for a "rescue," many people expect a helicopter in the Alps like they'd expect an ambulance in a city.

But what about the Himalaya or the Karakoram or the Andes? We don't go to these mountain ranges to find the First World life. We go, or at least we used to, in large part to experience ancient ways, to feel remote, cast off in time, in touch with a more traditional way of being. And to climb peaks that are so big and wild that we're on our own up there, reliant entirely and exclusively on ourselves and our partners. We don't, or didn't, even want the safety net of the Alps. It was *supposed* to be serious.

The editors of the *AAJ* have been discussing whether to publish an article about helicopter use in the Himalaya ever since 2005, when Tomaz Humar called for a rescue from Nanga Parbat. Some people were grumbling that if you're going to solo in the Himalaya and get in trouble, maybe you should just "suck it up and die."

We editors dithered, not least because we realized that modernity is coming to the big mountains. Still, there's much to think about, and this year we were enraged and engaged afresh by developments in Nepal, which Elizabeth Hawley summarizes on pages 312 and 334. And consider Simone Moro's comments in an interview on planetmountain.com: "Many of these [rescue] calls come from people who perhaps could avoid getting into trouble in the first place, people who shouldn't really be on these gigantic mountains. I see people who are simply too close to their limits.... I don't want to sound arrogant, but unfortunately that's the way things are." And then consider that Moro, both a top-notch Himalayan veteran and a helicopter pilot himself, plans to help develop an efficient rescue service for Nepal.

I dislike the Alpification of the Himalaya and other remote ranges. But if I were dangling from one of its peaks with broken feet and Moro's chopper-ride-to-life was a mere phone call away?

John Harlin III
Editor

Photo: A body being transported in 2011 from Manaslu to Samagaon, Nepal. *Simone Moro Collection*
Inset: Rescuers arriving for John Harlin on the Aiguilles Rouge du Mont Dolent, Switzerland. *Cameron Burns*

If you like the AAJ, you'll love the AAJ Online. There you'll find extra panoramic photos, topos, longer reports, and more. Space in the printed AAJ is very tight, so we can't include everything. When you find a report about a place you're interested in, be sure to check out aaj.americanalpineclub.org; you might find a lot more good info. You can also leave comments and see corrections.

The American Alpine Club
From the 2010 Annual Report.

2010: The birth of a new AAC. As we continued to grow membership and deliver on our mission, we also devoted extraordinary effort to the foundations of our new Five-year Strategic Plan. Indeed, "Double Duty" is the phrase that best defines fiscal 2010 for The American Alpine Club.

2010 was an extremely busy year in the policy arena. We worked with Yosemite National Park on the Merced River Plan and found climber-friendly solutions to the cliff closures in Minnewaska State Park, New York. Denali and Rainier National Parks both proposed substantial increases to their special-use climber fees. We worked very hard—and successfully—to obtain a public process to debate those intentions. Rainier finally settled on $43, an increase at the lowest end of their proposed range. We are still working hard on the Denali issue and will continue to press for more transparent and iterative processes when climbers are singled out for special fees.

Craggin' Classics multiplied out to three new locations (New Paltz, Chattanooga, Truckee), and we continued to learn that local engagement is the most essential ingredient to successful events. At our 2010 Annual Benefit Dinner we announced that future benefit dinners would move around the country (2011 Seattle & 2012 Boston) as part of our goal to deliver more programs locally. Climber and business leader Jim Collins was our 2010 keynote speaker. His remarks were particularly fitting as the AAC enters this exciting time of change.

The American Mountaineering Museum hosted its first Hall of Mountaineering Excellence Gala and Awards Dinner. Bob Craig and Yvon Chouinard were inducted as the first recipients of this new award along with posthumous inductees Bob Bates and Charlie Houston. Ed Viesturs was the keynote speaker for a wonderful evening that also raised $15,000 and led to a year in which the museum was fully self-funded.

Just next door, the AAC Library shelved the first half of its new 30,000-volume Central Asia Library, plus new guidebooks and one-of-a-kind archives. With the help of volunteer Jason Albert, the AAC Story Project—a collection of podcast interviews with notable climbers'—launched in September 2010, heralding our efforts to put more resources online.

The Grand Teton Climbers' Ranch had a very good year in which its total revenues completely covered its direct expenses. Part I of our climbers' exchange with Iran was hosted in the Tetons and was a tremendous success, and GTCR Work Week again pulled in eager climbers who improved basic amenities. 2010 was John Clegg's last year as Ranch Manager. The torch passes to his Assistant Manager, the enthusiastic Robert Montague. The Ranch also supported our continued distribution of free Restop bags in the Tetons as part of our larger conservation work.

The year's conservation highlight was hosting Exit Strategies: a conference on managing human waste in Wilderness. Roger Robinson was tireless in organizing a gathering of scientists, land managers and NGO leaders from over 17 countries to talk

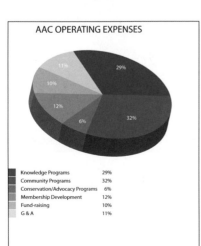

AAC OPERATING EXPENSES

Knowledge Programs	29%
Community Programs	32%
Conservation/Advocacy Programs	6%
Membership Development	12%
Fund-raising	10%
G & A	11%

about this important issue in a three-day conference held in Golden.

AAC Research Grants, along with the Nikwax Alpine Bellwether Grant, gave away a total of $11,700 to 18 researchers for research work in 2010. And AAC Climbing Grants totaled $27,700 to 23 individuals.

2010 also cemented the case for substantial change at the AAC. We had another year in which—while membership revenue grew by 5%—retention waned, and we spent a greater share of our total budget acquiring new members to replace the old. This, combined with expenses associated with the outreach to build the Strategic Plan, led to an operating loss of $75,596. 2010 was financially difficult and a terrible year for non-profits. I do not, however, attribute our loss to the economy. Instead, it is a clear statement that the AAC's relevance to the climbing community and value for members was not what it needed to be. That had to change.

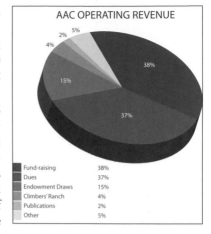

AAC OPERATING REVENUE

Fund-raising	38%
Dues	37%
Endowment Draws	15%
Climbers' Ranch	4%
Publications	2%
Other	5%

Looking Ahead

2009 was the year we solidly determined it was time to remake the AAC to be more relevant for today's climbers. 2010 was the year we decided what to do about it. Throughout the year, we spent staff and volunteer time asking: How should we rebuild America's national climbing organization?

After reaching out to over 2,000 climbers through surveys and focus groups, we built a draft Five-year Strategic Plan and submitted it to the board as the 2010 fiscal year came to a close.

The effects of the final plan, ratified in February 2011, have been positive and sweeping. Now our staff structure is united through five groups: Membership, Community Programs, Information & Marketing, Conservation & Policy, and Development. Each group's leader and staff are focused on the most critical parts of the AAC mission: putting our members and the places we climb at the forefront. The plan breaks down into the following strategies:

1. Improve member benefits
2. Develop community programs
3. Regain leadership as a climbing information resource
4. Improve and create new grants
5. Strengthen commitment to conservation through community programs & grants
6. Provide lodging facilities where needed at climbing destinations
7. Build a separate strategy for the American Mountaineering Center

The full plan is available for download at americanalpineclub.org/p/5-year-plan

Now, as the AAJ goes off to the printer, we are launching that plan—a plan that builds our AAC like never before.

Phil Powers
Executive Director

I-TO

The first ascent of the immense south face of Mt. Logan, Canada.

KATSUTAKA "JUMBO" YOKOYAMA

The south face of Mt. Logan with the line of the new route I-TO. In the foreground is the Warbler Ridge (Baumann-Bucher-Jones-Page-Thiessen, 1977). Okada and Yokoyama descended the east ridge on the right skyline. *Katsutaka Yokoyama*

It was July 2009 when Christian Beckwith showed me a picture of Mt. Logan. Captioned "The 3,000-meter unclimbed south face," it immediately captured my imagination. The attractive phrase was part of it, but so was the mysteriousness of the mountain itself: I had absolutely no idea where Logan was.

My climbing partners and I have climbed in the Alaska Range over the last several years. These experiences have been significant for us, and there are still many objectives that I am itching to try. Still, the mountains around Denali have been losing their appeal. Here it's easy to find information, route descriptions, and reasonably accurate weather forecasts, all of which lessen the adventure. Also, the commitment is relatively low because escapes are easy. Even though it is a joy to climb in such an accessible environment, I was starting to think that for me real climbing would be in a truly wild arena with more unreliability, uncertainty, and anxiety. Christian's photo of Logan stirred these feelings.

The south face of Mt. Logan has a notorious history, having turned down several

Katsutaka Yokoyama on the morning of the third day on the south face of Mt. Logan. *Yasushi Okada*

Yokoyama on thin AI5 just above the route's crux on the third day.   *Yasushi Okada*

attempts by strong North American climbers. Its technical difficulty was not the only reason this wall remained one of the greatest unclimbed projects throughout the years. It has a fearsome reputation for unpredictable weather, serac fall, remoteness, and the sheer magnitude of its landscape. These are difficulties that cannot be described by a number or grade. I see mountains as yardsticks for measuring the hardships a person can endure, the physical and mental toughness a person may—or may not—possess. On Mt. Logan, pure luck would also be required. To climb Logan's south face, I would have to look deep for strength. But I told myself, "OK, I will face and accept everything this mountain has to offer."

"HUGE!"

That was the first word our little group blurted out as we exited the plane onto the glacier under Mt. Logan. The hugeness was well beyond our expectations and even our comprehension. When Yasushi Okada, Genki Narumi, and I had left Japan we already felt ecstatic, like it was our first overseas expedition. Being here under the face created an indescribable energy.

The first order of business was acclimatization. However, from the Seward Glacier, even after a thorough search, we couldn't find routes safe enough to acclimate on. As we reexamined our options, we decided that the east ridge of Logan, accessed from Hubbard Glacier, would be the safest and quickest way to get high. We left basecamp three days after landing. Two hours of walking took us to a col where we could look back toward camp. The sight sent shivers down my spine. Our camp was just a tiny dot in the vast icefield, and then clouds rolled in and the tent disappeared. I wondered how we would be able to find it again if it snowed while we were climbing the east ridge. We would be lost in a vast sea of white.

We saw how stupidly optimistic we had been, and promptly headed back to base camp. Our priority was to "secure the port." But without a camp keeper or GPS, we were limited to primitive methods of marking our camp. We

The gear stash left by Jay Smith and Jack Tackle for a future attempt. *Katsutaka Yokoyama*

placed a tent pole upright and hoped that we could locate camp with a map and compass. The first storm came and went, and on day six we turned again toward the east ridge.

As expected, acclimatizing turned into an adventure. First, there was the 30-kilometer walk just to reach the route. And while the east ridge is a beautiful line stretching nicely to the summit plateau, it proved a bit too technical for an easy acclimatization outing. To make matters worse, stormy weather forced us to spend three hours each night digging snow shelters. If we didn't pitch our tent inside a cave it would be buried under the falling snow.

After eight tiring days, we had finished acclimatizing and were headed back to base camp. Just before reaching camp, fog rolled in and we lost all visibility. We had to go inch by inch while closely checking our compass. By 9 p.m., a slight opening in the dense fog allowed us to finally catch a glimpse of our tents. We shouted for joy.

I found myself strangely excited. The east ridge and the foul weather might have been tough for acclimatizing, yet on Mt. Logan we were finding the adventurous mountaineering I had been longing for. Yasushi felt the same, and we agreed on how great it was to be here. Genki lacked our excitement. It was not discord in the team, but a difference in how we perceived the mountain. As we scouted the south face, Genki's reservations became clear. He was overwhelmed by the situation. Yasushi and I understood; his negative feelings made complete sense to all of us. The question was, do you embrace those negativities and focus them into upward progress, or do you let them hold you back? Genki chose not to accept them. He opted to remain at base camp, lessening the climbing team to just Yasushi and me. With only two, we needed to change our tactics and equipment—but our objective remained the same.

Yokoyama on the third and last day on the south face. *Yasushi Okada*

On May 4, we crossed the glacier under a bright moon. As day broke, we managed to navigate through seracs and reach the base of the wall. As we gazed up, Yasushi half joked, "We can climb it in a day, can't we?" We are always like this, half serious and too optimistic.

We simul-climbed the initial gentle snow slope. Our progress was so quick that I almost believed we could finish this wall in just one day. When we reached the rock, route finding became less obvious, and we traversed left with difficulty.

After the traverse we looked up to a distinctive chimney. It was our planned high point for the day, but it was still far above us. We had been slowed by snow falling on and off throughout the day. As night drew near and the stars began to twinkle, we carved an unexpectedly comfortable bivouac site and settled down to sleep, satisfied with our progress.

On the second day we struggled upward into the early afternoon and the looming crux chimney. The unrelenting steepness, thin ice, and loose rock all conspired to slow our progress. The follower suffered with a heavy pack, especially during delicate traverses without adequate protection. I suffered a big whipper after too many vain attempts to tiptoe toward the chimney, and it was dark by the time we topped out from the chimney. There was not enough space to pitch our tent, so we rigged our rope into a makeshift hammock to set the tent on. Even in such miserable conditions, Yasushi was cheerful. I believe that if we can accept all that nature has to offer and enjoy our own presence in mountains, there is no pathos, only laughter.

Day three opened with a perfect blue sky, but we were skeptical of the continuing fine weather. We kept mulling over all the stories of ferocious sudden storms, "dumping snow to neck height in just one night," and the fearsome reputation Logan had of being the "worst weather mountain." In addition to those doubts and fears, our planned descent of the climbing route was out of the question. The traverses, rotten rock, thin ice, and avalanche danger made it too slow and dangerous. Even if we loathed repeating the lengthy east ridge and 30-kilometer hike, it was the most reliable way back to base camp.

The wall would not give up an easy path. We had already passed through the most technically demanding sections of the route, but high altitude and heavy packs reminded us that we were not yet finished. Finally, after navigating through the last serac barrier, we topped out the face at 11 p.m. Luckily, we found a well-protected crevasse to settle into for our third bivouac. Taking off our sturdy double boots, we found our socks were frozen. Throughout the night, penetrating cold kept me awake. To make matters worse, we dropped a fresh gas cartridge into the bottom of the crevasse. This loss reduced our supplies by one-and-a-half days.

It seemed impossible, but the fourth day dawned with another beautiful blue sky. Despite our euphoria over the ascent, we were anxious about weather pinning us down on the summit plateau. A big storm had to come soon.

If we were thinking rationally we should have begun our descent immediately. But Yasushi and I agreed that the true goal should be the summit, not just the monstrous wall we'd just climbed. So, we proceeded to traverse four kilometers westward with 800 meters of elevation gain just to stand on the summit. It took three hours to get to the final col. Trail breaking and our accumulated fatigue was beyond our expectation. Physically and mentally we were approaching our limit, but 600 meters of vertical gain remained. Looking up at the beautiful blue sky, we obsessed over our fear of a storm. To be honest, we used our fear as the excuse to give up on the summit.

We deliberated for about 30 minutes before deciding to turn around. I instantly regret-

Okada nearing the top of the south face. *Katsutaka Yokoyama*

Okada descending the East Ridge after grinding it out to the summit. *Katsutaka Yokoyama*

The Seward Glacier is staggeringly big country. *Katsutaka Yokoyama*

ted our retreat, but tried to keep my mouth shut. It was *our* decision. The very moment we began our descent, I could not stop sighing. When Yasushi caught my sigh, words poured from his lips: "No Jumbo. Let's go to the summit. This is not good. We should go."

Three hours later, we stood on top of the east summit. People may say there was no meaning in our slog, or they may question why we did not go to the main summit. Between the east and the main summits there was one more big dip, and we had to admit it was beyond our limit. But being on the east summit, I felt there was neither more nor less. The summit on which we were standing was our final, proper destination. That feeling has not changed, even now. It is hard to say that the last stretch to the summit added value to our climb of the south face, but we had promised to accept everything Mt. Logan had to offer. The last half day of slogging and the accompanying mental conflict was an indispensable spice to our journey.

Now we just had to get back to base camp where Genki awaited our safe return. Descending the east ridge was not easy, and 30 kilometers of trail breaking without skis or snowshoes was a cruel punishment. But, it was simply walking.

SUMMARY:

Area: St. Elias Range, Yukon Territory, Canada

Ascent: The first ascent of the south face of Mt. Logan (5,957m), continuing to the east summit (May 4–8, 2010, including the descent). Yasushi Okada and Katsutaka "Jumbo" Yokoyama called their route I-TO (2,500m, ED+ M6 WI5), meaning "thread, line, relationship," partly in honor of Jack Tackle and Jay Smith, who had attempted the route two times and shared the details with Yokoyama. The Japanese climbers descended the east ridge, aided by the unexpected fresh tracks of another team of climbers.

ABOUT THE AUTHOR:

Katsutaka Yokoyama is nicknamed Jumbo because, well, he's big. He hails from Japan, where he is a member of the Giri-Giri Boys, an informal group of alpinists who have been systematically ticking off impressive unclimbed routes all over the globe. Yokoyama is well known to North Americans for his new routes in the Alaska Range, including a massive link-up of the Isis and Slovak Direct routes on Denali in 2008, about which he wrote a feature article in the 2009 American Alpine Journal, *"Pachinko on Denali."*

Yasushi Okada and Katsutaka "Jumbo" Yokoyama on the summit of Mt. Logan. *Yasushi Okada*

Translated by Jiro Kurihara. This article is shared with the 2011 Canadian Alpine Journal.

DODO'S DELIGHT

*The Wild Bunch slays one virgin wall after another on the
Greenland 2010 – Tilman International expedition.*

BOB SHEPTON

Dodo's Delight waits for the climbers' return in Torssukatak Fjord. Behind, on Pamiagdluk Island, stands the Baron (1,340m) with its lower west summit, the Baronet. These formations were blitzed in 2004 (*AAJ 2005*). *Bob Shepton Collection*

The email read, "Bob, do you know where there are any big walls to climb in Greenland? We did some on Mt. Asgard in Baffin last summer and would like to do some in Greenland in 2011."

To which I responded, "Well, yes I do know where there are some big walls on the west coast of Greenland but I am not going to tell you where they are as I want them for myself and my teams. But … it so happens I left my boat in Greenland for the winter, what about this year?"

The first pitch of The Impossible Wall And The Devil's Brew. *Bob Shepton Collection*

The Red Wall (left) and the Impossible Wall. *Bob Shepton Collection*

"Ah, we'll have to think about that, and get back to you."

To parody Julius Caesar, they thought, they came, they conquered.

So my crew in 2010 consisted of the Favresse brothers, Nico and Oli, from Belgium; Sean Villanueva O'Driscoll, of Irish, Spanish and Belgian descent; and Ben Ditto, American. I dubbed them "the Wild Bunch" after all those high fives and yells at the top of climbs on their website—and to keep them in their place, of course. They enjoyed that. So "Greenland 2010—Tilman International" was born. International because of the nature of the team; Tilman, because all my expeditions have followed the example of this British explorer/climber of yore who in his latter years sailed his boat to remote places and climbed from the boat.

The climbers arrived by plane in Aasiaat and that afternoon took over the Greenland National Day celebrations at the boatyard party, entertaining the staff with their musical instruments and song. Are Greenlanders tolerant? Yes, but the team *was* excellent. Next day we went out for an afternoon's sail in my boat, *Dodo's Delight*, a 10-meter Westerly Discus, to learn the ropes, as two of them had never sailed before. Soon enough, we put out to sea for the passage to Upernavik.

It proved a rather arduous passage for us all, especially the two novices. After we motored across Disko Bay, a breeze came up at last, so we turned off the engine and sailed. But thereafter the engine would not start and we had to sail whether there was wind or not. There was the occasional iceberg looming suddenly out of the mist. It was particularly frustrating in the dead calms, of which there are many in Greenland owing to the Greenland High. Sean was heard to comment, "This must be the low point of the expedition." I hoped he was right and there would be nothing worse. It took us five days to sail the normal two and a half day passage. We had to endure the final indignity of sailing very slowly through a lot of icebergs in full view of all in the settlement of Upernavik, and then to negotiate coming alongside the wharf on sail alone. "Well, you wanted to learn how to sail, lads, didn't you?"

Solving the engine problem proved easy; the alternator, however, was broken. But obviously the team wanted to get climbing, so I bought a portable generator to charge the batteries. It was far too big and heavy for a small boat, but was all I could find, and we set off for the big walls. We started on Red Wall as I had dubbed it, the headland of Agparsssuit, at the southern end of the Sortehul fjord. Apparently the Greenlanders call it "the cliff where the guillemots stand in line," and they did, like black sentinels on parade. I got the impression that the Wild Bunch were not used to sea cliff climbing, as they seemed disturbed by all the seagulls wheeling and squawking around them. But they stepped from the boat to the dinghy to the rock to start their climbs. They chose two dihedral and crack lines that went straight up the cliff, and in one big 30-hour push completed two routes of 350 meters and 400 meters respectively. So Seagulls' Garden at E5 6a sustained (5.11) and Red Chilli Cracker at E6 6b sustained (5.12a) were the first routes ever to be done on this wall with all its potential. The only problem was that to save weight they had chosen not to take a hand-held radio with them, so when finished they had to walk all the way round the fjord behind the headland to where I had anchored the boat. The first I knew of it was when Sean swam, in the nude in arctic waters, across to the boat in the early hours next morning.

"Oh, I'm sorry, I was asleep."

"Not at all, I wanted a swim."

After a brief visit back to Upernavik, I dropped them off for another climb on a dramatic face halfway between Upernavik and the Sortehul, this time by a short dinghy ride to shore. I returned to Upernavik to deal with the alternator problems whilst they set up camp, and then after a rather intricate approach, they put up another superb route on this face, Brown Balls at

Ben Ditto jamming on Seagull's Garden on the Red Wall. *Bob Shepton Collection*

Routes on the Red Wall: Red Chili Crackers (left) and Seagull's Garden. *Bob Shepton Collection*

5.12a (sustained 5.11, with two pitches of 5.12a) and 450 meters. It became a whole team effort, as Nico had come up to a huge pillar that looked too unstable for comfort, so he and Sean rappelled down to the high point the other two had reached on their route. They then abseiled off and left Nico and Sean to finish the route. So the final route takes the continuous line just to the right of the obvious central pillar. They described it as "a superb line with Yosemite type cracks," and noted that this first ascent was harder because they had to clean sand and earth from the cracks. It was then a combined onsight free ascent, though Nico confessed to pulling once on gear on a 10-meter wet section.

But the tour de force of their climbing in this area was the first ascent of Impossible Wall. I have had my eye on that wall for many years now as I passed underneath it, but, as I told them, I have never had a team good enough to climb it before. Hence the name. Their route, Impossible Wall And The Devil's Brew (there is a story behind the addition) at E7 6c (5.12d) followed the steepest and hardest line on the wall, and probably in this whole area, ascending 850 meters in 19 pitches with each pitch sustained. They started this time by simply stepping off the boat, moored alongside the wall with a couple of cams in cracks. This was the first time a veritable "Garden of Eden" had been planted on my boat from all the grass and earth that fell as they climbed and cleaned the start of the route. There was no let up in standard, and it took them 11 days to complete the climb with three portaledge encampments along the way. True, three of those days were spent stuck on their portaledges in bad weather, but this was initially no problem as they had included their musical instruments in the haul bags. They fell to "jamming" and composing new songs! But gradually the infamous black hole (coincidentally, Sortehul also means Black Hole) began to drip more and more water on top

The Impossible Wall And The Devil's Brew. *Bob Shepton Collection*

Ben Ditto starting The Impossible Wall And The Devil's Brew   *Bob Shepton Collection*

of them. Three days later Sean, the acknowledged expert on loose rock, wet rock, grass, and lichen who said "it doesn't matter as long as you can just keep on climbing," managed to lead the black greasy hanging chimney crack. Nico also had his moments on this climb. The Greenlandic name for this wall is Seagull Cliff or Bad Seagull Cliff, and bad they were. He *had* to get onto a certain ledge, but a fulmar wasn't having any of it and kept ejecting foul-smelling slime all over him. It took repeated swings with a number four cam before the fulmar finally relented.

The penultimate pitch also proved interesting, especially since by this time Nico had to empty the contents of his own stomach rapidly and repeatedly. It seems the water supply running down the wall had been polluted by seagulls. He then hooked his foot high up in a crack to lever

Olivier Favresse about to negotiate steep grass on The Impossible Wall And The Devil's Brew. *Bob Shepton Collection*

himself up with an "impossible" move to start the pitch. But after 11 days they topped out, this time to a well deserved dance together on the top, and a toast in champagne when I picked them up round the back of the mountain the next morning. Funnily enough it had only been eight days as far as they were concerned, as their days were 30 hours long!

Nico remarked to me later, "I think that must be the greatest adventure of my life so far," and a knowledgeable authority has subsequently commented that it was "probably the hardest climb done in Greenland to date."

It certainly was a landmark climb, and hopefully these ground-breaking ascents will open up the tremendous climbing potential of this area, at almost any standard. This latter point was illustrated for us a few days later. After I picked up my crew from the base they had established round the back before they started the wall, we retired to the only safe anchorage in the Sortehul—at its northern end—where we fortuitously met up with another bigger and smarter yacht, *Saxon Blue.* Also soon to arrive were a group of three kayakers from Wales—this was positively crowded for Greenland. After we had all been generously entertained one evening aboard the luxury of *Saxon Blue,* including the inevitable musical ensemble with my crew singing for their supper, they put up some pleasant, shorter, and not quite so extreme routes in the area, reached by kayak.

Bob Shepton and the *Dodo's Delight* coming to check on the climbers.
Bob Shepton Collection

But the team was keen to press on for the southern tip of Greenland. We started the long trek, some 850 nautical miles, to the Cape Farewell area. Early on we inspected a wall I had reconnoitered whilst they had been on the big wall, but this was finally rejected for various reasons. This became the story of this passage south. At one stage we turned toward the Ummannaq area to have a look—were any big walls lurking there? In times past there had been a lot of mountaineering in that area, including by some famous names, and subsequently I did hear from a group who rock climbed there last summer. Yes, there are rock routes to be done, but beware the considerable loose rock. It was fortuitous therefore that we decided not to inspect it after all. Instead we turned round and continued on to Aasiaat, from where we had started. Here we dispatched some extra gear via the Royal Arctic Shipping line, and then proceeded further south.

Again we diverted to inspect possible big walls we had been told about. This is one of the great advantages of climbing from a boat: you can explore while living on a mobile but firm base that goes where you want. We put into a fjord to the north of Sisimiut and another to the south of Paamiut on our way, but both walls were rejected as being not long or steep enough for my expert team. Instead they got their kicks by jumping into the arctic waters for a swim and sitting on ice floes in still life pose, with no protective clothing, shall we say. It was a long haul, especially as what little wind there was came "in our faces." We had to motor practically the whole way. But eventually we arrived in Nanortalik in the far south, where we restocked and read reports from past expeditions kindly lent from the Tourist Office, before making our way round to the Cape Farewell area.

We immediately noticed the difference. Upernavik involved big sea cliffs; here the terrain was alpine in character. As this area has received quite a lot of attention in the past, it is more difficult to find new routes. We managed five in the end. The first two were on a wall beneath an unnamed peak northwest of Tikaguta on the Saga map, which they only found because they got lost in the morning mist and suddenly there it was in front of them! It had required a five-kilometer walk in, carrying all their gear, leaving the skipper and boat anchored in the Torssukatak fjord. This cliff provided "two classic, clean, direct lines on excellent rock" at E4 or 5.11, both of 450 meters. They then completed the ridge traverse at D/TD and were kind enough to name the summit Shepton Spire.

Next came two routes on the obvious wall at the northern end of Quvnerit Island. Both were offwidth cracks: Chinese Gybe, E5 6b or 5.11+ at 550 meters, and Chloé, also E5 6b or 5.11+, 550 meters. The names? A Chinese Gybe is a sailing maneuver you try at all costs to avoid. Nico, eight meters above a stance with no intermediate protection, pulled on a huge block of some 200 pounds that came away in his hands. He struggled to hold onto it and find purchase on the cliff somehow somewhere, but in the end he had to push it away and take the 16+ meter fall, finishing upside down with a 400-meter void below. He felt himself all round and was ecstatic to be alive and unharmed. The rock had hit the wall and burst, but mostly missed Ben on the stance, who only took a badly grazed ankle, though he later discovered the blade of his pocket knife in his pack had been snapped in half, presumably by a projected missile. Both were considerably shaken, and stirred. Chloé was named after the Belgian bouldering champion, who was a close friend of the group; she was killed by a fall in the Alps on the very day of these Quvnerit ascents.

Nico and Ben were puzzled to find a bolt and some tat on their route and wondered whether it had already been climbed. We discovered later that a strong Swiss team had been here in 2004 and climbed some routes, but not these two. They had used the bolt to escape, as they had found the crack above to be wet and greasy. Honor was satisfied. My team, after shivering away the rest of the darkness (it was late August by now) in a bivy at the top, went on to traverse the whole of the ridge, but did not claim it as a first as they found more tat on the way.

The final ascent was a mistake, at least as far as the skipper was concerned, who foolishly allowed himself to be persuaded to go out with Nico and Sean. The route on the southeast

Shepton Spire, with routes Corned Beef and Condensed Milk plus the ridge traverse. *Bob Shepton Collection*

corner of Angnikitsoq, at E2 (5.10) and 500 meters, was far too long and far too hard for an old man, however expertly he may have been guided. The old skipper survived, quite exhausted, and immediately named the route Never Again! Seventy-five seems a good age to retire from that sort of thing (again). However, he was able to join the Wild Bunch in their victory dance at the top and thus become a full member.

We stopped at Saft Wall on the way out, but the weather turned gnarly and only bouldering was done. Again, it looked as if most worthwhile routes had already been climbed here. We made our way down Prins Christian Sund, enjoyed the hospitality and Danish pastries at the Weather Station at the far end, before making our way out for the Atlantic crossing. The lads were keen to do this "for the experience." They were not disappointed; it proved a tough crossing with a lot of headwinds before eventually we could work south and pick up favorable westerlies to bowl us along to Scotland. We hove-to to sit out Post Tropical Storm Danielle, and later another vigorous double depression. And yet again to repair the steering at sea, which had worked loose. We finally came up to Mingulay and Pabbay in the Western Isles of Scotland and inspected the cliffs with a view

Sean Villanueva in the middle of the Atlantic Ocean. *Bob Shepton Collection*

to climbing ("it would be cool to climb this side too"), before anchoring off a remote beach with a huge colony of seals lining the waterline. But the next day the skipper overruled the climbers for fear of weather, and we eventually arrived in Oban in a full gale. Welcome home!

All of this weather had nothing to do with the fact this was my thirteenth crossing of the Atlantic, we arrived on the thirteenth day of the month, and a large 13 was the number on my storm trysail. As I told them, "It's lucky you are not superstitious, lads!"

It had been a successful and happy summer. And I couldn't have had a more pleasant bunch aboard.

Summary:

Area: West Coast of Greenland (Upernavik region) and Cape Farewell region.

Ascents: Nine new routes by climbers Nicole Favresse, Olivier Favresse, Ben Ditto, and Sean Villanueva, with Bob Shepton skipper and climber on one route.

In the Upernavik area, on the "Red Wall" on the headland of Agparsssuit, at the southern end of the Sortehul fjord: Red Chili Crackers (350m, 5.12- R or E6 6b), by Olivier Favresse and Villanueva, in 30 hours beginning July 2, 2010. Seagull's Garden (400m, 5.11 or E5 6a), by Ditto and Nico Favresse in 30 hours beginning July 2 (one bolt was placed on lead to protect a slab—the only bolt placed on the expedition). On a dramatic face halfway between Upernavik and Sortehul: Brown Balls Wall (400m, 5.12-; all free except for one pull on a 10-meter wet and dirty section), by Olivier Favresse and Ditto on first 3 pitches; Nico Favresse and Villanueva on the rest, July 6. Back at Sortehul fjord: Impossible Wall And The Devil's Brew (850m, 19 pitches, 5.12+ or E7 6c), by Olivier and Nico Favresse, Ditto, and Villanueva, in 11 days with three portaledge camps (no bolts), July 11–22.

In the Cape Farewell Area, on a wall beneath a previously unnamed peak northwest of Tikaguta on the Saga map, 5km walk from Torssukatak fjord: Corned Beef (450m, 5.11 or E4), by Ditto and Villanueva. Also Condensed Milk (450m, 5.11 or E4), by Nico and Olivier Favresse. Both routes were climbed on August 16 and followed by a long scenic ridge (D/TD) to another summit on the east side of what they named "Shepton Spire." On Quvnerit Island: Chloé (550m, 5.11+ offwidth or E5 6b) on Angegoq Tower followed by the ridge to the summit of Morel Tower and then the summit of Asiaq Tower, by Olivier Favresse and Villanueva on August 20. Also on Angegoq Tower on August 20: The Chinese Gybe (550m, 5.11+ offwidth or E5 6b), by Ditto and Nicolas Favresse. They found one bolt and rap anchors on the lower part of the wall, but no sign of previous climbers above that point. On Angnikitsoq: Never Again! (500m, 5.10 or E2), by Shepton, Nico Favresse, and Villanueva on August 21.

About the author:

Considered an institution in northern waters, the Reverend Bob Shepton (76) many years ago left the pulpit for the cockpit of his yacht. He has become a leading expert on the waters around West Greenland and is the only person to have won the Royal Cruising Club's Tilman Medal twice. His boat Dodo's Delight is a Westerly 33-foot Discus built in 1980. Shepton spearheaded the development of rock climbing in the Portland area (UK) during the 60s and 70s, and climbed new routes on the Little and Great Ormes. He is now a proud holder of a Piolet d'Or 2011 with the Wild Bunch for this expedition. He can be reached via bobshepton.co.uk.

Bob Shepton at the wheel in Torssukatak, Cape Farewell. *Bob Shepton Collection*

THE ROSE OF
NO-MAN'S LAND

Eight days under threat on the east face of Mt. Edgar, in Sichuan,
yields a route almost too dangerous to be proud of.

BRUCE NORMAND

Edgar viewed from Yanzi Gou to the east-southeast. Marked is The Rose of No-Man's Land climbed by Kyle Dempster and Bruce Normand. The smaller inset face to the left, rising to the lower south ridge, was likely the goal of the ill-fated American expedition. *Tamotsu Nakamura*

There's nothing neutral about Mt. Edgar. It's stunning and savage. It's beautiful and deadly. It's amazing climbing with incredible dangers. Kyle Dempster and I stepped into the Casino Edgar in November of 2010. We didn't lose our shirts, but the old adage always holds true: nobody beats The House.

The Minya Konka Range in southwestern China's Sichuan province is barely larger than the Mont Blanc massif. However, it hides more than ten 6,000-meter summits, each with only a single ascent, or fewer. The place offers serious potential for alpine-style new routes on little-known and highly committing peaks.

This sort of adventure is precisely what Kyle Dempster and I were looking for when we planned another sortie into the remote summits of Western China. We'd found plenty of it on the Xuelian peaks in 2009, and we'd talked a lot about climbing philosophy as a result. In 2010 we were after more of the same, minus the talking.

It's not easy to think about hard alpine-style climbing around Minya Konka without running into the specter of Edgar. Though the peak was climbed by Koreans in 2002, the climbing world didn't sit up and notice until 2008, when Tamotsu Nakamura published his iconic picture of Edgar's stunning east face. Two teams tried to climb it the following spring. The first—Alexandr Ruchkin and Mikhail Mikhailov—failed even to find it because of weather. The second—Johnny Copp, Micah Dash, and Wade Johnson—was killed in an avalanche after they'd decided the face was too dangerous to climb.

Kyle and I complement each other. I'm the scientist and he's the artist. I have all the details under control; he has the big picture. I get stuff done; he has fun doing it. I'm your guy for the drudge work; he's your guy for the spectacular finishing moves. This said, we both had exactly the same feelings about the east face of Edgar: equal parts attraction and repulsion. Kyle's emotions were even stronger than mine, not least because he felt a deeper connection to Johnny and Micah through shared American climbing circles. After a lot of talking, we decided we'd have to go. We opened the door and, in its all-or-nothing way, Edgar sucked us in.

We knew the approach to Edgar would be no place to hang around, so we decided to climb in a single push from the base. That meant acclimating somewhere else, and for this we chose the high valleys on the western side of the Minya Konka Range. We were accompa-

Mt. Grosvenor (a.k.a., Riwuqie Feng, 6,376m) from the west. Kyle Dempster and Bruce Normand climbed the obvious central line in the face, making the peak's second ascent. From the top they climbed a little way down the left skyline before rappelling the north face, part of which is visible in shadow. Julie-Ann Clyma and Roger Payne climbed the right ridge in 2003 for the peak's first ascent (AAJ 2004, pp. 418–420). *Bruce Normand*

The east face of Edgar showing The Rose of No-Man's Land as seen from ca 4,200m in the dangerous approach gully.
Bruce Normand

nied by accomplished French alpinists Jean Annequin and Christian Trommsdorff, climbing as a separate pair, and by premier Chinese alpinist and logistics expert Yan Dongdong.

We made all our preparations in Chengdu and Kangding, and then trekked in two very short days to a base camp in Shang Riwuqie (4,300m). Dongdong and I had been there the previous winter, and we knew it would be a good place to spend two weeks hiking, climbing, and eating. The local peaks, including Little Konka (5,924m), Jiazi Feng (6,540m), Mt. Grosvenor (Riwuqie Feng, 6,376m), and Leduomanyin (6,112m), offer plenty of climbing challenges, spiced up by biting west winds that blow off the Tibetan plateau.

In addition to the hiking and eating, we did one piece of climbing: the central couloir on the west face of Grosvenor, which rose directly above our camp. This route had been tried twice before, including by Andy Cave and Mick Fowler in 2003, but the parties had been turned back by dry conditions. When Roger Payne and Julie-Ann Clyma made the first and only ascent of Grosvenor in November 2003, they took shorter couloir leading to the southwest ridge.

In Sichuan most snow falls in summer, which makes autumn, when we were there, the season to find ice. Kyle and I decided on a single-push strategy and left base camp at 3 a.m. We cruised unroped all the way to the crux (at 5,800m), and by noon had climbed its two thin pitches. Unlike all our preparation days, this day turned cold, with clouds, strong wind, and occasional snow. We simul-climbed the upper couloir all afternoon until some nice exit moves. A little sunshine through the wind-torn clouds greeted us on the summit at 6 p.m. Off to the east, Mt. Edgar looked menacing.

Dempster enjoying some of Edgar's best ice. *Bruce Normand*

The descent was no giveaway: like the first-ascent party, we made a little progress down the increasingly corniced northeast ridge until dark. Then we launched into 15 rappels down the precipitous north face, arriving in the upper glacier basin at 2 a.m., where a little walking took us to an icefall. We'd been on the go for 24 hours in the cold and the wind, so we stopped to bivouac, returning to base camp the following day.

Mt. Edgar was an altogether different story. On the east side of the range, its approach begins on verdant valley floors at only 1,500 meters. Misty, rainy weather is the norm for about 300 days of the year. With over 2,000 meters of precipitous forested slopes and blown-out river gorges between the fields and the mountains, this region shrouds its peaks in a special brand of mystery.

Sure enough, we had to start our approach blind, spending the first day in a landscape of cloud-forests and moraine-like canyon walls. We'd asked a porter to help with a gear bag, and his cluelessness about where we were heightened the mystery. On the second day, one porter lighter, we were still navigating in mist up unstable, vertical-sided river cuts. Occasional rocks would fall and bounce toward us. This place would be hell in the rain. Light snow started falling as we pitched camp on the edge of a small glacier at 4,100 meters. The cliffs above us were veiled in clouds.

On the third day, everything became clear. Glistening in the sunshine of a cloudless morning, a massive, rimed-up rock face towered directly above us. The east face is a shallow scoop with a dry, vertical, southeast-facing side below the true summit; a shaded, northeast-facing side seamed with several thin ice lines; and a central drainage gully catching everything that falls off the cornice line rimming the face. The narrow access glacier-gully avalanched as we watched, a wave of powder billowing down and over us.

We waited two hours until the sun was off the glacier and then we continued up the approach, the air still threatening. We found a huge slide line, which at least made it easy to tell where the dangers were. My heart was hammering from more than just our speed. Later we saw the serac that caused the slide, and at 5,000 meters we were beyond it, post-holing in knee-deep snow. The relief was worth the extra effort. We slogged on up the steepening gully, pulling ever closer to the face. We pitched camp by digging a semi-cave at the foot of the first ice ramp, astonished to find ourselves already at 5,500 meters.

Two atmospheric pitches up the ice ramp in the morning sun, followed by more steep snow, took us to 5,800 meters. The serac behind us calved again, sending another wave of blocks down the glacier. We didn't need the hint. We had to stay out of harm's way by sticking to the left wall. Kyle chose to start the serious climbing in a faint dihedral, which turned into M6 dry-tooling. The climbing was thin and punishingly steep, and the exit moves tenuous, but at least the rock was solid and took protection much better than we'd feared.

While Kyle was working steadily on the lead, the easier option in the main drainage gully was getting pounded by a falling cornice. We'd definitely made the right choice, and a quick flash of relief moderated my trepidation about the climbing to come.

Despite the heavier pack, following was fun: small but positive edges and good hooks. Three pitches of steep thin ice followed. Kyle stayed on lead, climbing delicately to leave at least a little ice still glued to the slabs beneath. More fun for me, solving a different balance problem in his tracks. At nightfall we pulled into the snowfield we'd been aiming for, but it was steep and icy. The only option was a sitting

Dempster leading the M6 mostly dry-tooling pitch on Edgar. *Bruce Normand*

Dempster on rocky M6 with typical Edgar action in the background. *Bruce Normand*

bivouac on two shelves we hacked out. The night was calm and clear as we brewed up while watching the stars, but in the morning the winds rose slightly and we found we were sitting in a spindrift funnel.

The fifth day served up some new threats. The first was the weather, cloudier with wind whipping around the ridgeline above us. The second was the ice, which was thin, then breakable, and finally non-existent. Kyle, leading over the tenuous, slabby ground, was forced to remove almost every vestige of white stuff to dry-tool the features beneath. It was a taxing day, both from the nature of the climbing and from the ever-present possibility of a checkmate, followed by that horribly dangerous descent yawning beneath us. Finally we worked our way up a shallow dihedral below a roof and pulled out onto a snowy col in a howling gale. We were through. We threw up the tent and dived inside to rest and refuel.

The wind did not relent. Our perch, at 6,200 meters, had a stunning view of Minya Konka trailing a wind cloud and up the summit ridge of Edgar. Reaching the summit ridge required a long ice traverse into the south-facing slopes and up through a serac line to the rounded south ridge. Now the threat was exhaustion, which was prowling close by. We summoned reserves and pushed on to the summit, arriving at 2:30 p.m. on hands and knees to make sure we found the cornice line before it found us. By this time the stormy wind had brought in a full white-out: There was no view and no celebrating, only the stock two-man photo shot at arm's length.

One of the long ice pitches on Edgar. *Bruce Normand*

We launched into a fast and blind descent, aiming for a high glacier basin we'd mapped out from above. Easy slopes brought us down to 5,700 meters, out of the worst of the wind, but the snow thickened as the angle dropped. We ground to a halt in a bivouac spot under a rock as fresh snow started to fall. The threat that night was that we had no idea where we were.

Another sunny morning gave hope that the glacier might not be too bad. Hours of deep snow, deep slots, down-climbing ice fins, and rappelling into crevasses dashed these hopes.

The difficult climbing continued even on the south ridge. *Bruce Normand*

The weather gave out and we were on a first-descent in zero visibility. The threat grew of starving to death lost in a maze. For a while we found the easiest going was between rock and ice on the true left, but as night fell we found ourselves marooned on steep, dirty slabs with icing ropes and nothing at all for a rappel anchor. We were still at 4,300 meters.

Our eighth day dawned as misty as ever, with thickly falling snow adding avalanche danger to the mix. We ate the last of our food—one way or another, we wouldn't be needing it later. We found an anchor, nearly failed to pull the icy ropes, and down-climbed through endless steep, loose boulders and gullies. At 3,600 meters things flattened out, the snow deepened, and then we were thrown into a streambed like the ones we'd climbed a week earlier. At 3,300 meters the river gave suddenly onto a road. We were down. We walked for a bit, then hitched a ride out with some construction workers in a classic Chinese Dongfeng truck, which left us feeling a little seasick when we finally walked on Moxi's main street.

On the surface, we got what we came for: a hard line on a hard peak, which we climbed in pure alpine style (we left only some rappel slings and two dropped items on the mountain). For both Kyle and me, however, the result was at best a tie—a borderline-epic adventure in a permanently threatening atmosphere. We might have done the hardest technical climbing yet attempted in the Minya Konka Range, but the outcome was not a feeling of success, or even of satisfaction, but rather one of relief to have made it up and off this mountain in one piece.

I try to picture how we'd have felt about Edgar if it had not claimed the lives of Johnny, Micah, and Wade. Our heads would have been lighter. We'd have cracked more jokes. We might have taken the bouncing rocks and calving cornices, each snowfall and each wind gust, more lightly—just parts of a package we felt we could deal with if we didn't already know this mountain was mean. Or maybe we'd have been shocked and frightened away, completely overwhelmed by the savagery of the place, if we hadn't had some idea of what to expect. I will never know. As I write this four months later, I can still feel the climbing, the teamwork, and the mountain atmosphere of that face. I no longer feel the same immediate dangers, but I still feel the threat.

Although not a very direct line, our route, The Rose of No-Man's Land, may be the only safe one on the east face of Edgar. Kyle and I would like to dedicate this route to the memory of Johnny Copp, Micah Dash, and Wade Johnson. We dedicate it not to the dark side of Mt. Edgar—the experiences they faced there—but to its light side: the spirit of adventure, the quest for beauty, and the infectious enthusiasm for the mountains that they brought to their friends and to the entire climbing community.

SUMMARY:

AREA: CHINA, SICHUAN, MINYA KONKA RANGE

Ascents: First ascent of the east face of Mt. Edgar (6,618m). The Rose of No-Man's Land (WI5 M6) was climbed by Kyle Dempster and Bruce Normand during an eight-day round-trip from the nearest town, summiting on November 12, 2010. The previously untouched east face and upper south ridge of Edgar rises 2,500m and features an objectively threatened approach couloir. The smaller southeast face to the left was where Jonny Copp, Micah Dash, and Wade Johnson were killed by an avalanche in 2009. Dempster and Normand made a difficult descent of the south ridge and complex south glacier in generally poor weather. Mt. Edgar had been climbed only once before, in 2001, by a Korean team that ascended the west face. Prior to Edgar, Dempster and Normand made the second ascent of Mt. Grosvenor (Riwuqie Feng, 6,376m). They climbed it via the central couloir on the west face, which had stopped two previous attempts due to dry (no ice) conditions.

ABOUT THE AUTHOR:

Bruce Normand, 44, is from Scotland but lives in China, where he works as professor of physics at Renmin University (People's University) in Beijing. Author of more than 20 first ascents and new routes on 6,000m peaks in the Trans-Himalaya, he has also climbed K2.

Kyle Dempster (left) and Bruce Normand on the summit in a white-out. *Bruce Normand*

SEASON FINALE

*In today's Yosemite, a good half-day is an ascent of Half Dome and
El Cap, both solo. But climbing three El Cap routes still takes a full day.*

ALEX HONNOLD

Yosemite Valley showing El Capitan and Half Dome. El Cap's routes, left to right, are Lurking Fear, Salathe Wall, and the Nose; in the distance is the Regular Route on Half Dome. Alex Honnold's half-day of solo climbing began with the Regular Route and finished with the Nose. His full day with Sean Leary climbed the Nose, Salathe Wall, and Lurking Fear. *John Harlin III*

Every year in Yosemite seems to bring fresh challenges, starting five years ago with my first long trad climbs and continuing year after year into longer and harder routes. This summer in the Valley was my season of aid climbing. And since I have not yet learned how to nail or haul, aid climbing for me means speed climbing. The whole season can be summed up in two glorious days.

Both days stemmed from the same idea. Sean Leary had proposed doing the Triple: three El Cap routes in one day. We'd done something similar the year before, so we had a pretty good idea what it entailed and how long it would take. But while we were planning the Triple, I stumbled across the idea of doing a solo Half Dome–El Cap link up. It had always flittered around in my mind, though I never really believed I could do it. But I'd already done several laps up the

Sean Leary and Alex Honnold checking out the topo for Lurking Fear after getting down from the Nose and the Salathe. *Tom Evans*

Nose that season and I knew it pretty well. All the pieces were in place for both ascents—a fortuitous timing in terms of psyche, fitness, and opportunity.

These link ups offered the opportunity to break speed records. The one that I cared about most was the record on Half Dome, which stood at about 1:50 for a pair simul-climbing. I hoped to break it solo, largely as a matter of style. I would just climb like normal, without checking a watch or hurrying my pace. But I hoped that normal soloing would be faster than paired speed climbing.

Hans Florine's solo speed record for the Nose of 11 hours also seemed like a reasonable goal, but simply getting to the top was much more important to me. Having never soloed El Cap and, for that matter, having hardly rope-soloed at all, it seemed like a very big undertaking. Climbing the Nose alone would be a great adventure; climbing it quickly would be a bonus.

Our goal for the Triple was simply to climb all three routes in a day. We weren't worried about records or style or any of the subtleties, we just wanted to do a ton of climbing. The year before, we'd attempted to climb the Salathe, Nose, and Half Dome in a day, but stopped after just the two El Cap routes. There had been enough time left in the day that we knew it was possible to climb more; it was just a matter of doing it.

Sean and I planned to climb the Triple on a Thursday. This would be the culmination of my season, so I figured I should do the solo link-up first. I hoped to squeeze it in on Tuesday and then have a rest day before climbing with Sean. I hiked up to the base of Half Dome on Monday afternoon and bivied at the base so that I'd be less tired for Thursday's climb on El Cap. This was "cheating," since Dean Potter and Hans Florine had each done this link up Valley to Valley, but I wasn't too troubled. The important part to me was just being able to do the climbing.

My plan was simple: I would free solo all the easy stuff—anything up to about mid 5.10—and pull on gear for the rest. I had a double set of thin gear for the upper dihedrals, but no hand-sized gear. I would also carry a backpack with my shoes, food, water, and a 30-foot piece of cord, just in case I needed it for the Robbins Traverse or anything else unexpected.

I was awake before the sun, waiting impatiently below the route for enough light to begin climbing. A massive snow cone still covered the base of the route, so I didn't start my timer—or even put on my climbing shoes—until midway up the first pitch, where I crouched on a small ledge and prepared for the rest of the adventure. From there I climbed almost without stopping all the way to the summit. I had no aiders, but I used daisies to pull on bolts and clip into gear during the hard sections. (I've since been informed by a friend at

Black Diamond that this is an entirely unsafe practice, since daisy chains aren't designed to hold a fall. Thankfully, I never fell on them.)

Having already free soloed the route a few years before, rope soloing it felt like a vacation. I use rope soloing as the general term for my style on both Half Dome's Regular Route and on the Nose, even though I almost never used a rope. To me, rope soloing includes all styles of soloing that involve gear. Being ropeless on Half Dome reminded me of the fun and the freedom of movement that comes from free soloing, but the gear made it much less committing. I could relax and enjoy the climbing, knowing that at any point I could choose to place gear or put myself on belay. In many ways, it combined the best of both styles: I could be up on a big wall by myself yet still feel safe.

The descent from Half Dome felt pleasantly short and cool. The climb had taken about two hours, so I hiked in the early morning shade while I thought about the next route of the day. The Nose would require somewhat more complicated tactics, since the climbing is a little more difficult and I was getting tired. I still planned on the same overall strategy—free soloing the easy pitches and improvising on the rest—but since there is much less easy terrain on the Nose, I decided to take a full-length rope and a standard double rack. I borrowed a skinny half-rope from a friend because it would be much lighter, but hopefully still sufficient in case of a fall. Unfortunately, the rack proved to be a burden. I hadn't realized that with soloing—especially daisy soloing—you never leave any gear behind. So I wound up carrying the whole rack, rope, and pack up every pitch, which added up to a lot of weight.

I mostly free soloed to the Great Roof, though I tied into the rope so that I could use it on the pendulums on the lower pitches of the route. I also rope soloed the short aid climbing section to the Boot Flake, though as soon as I made it to the hand crack on the Boot I took off my belay and went back to free climbing. The line kept tangling, and loops of slack would catch on things, so it was simpler to just do without the rope as much as possible. But when I reached the Great Roof, I didn't even think about free soloing or using daisies. Instead, I rope soloed the pitch in a traditional style. I've always found the Great Roof, with all its thin gear, very intimidating. So I aided it, then rapped down and jugged back up to clean it. By the time I'd finished jugging the pitch my fatigue was starting to catch up with me. I decided that all

the jugging that traditional rope soloing requires was too tiring, so I put the rope away for good and daisy soloed the rest of the route.

As I climbed higher and began feeling more tired, I clipped into gear more often. I would climb a hand crack pushing a #1 Camalot in front of me. Or I would pull on the cam with one hand and jam with the other. It was a very fluid style, constantly changing as I went. Basically, I did whatever I could to make the climbing easy while also feeling secure.

When I topped out I was

Honnold and Leary crossing the El Cap Bridge on their way to Lurking Fear. *Tom Evans*

Honnold on the Pancake Flake above the Great Roof on the Nose. *Tom Evans*

surprised to find that only six hours had passed since starting the route. I felt vaguely foolish for having brought extra food, water, clothes, and a headlamp, only to finish climbing in mid afternoon. My worries of spending the night on the route were now replaced by a more pleasant concern: where to go for dinner that evening. My overall time on the link-up was about 11 hours, which was a very satisfying half-day of climbing.

Following the solo link up, I had a hard time feeling motivated to climb another link up two days later with Sean. My feet hurt and my legs were tired. But mostly my appetite for climbing was sated. I'd had a large helping of big walls and wasn't sure if I could handle any more so soon. So I left the Valley for a few days to see my girlfriend and let the batteries recharge.

When Sean and I met in El Cap Meadow the next week, it felt like the season had changed. It was officially summer. It was blazing hot and there were almost no climbers on any of the walls. We planned on starting in the dark and climbing the Nose first, since we both knew it well. We would then climb the Salathe, since it gets morning shade. And finally we would suffer up Lurking Fear in the crushing afternoon sun. We knew it would be brutal to do our last route in the worst heat of the day, but we rightly assumed that by that point in the Triple we would be suffering anyway, so a little more wouldn't matter.

We started climbing around 8:30 p.m., as soon as the sun left the wall. Sean led the first half of the route with me simul-climbing behind him. After the King Swing I took over the lead and short fixed the rest of the way to the top. We woke up a party on Camp 6, but otherwise had the route to ourselves. It was pleasant how smoothly everything went, taking us only four hours even though it was dark. Our descent was also quite fast, taking only a little more than an hour to get back to the bear boxes where we'd left food and water.

The details of the Salathe aren't very important. We climbed the route. We felt more tired. We descended. We felt even more tired. By lunch time we were at our bear box in El Cap Meadow again, trying to cram as much food down as possible. There were a bunch of "monkeys" around—wall climbers and dirtbags living in the Valley. It was good to have some people to talk to, just to keep us motivated. That's always a problem with link ups: the down time in between routes, when it feels so good to relax that it's hard to start again. At one point I looked over to see Sean wading in the river and I feared he wouldn't want to get back out.

One of the highlights of our lunch break was talking to Steve Schneider, who climbed

El Cap three times in a day with Hans Florine back in the day (1994). They climbed slightly different routes and used fixed lines to get back down, which must have saved some energy. But either way, climbing El Cap three times in a day is a ton of climbing. Steve gave us some last-minute beta for Lurking Fear before we started hiking, which we really appreciated. By that time, with the stifling afternoon heat settling over the Valley, we were both feeling a sluggish. We hiked a lot slower, heads down, concentrating on just grinding out one more route.

The Nose had been good fun, the Salathe a little more tiring, but Lurking Fear was simply hard work. Just like all the popular sayings about alpinism being more suffering than climbing, I felt that climbing a third grade VI in a day was definitely more work than fun. I short-fixed the majority of the route and then Sean lead us simul-climbing to the summit. The most memorable thing about the route was the pain in my feet, which was so bad at one point that I popped off the heels of my shoes mid-lead and finished the pitch with only my toes.

The final descent felt completely surreal. As we hiked past the top of the Nose on the way to the East Ledges, the physical and mental fatigue was immense. I felt like we'd climbed the Nose a week ago, not that morning. Sixteen hours of simul-climbing/short fixing and seven hours of hiking reduced the world to a blur.

The solo link up was perhaps a greater mental challenge, since I wasn't sure I could do it and there was a bit more risk involved. But the Triple was a far greater physical challenge, pushing both Sean and me far past any of our previous levels of fatigue. And while neither of these days were truly ground breaking, they both broadened my own relationship with climbing and expanded my future possibilities. Solo El Cap two or more times in a day? Possible. Solo even bigger walls someday, using the same kind of improvised style? Probably. Climbing with Sean for so many pitches proved that we could go longer than we might have thought,

Honnold leading the seventh pitch of Lurking fear as Leary cleans the short-fixed sixth pitch. *Tom Evans*

that even when my whole body was crying out to stop and rest, I could still climb for hours.

Honestly though, the Triple wasn't much of an adventure, since the outcome was almost certain from the start. We knew how long the routes would take and we knew we had enough time in the day. Actually executing it was just a matter of hard work. The solo link up was much more of an adventure, since I didn't know if I could do it. It's that kind of adventure that draws me to soloing. I like a challenge that pushes me past my previous limits, but hopefully not so far past as to be dangerous. It's walking that fine line of "just enough challenge but not too much" that makes soloing such an exhilarating mental game. Not everyone feels the need to push all the time, and I think that's partly why so many people disapprove of soloing. I tried to be safe and to enjoy the climbing without rushing; all my hurry was reserved for the Triple, where we hustled as fast as we could all day. We didn't break any records with that link up, but we set a new example for how much climbing can be done in a day using normal Yosemite speed tactics.

Many other climbers have already done similar kinds of link ups: Dean Potter, Timmy O'Neill, Hans Florine, and Steve Schneider are but a few from recent Yosemite history. But even if nothing about our link ups was truly ground breaking, they were two of my best days of climbing. In both cases there was a slight improvement in style over past ascents, and a definite increase in pace, but what's more important for me is that I did my best, that we did our best. Someone will improve upon our ascents soon enough, but they were a pleasure for us.

Summary

Area: Yosemite National Park, California.

Ascents: Half Dome's Regular Route and El Capitan's The Nose. On June 22, Alex Honnold combined a solo link-up of Half Dome's Regular Northwest Face (2,200', 2:09) and the Nose on El Capitan (2,900', 5:59), which halved the solo speed records for both routes. El Capitan Triple: In 23 hours between June 30 and July 1, 2010, Alex Honnold and Sean Leary climbed the Nose (2,900'), Salathe Wall (2,900'), and Lurking Fear (2,000'), including hiking down between ascents.

Alex Honnold on his way to the Nose after completing the Regular Route on Half Dome. *Tom Evans*

About the author:

Alex Honnold (25) was born and raised in Sacramento, California. He looks forward to climbing elsewhere in the world, but so far he's been happy in Yosemite and excursions to Zion, where he free soloed the Moonlight Buttress (1,200', 5.12+). He onsights 5.13+ sport climbs in addition to his many hard free solos. Alex says that "When I'm in the Valley, I like making it down in time for the pizza deck. That's when you know you've really done it in a day. Very civilized." But he also says, "When I get older I'll become an alpinist. Seems like the only way you can continue to climb bigger and bigger routes is to go to the real mountains. But for now Yosemite is big enough."

Takargo

*Nepal's Rolwaling Valley delivers a paradise of unclimbed
waterfall ice and a 6,771-meter virgin summit.*

Joe Puryear

The route line followed by David Gottlieb and Joe Puryear on the east face of Takargo (6,771m). *Joe Puryear*

I screamed down to David as I desperately groped for a hold below me, trying to reverse the move I had just made.

"I'm coming off!!!"

The screech of my crampons against rock echoed across the ravine. I was keenly aware of the double-zero Camalot three meters below and a half-driven Lost Arrow piton just below that. These were the only pieces that could possibly keep me off the deck. My mind raced as I thought of an old saying.

Rule #1: don't fall while ice climbing.

Rule #2: don't fall while ice climbing in a super-remote location in the middle of nowhere in a Third World country.

Shorty thereafter, I pitched….

△

I'd never done the first ascent of a waterfall before. Ice climbing had always been a means to an end. I used it to train and to hone my skills for what I always considered the more dignified objective: alpine climbing. But now things felt different. This place was filled with

Gottlieb at the final point of the ridge crest. *Joe Puryear*

Nemari Left, one of the many waterfalls climbed by Gottlieb and Puryear near Beding, in the Rolwaling Valley.
Joe Puryear

beautiful unclimbed waterfalls, perhaps a higher concentration than anywhere else in the Himalaya. And there was also a major unclimbed peak near the head of the valley. This journey was like no other.

It began in the autumn of 2008, when David Gottlieb and I were fresh off our first ascent of Kang Nachugo in the Rolwaling Himal. While planning this expedition we had the choice of two major unclimbed peaks in the valley, Kang Nachugo (6,735m) and Takargo (6,771m). Kang Nachugo seemed like the obvious choice for our first trip. It was more accessible, more prominent, and logistically easier. During our acclimatization we made numerous climbing and scouting ventures to the south side of the Rolwaling Valley. Here, a small sub-range of peaks rises to a modest 6,259 meters at its highest peak of Chugimago. The range's many glacial cirques drain to the north into the U-shaped Rolwaling Valley. This valley falls over a cliff band, and it is here that the waterfalls prevail. Just as we were leaving the valley in late October to hike over the rugged Teshi Laptsa pass, we noticed the waterfalls were starting to freeze. It was at that moment that we conceived a future expedition. Wouldn't it be great to combine a winter ice climbing trip with a winter expedition to attempt Takargo? The dream was in place; plans were soon made; 2010 would be the year [in 2009 Gottlieb and Puryear climbed nearby Jobo Rinjang (6,778m), a feature article in the 2010 *AAJ*].

△

The low winter sun shone brightly across Gauri Shankar, revealing inner ridges and hidden couloirs across its intricately weathered slopes. A dearth of winter snow had left it looking dry and barren, unfitting for such a brilliant and sacred mountain. The fresh smell of pine and rhododendron filled the air as we made our way up from the 900-meter village of Singati to the 3,800-meter village of Beding, hiking in T-shirts in unusually warm conditions. Another dry winter in the Himalaya, I thought to myself, wondering if we were to find any of the ice that we'd flown halfway around the world to climb.

An early blooming rhododendron caught my eye amidst a sea of green forest. Behind it in the distance shone a curious swath of white. Could that be what I think it is? The multi-pitch waterfall in the middle of a dry forest seemed peculiar, but it confirmed what we were in for. There were to be frozen waterfalls, and lots of them.

"Wow, look at all that ice!"

I excitedly asked my friend Yangzum, "Do you have a name for those? Have they been climbed?" On our prior trip to the Rolwaling we met a Sherpa girl who had just started her training to become a mountain guide. Her small size belied her strength and tenacity, and her infectious smile exuded enthusiasm. When we asked her to help in setting up logistics for the trip, she offered that we could stay in her father's home. In return we asked her if she would like to come explore her own backyard for ice climbing objectives, and she eagerly accepted. Yangzum saw the value in getting experience away from the regimented official training she was receiving. We were more than pleased to have her on the rope for part of our ice explorations, not only because she was fun to climb with, but also because we gained instant credibility with the locals by including one of their own in our pursuits.

Immediately we set our sights on the most obvious and easily accessible objectives. Although there had been a couple of Nepali guide-training courses in the valley in years past, none of the locals could recall there ever being any foreigners here simply to ice climb. The locals keep a keen eye on outsiders, including visiting Nepali guides, and they affirmed that nearly every waterfall in the valley had not even been attempted.

The first day we warmed up on a nice waterfall directly above the village, a four-pitch WI4. Yangzum was immediately astounded by the length, steepness, and quality of ice, saying that the climb was the "grandfather," meaning much greater than any of the ice she had encountered on a previous climbing trip to the Langtang region. We named the climb Pagaga Falls, meaning grandfather in Sherpa, which also spoke to its prominent position above the village.

Near Pagaga, we noticed a pitch of ice flowing out of an immense gash in the hillside. No ice was visible above, but we wanted to explore the enticing possibility that the ice continued upward. The next day we embarked on incredible ice-canyoneering adventure that would surpass our wildest dreams. After climbing the initial pitch, the waterway sank deep into the mountain's side. Vertical and sometimes overhanging walls loomed over our heads and a ribbon of

Gottlieb breaking trail below the hanging glacier. *Joe Puryear*

Gottlieb tackling the summit headwall. *Joe Puryear*

ice snaked its way upward in steps. Pitch after pitch of quality ice revealed itself, mostly in short steps of 20–30 meters, but occasionally full pitches of water-ice choked the chasm. In places the canyon was so narrow that light barely penetrated its depths. We climbed nearly 350 meters before emerging onto an upper plateau below the Chekigo Glacier. From here the canyon split and several more ribbons of ice continued to the glacier's edge. We picked the deepest one with the most ice and continued up another 350 meters, topping out below the edge of the glacier's moraine. We named our climb Beyul (700m, WI 4), which throughout the Himalaya means a secret and sacred valley. The climbing in the Rolwaling had already exceeded our expectations—and we were only on our second day.

Both these climbs were located on the south side of the Rolwaling Valley, which is subject to intense sun. In a better ice year, or perhaps earlier in the season, there must be massive potential for long ice routes here. The two routes we climbed were in deep gullies and were thus shaded. The rest of the ice climbing we did was focused on the shadier and snowier northern side.

Directly across the valley from the lower village of Nemari was one of the best and most extensive displays of ice in the valley. Fourteen distinct lines rose in upward of five pitches of steep water ice. At least one of these lines had been attempted by Nepali guides. The locals told a broken tale of failure and an accident, but we couldn't get any concrete information other than: "Everything over there is unclimbed." Two long waterfalls stood out more than any other, so over two days, we established Nemari Left (4 pitches, WI5+) and Nemari Right (5 pitches, WI5). On Nemari Left, the climbing seemed a bit too dangerous to have Yangzum with us; in any case, she was keen to have a day off with her friends. Unbeknownst to us, the Sherpas had a betting wager on whether we would succeed. They eagerly watched all day as we picked our way up the waterfall. In the end Yangzum, the only one to have placed her bet on our success, walked away with a handsome share of rupees.

△

By falling I broke the rules of ice climbing, but this time I escaped punishment. David lowered me to the snow and I sat down to recover and assess myself for trauma. The pain in my hands from the cold and from over-gripping my ice tools was intense, and my whole body felt tweaked. Fortunately, it had been a clean fall and my crampons skated down the rock wall without catching on anything. I was okay, but I wasn't keen on trying it again. The line was inspiring, but it would have to wait for another day.

Gottlieb on the summit ridge of Takargo. *Joe Puryear*

In the upper valley, an hour and a half hike from Beding, David and I had walked into the mother lode of ice climbs. We opened a two-pitch WI6, a handful of two- to three-pitch WI5's, and some fun WI4's. And we found a spectacular side gully containing a host of high-end ice and mixed routes. We named the gully Samsāra, a Buddhist term that can indicate the suffering that occurs while traveling through the cycles of life and rebirth. With my near-death experience and the agony that ensued, we thought it appropriate.

In all we climbed 13 waterfalls, with 12 of them likely being first ascents. The potential of the area is much larger. In a year of good ice conditions, or maybe just earlier in the season, there could be as many as 50 high-quality ice routes, all within a two-hour walk of Beding. We saw even more huge waterfalls in remote and obscure locations. The Rolwaling truly is one of Asia's greatest ice-climbing venues.

Toward the end of February temperatures started rising and we witnessed several ice collapses. Ice climbing season was over. It was time to focus on Takargo.

Rays of sun filtered through the small crosshatched windows, weaving patterns in the incense smoke that filled the large room. Boom, boom, boom, clang, clang. The sound of ancient ceremonial drums and symbols combined with a monotone chanting put us in a deep trance. We sat cross-legged on the floor for several hours receiving the puja, a Buddhist blessing ceremony, for our upcoming expedition. The lamas of Beding determined that the auspicious date for our departure would be March 4. This was a bit later than we wanted to leave, but we waited until that day because of the importance of this ancient tradition. Stormy weather dominated right up to that date, and we departed Beding with clear skies and clear heads.

The busy clamor of goats and sheep echoed across the hillside and the poignant smell of yaks filled the crisp clean air. Sherpanis vigorously worked the prolific potato fields that enveloped every usable flat space. The Sherpas were starting to move out of their lower village and make their seasonal move up to Beding and then Na, the highest summer village, in order to plant more potatoes and prepare for the upcoming tourist season. But where we were headed, there would be no tourists, nor any Sherpas. Though normally staged with an average of one trekking group a day in the high season, the way east was totally deserted. We did not encounter a single tourist from the time we left Kathmandu until we returned. The reason was plain: The Trakarding Glacier was gripped by snow.

We made slow but steady progress and in three days established an advanced base camp at 4,700 meters, intending to climb the mountain's west face. Here the narrow hanging valley between Chobutse and Takargo actively spills rocks into the Trakarding Glacier.

The next day dawned clear, and we made a reconnaissance trip up into the valley to scout our route. Our fears of a dry Himalaya came true. While the lower elevations were collecting snow, the higher wind swept faces looked dry. Research photos had led us to believe the face would be covered in ice; instead it was dry and barren. Rockfall clattered down the face.

We spent the night near the mountain's base in order to make a complete assessment, and the next morning it was obvious: We did not want this risk. We quickly retreated back to our advance base camp and reformulated our plans.

We had seen pictures of the mountain's east side, but were unsure whether it would offer a better alternative. There was only one way to find out, which required a long hump to reach. We packed seven days' worth of food, leaving just a couple days of supply at our advance base camp, and then we headed up the glacier.

We began by hiking the normal route toward Tashi Laptsa pass. Up to the head of the Trakarding Glacier, then up a steep rock headwall to gain the detached Drolamba Glacier, then a long trudge up ice fields and moraines past Takargo, then back up a side-glacier to the mountain's east face. It was a grueling two-day journey, but we were pleasantly surprised when we arrived at the base and saw that there might be a feasible route. The face was complex. A colossal hanging glacier guarded most of the middle face. Above that, a fortress of rock and icy flutings extended across its entirety. We would have to pick our way through it like an obstacle course.

The next morning we made the final approach to the base over hard glacial ice. There was no snow accumulation on the wind-swept glacier at this elevation. Threatened by the massive hanging glacier that drew across most of the face, we were nervous about finding a safe way through the initial rock band that immediately impeded progress. Immense amounts of rocky and corniced terrain rose above our heads. Fortunately, cool temperatures on the face kept everything in place.

In a couple leads we weaved in and out of rocks, made some tricky moves, and soon broke free of the rock band and onto easier slopes. Now unroped, we continued up snow slopes heading for a couloir that bypassed the hanging glacier on its right side. The way became arduous again as deeper snow slowed our progress.

Late in the afternoon we finally broke over the glacier and onto a long bench that took us back south to a bivy near the mountain's east ridge. The east ridge is fairly prominent down low, but at the point where it meets the hanging glacier the ridge disappears into the eastern headwall of the peak. We dug out a bivy and settled in for a long, cold March night.

Right in front of us, a comprehensive view of the Khumbu unfolded. In the glow of the fading evening, bands of yellow and pink light and contrasting blue shadows brought brilliant intensity to the world's most famous peaks. A luminous sunset on Everest and Lhotse was matched only by a radiant sunrise the next morning over Makalu.

On March 12 we awoke at first light and geared up for our final push to the summit. The first obstacle was a stubborn serac that blocked the way to the upper headwall. David made quick work of two pitches of 60° glacial-ice. Low-angle snow led to the final headwall.

The first lead was mine and I dispatched a ten-meter 80° bergschrund followed by 60° alpine ice, for a full 60-meter pitch. David swapped leads and continued up the ice, making a tricky traverse past some rocks. I led two more pitches of ice, with an abrupt 80° serac break-over into a nice 65° runnel. Things were going well; we felt strong and climbed efficiently.

David took the last lead to the ridge crest, which was perhaps the most interesting. Seventy-degree serac ice led to the base of a massive cornice/ice cliff. Traversing under it to the right, he made tenuous moves through weird snow and ice features, digging a path upward and finally climbing through a natural break that led to the 6,756-meter southern sub-peak on Takargo's south ridge.

The summit was physically close, but before us was the mental crux of the route. We were now tired and feeling the high elevation, and a bitterly cold wind swept up from the west. A lack of protection meant we had to be extra cautious, as one slip would mean a 1,200-meter ride down the west face.

We carefully picked our way across the corniced crest and an hour later arrived at the true summit. There were three high points, each about 60 meters apart, that all appeared to be equal height. In order to be thorough, we visited each one and tried to gauge which was the true summit. In the end, we settled on the middle point as being the probable highest. Here a huge detached cornice on the other side of the ridge crest allowed a small reprieve from the wind. We sat and enjoyed our success for about 20 minutes.

The weather was changing fast. Huge billowing clouds poured in from the west. Already, Kang Nachugo and Melungtse were no longer visible. It was time to leave.

We vigilantly retraced our steps back across the ridge. From the sub-summit, we down-climbed 30 meters of snow in order to reach a suitable spot to sink our first V-thread anchor. Using our standard technique, we pulled the rope through the V-thread hole, thus leaving no trace of

The southwest face of Takargo, which Gottlieb and Puryear rejected as being too dangerously loose. Joe Puryear

our ascent on the mountain. After two rappels it started snowing lightly, causing spindrift to pour down the face. Seven 60-meter rappels brought us to the safety of our high bivy.

We were nervous about our location. If it snowed heavily, our descent would be extremely avalanche prone, leaving us stuck waiting for better conditions.

"What to do you think about the weather?" I asked David.

"Let's just not talk about it right now," he replied.

He was right, no reason to get worked up about it, since there was nothing we could do. We were way out in the middle of nowhere with very little supplies. The situation could become dire.

Luckily it stopped snowing during the night. We awoke to clear skies and let out a huge sigh of relief. At this point we were on a mission to get out of there. We crossed the bench and carefully descended slopes next to the hanging glacier. We down-climbed and rappelled through the rock band, eventually reaching the relative safety of the glacier below.

We felt great satisfaction with the accomplishment, but knew what lay ahead: three very long days of laborious slogging. Intense afternoon snow and lightening storms plagued our exit from the upper valley.

We arrived safely in Beding to a warm welcome from the community. We told tales of our adventure, showed pictures, and drank chang for three days before making our final departure. It was a successful trip on so many levels. The ice climbing and the peak's first ascent mattered to us, but equally important was the relationship with our new Sherpa friends. These experiences will long outlast memories of the climbing, and the falling.

SUMMARY:

AREA: ROLWALING HIMAL, NEPAL.

Ascents: After discovering an untapped ice-paradise in the upper Rolwaling Valley and putting up a dozen new waterfall routes, David Gottlieb and Joe Puryear made the first official ascent of Takargo (6,771m), March 11–13, 2010. They climbed a gully on the right side of the east face to reach a large glacier shelf, traversed this left, and then climbed seven ice pitches to the south summit before following the ridge north to the main top (1,000m, TD). The snowy alpine-style approach added another week to the adventure.

ABOUT THE AUTHOR:

On October 27, 2010, Joe Puryear was attempting an unclimbed line on Labuche Kang in Tibet with David Gottlieb when he broke through a cornice low on the route. Unroped, he fell 700 feet to his death. His wife, Michelle Puryear, found this article and these photos on Joe's computer. His obituary is in the In Memoriam section of this Journal.

Joe Puryear (left) and David Gottlieb on the summit of Takargo.

The Serpent King

The first ascent of the west face of Vasuki Parbat, India.

Malcolm Bass

I really wanted this one. So far, the great mountains of Asia had largely defeated me. Six big trips over 18 years had produced two summits and plenty of abseiling practice. In the last few years I had begun to question the investment, to consider giving up long trips to the Himalaya and Karakoram in favor of Scotland, Alaska, and the Alps. But a question kept reappearing: "Do you want to walk away a failure?" And I knew that I didn't. I knew that if I stopped at that point I'd live the rest of my life knowing I had been bested by the big beasts. I wanted to climb a great new route to a high Himalayan summit, and then be free to choose my future. Until then I'd just have to keep trying. I really wanted this one.

So I wasn't pleased to be lying on a bed in a guesthouse in Gangotri, two days behind schedule, listening to rain hammering on the roof and watching the snow line creep ever closer to the Ganges. The rains that had devastated the subcontinent throughout the summer were still falling, now as a late monsoon. The authorities had closed the track towards the mountains, while landslides blocked the road to Gangotri. I was glad of our team: New Zealander Patricia Deavoll, my friend and stalwart climbing partner of many fine trips since our chance meeting on Alaska's Tokositna Glacier, who possessed a much better Asian hit rate than mine. The indomitable Paul Figg, veteran of shared Alaskan epics, returning for a second round with the Garhwal. Rachel Antill, our expedition artist, hugely enthused by her first trip to India, making the best of our enforced halt with her sketchpad. And Satyabrata Dam, our multi-talented liaison officer: Everester, polar traveler, and exploratory mountaineer. Between us we'd logged a lot of days in Scotland, Alaska, India, and New Zealand. We knew how to wait out bad weather.

Our patience was eventually rewarded with a beautiful morning, an early chill in the air, and perfect blue skies. Porters congregated and we were under way. Two hours later I caught my first glimpse of the west face of Vasuki. It looked hideously steep. Luckily the face was soon hidden by intervening peaks, making it easy to retreat back into the comforting delusion I use on Himalayan walk-ins: We're just going for a nice trek with someone cooking us lovely food each night before a long sleep in a warm bag.

My delusion crumbled two days later as we dug base camp into a couple of feet of fresh snow. The great dark face drew our gaze, and we'd pause in our digging long enough to imagine ourselves up there. The mountains were laden with fresh snow, but Vasuki's west face looked the same as it had in all the photographs. We'd chosen wisely: It was too steep to hold fresh snow.

Vasuki Parbat (6,782m), named for Lord Vasuki, the serpent king of Hindu mythology, lies between the huge pyramid of Satopanth (7,075m) and the famous Bhagarathi chain. It has

The west face of Vasuki Parbat, showing the Bass-Figg line and their camps. The descent continued along the left skyline. *Satyabrata Dam*

Malcolm Bass and Paul Figg on the first pitch of the first day. *Pat Deavoll*

a mysterious climbing history. The Indo-Tibetan Border Police claim to have made the first ascent in 1973, route unknown. The scant details have caused some to doubt the claim. A Japanese team made the first ascent of the broad, icy east face in 1980 after fixing ropes up the lower 600 meters of the route. In 1983 a French team made a siege attempt on the northwest ridge; a Welsh team attempted the same line in alpine style. No one had attempted the steeper west face until a Harish Kapadia photograph lured Mick Fowler and Paul Ramsden in 2008 to have a go at the compelling ramp and buttress cleaving the face. Heavy snowfall began on the day after they reached base camp and continued for 48 hours, putting paid to any chance of acclimatizing on easy ground. As they started up the face, which had remained in good condition, temperatures plummeted. They climbed over half the face, including most of the steep middle section, before lack of acclimatization and incipient cold injuries forced a retreat.

Our team's original goal had been an unclimbed peak elsewhere in the Garhwal. But while the Indian Mountaineering Foundation had issued us with their permit, the state government of Uttarakhand refused the local clearance. With plane tickets to Delhi already bought, we needed a new Indian objective, one that was at least as attractive to generous grant-giving bodies as the original had been. Emails zipped between the UK, New Zealand, and India. Unclimbed peaks in Pakistan and long overland journeys got brief looks before early drafts of the 2010 *AAJ* told us they'd been climbed. Eventually we had a short list. Nothing on that list was of the same level as our original objective—except the west face of Vasuki. A 1,600m face, with glaring technical difficulties on a big hill, it had turned back one of the most effective alpine partnerships of our generation. Quite frankly, it scared me. Pat's courage decided the issue. She wrote: "Let's go and see what the good guys do." And so, after confirming that the good guys weren't planning to go back for another shot, we turned our faces toward Lord Vasuki.

W.H. Murray was thinking about the Garhwal when he wrote: "Until one is committed, there is hesitancy, the chance to draw back, always ineffectiveness. Concerning all acts of initiative (and creation) there is one elementary truth, the ignorance of which kills countless ideas and splendid plans: that the moment one definitely commits oneself, then Providence moves too" (The Scottish Himalayan Expedition 1951). That was exactly how I felt when we finally committed to Vasuki. I began to believe that we could do it.

The weather was superb as we acclimatized on the lower section of the normal route on Bhagirathi II, but Pat was having a hard time; she felt cold and out of sorts, plagued by a persistent cough. And then I developed a head cold. But finally Pat, Paul, and I left base camp carrying seven days' food, nine days' gas, and, as the nights were bitterly cold, our warmest sleeping bags. This wasn't going to be an elegant dash. It would be a grinding war of attrition. I found that oddly reassuring.

Pat led off from the top of the snow cone in the first light of a cold dawn. A thin runnel of water ice snaked down a narrow gully, an oddly intimate start to a 1,600m face. The gully bed and sidewalls were worn smooth by water and rock fall. We needed to be out before the sun came onto the face at noon. Pat flowed smoothly up the pitches, a consummate ice climber, while Paul and I struggled along behind with big rusacks and screaming calves. The sun was just coming onto the face as we left the gully to climb up and right onto the buttress crest where we planned to spend the first night. Deep snow exhausted us on the buttress, but still, the first day went as planned.

The next day began with arduous snow plodding up the ramp. Pat was having a grim time. She'd broken her back in a fall only five months before the trip, and now both her back and her knees were protesting. She wasn't acclimatizing and felt constantly cold. We sat on our packs discussing what to do. Pat worried that she was holding us back; we reassured her this wasn't the case. None of us were ready to consider breaking up the team, so we decided to press on together.

By mid afternoon the ground began to steepen as it ran up against the obvious crux: the rocky buttress that comprises the middle third of the route. We decided to bivouac early as

Mick Fowler leading on day 3 in their attempt in 2008. *Paul Ramsden*

sites would be scarce above. The next morning was fiendishly cold. A light breeze blew frigid air down the ramp, and we windmilled vigorously as we tried to keep some sensation in our digits. It wasn't working for Pat, who had several numb fingers and toes. We moved up and left into a broad couloir, where we uncoiled the ropes to start pitching.

Pat said, "I could get down from here on my own."

"Are you joking?"

"No. I'm serious."

A pause, then, "I'm going down."

We had no time for debate. The sun was about to hit the face. We had to make do with brisk, functional communication.

"I'll take the haul line"

"Take the spare stove."

"I'll need an ice screw."

We shunted gear from one to another. Is this the right thing? I rigged our climbing ropes for Pat to abseil on.

"Be careful."

"And you."

And she was gone. A shout to say she was off the ropes, and as we tied back in we watched her climb carefully down and across, out of the couloir's line of fire, making for last night's bivouac ledge.

The ice traverse on day four of Fowler and Ramsden's attempt in 2008. *Mick Fowler*

The next pitch was horrible. I was still rattled from the events of the last half hour. I knew that rock fall might start any minute. I tried to climb fast, but couldn't find a piece of gear to protect the belay. The climbing was steep and insecure, with loose blocks and dirty black ice that shattered far too readily. Eventually a tricam behind a creaky flake gave me enough confidence to hook a series of dusty edges onto decent ice and belay underneath a reassuringly protective roof. I had just started taking in the ropes when a huge block hurtled down the gully. It hit the top of the wall below me, spun out into space, then described a gentle arc toward Paul, who had nowhere to go. I saw him hunch under his pack just before the rock hit. He crumpled and slumped sideways. I thought he was dead.

"Paul, Paul!"

Nothing but the distant clattering of the rock completing its journey to the glacier.

"Paul!"

No. No. No. This hasn't happened.

"Paul!" Shouting so hard I could feel my throat tearing.

Movement, then groans. Slowly he righted himself and stood back up to the belay.

He's alive at least. Thank fuck for that.

"Are you OK?"

"I think so."

"Can you climb?"

"I think so."

The ice traverse on Fowler and Ramsden's fourth day. *Paul Ramsden*

Paul is made of an indestructible material. Descending the west ridge of Mt. Hunter roped together in thick fog in 2001 we fell over a serac. Paul went a good 70 meters, 10 of them vertical. Yet within a few hours he was back to normal. And this time he appeared to have suffered even less damage. Treatment consisted of anti-inflammatories. Although we were both in reasonable physical shape, our nerves were frayed. Rocks, loosened by the afternoon sun, flew down the couloir. We put a brew on and whiled away the rest of the afternoon beneath the safety of our overhang. Back home Fowler and Ramsden had been generous in sharing their photographs and suggestions. We'd brought along laminated copies, and we got them out now to review the key ramp that would take us onto what Mick had referred to in the *Alpine Club Journal* as "great squeaky white ice traverse pitches."

We never found that ramp. Perhaps that was an inevitable outcome of waiting till dark before continuing up the couloir. It was my leading block, and although the climbing was a brutal fight with gritty black ice, I felt a surge of optimism as we gained height. We were getting up this thing. At about 11 o'clock I reached the top of the couloir. Above me a free-hanging ice pillar dropped from an overhanging wall. So I swung out right, dry tooling onto the front face of the buttress and a series of sloping rock ledges. One sloped more gently than the rest.

"I've found our bivouac. Safe."

If Paul was disappointed by my find he didn't show it. Nor did he give me a hard time when I told him that I'd just dropped our only camera off the ledge while arranging the belay. An understanding partner is a great asset in these situations.

We were too tired to cook that night, but we did the right thing by making lots of drinks before trying to sleep. We would sleep for a bit, slide off the ledge, wriggle back up, sleep some more.... We found out later that 300 meters below, Pat was also trying to sleep. Cold and lonely, lying in the open on the previous night's narrow tent platform, she was wondering whether she'd made the right decision.

I woke properly with the first light of dawn. Paul, a resilient sleeper, slumbered on. How amazing it was to be perched on a tiny ledge halfway up a huge face in the vastness of the Himalaya. Things certainly weren't going to plan, but they were going well enough. We could do this.

As we drank our morning coffee we watched Pat climbing down from the first night's tent platform. We packed up and Paul led a descending line that took us neatly onto the ice traverse. He seemed to have forgotten how to place ice screws, and was taking several minutes to place each one. When I reached his stance he told me they had all been blunted by the gritty ice we'd climbed last night. Despite this it was good to be back on the route pioneered by Mick and Paul R., and even better to reach the instantly recognizable "pinnacle bivouac," a magnificent spot right on top of an overhanging wall. A snow pillow forms on top of the pillar, and it doesn't take much work to carve off the crest to form a perfect flat tent site. It has become customary to spend two nights here.

Day six for Fowler and Ramsden consisted of superb mixed climbing. Paul Ramsden

Mick and Paul R. had made good use of their stay. Despite numb toes and blistering fingers they'd pushed on up fantastic mixed ground to a ledge beneath a steep rock tower. But then things started to go wrong as a long traverse left failed to outflank the tower. Running out of daylight they abseiled back down to the pinnacle bivouac.

I didn't make such good use of the first day of our stay. I just fell off.

I wasn't far up the first pitch above the bivouac when I leaned down to place a nut and suddenly I was falling, a nasty clattering fall out over the ice traverse and then down the horribly steep wall below. A small nut just above the traverse stopped me from shock loading the belay. I hung there for a few seconds, my dilated pupils trying to take in the immense drop below. I was terrified. The thought of the nut popping

The incredible Pinnacle Bivy, where Bass and Figg spent their fourth and fifth nights on Vasuki. This photo shows Paul Ramsden in 2008; he also spent his fourth and fifth nights there. *Mick Fowler*

was hideous, and I began to scrabble frantically to get back up the wall onto the safety of the ice traverse. But the moves were too difficult, and it was just too soon, so I sagged back onto the rope gasping from fear and exertion until I could try again. More thought, less pedaling, and a very hard move gained me a placement in the ice ledge, and then I was up. I tottered back to Paul on the pinnacle, where I burst into tears.

"I'm sorry, I'm sorry."

"It's OK. You're OK. We're all OK."

"I'm sorry. I really want to get up this."

"We will. It's OK."

I became convinced that Paul or persons unknown, having seen me fall, would ban us from going any higher. My head and neck hurt, and I felt confused and emotional. I'd clearly bashed my head. Paul wisely declared a rest day and began to put the tent back up. He evened-up the gear-dropping score by dropping a tent pole. The tent worked fine without it.

A long sleep seemed to sort me out. Paul was in the lead as brilliant icy mixed climbing took us to the base of the rock tower at about 6,000m, where Mick and Paul R. had traversed fruitlessly left. They had suggested that we try a direct line up the crest of the tower instead. The sun came onto the rock tower as we racked gear at its foot. I took off a glove and tentatively touched the rock. It was warm enough. I hung my pack on the belay and climbed with bare hands and crampons. I'm no geologist, but it seems to me that Vasuki is made of some sort of

The west face of Vasuki. Bass and Figg's descent route followed the left skyline. *Satyabrata Dam*

limestone, most of which is solid and compact. But the rock tower is horribly loose. I sent a steady stream of blocks and flakes over the edge of the buttress, careful to avoid testing Paul's indestructibility any further. We climbed the tower in short pitches to make hauling easier, but the packs resisted all the way.

The tower was connected to the main face by a narrow, nearly horizontal, snow crest interrupted by short rocky steps. Above the crest's junction with the main face was a blank looking rock wall that we believed was the penultimate barrier, the last being a hoped-for jink under the headwall.

The snow crest was the wildest bit of climbing I've ever done. The light faded and the evening wind blew strongly up from the huge voids each side of the crest. My face stung from airborne ice crystals as I shuffled *à cheval* along the crest. I was suddenly filled with joy at our situation: six days up an unclimbed face in a tremendous place, deeply committed, and moving forward in the most ridiculous way. I laughed and shouted for the love of our stupid, serious adventure.

By the time I reached the next rock step it was dark and the wind had strengthened. We needed shelter. It took us an hour to dig the narrow snow ridge down far enough to make something approaching a tent platform. Luckily we'd recently converted our tent to a Super Lite One Pole Narrow Pitch model, so it fitted well. As had become routine, Paul crawled in first, and I stood outside throwing in a random assortment of kit that I expected him to have sorted by the time I entered.

It was always delightful to crawl inside out of the wind. With the stove burning the tent soon warmed up, and we'd peel off layers and relax. The reality of the mountain and the climbing would vanish, and we'd talk abstractly, as if in a pub back home. We slept well in our big bags, keeping civilized hours since it was far too cold to do useful climbing done in the early morning (or so we told ourselves). These snug nights were perfect for physical and psychological recuperation.

The next morning began with more cowboy action before the arête ran up against the rock wall. This did not look promising. It was smooth, compact, and slightly overhanging at the top. Would this measly little wall stop us after so much effort? We moved left, searching for a way through. Just around the corner a short, steep groove with a more helpful look about it gave hard, delicate moves up rock to reach fluffy rubbish snow. Thump, useless, a bit higher, thump, powder, then finally, at full extension, a solid stick in ice. I committed everything to that placement, hauling with both hands on the one tool till my foot was held by something in the powder zone and I got another good placement and pulled onto the huge upper snowfield.

The altitude took its toll as we moved slowly up the snow. Eventually we were unable to resist a well-protected campsite under the impending headwall. The wall above us was obviously impossible, so before turning in for the night we sneaked a look along the ramp. Further upward progress depended entirely on finding a way round the wall into the final gully. Our hearts were in our mouths as we explored. The snow ramp gradually narrowed till it was no wider than a boot, where a helpful flake allowed us to lean out and peer round the corner. There it was: A step down would be enough to reach the gully floor and outflank the wall. We were on.

Our world instantly expanded when we reached the summit ridge in the late afternoon of our eighth day on the mountain. The great pyramid of Satopanth dominated the southeast, while to the northeast we could see right over the Himalaya to the brown hills of Tibet. Look-

ing down the east face of Vasuki we didn't like what we saw: a steep snow and ice face, lots of seracs, and hidden ground. The summit rose to the north along the broad, undulating ridge. We set off that way, more relaxed now that we were off the face, enjoying the late afternoon sun. We camped in a little col between rocky steps just south of the summit, ate our last proper food, and talked about the descent.

Buss and Figg on day eight, just below the crest of the face. *Satyabrata Dam*

"I don't fancy the east face."

"Not with blunt ice screws."

"Would we have enough gear to get back down the route?"

"Not sure."

"Northwest ridge?"

"It's a long traverse to get to it. Looks OK once we're on it."

"Looks safe."

"Northwest ridge it is then?"

"Agreed."

"Paul, about the summit tomorrow. Would you mind if we didn't stand right on top? I've sort of promised Lord Vasuki that we wouldn't."

"So have I!"

Our ninth day began with a moderate rock pitch. From its top we saw that the slightly higher point ahead was the summit. We avoided it by skirting a couple meters below on the west side. The summit seemed an irrelevance, just another rise on the ridge that led to our descent, and it was easy to keep our promise.

From here on we were on a sharp crest, surprisingly free of cornices, and its undulations gave us a magnificent day's mountaineering. For long sections we were moving crab wise, our tools planted on the top of the east face, and our feet on the west. We were very happy. We'd climbed the west face, reached our summit, and were reveling in our three-kilometer skywalk. Although we'd been out a long time we still felt firmly in control. In the late afternoon we reached the junction of the northwest and northeast ridges, made a few rappels, and found a campsite. Quite unexpectedly this became the first miserable night of the climb. Although the traverse of the summit ridge had been superb, we had been moving in deep, very cold snow all day. With nothing left to eat, our bodies refused to warm up. We slept fitfully, waking to long periods of shivering. We were starting to weaken.

The steep sections were the easy bits. Continuing our descent the next day we abseiled down rocky steps among tangles of rotting fixed rope, and down-climbed snow couloirs. But each time the ridge leveled out we found ourselves in thigh-deep snow through which we made terribly slow progress.

I didn't have much time left to secure my position as the champion kit dropper of the team. I bided my time, then seized the moment. Paul had just down-climbed a pitch of evil, shiny, snow-covered slabs. I was totally unable to follow and insisted on a rope. Balancing precariously on tiny edges, I swung my pack off, fished out a rope, and swung the pack on again without doing it up. One leaning move was enough to do the trick. Soon a stuff sack containing a headlamp, compass, map, and my beloved orange hat from the Dolomites sped down the north face.

As the angle of the ridge eased, our progress slowed until Paul had an idea:

"Why don't we just drop off the north side of the ridge?"

"But that looks much steeper."

"Exactly."

The extra angle proved enough to keep us moving. We rolled, fell, bum slid, and floundered, accompanied by great sloughs of snow, down to the foot of the north face, where we stumbled around in the darkness in the general direction of Vasuki Tal, the lake at Satopanth base camp.

Eventually we found tracks made by climbers on their way to and from Satopanth, and we followed them back to the lake shore. We stopped by a little stream to fill our water bottles. The snow around the stream had melted, revealing grass. We sat on our packs and took off our crampons. The sky was full of stars. We said thank you to one another for keeping each other safe, for keeping going, and for getting up it. The marshy ground smelled of mud. It felt like Scotland, not the Himalaya, like the end of a hundred climbs before it and hopefully hundreds more to come. Where those climbs will be I don't know yet. Climbing Vasuki has left me free to choose.

Postscript: After we lost sight of Pat on the morning of the fourth day, she down climbed into the initial ice gully and then abseiled (using the haul line and V threads) and down climbed to its foot. When we unpacked Paul's pack we found that one gas bottle had been crumpled by an enormous blow. It was this propane-butane air bag that had saved Paul from significant injury or worse from the falling rock.

SUMMARY:

Area: Garhwal Himal, India

Ascents: The first ascent of the west face of Vasuki Parbat (6,782m), by Malcolm Bass and Paul Figg (1,600m, V,6 Damilano system: the crux was Scottish VI,7), October 4–13, 2010. They traversed the three-kilometer summit ridge and descended by the northwest ridge. This was the first alpine style ascent of Vasuki, and the second or third ascent overall. Other expedition members were Patricia Deavoll (climber), Rachel Antill (expedition artist), Satyabrata Dam (Liaison Officer), Chandar Singh Negi (cook), and Shankar Thapa (assistant cook).

ABOUT THE AUTHOR:

Malcolm Bass is a clinical psychologist specializing in people who self-injure. He lives with his partner Donna James on the edge of the North York Moors in the United Kingdom, where he climbs the soaring sandstone spires of Scugdale.
He would like to thank the Mount Everest Foundation, the British Mountaineering Council, The Alpine Club, and W.L. Gore (The Shipton Tilman Grant) for financial support of his expedition. Also DHL (freight), Wayfarer meals, and Mountain Hardwear for their support. Finally thanks to Anita and Mandip Soin and Khem Singh, all of Ibex Expeditions, for their kindness, efficiency and hospitality.

Paul Figg (left) and Malcolm Bass after their ascent.
Rachel Antill

DRACULA

*Seventy-one sleepless hours during a first ascent on the
southeast face of Mt. Foraker, in the Alaska Range.*

BJØRN-EIVIND AARTUN

Mt. Foraker (17,400'), showing the complete odyssey for Colin Haley and Bjorn-Eivind Aartun during their first ascent of Dracula (10,400', AI4+ M6R A0). From the KIA camp they skied to the base of the southeast face, where they spent the night. From there it was 71 sleepless hours back to KIA. The French Ridge is the left skyline, while the Northeast Ridge is the right skyline. Bjørn-Eivind returned afterward to retrieve their skis. *Bjørn-Eivind Aartun*

Sometimes you meet someone who easily shares your dreams. On first meeting Colin Haley I could see that he was an open minded, highly motivated climber not easily distracted by mere obstacles. He was keen to explore all the possibilities within singlepush climbing. While together in 2009 on Mt. Hunter, we discussed our ambitions, discovering a shared goal of climbing the Cassin Ridge on Denali in a day. The weather during our final week in Alaska that year didn't allow for anything big, so we skied over to the southeast side of Mt. Foraker to scope a line on the unclimbed rock face leading to the crest of the French ridge. The seeds of next year's climbing had just been planted.

Haley starting up the first, left-trending ramp on Dracula. *Bjørn-Eivind Aartun*

May 2010. The constant roar of Talkeetna Air Taxi's powerful Beaver engine left each of us in our own thoughts as we flew back into the Alaska Range. During the flight in, we passed directly in front of the southeast face of Foraker. As it came into view I could feel it right in my stomach. We planned to climb this huge wall without bivi gear. Treating such a route as a day climb was a step up for me. But based on our experiences last year on the north buttress of Hunter, it seemed the right thing to do, a perfect dose of the unknown. Could we quickly unlock its steep, rocky secrets on our way to the ice slopes above?

Aartun on the right-trending ramp on Dracula. *Colin Haley*

Immediately after landing on the Kahiltna Glacier, we started skiing toward the 14,200-foot camp, where we would acclimatize. Our time there was both fun and a test of my patience. Camp life had its own challenges. The toilets were both funny and disgusting. It seemed like the rangers had deliberately exposed them to the living area, placing them directly in the path leading to the board where weather forecasts were posted. Images of old men doing their thing are still horribly burned into the back of my eyeballs. But eating pancakes and fighting with the Dutch and Belgians was fun, as was learning about "zvaffeling." To acclimatize, we skied a lot and climbed Denali twice by different standard routes, but the weather never gave us much to work with. Time was running out and we worried that we'd leave the range without even attempting our dream climbs.

Finally we had to take action. Despite a less than ideal forecast, we left for the Cassin Ridge with a couple of screws and a 20-meter rope for the approach down the Seattle 72 Ramp. We stopped at the bergshrund below the Japanese Couloir to brew and rest before starting out at night.

The first half of the Cassin was great fun, as there were sections of technical climbing. It was intense and invigorating: going "naked" required focus. Being able to move with a very light pack and no gear on a big mountain is pure pleasure for the freedom of movement it allows, much more than mere speed or record-chasing (we hoped to beat Mugs Stump's 15-hour ascent, set in 1991). But at some point above the Knife Edge ridge it started snowing, which slowed us considerably. The upper half of the climb was easy snow and ice slopes, which would be fine if the weather were good. But wallowing in deep fresh snow was not fun. We summited totally exhausted 17 hours after leaving the shrund.

After descending to the 14,200-foot camp, we felt the only reasonable thing to do was pack up immediately and ski down (thank god for the skis) to Kahiltna International Airport, where we could start looking up at Mt. Foraker while counting the hours to our flights back home. Or was there still a slight chance of trying our main objective?

On June 12, three days before we had to fly out from KIA, we crossed the Kahiltna Glacier on skis to the foot of the face just to "have a look." The forecast called for a single day of good weather, coming tomorrow. It snowed during the night, but we woke up at 4 a.m. to clear skies. After careful consideration, we decided to go for it.

Knowing we could expect deteriorating weather on the descent, we brought two full 225-gram gas canisters just in case. We discussed taking only one rope, but decided on two ice

Haley approaching the precarious cornice near the top of the right-trending ramp. *Bjørn-Eivind Aartun*

twin ropes to have an extra margin there as well.

With such small backpacks containing no bivi gear, it took us only two hours to cross under the dangerous seracs vvguarding access to the wall itself. Going all out for safety, acid burning in our legs, our hearts pumping at full speed, we continued past crevasses and then easy runnels and ice steps up past the seracs until we were just under the wall. While jumping one of the gaps down low, I lost my sunglasses, so I pulled my beanie down whenever I could to protect my eyes.

A brew stop at the start of the big rocky wall gave room for thoughts about what lay before us. From the tent we had seen that this first part would be easy climbing with serac danger. The wall itself was harder to predict. It was a thrill to sit there, getting ready to venture into the unknown.

Haley on the route's second crux pitch. Not as steep as the first, but with rotten rock and bad protection. *Bjørn-Eivind Aartun*

Haley nearing the end of the "never-ending" 60° ice slopes, in the first rays of the sun. They were desperate for water at this point. *Bjørn-Eivind Aartun*

Colin started leading. The first part was really nice: ice runnels with trickier mixed bits in between. A couple of pitches up, I followed a dead vertical dihedral. My picks found good slots, while front points rested on small edges. It was good climbing, with good protection; I felt inspired and happy. This was what we had come for. Smiling, I joined Colin on the belay, and he immediately off for a steep pitch of ice.

The sun disappeared behind the French Ridge and it was my turn to lead. The terrain was easier here. Mostly moderate ice took me to the big right-trending ramp in the middle of the wall. We simul-climbed a lot on this section, making good speed. I was excited to have reached the ramp. Studying everything from below, we had predicted the difficulties quite accurately. Reaching the ramp resolved one of the mysteries. We expected that the last part up the wall and out onto the icefields would also have a crux.

At the end of the ramp, fun mixed climbing took me onto steep snow—really steep at the end. This should have been Colin's lead: he's good at it. He even likes it, whereas I don't. Almost through, I got a creepy feeling and peered out over the edge to the right. Yes, it was just as I feared: I was about to ascend an overhanging mushroom as big as a car. My heart raced and I quickly tried to move left. There was no protection. My last screw was 20 meters away when finally I could build a belay in sound ice. Looking down, I was awestruck by the precarious snow formation. It looked like it was hinged in 30 cm of loose snow; my tracks cut through just where it would someday break.

"I think we can take a brew stop after this last steep pitch," Colin said as I re-racked, heading up. I had to climb a belt of rotten rock to get to a fine corner higher up. Gently balancing on my crampons, I tried to kick away loose stones to find secure footholds. I felt a rush of warmth to my head. With next to no protection, falling was out of the question. It wasn't really hard, but delicate and dangerous. Eventually I wiggled onto an ice tongue, put in a good screw, and once again felt invincible. But there was no ledge on top, so when Colin arrived, we continued without a brew. This proved unwise; we should have forced a hydration stop, even if it meant a semi-hanging belay. Colin developed frostbite on his big toes during the torture of the never-ending 60° ice up to where we met the French Ridge. It's hard to know if he could have avoided it by drinking more, but I think it would have helped.

The first rays of morning sun hit us some 200 meters below the ridge. We were totally worked when we finally finished the last simul-climbing pitch and could lie down on the ridge crest. I hitched a sling around my waist and clipped it to my tool to get a couple of minutes of sleep while waiting for the snow to melt.

Later that morning, after 31 hours of climbing, we stood on top of Foraker. The last part had been easy snow plodding. Smiling as we looked around at nearby Hunter and Denali, we felt happy but anxious to get as far down as possible before bad weather might catch us.

Our first goal was to reach the saddle where the Sultana Ridge traverses toward Crosson.

The crevasse shiver-bivy at 12,000 feet on the Northeast Ridge, where they spent a miserable 12 hours waiting for the blizzard to abate. *Bjørn-Eivind Aartun*

From there it should be "easy" to follow the distinct Sultana Ridge without getting lost in foul weather. We moved as fast as possible, butt-sliding crevasses. This was really painful for Colin, as by now his toes had warmed up again and they hurt badly. I fed him painkillers, but that didn't help much.

When we reached the saddle, we found a sheltered crevasse in which we could make dinner and melt snow. Happy to have made it down there, we felt secure and upbeat. So far, the weather was holding. But when we tried to exit and continue our descent everything had changed. A full-on blizzard raged outside.

After two attempts to continue along the ridge, we had to escape back into the crevasse. It was impossible to go on. Strangely enough we felt quite calm. My Norwegian background— filled with cold mountains—allowed me accept the fact that we just had to wait it out, even if we weren't equipped. Sooner or later there would be a small break in the storm and we'd have just enough visibility to get us going again. Inside, we alternated between small jokes and big worries. Most of the time we had to work hard to stay warm. We could never lie down; instead we did knee bends and swung our arms in endless repetitions.

I frequently went out to have a look at the weather, afraid to miss improving conditions. After 12 hours, a new day brought some visibility—just barely enough to find our way along the ridge. By now we had decided to try down climbing the original northeast ridge route, established in 1966 by a Japanese team. It had not been climbed in decades, but it was more sheltered from the wind and seemed the only feasible option.

Navigating crevasses and down-climbing ridges, we slowly got out of the wind. Colin did a great job of finding the way. During a little down climb on a loose and steep ridge, I noticed that when tired Colin became even more careful. That made me trust him even more. I'm also like that. Whenever I'm tired or exhausted, I keep calm and put extra energy in to making things

Aartun on the last rappel: 50 meters of overhanging rotten rock into the biggest moat they'd ever seen. They climbed a pitch of steep ice to exit. *Colin Haley*

safe. It was a long and arduous journey down to the glacier, including overhanging rappels down a rotten rib of rock flowing with water. The last rappel fed us into the Big Moat of Evil. It took us a vertical pitch of ice climbing to escape. While running between fresh ice blocks dropped by hangers on both sides of the rock rib, I leaned all my weight into the rope in order to ease the load on Colin's frostbitten toes. Finally out of the danger zone, we used our last gas to melt water. We were now safe, although we didn't look forward to the slog back to KIA.

When Colin suggested naming our new route Dracula, I felt it was good. We had both read Bram Stoker's *Dracula*, about a dark and powerful figure who operated at night, recruiting souls to his frightening empire. During our massive descent, our minds and bodies moved ever closer to another reality. I'm not saying we were becoming vampires (though that could have been interesting), but we were slowly exceeding our limits both physical and psychological. As we crossed the Kahiltna Glacier in rotten snow, dodging hungry crevasses, every step took us closer to real life, but also brought us deeper into a parallel universe. Our bodies buzzed with fatigue, our minds hallucinated. When we finally saw camp I felt greatly relieved, and yet strangely out of place, as if I belonged somewhere else. Camp, once so familiar, was now the unknown landscape. This experience was both scary and alluring. Flying home to Norway, I felt like I was sitting in a spaceship returning from another dimension.

SUMMARY:

Area: Alaska Range.

Ascents: Denali: Simul-solo of the Cassin Ridge in 17 hours from bergschrund at the base of Japanese Couloir (28 hours round-trip from 14,200-foot camp) on June 7, 2010, by Bjørn-Eivind Aartun and Colin Haley.

Mt. Foraker: First ascent of the rock wall on the southeast face. Dracula (10,400', AI4+ M6R A0) starts by climbing the hanging glacier on False Dawn before reaching the prominent rock wall. Aartun and Haley then descended the rarely climbed 1966 Japanese northeast ridge route. They carried no bivouac gear and made the round-trip from camp in a sleepless 71 hours, June 13–15, 2010.

Colin Haley hiked out the last section in his boot liners because his frostbitten toes hurt so bad. The Viking on the right is Bjorn-Eivind Aarturn. *Jacob Schmitz*

A NOTE ABOUT THE AUTHOR:

According to Colin Haley, Bjorn-Eivind Aartun resembles an archetypical Viking with his angular face, blue eyes, and shaggy blond hair. Only 44-year-old Bjorn-Eivind is "gentle, polite, and kind." A professional photographer by trade, he lives in Oslo, Norway.

A JOURNEY TO WESTERN SICHUAN

A return visit to the Shaluli Shan reveals troublesome changes in the mostly unclimbed peaks of the Litang Plateau, China.

TAMOTSU NAKAMURA

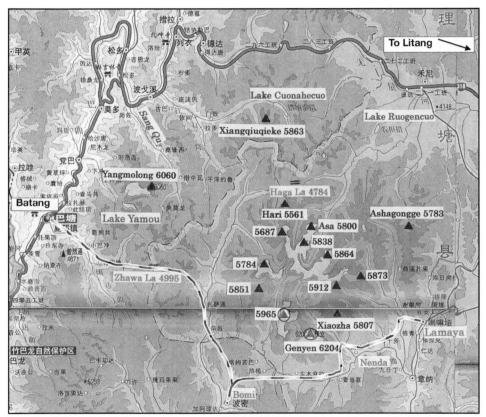

Peak identification of the Shaluli Shan, on the Litang Plateau of the West Sichuan Highlands. Nakamura believes only four or five peaks in this region have been climbed, including Dangchezhengla and Central Peak, both lower summits of the Yangmolong massif. The dashed line south of the peaks is Nakamura's horse caravan route in 1999 to retrace the footsteps of early explorers from Lamaya to Batang. *Tamotsu Nakamura*

After a fascinating visit to the eccentric collection of Christian churches in the upper Salween basin of northwest Yunnan, this pair of old explorers, Tsuyoshi Nagai (77) and I (75) headed to the Litang Plateau. We wanted to explore the Xiangqiuqieke massif (5,700–5,800m) from the southern side, which no climber has visited, and Yangmolong (6,060m), which no climber has summited. We then planned to horse-caravan through the heart of the Litang Plateau from west to east in 10 days, crossing two high passes between 4,800m and 5,100m.

Things went wrong very quickly.

First, hostile Tibetans blocked us from entering one southern valley. Then, we could not organize a caravan across the Litang Plateau because a nomad chief refused us horses and muleteers, saying that villagers would not travel to distant places no matter what we paid them. This seems to be the paradox of development in Tibet and West China: the frontiers are becoming less accessible.

Two decades have passed since I started my odyssey of discovery to the borderlands of West China. The changes have been drastic. When I think of my early visits, beginning in 1990, it feels like a different world. The Chinese national project called the "West Development Drive" has transformed the lifestyle of Tibetans in remote regions.

Twenty years ago there was only one shabby rest-house in Lijiang, a homeland of the Naxi Minority's Dongba culture, located at 3,200 meters near the foot of the Jade Dragon Snow Mountains (Yulong Xueshan) in Yunnan. Originally an arid, windy, dusty Tibetan town like you might see in a Western movie, Lijiang is now a large city with new Tibetan-Chinese buildings designed for visitors. The old town of Lijiang is listed as a UNESCO World Heritage Center and attracts thousands of tourists each year. But artificial Tibetan villages have sprung up specifically for sightseeing. Purely for marketing reasons, in 2001 the Chinese government changed the name of another town on the Zhongdiang Plateau from Zhongdiang (the historical local name) to "Shangri-La." And then there is the newly registered UNESCO World Natural Heritage protected area called the "Three Parallel Rivers of Yunnan"—the gorges of the Yangtze, Mekong, and Salween rivers—which are surrounded by the sacred "Meili Snow Mountains" on the Mekong-Salween Divide near Deqen County. These areas, too, are in a great bustle today.

Near Chengdu in Sichuan, Siguniang National Park is crowded with trekkers and climbers. Modern hotels provide every comfort. Minya Konka and neighboring mountains in Daocheng County are in the same situation. Access roads now speed domestic and foreign tourists from site to site and sight to sight.

East flank of Genyen (6,204m) and neighboring peaks to the northeast, including the spectacular unclimbed Peak 5,873m. Photo taken from Three Smith Brothers Pass, 4,830m. *Tomas Obtulovic*

Ironically, as development progresses with modern conveniences, many of the remote areas are growing more isolated and depopulated. Old trade paths are abandoned in favor of modern roads. Motorbikes replace horses.

In the autumn of 1999, our already

South-southeast face of Xiangqiuqieke (5,863m). *Derek Buckle*

elderly team retraced an old trade path westward from Lamaya (southwest of Litang) to Batang. It required a weeklong horse caravan detouring south of Genyen (6,204m) over two high passes. Many early explorers who traveled to Lhasa from Chengdu (or vise versa) used this difficult trunk route, including Gabe and Yuc, Hamilton Bower, T. T. Cooper, William Gill, F. M. Bailey, Japanese monks, and more. A Nepalese delegation followed this path to reach Beijing. However, in recent years the only travelers you'll see on the historic route are nomads pasturing their yaks. Everyone else, including local Tibetans, reach Batang from Lamaya in an easy day by driving a well-maintained road.

Another change is that villagers are growing rich off the caterpillar fungus, a strange fungal growth that consumes moth larvae at a certain altitude. The fungus-caterpillar is used in traditional medicine to provide energy, especially of the male erotic kind, along with other medical benefits. Younger generations of Tibetans have been infected with a worship of money from the caterpillar-fungus trade. The young Tibetans want very high rates for hiring their motorbikes, while horses are no longer available. A 2009 British expedition suffered serious robbery at their base camp in a valley beneath Yangmolong in the northern side.

Tibetan villages used to welcome us into their houses, where we could spend the night. But now the government's control over eastern Tibet is tight and strict, so everything is much more sensitive. In 2009, we were not allowed to stay in any Tibetan villagers' houses in the upper Yi'ong Tsangpo, presumably because of an order from the Public Security Bureau. Permits for foreigners to unopened areas in eastern Tibet are affected. We did not hear of any expedition, either climbing or exploration, in eastern Tibet in 2010.

Compared with the serious flood damages from extraordinary weather in Yunnan, the 2010 climate in the West Sichuan Highlands was rather stable. At least the roads were not blocked up. On July 27, before we even imagined our troubles to come, Nagai and I departed Chengdu in the company of staff from Sichuan Earth Expeditions Inc. Our guide was Pan Yayu (47, Han), our cook Zhong Jinbing (41, Han), and our driver Wang Yonglian (43, Han). Pan Yayu speaks perfect Japanese and has an excellent reputation as a guide. Unfortunately, his

South face of the still-unclimbed main peak of Yangmolong (6,060m).
Tamotsu Nakamura

Dangchezhengla (5,833m) on left, and the central peak (Makara, 6,033m) on right. Both are lower peaks of the Yangmolong massif and have been climbed, though the ascent of Makara has not been confirmed.
Tamotsu Nakamura

Northeast face of the main peak of Yangmolong. *Derek Buckle*

Han Chinese ethnicity makes it hard for him to negotiate with Tibetans, which makes him unsuitable for the sensitive areas of eastern Tibet. As the great British explorer F. M. Bailey suggested a century ago, you had better employ a Tibetan guide while traveling off the beaten track in Tibetan regions.

We drove 520 kilometers to Yajiang in a day. On the next day, July 28, we reached a village north of Batang by driving the Sichuan-Tibet Highway through the fertile Litang Plateau. The plateau's summer landscape is stunningly beautiful: green pastures, gentle streams, and hundreds of grazing yaks, all at 4,000–4,600m of elevation. We were surprised to see many Chinese university students bicycling to Lhasa. They told us that it would take 25 days to get there from Chengdu and that this has become a modern pilgrimage. We also found an abundance of blue poppies (Meconopsis). The Sichuan-Tibet Highway has received new tunnels between Haizi Shan Pass and Batang, an important shortcut.

The world-famous "Litang Horse Festival," which draws foreign tourists on the first of August each year, was suddenly canceled in 2010 for reasons unstated, but probably political. The authorities may have seen signs of unrest and resistance among the warlike Khampa people (ethnic Tibetans), but no one responded to my questions on the topic.

When we reached the access to Tarilong Valley at road maintenance station 336, a local district secretary advised us against entering this valley because the villagers were excluding outsiders. He told us that not even the villager's chief could administrate them. This is where we gave up on our plan to unveil Xiangqiuqieke.

"Anything happens in China; nothing is impossible in China."

When faced with difficulties during my Tibetan travels, I always repeat these words. I cannot return home from an expensive expedition to the eastern Tibetan plateau without some kind of fruit. Having resigned our original plan to explore the Xiangqiuqieke massif from the south and to traverse the Litang Plateau from west to east, we decided to survey and identify peaks of the Shaluli Shan in Litang Plateau as best we could, since many peaks here remain unknown. As usual, I carried with me maps of the mountains for the identifications.

The southeast face of Peak 5,687m, as seen from Zhawa La (4,995m). *Tamotsu Nakamura*

West flanks of peaks 5,838m (left) and 5,784m. *Tamotsu Nakamura*

North face of Asa (5,800m) on left and northeast face of Hari (5,561m) on right, taken from Heranseba. *Tamotsu Nakamura*

Telephoto of north face of Ashagonge in summer. *Tamotsu Nakamura*

North face of Ashagonge (5,783m) in autumn. *Tamotsu Nakamura*

In order to make this survey, I viewed the Xiangqiuqieke and its eastern peaks from the Sichuan-Tibet Highway, taking pictures of as many as I could. I also visited the Genyen massif to photograph its little-known rock peaks. And I gathered and reviewed as many pictures as possible from past expeditions to Genyen, Xiangqiuqieke, and Yangmolong. Very helpful for peak identification were a panorama from Genyen in 1988, my journeys in 1999 and 2000, photos from the 2005 Yamanashi expedition, Tomas Oblutovic's visit in 2009, Derek Buckle's in 2009, and Tim Boetler's in 2010.

After we changed plans, we first ascended from a monastery in the new nomad village of Muye (Deda District, Batang County) to 4,700 meters. From here we could take photos of the north face of Xiangqiuqieke massif. The next day we reconnoitered the prominent three peaks south of the Sichuan-Tibet Highway. My pictures were taken from a Tibetan village at 4,310 meters. After that we drove to Lamaya to have a grand panoramic view of the east face of the Genyen massif from Three Smith Brothers Pass, at 4,830m. Road conditions have improved considerably from my previous visit here in 1999. The driving time in 2010 was one-fourth what it had been.

APPROACHES TO XIANGQIUQIEKE AND YANGMOLONG

I would like to describe the available information about these exceptional and little-known neighboring massifs with their collection of peaks.

Only two parties familiar with climbing have approached the peaks of Xiangqiuqieke (5,863m), the first being Nagai and me in the autumn of 1999. We saw two 5,700m peaks from the south while making the horse caravan journey from Lamaya to Batang. Next came a Japanese party from the Yamanashi Mountaineering Federation, in 2005; they reconnoitered the northern side. From the Sichuan-Tibet Highway, they reached a lookout point with a panoramic view of the north face beyond Lake Counahecou. But their weather was not very good.

In 2009 a British expedition to Yangmolong did not approach Xiangqiuqieke, but they managed to photograph its southwest face from their advanced base camp. A New Zealand team plans to attempt the main summit in September-October 2011.

Peak ca 5,600m in the Garmunei Gou drainage. *Tomas Obtulovic*

There are five routes for approaching the massifs of Xiangqiuqieke and Yangmolong. Though all are inhabited by ethnic Tibetans, their nature and attitude toward foreigners varies from valley to valley. I'll introduce the valleys from north to south.

West face of Peak 5,851m from trail to Zhawa La. *Tamotsu Nakamura*

XIANGQIUQIEKE:

1) One can reach the north side of Xiangqiuqieke from the entrance to a new nomad village at 4,300m on the Sichuan-Tibet Highway, 10km east of the Haizi Shan Pass. A Japanese team from Yamanashi followed this route with no problem in 2005.

2) One can approach both the north and south sides from road maintenance station 336, which leads to the Tarilong Valley. This is where Tibetan intransigence forced us to abandon our plan.

YANGMOLONG:

3) Geographically, the Sang Qu–Sanglongxi valley between station 336 and Dongba is the best route to reach the north side of Yangmolong. But it is the most dangerous due to the bad nature of villagers. This is where in 2009 a British party was robbed and levied extraordinary expenses for motorbikes. That same year American and German parties were forced to turn to the southern side of Yangmolong. Villagers told them that foreigners would cause catastrophe. Since then the Batang County government has prohibited foreigners from entering this valley. Several years ago a British party encountered a similar reaction from locals who had been agitated by lamas when they entered a valley to attempt the unclimbed Kawarani (5,992m) in the Gonkara Shan range.

4) A route from Dongba in the east leads to the northwest side of Yangmolong. In this valley the Tibetans are friendly and welcome foreigners. In autumn of 2010 two groups used the route: a Japanese student party from the Waseda University that reconnoitered an unclimbed 5,850m peak and an American-Chinese expedition that went to the north face of Yangmolong.

East face of Peak 5,912m. *Tamotsu Nakamura*

5) The easiest access is from Dongba in the east via Zhongba to reach the south face of Yangmolong. Villagers here are cooperative and support expeditions. Nagai and I followed this route to reconnoiter the south face of Yangmolong in June, 2000. Since then several parties have used this approach. A Japanese party from the Hengduan Mountains Club reached the south side and made the first ascent of Dangchezhengla

Southeast face of Peak 5,912m. *Tamotsu Nakamura*

(5,833m) in October, 2002. They experienced no conflicts with villagers.

A BRIEF HISTORY OF CLIMBING IN THE YANGMOLONG MASSIF

The following is a brief chronicle of climbing and explorations in the Yangmolong massif. The high points of the Yangmolong massif consist of Yangmolong (6,060m) in the east, Dangchezhengla (locally known as Bongonzhong, 5,833m) in the west, and Central Peak (locally known as Makara, 6,033m) in between.

1991: A Japanese party from Nippon University approached from the north and attempted the north face of Yangmolong's main peak (6,060m). Bad weather and avalanche danger forced their retreat from about 5,400m.

2000: In June Tamotsu Nakamura and Tsuyoshi Nagai reconnoitered access to the south face.

2002: In June a Japanese expedition of the Hengduan Mountains Club (Kyoto) made the first ascent of Dangchezhengla at the western end of the Yangmolong massif. They climbed from the south via the central glacier between Dangchezhengla and the central peak (Makara), and reached the summit via the east ridge from the col. There is a detailed account of this climb in the 2008 *AAJ*, pg 422.

2003: There is information that a Korean party made the first ascent of the central peak (Makara) from the south via the central glacier and west ridge. The 2010 *AAJ* mentioned this briefly (pg 338), but the information has not been confirmed.

2007: In March a three-person Chinese team unsuccessfully attempted Makara, probably on their way to Yangmolong. Liu Xinan, a top Chinese climber, fell to his death during the descent (originally reported in the *AAJ 2008*, pg 422, and corrected in the *AAJ 2010*, pg 338).

2007: In October four members of a British-American expedition led by Dave Wynne-Jones approached from the north. During their acclimatization they made the first ascent of a 5,600m snow peak south of Peak 5,850m. They then made the second ascent of Dangchezhengla, via a new route on the northeast ridge to east ridge. They also challenged the main summit (6,060m), but gave up at 5,400m due to cold and unstable snow conditions (*AAJ 2008*, ppg 420–422).

2009: In autumn the British party of Dave Wynne-Jones, Derek Buckle, and friends revisited the north face of Yangmolong's main peak. This is when they encountered serious trouble with the villagers of Sang Qu, who had treated them well in 2007. They then attempted the north ridge but again failed (*AAJ 2010*, ppg 335–336).

Also in 2009, an American-Chinese team led by Jon Otto attempted the south face of Yangmolong's main peak. They started to climb the south face just beneath the summit, but were unable to break through the lower part of the fragile and dangerous rock wall (*AAJ 2010*, ppg 336–338). A German party also came to the south side, but left with no result.

2010: In November, Jon Otto, Tim Boetler, and Chinese climbers again challenged the main summit. They entered the north side from a valley east of Dongba after crossing a high pass at about 5,000m. The descent from the pass was so steep that they had to rappel into the valley. They attempted the north ridge but did not surpass the elevation reached by the 2007 British expedition. Dave Wynne-Jones appreciates that they found an alternative access route to reach the north face.

The Yangmolong main peak has refused several attempts and still remains untrodden. Who will challenge it next?

Climbing Paradise of the Future

Thanks to its easy access from the large city of Chengdu, the Qionglai Mountains of Mt. Siguniang National Park have become very popular for tourists and rock climbers. Almost all the outstanding rock peaks above 5,500 meters have already been climbed here. To the best of my best knowledge, only Goromity (5,609m) remains virgin now that attractive Se'erdenpu (Barbarian Peak, 5,592m) was scaled by an American party in 2010. [Also in 2010, a Japanese party put up a beautiful new route Niuxinshan (4,942m). Both ascents are in the China section of this *Journal*.]

One of the finest climbing fields after the Qonglai Mountains is a group of rock peaks in the Genyen massif of the Shaluli Shan, also on the Litang Plateau. The main peak of Genyen (6,204m) was first climbed by a party from the Himalayan Association of Japan in 1988. The next visit by climbers came in 2006, when an Italian party led by Karl Unterkircher made the second ascent via a new route on the north spur (*AAJ 2007*, p. 408 with summary of 1998 Japanese ascent on p. 409). The Italians thought they had made Genyen's first ascent, leading to some confusion in the initial reporting. Later that year, a party of Americans climbed Sachun (5,716m), as well as a peak they called Phurba (ca 18,650'/ca 5,685m) and came within eight

East face of Peak 5,873m. *Tomas Obtulovic*

Peak 5,965m (left) and west face of Genyen (6,204m) from Zhawa La. *Tamotsu Nakamura*

The southeast side of the Genyen massif seen from about 4,500m near Daocheng. *Tamotsu Nakamura*

meters of another summit they called Damaru (ca 18,550'/ca 5,654m). In Molly Tyson's feature article in the *AAJ 2007* (p. 79), Sachun is given the erroneous height of 19,570' (5,965m); in fact, Sachun is a neighboring summit connected to Peak 5,965m by a long ridge. Even later in 2006, Americans Charlie Fowler and Christine Boskoff were killed by an avalanche on Genyen.

The Genyen massif's second highest summit, Peak 5,695m, was climbed by Peter Inglis and Joe Puryear in 2007 (*AAJ 2008*, p. 427). These seem to be the only 5,500–5,900m peaks that have been climbed in the entire massif.

The whole northern aspect of Genyen is a climbing paradise, with outstanding granite towers surrounding a beautiful valley with a 600-year-old monastery, Rengo Gompa. Most of these fantastic peaks have never been touched by climbers. In the near future they will surely become known as an alpine rock paradise like the Qonglai Mountains.

Unfortunately, the rules and official prices for climbing in Sichuan have just increased significantly (see "New Regulations" on p. 343 of this *Journal*). This might be a good time to remember my motto, "Anything happens in China; nothing is impossible in China."

Editor's note: The AAJ will compile an extensive collection of photos of the Genyen massif from various expeditions, including panoramas from the summit of Genyen. Look for this on aaj.americanalpineclub.org late in 2011.

SUMMARY:

Area: Shaluli Shan (mountains), Litang Plateau, Ganzi Prefecture, West Sichuan, China.

Events: A survey of development and cultural trends in West Sichuan as they affect climbers and explorers, along with a review of access, history, and mountaineering potential on unclimbed peaks in the Shaluli Shan, in particular the Yangmolong (6,060m) and Xiangqiuqieke (5,863m) massifs, along with the granite peaks north of Mt. Genyen (6,204m).

ABOUT THE AUTHOR:

Tamotsu (Tom) Nakamura (75) is an honorary member of the American Alpine Club, and was recently elected an honorary member of the New Zealand Alpine Club. He has received many awards from exploration and alpine clubs around the world. He has made 32 exploratory journeys into what he calls "East of the Himalayas – the Alps of Tibet," which more broadly include the mountains of east and southeast Tibet, the Hengduan Mountains of northwest Yunnan, and the peaks of West Sichuan and Qinghai. Nakamura's work is almost an annual fixture of the American Alpine Journal, but our most extensive look at this region is his definitive compilation "East of the Himalaya" in the 2003 AAJ. Nakamura has written, "Some convince themselves that veiled mountains in the greater ranges are an experience of the past. But [the eastern] Tibet [Plateau] has an incredibly vast and complex topography that holds countless unclimbed summits, and beckons a lifetime's search. The peaks there are stunning and magnificent, and many of them will remain enigmas for generations."

Climbs and Expeditions

2011

Accounts from the various climbs and expeditions of the world are listed geographically. We generally bias from north to south and from west to east within the noted countries, but the priority is on a logical flow from one mountain range to the next. We begin our coverage with the Contiguous United States and move to Alaska in order for the climbs in Alaska's Wrangell Mountains to segue into the St. Elias climbs in Canada.

We encourage all climbers to submit accounts of notable activity, especially long new routes (generally defined as U.S. commitment Grade IV—full-day climbs—or longer). Please submit reports as early as possible (see Submissions Guidelines at aaj.americanalpineclub.org).

For conversions of meters to feet, multiply by 3.28; for feet to meters, multiply by 0.30.

Unless otherwise noted, all reports are from the 2010 calendar year.
Longer versions, extra photos, and additional information for many of these reports can be found at aaj.americanalpineclub.org

Contiguous United States

WASHINGTON

Colchuck Balanced Rock, Let It Burn. Colchuck Balanced Rock, tucked between the river valleys and high glacier plateaus of the Stuart Range, has become firmly established as one of Washington state's premier alpine free-climbing zones. Max Hasson and I were thrilled to add a new route to this inspiring chunk of stone in late August and early September, working ground up, without fixed lines, between work stints in Leavenworth.

The route closely parallels the relatively popular West Face route, sharing the approach and first pitch of that route, before splitting left and following a fairly obvious thin crack system. Every pitch of the line is sustained and challenging, with a 130' 5.12a providing the crux. Like many of the Enchantment's new lines, wild knobs just barely connect incredible crack systems. Though the stone was next to perfect there were some exciting large features to trundle, with the belayer usually a sitting duck underneath. Very little loose rock exists on the route now. We named Let It Burn (IV 5.12a) after a forest fire we watched smolder for weeks in a neighboring valley, adding a spark of flavor to the already stunning views.

JENS HOLSTEN, *AAC*

Jens Holsten following the wild second pitch of Let It Burn. *Max Hasson*

Le Petit Cheval, First Amendment. In September 2009, Chris McNamara and I climbed First Amendment (IV 5.11a), a new route just right of center on Le Petit Cheval's northwest face. The rock is excellent, but, as is normal for the area, many cracks were filled with dirt. We approached as per Spontaneity Arête (II/III 5.7, Goldie-Johnston, 2004), then, from its base, we traversed about 250 yards toward the middle of the face on 3rd- and 4th-class ledges. Our route begins with a 100' 5.4 chimney and hand crack to a large ledge. P2 (150') is a slightly vegetated 5.8 hands-and-fists corner that starts around the corner from a 5.10 splitter finger crack. P3 (120') is 5.9 and follows the same corner before breaking right on thin face climbing and gaining a ledge with a cave. P4 (120') climbs sweet 5.8+ finger cracks to a large, slabby ledge. P5 traverses around right to a ledge (after many attempts to go left failed). P6 is a sweet 5.9 finger crack. P7 (150') is a 5.10+ series of corners and roofs that take very thin protection (knifeblades and Lost Arrows would be useful). P8 is 5.11a and starts in the same super-thin cracks, with the crux right off the belay, and tackles another series of corners and roofs. P9 is 5.6 and mostly easier terrain, then joins Spontaneity Arête for its final one-and-a-half scrambly ridge pitches to the summit.

Ian Nicholson, *AAC*

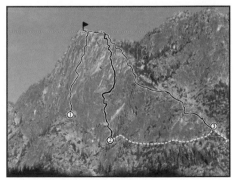

The northwest face of Le Petit Cheval: (1) Paul Revere (II+ 5.9+, Allen-Mitchell, 2006). (2) First Amendment (9 pitches, IV 5.11a, McNamara-Nicholson, 2009). (3) Spontaneity Arête (II/III 5.7, Goldie-Johnston, 2004). *Ian Nicholson*

CALIFORNIA
YOSEMITE NATIONAL PARK

El Capitan, The Prophet. On October 27, Jason Pickles and I completed our nine-year quest to establish a new free route on El Cap. The Prophet (E9 7a, 5.13d R) is on the far right side of El Cap, home to many of Yosemite's scariest and most technical aid routes. Jason and I made it almost halfway up the route in 2001, in a ground-up attempt using no bolts, no aid, no port-a-ledge,

and no fixed rope that ultimately proved too ambitious. After several other unsuccessful ground-up attempts, we returned in 2010 for a more conventional, top-down approach. We invested many days preparing ourselves and the climb before, at long last, a successful redpoint.

The 600m, 13-pitch route demands continuously difficult, bold climbing. It frees the first five pitches of the aid route Bad to the Bone; climbs three pitches of entirely new terrain and a traverse pitch, the Devil's Dyno (which shares 10m of climbing with Nico Favresse and Sean Villanueva's free route, The Secret Passage); then frees the last four pitches of Eagle's Way, including the stunning A1 Beauty. We added eight protection bolts and four bolts in belays.

The most extreme difficulties come high on the wall. Pitch 9 (5.13c R), the Devil's Dyno, involves a wild, 2.5m, no-points-of-contact sideways jump. The A1 Beauty, a hairline crack splitting an immaculate golden headwall in an extremely exposed position, forms the crux of

Leo Houlding near the top of the crux A1 Beauty pitch on The Prophet,   the route. Matchstick edges,
El Capitan. *Alastair Lee*   non-existent footholds, and

sustained desperate moves create an incredible pitch protected exclusively by natural gear.

I led all of the pitches during the continuous free ascent, with Jason seconding everything cleanly except the A1 Beauty. During the six-day ascent, we were hammered by a severe four-day storm. After 80 hours of squalor on the port-a-ledge, the A1 Beauty pitch (free at 5.13d R) pushed me to my limit. It is the most perfect pitch I could ever have imagined—such an aesthetic line in an unequalled position, so desperately thin, and painfully close to my limit. If I never climb anything harder, I will not be disappointed. The Prophet was a dream come true.

LEO HOULDING, *U.K.*

The Prophet, El Capitan. *John Dickey, Rock and Ice*

Liberty Cap, Scarface. In late June, Steve Bosque and I completed a 13-pitch independent line on the west face of Liberty Cap. The route follows a long crack system that shoots straight through a huge, white scar, the wall's most prominent feature. Steve and his wife, Paula, started the climb in 2004. Soon after, Chuck Clance joined them before an injury forced them to fix and descend from the top of pitch three.

Steve mentioned the line in early spring and we headed straight for it, replacing the fixed lines and establishing a fourth pitch, which brought us to the base of the scar. We returned in late June for the final push.

We were greeted by impeccable cracks cutting through the bulletproof rockscar. Late on the third day, with a heat wave moving in, Steve made a great effort on pitch seven by drilling eight rivets and then nailing straight up into an A2 corner crack that ended at the base of the "Cubano Corner." After adding a belay bolt, we hauled the bags and I racked up for the most impressive corner I have climbed. Laser cut and vertical, the corner leads to very thin A3 beaking and a bit of loose free to a belay on a decent ledge. By then we were cooked. White rock, nuclear sun, and long days

Josh Mucci on pitch 8 of Scarface. *Steve Bosque*

Scarface, on the west face of Liberty Cap. *Joe Hornof/qitnl.com*

had zapped us. Steve made his way up an A3 ramp, reaching a small tree after 75' and a belay that escaped the sun's rays.

Very low on water, we were desperate. We were hundreds of feet from the summit, with mixed climbing the entire way. I set off at dusk. After a difficult pendulum, I free climbed and placed beaks in a tiny seam that split a watercourse ramp. I came down in the dark, and we agreed to stash the bags and gun it in the morning.

Morning came and Steve handed me the last fruit cup for energy to climb the 600'+ to the summit. The next four pitches were a blur for weeks afterward; we moved fast and tried to beat the sun to the summit. Parched, we collapsed under the first shade in five days, not looking forward to the slabs and descent. It took us hours to reach the river. A fine gentleman saw us coming out of the woods and immediately offered his water pump.

We returned soon after and retrieved the bags and got a sober look at the upper four pitches. Not so bad! Scarface (13 pitches, V 5.8 A3).

JOSH MUCCI

Ari Menitove on the crux pitch of Tehipite Sanction. *Andrew Burr*

SIERRA NEVADA

Kings Canyon National Park, Tehipite Dome, Tehipite Sanction. California sunshine, stable weather, and perfect Sierra granite were the ingredients for our new route, Tehipite Sanction (5.12 C1), on Tehipite Dome. The massive south face and upper dome rises out of the majestic and lonely Kings Canyon. In July, Ari Menitove, Mike Brumbaugh, and I horse packed 13 miles to a base camp in the forest below the upper dome.

We were alone in the recently burned wilderness, and an eerie feeling lingered in the dead forest as we hiked back and forth to camp during our five-day stay. To start, we hiked down a gully to the ledge system just above the middle of the wall and rapped to the base [Farther east, the rock drops to the toe of the complete 3,400' south face—Ed.]. From there we scrambled about 600' up an obvious gully, then established 12 pitches connecting the steepest part of the wall to the upper dome. Ari and

I nearly freed the crux fifth pitch—we climbed it with one hang—which should go at 5.13-. Other than anchors, we only needed to add about six bolts. Where our route ends, at the big ledge system below the upper dome, one can walk off or continue on one of the upper dome routes. We finished with six rope-stretcher pitches on the upper part of the 1997 route, In the Niche of Time (Felton-Joe-Zielsky).

The route has every type of crack climbing on it, from tips to hands to offwidth—and no hanging belays! The wall required little to no cleaning and was a spectacular experience. Dust and ash covered us daily and the hours on the wall were long; but when it came time for climbing, the soreness and pain went away and were replaced by the joy of climbing an amazing line in a wonderful place.

ROB PIZEM, *AAC*

Tehipite Dome: (1) South Face/Time Warp (Beckey-Swedlund & Ahern-Weeks, 1963; FFA Bard-Harrington-Leversee, 1983). (2) Southwest Face (Chadwick-Kroger-Weeden, 1970). (3) Too Hip (Felton-Leversee, 1996). (4) In the Niche of Time (Felton-Joe-Zielsky, 1997). (5) Wall of Ages (Fehrman-Nettle-Sweeney-Thau, 2001). (6) Tehipite Sanction (Brumbaugh-Menitove-Pizem, 2010). *Jay Wilkerson*

Sequoia National Park, Tamarack Lake area, new routes. On a winter trans-Sierra attempt in the coldest week of 2007, Chris LaBounty, Neal Harder, and I spotted a beautiful granite tower, surrounded by snow and set against a blue sky above Tamarack Lake. Even from a distance, we could see scoops, knobs, and chickenheads. It was like falling upon an unclimbed Charlotte Dome. We returned in the summer, and on July 13, 2007, we established the first route on the Prism (our name for the tower). The Left Facet (13 pitches, 5.10a R) starts on the lowest part of the tower and follows the left skyline to the pointy summit block. The route climbs featured slabs, cracks, runnels, and a steep face up high. Once atop the summit block we were surprised that the climb wasn't over. Another four pitches of ridge traversing and downclimbing up to 5.8 were required to descend.

New climbs above Tamarack Lake (the first three are on the Prism): (A) Left Facet (Harder-LaBounty-Thau, 2007). (B) Pig with Lipstick (LaBounty-Thau, 2010). (C) Right Facet (Harder-LaBounty, 2009). (D) Saber Ridge (Dille-Thelen, 2008). *Brandon Thau*

Brandon Thau leading the 5.9 crack on pitch 5 of Left Facet Crack. *LaBounty-Harder photo*

Since then, among the three of us, we've established two more routes on the Prism. In July 2009, Neal and Chris climbed the right skyline (Right Facet, 11 pitches, 5.9). Last July, Chris and I established Pig with Lipstick (11 pitches, 5.9 R), a distant reference to Charlotte Dome that starts near Right Facet but heads up and left on golden knobs, chickenheads, and flakes. During the same trip, Chris and I also climbed the giant rock ridge right of the Prism. Our plan was to remain roped up for the nearly half-mile ridge, but after difficulties up to 5.7 on the first third, we coiled the ropes and continued. Spots require hand traversing on a knife-edge ridge with big air beneath, and once you start, the easiest way off is continuing to the other side. Unlike other ridge traverses in the Sierra, this ridge doesn't have any spots to bail from easily. We called the climb Saber Ridge (~20 pitches, 5.7), though subsequently learned that our friend Scott Thelen had climbed it in 2008, with

Justin Dille. He thought the name appropriate, and agreed with our thinking that it's one of the best ridge traverses in the Sierra. One could argue that Saber Ridge is better than Matthes Crest in terms of exposure and commitment. It's nice to know that Beckey and Rowell left a few Sierra plums for the rest of us to pick.

BRANDON THAU, *AAC*

Fourth Needle, East Face. Over the summer, Greg Corliss, my wife Hjördis Rickert, and I climbed a new line on the thin spire just south and essentially part of the Third Needle along the Whitney Crest. The route goes through two roofs and corners on the east face of the narrow pillar. We did a couple of exploratory trips in June and July and climbed the route on August 21. The rock gets better and better going up. We used a little aid through the roof sections, but it may well go free. As it stands, the free climbing pitches are good fun and go from 3rd-class scrambling to about 5.11. We are referring to it as the East Face of Fourth Needle.

Hjördis Rickert on pitch 9 of the East Face of Fourth Needle. *Bernd Zeugswetter*

The first two pitches are very long on steep and varied terrain through a massive quartz band. Pitch three leans back with 3rd-class scrambling to gain the base of the main pillar. The next three pitches climb the central part of the gray pillar by cracks and off-width up to 5.11. Pitch seven traverses back left a little and goes up a finger crack and arête to an alcove. Then come two crux pitches that follow a thin crack (micro-nuts and knifeblades) through a series of corners and roofs and up the center of

The East Face of Fourth Needle, along the Whitney Crest, which includes the Fourth Needle, Third Needle, Day Needle, Keeler Needle, and Mt. Whitney. *Bernd Zeugswetter*

the pillar. One more pitch of easier climbing gets you to the top (10 pitches total). Two knifeblades went in the narrow seams of the roof and one bolt was placed at the top of the roof pitch.

BERND ZEUGSWETTER, *AAC*

Mt. Chamberlin, Innominata. On July 3, 2009, Dave Nettle and Reuben Shelton climbed a new route on the central buttress of the northeast face of Chamberlin. Innominata (5.11 A1) is mostly free, with two points of aid, and climbs all independent terrain. It starts with two vertical, wide-crack pitches just right of Breaking Point, continues straight up on the far right side of the central buttress and then into big, steep corners just right of the number "3" in the photo on p. 147 of the *AAJ 2007.*

From communication with DAVE NETTLE, AAC

Dana Plateau, Butterflies and Rainbows; Mt. Chamberlin, various routes. In July, Chris Brown and I set our sights on a large, east-facing dihedral on a broad wall just northeast of the famed Third Pillar of Dana. When viewed from the edge of the Dana Plateau, this "wall" reveals itself as a long and complex ridge reaching east. We approached as per the Third Pillar, descending the rock ridge to its immediate north and then east across talus and scree to the base. A brief 5.9 section past a chockstone led to rambling terrain and a large ledge at the base of another large dihedral, from where we climbed 200' of splitter cracks on the face to the right, gained another big ledge, then climbed another 200' of fun 5.6 on the ridge that forms the left margin of the main dihedral. We moved the belay to a large tree in the main dihedral and traversed a hairy butt crack right, and then back left, to a ledge. That led to a long 5.10- corner, followed by a classic 5.10+ ropestretcher to the ridge crest. We hopped boulders along the ridge back to the Third Pillar approach/descent ridge, and scrambled back to the Plateau. Although it's unlikely that our route, Butterflies and Rainbows (1,000', IV 5.10+), is the first line on the wall, a search of the *AAJ* online database returned no other routes. This wall, however, certainly holds potential for many other interesting lines.

In mid-August we met our friends Mike Pennings and Jimmy Haden in Whitney Portal for what Mike described as a four- or five-hour approach to the northeast face of Mt. Chamberlin [The *AAJ* has misspelled this peak as "Chamberlain" in some previous editions—Ed.]. They started hiking around noon. We opted for burgers and beer at the Whitney Portal Store while waiting for the oppressive sun to drop. We figured we could leave at 4:30 and still make camp by dark.

The prescribed five hours of hiking found us at Consolation Lake, still a few hours below the Sierra crest and several more from Chamberlin. A day-and-a-half after leaving Whitney Portal, we arrived in base camp. "Where you guys been?" they chuckled. They had done a new route—Where's the Boys (IV 5.11-)—on Chamberlin's previously unclimbed east buttress. We, on the other hand, had been roundly sandbagged.

Chamberlin's northeast face comprises three buttresses separated from one another by deep clefts: the leftmost, or eastern, had no known routes; the central buttress had several existing lines [See *AAJ 2007*, p. 147, although

The routeline of Butterflies and Rainbows, with the Third Pillar of Dana (3D) for reference. *Chris Brown*

we've subsequently learned of additional significant routes on the buttress—Ed.]; the rightmost, or western, is home to Rowell's North Pillar route and the 2006 route Barracuda (Nettle-Thau).

The next day Chris and I climbed a line, Safety First (1,500', IV 5.10+), on Chamberlin's western buttress, starting a little right (west) of the North Pillar route. Ours is probably a variation to Barracuda, and trends right for a few easier slabby pitches, then steepens for three pitches of 5.10 before the angle eases again toward the top.

Where's the Boys (Haden-Pennings, 2010), the first known route on the east buttress of the northeast face of Mt. Chamberlin. The next buttress right (central buttress) and the rightmost buttress/pillar have multiple routes and variations, many of which are shown in the AAJ online report. *Josh Finkelstein*

We rested and fished for golden trout the next day, while Mike and Jimmy explored the Hitchcock Lakes basin, one drainage north. The following day we started up a line in the middle of Chamberlin's central buttress, about 100' west of Fiddler and Harrington's original Northeast Face route (1980) and below a striking 5.10+ changing corner. From binoculars in camp, all of the features of our intended line appeared to connect, with the exception of one dubious crack. Leading up an amazing 5.10 crack on pitch four, the mystery crack revealed itself: overhanging hands and fingers! We climbed it at 5.11-, grinning the whole way. Two more long, excellent pitches in steep, knobby corners brought us to slabbier terrain, then the top. We called our route The Sword in The Stone (V 5.11-) after an oddly shaped block we trundled. In the upper corners we found a fixed nut, left by Jonny Copp and Nils Davis during their 2006 first ascent of I Fink Therefore I Am (*AAJ 2007*), with which we shared some pitches. A strange coincidence given that friends nicknamed me "Fink" when I was in grade school. My nickname and Jonny's ability to inspire survive to this day. All of the routes were climbed hammerless, free, and onsight.

JOSH FINKELSTEIN, *AAC*

NEVADA

Mt. Wilson, Lady Wilson's Bush. This climb is a long, sketchy-but-easy, rockaineering ascent of Mt. Wilson. In mid-April, Oliver Deshler and I hiked two hours to the base, up a gully toward Resolution Arête and Inti Watana, past the Inti Watana ravine, and bushwacked another 100' up the main gully. Then we hooked left, scrambling up to a broad shelf with an obvious vertical crack (looking south you can see the ponderosa on the shelf at the base of Resolution). From there we climbed 13 pitches to the summit: P1: 200', 5.9, mossy hands and fingers to top of buttress, belay off a bush. P2: 200', scramble up and left toward the very wide, leftmost crack 40' right of Inti Watana. P3: 170', 5.8, avoid chimney by climbing vertical finger crack on right. P4: 160', 5.9, stem chimney up through mossy handcrack roof.

Lady Wilson's Bush, on Mt. Wilson. *Mark Jenkins*

P5: 150', 5.7, stemming, handcracking through two easy roofs. P6: 200', 5.6R, stem chimney. P7: 170', 5.7R, stem chimney, airy, go left to big bushy belay. P8: 200', 5.6R, chimney. P9: 200', scramble through keyhole on right, then left up chimney, circling around to top of giant white block leaning against face. P10: 200', 5.9X, climb straight up white face on sketchy white flakes that provide psychological pro, past the tree on the left. P11: 200', 5.9, don't go to next tree up and right, instead climb finger crack straight up. P12: 100', scramble straight up to big tree. P13: 200', scramble rightward, above Aeolian Wall, tree-to-tree, finally passing left through chimney to wide, cactus-covered ledge. Hike 400', starting on a ledge south and then curling up and around to the saddle and summit. Lady Wilson's Bush (a.k.a. Skeazy, 2,000' 5.9+ R/X).

MARK JENKINS, *AAC*

UTAH

The Titan, Gimp Warfare; Echo Tower, Sidewinder. In early March, Jeremy Aslaksen and I explored the virtually unclimbed east face of the Titan in the Fisher Towers. The only route on the face is an old Jim Beyer route, World's End, which climbs the extreme left margin. After climbing four new pitches we hustled back to the car in an amazing rain, thunder, and lightning storm. A return trip in April was thwarted when I pulled off a block on a downclimb while hiking back to the car, fell 10 feet, and broke three bones in my foot. Over the next few months Jeremy added a new pitch, solo, to keep up the progress. After my foot healed enough to climb again, we returned in August, in 100°+ temperatures, to finish Gimp Warfare (8 pitches, VI 5.10 A3). The route is characterized by much beaking.

In December, we climbed Sidewinder (5 pitches, V 5.9+ A1++), a new route on the right side of the south face of Echo Tower. The first

Gimp Warfare on the east face of the Titan. *Jeremy Aslaksen*

pitch had previously been climbed, as evidenced by a bolt and belay anchor. The route joins Run Amok one pitch from the top. The second pitch climbs a wide crack to a pedestal on the north face just left of Phantom Sprint, then a beak crack and a short six-bolt ladder back around to the south side of the tower. The route requires a significant amount of wide gear, and mostly climbs the tower on the opposite side of Phantom Spirit.

PAUL GAGNER, *AAC*

Paul Gagner leading pitch 7 of Gimp Warfare on the Titan.
Jeremy Aslaksen

MONTANA

Beartooth Mountains, various routes. Over three trips in October and November, Aaron Mulkey and I looked for ice and mixed climbs in the Beartooths. We managed a major route each trip, which made the long and remote approaches worthwhile. After speaking with several Beartooth climbers, we think these routes are likely new.

On Spirit Mountain, in Rock Creek Canyon, the Central Chimney (2,200', V WI4 M6R) climbs the large chimney right of Lunar Arête. We found compact rock that did not easily yield protection or belays.

On the Bullet, also in Rock Creek, Daniel Burson, Aaron, and I established Funeral For Another Friend (IV WI4 M6+), an extension to Funeral For a Friend (Jim Kanzler and Jack

Funeral For Another Friend, on the Bullet, Rock Creek Canyon. *Doug Shepherd*

Central Chimney, on Spirit Mountain. *Doug Shepherd*

Doug Shepherd on the crux pitch, Central Chimney, Spirit Mountain. *Aaron Mulkey*

Tackle, 1978). We broke out of the gully above the second pitch via a rock wall and climbed an additional five pitches of mainly moderate mixed and ice climbing, with a short M6+ crux at the headwall.

In East Rosebud, on the Giant's Belly of Mt. Inabnit (*AAJ 2009*, p. 123), to the far left of Ice Dragons (Mike Abbey and Ron Brunckhorst, October 28, 2000) Aaron and I climbed a three-pitch line. Ice Fairies (III WI5) follows an iced-up corner to a ledge and the end of the ice.

DOUG SHEPHERD, *Colorado, AAC*

WYOMING

Mt. Helen, La Mirada del la Gitana. In mid-October, Craig Pope and I made the quasi-annual pilgrimage from Bozeman to Pinedale with hopes held high for favorable mixed climbing conditions in the northern Wind River Range. The weather gods were on our side: We had just enough precipitation during the two-day march in to inspire confidence in the ice conditions and clearing just as we arrived in camp.

We'd chosen a direct line on the north face of Mt. Helen and were hoping for a series of ice runnels to follow through the gut of the mountain. We found lots of 60° black ice, moderate rock, and a series of enjoyable M4 steps where the runnels were supposed to be, punctuated with two distinct and back-to-back cruxes of well-protected 5.10/M6 followed by much spicier, dry 5.9 rock climbing with serious runouts.

We simul-soloed an approach gully over 45° black ice and névé, followed by the lower portion of the face through some M4 terrain, before roping up and using a running belay for the next 700'. We then pitched out the cruxes, running the second near 100m (some simuling) to reach a decent belay anchor. From here we joined previously established terrain, entering a deep left-leaning gully with mixed black ice

La Mirada del la Gitana, on the north face of Mt. Helen. *Pete Tapley*

and very loose rock to finish back right with a low-5th-class chimney that deposited us directly on the summit.

We were just under seven hours on the route, with a lot of time spent stopping to capture video and still images. A strong party could rally the line in five hours or so. La Mirada del la Gitana (The Look of the Gypsy, 2,500', M6). Do they give stars in the *AAJ*? If so: ****. Descent was the east ridge to the north col, then down the huge north couloir.

PETE TAPLEY

Mt. Hooker, free ascent. In August, Dave Sharratt, Pat Goodman, and I completed a free ascent of the northeast face of Mt. Hooker. The line generally followed Third Eye (VI 5.10 A4, Middendorf-Quinlan, 1993) in the lower half, then the upper corner systems of the Boissonneault-Larson (VI 5.11 A4, 1979). Details of the trip, including videos and stills are on both Dave's website (sharrattphoto.com/news.asp?ID=11) and Pat's website (bolderznwallz.blogspot.com/2010/12/mount-hooker-third-eye-free-var.html). By modern standards, our route (which we haven't named as it's not really a new route) is not very difficult. We neither did it very fast nor did we take the most difficult line; but we took an aesthetic line up one of the baddest parts of the wall. In short, the "new" free route is 13 full-rope-length pitches with lots of fun but spicy 5.11 and 5.12 climbing. Routefinding is generally straightforward except for one section with some funky downclimbing to access the upper corner system of the Boissonneault-Larson. Before reaching this downclimbing pitch, you may see an errant bolt (sorry, I thought it would go but failed) to climber's right. It would be a significant variation and a way to go straight up into the Boissonneault-Larson route rather than do the downclimbing pitch (good luck either way!). Though each pitch was onsighted or redpointed by one of us at some point, none of us made a continuous free ascent. While we added a couple of bolts to new free-climbing variations, we did not change the existing routes. We're pretty certain that they remain in original condition. A4 remains serious as ever.

TAKI MIYAMOTO

COLORADO
ROCKY MOUNTAIN NATIONAL PARK

Hayden Spire from Trail Ridge Road, showing the north ridge route (Dumbest Idea in the Park) on the East Pinnacle. *Richard Ryer*

Hayden Spire, East Pinnacle, Dumbest Idea in the Park. In early July, Chris Trimble and I had the brilliant idea of climbing the prominent north ridge of Hayden Spire's East Pinnacle, which looks great from high on Trail Ridge Road—except that it's a *long* way away. We convinced ourselves it wouldn't be so far if approached from the Flattop Mountain Trial, and so, bluffing with a pair of twos, we hiked in and then dropped down 1,500' into the spire's cirque. From the lowest point of the north ridge, staying mostly along the crest, we climbed to the top of the pinnacle in nine roped pitches, plus lots of scrambling (up to easy 5th class), and with a 100' rappel off the first tower. It's pretty clean, with three excellent pitches and the rest being, well, mountain-y. We scrambled off and slogged back toward the Divide and the Flattop trail, returning to the trailhead after about 22 hours and 25 miles roundtrip. We couldn't find any history of the route having been climbed before, so we informally named it after a friend's statement upon our return: "That sounds like the dumbest idea in the Park" (1,400', 9 pitches, 5.9).

JUSTIN DUBOIS, *Estes Park, Colorado*

Chief's Head, Flight of the Kiwi. Two pitches up the classic route Birds of Fire, I looked 400' left to a series of inviting cracks and corners. One more route appeared on my ever-growing to-do list. When the RMNP guidebook and other founts of local knowledge came up short regarding the line, it bumped to the top of my list. Graham Zimmerman and I began climbing on a cold and misty day in July, "Washington conditions" to us two Northwest natives. And despite our best efforts to find moss and wet cracks, an array of clean edges and dry stone abounded. The route's crux came early on pitch two, with a tenuous rightward slab leading to the clean cracks that had drawn us here. After six pitches of well-protected climbing, we topped out amid active storms. A week later, I returned

The northwest face of Chief's Head: (1) Papoose (Harlin-Wheeler, 1980). (2) Flight of the Kiwi (both variations shown; Herrington-Sambataro-Zimmerman, 2010). (3) Kachina Winds (Horan-Baldwin, 1992). (4) Seven Arrows (Fowler-Harlin, 1980). (5) Birds of Fire (Rossiter-Rossiter-Woolf, 1988). All lines except (2) are approximate, following vague features. *Blake Herrington*

with Joe Sambataro, another Washington native, who, like Graham and me, had spent formative climbing time in New Zealand. We repeated the route to the top of the face, with a better variation, on clean cracks to the right for pitches three and four, then climbed five more pitches (with a 3rd-class section in the middle) to the summit. The final pitches, along Chief's Head's north ridge, had likely been climbed before. In all, Flight of the Kiwi (IV 5.10+) provides a boltless alternative to Birds of Fire at a similar grade. We climbed the route clean and onsight, and the final five pitches can be reached from any route on the northwest face for those not seeking an "end of the technical difficulties" 500' below the summit.

BLAKE HERRINGTON, *AAC*

Longs Peak, Hearts and Arrows. Bruce Miller and I spent nine days on Longs Peak between July 27 and August 26 establishing Hearts and Arrows, a free route up the center of the Diamond. We climbed the first four pitches of the Enos Mills Wall (V 5.11 A3), already freed at 5.10, with a short new leftward traverse to a stance. We then added a new 45' face traverse pitch that climbs leftward into a prominent right-facing corner on Jack of Diamonds (V 5.10c A4). We added two bolts and one pin on this 5.11c traverse. The route overhangs slightly for the next 350'.

The sixth pitch climbs the corner (5.11a) to a semi-hanging stance where we added one bolt and one pin at the belay. The crux seventh pitch comes next: steep face (one new pin, 5.10- R),

Hearts and Arrows, on the Diamond, Longs Peak. A whole shitton of other routes exist in this image. *Chris Weidner*

Bruce Miller following the crux seventh pitch of Hearts and Arrows. *Chris Weidner*

then endurance crack climbing from fingers to fists for 90' (5.12b). Pitch eight is 100' of steep crack climbing (5.11b) ending with a spectacular hold-studded roof. The second half of this pitch is new climbing between Jack of Diamonds and Enos Mills Wall, including the 5.10d roof. The final pitch traverses right for 10' into the Enos Mills Wall for 100' of 5.9 offwidth and another 60' of easier terrain to the top of the Diamond.

Interestingly, the aid cruxes from the first ascents proved some of the easiest free climbing. For example, the 5.10- R start of the crux pitch was A4 on the first ascent of Jack of Diamonds, back in 1963.

Bruce and I rapped in from the top six different days, spending many hours finding the best, driest cracks and cleaning them of loose rock. Some days we were stormed off by 11 a.m., having hiked four hours to the summit just to get two or three hours on the Diamond (then another three hours down).

On August 26 we left the car at 1:45 a.m. We began climbing off Broadway at about 6:15 a.m. The crux was dry and we redpointed the route with no falls. We topped out at 5:15 p.m. after 11 hours of climbing, then hiked about 10 more minutes to the summit of Longs Peak. Our car-to-car time was 19:40.

Our line is objectively safe, relatively solid, and high quality for the middle of the Diamond. It goes at V 5.12b, nine pitches. We placed three bolts and three pins, in both cases two for lead protection and one at belays.

CHRIS WEIDNER, *AAC*

NORTH CAROLINA

Laurel Knob, Defective Sonar. Laurel Knob was purchased by the Carolina Climbers Coalition in 2006, which opened the cliff to legal first ascent activity. It is a beautiful granite dome hosting primarily slab climbing with some vertical sections. At the top it rounds off, as most domes do, into lower-angled fourth-class.

Arno Ilgner on Defective Sonar, Laurel Knob. *Dominic Smith*

I had not climbed on Laurel, but was interested in checking out potential new lines. Just left of the prominent right-arching feature of Fathom, I saw a beautiful, steep, diagonal crack midway up the face. Shannon Stegg told me Ralph Fickel and Burton Moomaw had started working on it back in 1991, reaching the top of the crack (about one-third up the wall) and still had dibs on finishing it. I contacted Ralph and Burton to find out whether or not this was true. I mentioned that I would like to join them to finish it. Burton hasn't climbed much due to physical reasons and wasn't interested, but Ralph was.

We asked Shannon to join us and in April 2008 we pushed past the high point, finishing four pitches. The angle lessened and we felt we were near the top. In May we climbed all day and into the night, adding three pitches, but with every pitch the angle of the rock didn't diminish. We had climbed about 1,000' feet and thought we were nearing the top, but in the darkness we couldn't determine where to finish the route. We returned in June, climbing the seven pitches, and realized that adding one more, easier pitch was all that was needed to finish it. After that the dome rounded off into scrambling.

Defective Sonar, on Laurel Knob. *Arno Ilgner*

Since then I worked on freeing the aid sections. After about six visits, ending on April 22, 2010, I freed it all in one redpoint effort (Defective Sonar, 1,000', 8 pitches, 5.12a). The climbing is varied from slab, to crack, to stemming, to crystal face climbing, to shallow and deep water groove climbing. All in all, it's a beautiful route.

ARNO ILGNER, *AAC*

Alaska

The online version of these reports frequently contains additional photos, maps, topos, and extended text. Please visit aaj.americanalpineclub.org

BROOKS RANGE

Peak 2,240m, first ascent and exploration. Due to lower elevations and poor rock quality, the Brooks Range does not attract a lot of attention. Doug Piehl and I were drawn to the range's remoteness and lack of other climbers. We focused on an area on the northern edge of the Endicott Mountains where, to the best of my research abilities, none of the mountains had been climbed. The area is mostly uninhabited, but archeological sites dot the area and wildlife abounds, most notably the huge caribou herds. Almost immediately after landing along the Killik River, a lone wolf ambled through our camp.

On the morning of June 3, we left base camp for Peak 2,240m, the third most prominent peak in the Brooks Range [Topographic prominence, behind Mts. Chamberlin and Igikpak. Peak elevations in meters, as per USGS maps for the Brooks Range—Ed.]. We first scrambled over a ridge and up an easy peak (approximately 68° 14' 30" N, 153° 48' W; 7,191' on our altimeter, and 6,824' based on converting the map contours), then scampered down scree on the east side of the ridge to the valley of the West Branch of the West Fork Okpikruak River. To reach Peak 2,240m we trekked downriver and around a group of mountains, then a short ways back up the East Branch. An easy river crossing took us to the 3,435' base (altimeter reading) of Peak 2,240m, seven hours after leaving camp. We began climbing the southernmost of three buttresses leading to the northwest ridge, encountering 3rd- and 4th-class terrain with a few spots of easy 5th (5.1–5.3). A thunderstorm, complete with lightning, slowed our progress to the main northwest ridge. Eventually an easy hike led to the summit (7,529' altimeter, 68° 17' N, 153° 33' W), for what we believe

The likely unclimbed Peaks 2,220m North (right) and 2,220m South (left), with the team's high point marked. They started on the opposite side of the ridge to the right of the X, joining the ridge about midway along its visible length. The team suggests that these peaks would offer the most exciting climbs in the area. *Erik Peterson*

is the first ascent. The night's rain turned our return river crossing—easy only 10 hours earlier—into a dangerous challenge. We returned to base camp 34.5 hours after leaving.

While Peak 2,240m doesn't offer much climbing, our scouting gave us a close-up of Peak 2,220m North, which we also attempted. The terrain was mostly 3rd-class scree, and we stayed along the ridge to about 6,500' where we met a tricky cornice in a col and deteriorating conditions, and we retreated. This mountain, with its several peaks, offers the best climbing in the area with several potential 5th-class routes on near-vertical rock. A badly sprained ankle prevented us from another attempt.

ERIK PETERSON

ALASKA RANGE

Geographical note: While the well-known peaks in Denali National Park are often called "The Alaska Range," these peaks form just one part of the immense Alaska Range, which contains many significant subranges, including the Hayes and Delta ranges, and the Revelation, Kichatna, and Tordrillo mountains.

HAYES RANGE

Mt. Hayes, Direct West Face; Mt. Balchen, Northeast Buttress to near summit. On May 22, Sam Johnson and I flew in to the Hayes Range portion of the eastern Alaska Range, looking for maximum adventure. We spent six perfectly cloudless days transporting tremendous amounts of gear around the Gillam Glacier, and then stood below Mts. Deborah and Hess, ready to launch. Watching water pour down our desired routes under the hot sun was disappointing, to say the least.

The Northeast Buttress of Mt. Balchen, and the descent (arrow). The East Ridge (Jagersky-Sumner, 1974) route is the left skyline, and Alchemy Ridge (Johnson-Klick, 2009) the right skyline. *Ryan Hokanson*

Fortunately, pilot Rob Wing, of Fairbanks, was able to shuttle us in his Piper Super Cub to the Hayes Glacier. Rob executed three absolutely spectacular landings on the rock-studded, double-cambered dry glacier ice at around 5,500'. After a short but heavy carry to the Hayes basin, we were greeted with colder, perfect conditions. First, Sam and I set our sights on a line attempted in the 1990s by Jon Miller and the late Keith Echelmeyer, and again in 2005 by Jed Brown and Kevin Wright (both parties turned back). As the high pressure amazingly continued through a second week, Sam and I established the Direct

Mt. Hayes (13,876') seen from high on the east ridge of Mt. Balchen: (1) North Ridge (Ferris-Hall-Hendricks-Montgomery-Shand-Washburn-Washburn, 1941). (2) Fairbanks Spur (Bull-Radford-Reynolds-Will, 1984). (3) West Face (Davis-Gowans-Hansen, 1976). (4) Direct West Face (Hokanson-Johnson, 2010). (5) West Ridge (D.B. Cooper and friends, 1978). (6) 1983 SW Face (Cheesmond-Tobin). (7) 1976 SW Face (Leo-McCarty-Ochenski). (8) South Ridge (Buchannon-Wheeler, 1977; 1975 Japanese to 50' from summit). *Jeff Benowitz*

One foot at a time, Sam Johnson and Ryan Hokanson get a leg up on the Direct West Face of Mt. Hayes. *Ryan Hokanson*

Sam Johnson leading the first real pitch on Mt. Balchen. *Ryan Hokanson*

West Face of Mt. Hayes (6,500', AI3 R) in a 24-hour, camp-to-camp push, which included a one-hour rest/brew stop. The route is exposed to seracs down low, but the climbing is easy enough that we soloed and simul-climbed the entire route, minimizing our exposure. The route consists mostly of thousands of feet of alpine ice up to 85° and several short, rotten rock bands up high. We descended the North Ridge for 1,000'+ until horizontal, corniced terrain posed an inconvenience, and then did 16 V-thread rappels down the west face, followed by 3,000' of downclimbing to our skis.

After a couple of rest days, we re-launched in the early morning of June 3 for a route on Mt. Balchen, establishing the Northeast Buttress (3,600', AI4 M6). After six fantastic granite mixed "pitches," some of which included significant amounts of simul-climbing, we continued up the East Ridge (Jagersky-Sumner, 1974). The weather had deteriorated to near-zero visibility with heavy snowfall, and by the final step below the summit we experienced very loud thunder and significant St. Elmo's Fire. With all of our metal equipment vigorously buzzing and the thunder now seeming to come from every direction, we decided it would be wise to forego the remaining 50–100' of linear distance to the tippy-top, and began a hasty descent down the snow/ice to the climber's right of our route. Twelve rappels and much downclimbing through heavy snow-fall and very robust spindrift brought us safely to our skis at the base, 16 hours after leaving. Photos of both routes can be viewed at www.ryanhokanson.blogspot.com. An expedition video as well as more photos and in-field expedition artwork can be found at www.alpineessence.com. Thanks to the American Alpine Club and the Copp-Dash Inspire Award for helping make this trip possible!

RYAN HOKANSON, *AAC*

DELTA RANGE

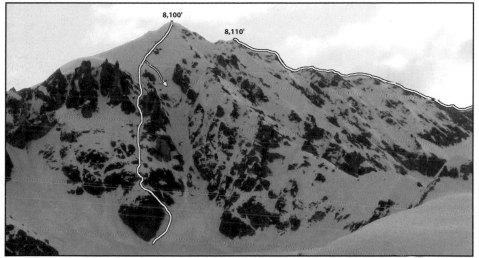

The routes on the southwest face of Peak 8,100' (arrow showing descent line) and the east ridge of Peak 8,110'. *Jeff Benowitz*

College Glacier area, various ascents. In the College Glacier region, numerous 8,000' peaks (the highest peaks in the Delta Mountains south of the Denali Fault) make for good late-April/early-May weekend outings with a small rack of pins and pickets for glacier travel. With various Fairbanks folks active in the area over the years, first ascent histories are largely unknown, thus the peaks lend themselves to the ever-common second, third, and fourth first ascents. [The claiming of new routes that have already been climbed—Ed.]

In 2009 and again in 2010, Sam Herried, Andy Sterns, and I climbed the southwest face of Peak 8,100' on the College Glacier, each time in about 36 hours round trip from the car, and climbing at night to avoid rockfall. At least one of those ascents is a second first ascent.

Also in 2010, Herried and I climbed the nearby Peak 8,110' via its east ridge, approaching on skis up the College Glacier and over a pass to the east onto an unnamed glacier, which we call "No Name Glacier." Again, the trip took us about 36 hours car-to-car, and we climbed at night.

JEFF APPLE BENOWITZ, *AAC*

Denali National Park

Denali National Park and Preserve, summary. In 2010, notable new routes and rapid repeats continued [see below], as did the inevitable rescues and tragedies. Thirty-five climbers were stricken with injuries or illnesses that required medical intervention by NPS rangers and volunteers, with cases ranging from climbing falls and altitude sickness to kidney stones and mental instability. Two climbers died in falls on Mt. McKinley (one each on the Cassin Ridge and West Buttress), and an avalanche in the Ruth Gorge killed two climbers.

Nancy Hansen, Felix Camire, and Doug Fulford were selected as the 2010 Mislow-Swanson Denali Pro Award winners for their assistance with a rescue and for helping a distressed solo climber.

Quick Statistics—Mt. McKinley and Mt. Foraker:
- *Mt. McKinley: Average trip length: 17.5 days. Busiest summit day: June 20, with 54 summits. Average age: 38. Women constituted 12.3% of all climbers.*
- *The five most represented nations on Mt. McKinley were: U.S. (673 climbers), U.K. (62), Canada (52), Poland (39), and Russia (36).*
- *McKinley was attempted by 1,222 climbers, with 55% reaching the summit; 1,135 attempted the West Buttress, with 56% summiting. Nine climbers attempted Mt. Foraker, with five summiting.*
- *The complete Mountaineering Summary can be found at www.nps.gov/dena/planyourvisit/ summaryreports.htm*

Summarized from the Denali National Park & Preserve Annual Mountaineering Summary

Mt. Foraker from the southeast: (1) Infinite Spur. (2) French Ridge. (3) Dracula. (4) False Dawn. (5) Southeast Ridge. (6) Viper Ridge (to junction with (5), no summit). *Colin Haley*

Mt. Foraker, Dracula. From June 13–15, Bjørn-Eivind Aartun and Colin Haley climbed Mt. Foraker by starting on False Dawn, then making the first ascent of a 3,000' mixed wall on the southeast face, and finishing via the French Ridge. Their climb, Dracula (AI4+ M6R A0), rises 10,400' from base to summit. They descended the Japanese Route, completing the round-trip in a sleepless 71-hour push. Beforehand, while acclimatizing on Denali, they simul-soloed the Cassin Ridge in 17 hours, coming close to the fastest known time for the route. See Aartun's feature article earlier in this *Journal.*

Mantok II, first ascent, Ladies' Couloir; Peak 10,020', northwest face to summit ridge. After reading trip reports and getting beta from Freddie Wilkinson, who along with various partners has established multiple climbs in the area, from April 8–20 Joey McBrayer and I explored the Northeast Fork of the Yentna Glacier. In mostly dismal weather we attempted several unclimbed features with limited success. Early in the trip we climbed the northwest face (3,000', AI4+ M5R) of an unnamed 10,020' peak, but did not continue to the summit. The peak is on the wilderness boundary just over two miles southwest of the Bat's Ears (Peak 11,044', *AAJ 2009*, pp. 130–132), and marked on the map on p. 153 of the 2008 *AAJ*.

After considerable cowering and a few more aborted efforts, we made what we believe was the first ascent of a ca 9,600' peak we called Mantok II. The peak sits along the same ridgeline (about 1.5 miles to the northeast) as Mantok I, a peak that Wilkinson, Gilmore, and Doucette summited in 2007. We took a moderate gully system on the left side of the southeast face to the southwest ridge and continued to the summit via broad, crevassed terrain, descended the same way, and named the route Ladies' Couloir (2,800', AI3+).

CHRISTOPHER WRIGHT, *AAC*

Ladies' Couloir on Mantok II. *Christopher Wright*

The northwest face of Peak 10,020'. *Christopher Wright*

Joey McBrayer descends Mantok II's summit ridge. *Christopher Wright*

RUTH GORGE

Moose's Tooth, Swamp Donkey Express. Zack Smith, Renan Ozturk, and I flew in to the Ruth Gorge on May 17, psyched to find perfect conditions: hard freezes at night but warm enough daytime temps to comfortably wear rock shoes. After a day to pack and scope, we left basecamp at 6 a.m. to do the dangerous approach to the Root Canal camp, beneath the south face of the Moose's Tooth, in the morning shade. I had navigated this same icefall seven years before, and was surprised at the amount of traffic it had received this year. Several distinct boot tracks left by different parties crisscrossed up the glacial canyon—some more exposed to hanging seracs and avalanche slopes than others.

We arrived at the Root Canal by 1 p.m., waited out a day of squally weather, then crossed the bergschrund and began soloing the snow slopes to the col between the Bear Tooth and Moose's Tooth. The south-southeast face of the Moose's Tooth is an obvious challenge that had been attempted sporadically for several decades. Badly rotten rock and a deceptive section of gendarmed ridge had defeated all teams within the first 100 vertical feet above the col. Our real challenge was not letting these discouraging reports affect our morale before we started.

After two hours of soloing and simul-climbing, we arrived at the base of the face. Zack transitioned to rock shoes and the show began. He found loose rock and runout climbing, but we made progress. Then came a significant aid pitch that demanded the efforts of two men, one hand-drilled bolt, and six hours to overcome. Several more wet and loose pitches with challenging routefinding followed. But then the angle lessened and soon I cramponed up a few easy mixed pitches to the southern end of the Moose's Tooth summit ridge. We stood just below the tip of the mountain's highest dollop of cornice at approximately 8 p.m., May 21 (Swamp Donkey Express, 5.9+ A2+ with some mixed).

We quickly rappelled Ham and Eggs (which, in its modern iteration, is equipped with rappel anchors every 30m) to return to the Root Canal camp around midnight. Though tired, we pressed on and descended to the Gorge in the cooler, safer, nighttime temps. An hour after we

Renan Ozturk at the belay below the "Bleeder Pitch" on the Swamp Donkey Express, Moose's Tooth. *Zack Smith*

exited the canyon and skied to the center of the Gorge, rockfall exploded off a wall, showering the glacier with debris. A week later, a team was hit by an avalanche and swept to their deaths on Freezy Nuts, a goulotte on nearby Hut Tower. If you're headed to the Ruth Gorge, or any of the excellent low-elevation venues for alpine climbing in Alaska, please be hyper-vigilant about temperature, conditions, and objective hazards.

Our special thanks and appreciation to the Copp-Dash Award for supporting our adventure, as well as the wonderful folks at Talkeetna Air Taxi and Alaska Mountaineering School for making it happen.

FREDDIE WILKINSON, *AAC*

Mt. Bradley, Vitalogy. Graham Zimmerman and I landed in the Ruth Gorge on March 28, and soon spotted a virgin line on the southeast buttress of Mt. Bradley. We made an initial attempt on March 31. On the evening of April 2, we left camp carrying 40 hours of food and fuel in a 20-pound second's pack and a 15-pound leader's pack, regained our highpoint, and established five more pitches. At mid-day we bivied on a prow, sheltered from what loomed above. The 1,500' day included Zimmerman climbing several M5 pitches and me dealing with sustained 5.9 rock, an A1 tension traverse, and a transition from boots and crampons to rock shoes and back.

Later that day the temps cooled and we climbed the beautiful ice ribbon that had initially drawn us in: 1,000' long and averaging WI4 with cruxes of M5+ and WI5. We climbed into the dark and established a second bivy. We awoke to lenticular clouds on the horizon and continued up a steep, blocky mixed ridge when the first of three storms hit. We climbed through to the base of a large 1,000' gendarme, which contained the crux of the route. The storm broke while we pushed seven pitches of sustained mixed climbing until we were spent. We fixed a line and rapped down to bivy on an exposed ledge. The next morning we finished the tower and simul-climbed steep, exposed snow slopes and spines.

At 4 p.m. on April 5, after 66.5 hours, we summited Mt. Bradley via Vitalogy (AK grade V, M6+ WI5 5.9R A1). Our 4,600' mixed route required 29 pitches, 19 of which were at least M5 or WI4. We finished our remaining food and began descending the west ridge, but a second storm closed in quickly, forcing us to downclimb and rappel 2,500' of uncharted terrain down a headwall and icefall to the Backside Glacier. We found ourselves under fire from increasing

Graham Zimmerman finishing a 140m unprotected snow wallow low on Vitalogy. *Mark Allen*

Mt. Bradley from the southeast: (1) East Buttress (Jochler-Orgler, 1987). (1a) Frieh-Johnson variation (2010). (2) Season of the Sun (Ichimura-Sato-Yamada, 2007). (3) Vitalogy (Allen-Zimmerman, 2010). The Bourbon Bottle (Crouch-Donini, 1996) starts on the left side of the lower shield that borders the start of (3), and the two routes weave similar terrain near Vitology's upper dots). Other routes exist to the left of the deep cleft left of the Bourbon Bottle. *Clifford Cochran*

spindrift and sluff slides. Lower, and still exposed to full-track avalanches, we found a safe bivy beneath a rock overhang at the base of the steep glacial-carved walls. The storm lasted an entire day, pinning us down without food and with little fuel, and brought 12" of new snow and waist-deep drifts. The next afternoon we were awakened by a sizable slide poring over the rim of our rock awning during a clearing. We used the break in the storm to wade through new snow for seven km, along the upper Backside Glacier, through 747 Pass, and down to the Ruth. Once in the Gorge a third and strongest storm hit, requiring us to navigate a whiteout at night to find our camp. After 99 hours away from camp, we began consuming the remainder of our 21 pounds of pork products. Visit www.markallenalpine.com for more details.

MARK ALLEN, *AAC*

Mt. Bradley, variation. On May 2, John Frieh and I climbed a new variation on the southeast face of Mt. Bradley, connecting the first third of Season of the Sun (Ichimura-Sato-Yamada, 2007) with the upper section of the East Buttress (Jochler-Orgler, 1987). The line departs from Season of the Sun just before that route heads left into the upper corner system, and continues up and right through 500' of previously unclimbed snow and mixed terrain (M6) to gain the East Buttress at roughly two-thirds height. On the upper East Buttress we found winter-like conditions (M5 C2); 12 hours after leaving the glacier we reached the summit.

DYLAN JOHNSON, *AAC*

Eye Tooth, new climbing to junction with Talkeetna Standard. During the last two weeks of April, Tim Dittmann, Dave Ahrens, and I attempted a new route on the west face of the Eye Tooth. We started up the obvious cleft between the Orgler route (Dream in the Spirit of Mugs, Bonapace-Haas-Orgler, 1994) and the Talkeetna Standard (Hollenbaugh-House, 2003). After the initial snow slopes, we roped up at the base of a chimney system cutting through the first rock band. This chimney was two pitches. The first: high-quality "frozen white stuff." The second: committing, low-quality "frozen white stuff" that proved as nerve-wracking for the belayers as for the leader. We simul-climbed the middle snowfield to the base of a second chimney system, which had been a big question mark from the Ruth Glacier. Upon arrival at the chimney we were psyched to find perfect, narrow, steep ice—an amazing pitch. Two more pitches of great, rolling ice in this shoulder-width chimney brought us to the southwest ridge and the intersection of the Talkeetna Standard, where we spent almost two hours creating a bivy platform.

Tim Dittmann in the perfect ice hose on the Eye Tooth. *Jared Vilhauer*

After a cozy night in our I-Tent, we continued up the ridge, climbing snow-covered rock for three pitches to the base of a giant rock wall. Here, we wandered the base of the wall looking for any weakness that would keep the Talkeetna Standard's 5.9 rating. Not having rock shoes or sufficient aid gear, we turned around. After many raps, some of which were from gear left by Hollenbaugh and House, we landed back on the glacier.

Being close to the Gorge landing strip, this route could become fairly popular. Those willing to hang it out in the first chimney system will be rewarded with great climbing in the second, and hopefully a summit.

JARED VILHAUER, *AAC*

The west face of Peak 7,400': (1) Bibler-Klewin (approximate line; 1989). (2) Optimist (Amano-Masumoto-Nagato, 2010), which likely shares the upper ridge with (1). *Giri-Giri boys*

The north face of Mt. Church: (1) For Whom the Bell Tolls (Bracey-Helliker, 2009). (2) Amazing Grace (Clapham-Pike, 2009). (2a) My Friends Forever (Amano-Masumoto-Nagato, 2010). (3) Memorial Gate (Ichimura-Sato-Yamada, 2007). *Jon Bracey*

Peak 7,400', Optimist; Mt. Church, My Friends Forever. Giri-Giri Boys Kazuaki Amano (leader), Ryo Masumoto, and Takaai Nagato established two new routes in the Ruth Gorge. On April 18–19 they climbed the Optimist (950m, 22 pitches, AK Grade 4, 5.9R M6), on the west face of Peak 7,400'. On April 25–26 on the north face of Mt. Church they established My Friends Forever (1,100m, 17 pitches, AK Grade 4, AI4+ M6R), named for their friends Tatsuro Yamada and Yuto Inoue, who died on Denali two years earlier.

HIROSHI HAGIWARA, *Rock & Snow magazine, Japan, based on communication with* AMANO

CHUGACH MOUNTAINS

Various new routes. On March 13, Ben Trocki and I climbed a new line on the east face of Awful Peak (the 8,170' peak that borders the west side of the unnamed glacier below the north face of Awesome Peak). We never came up with a name, so I've started calling it 13 Above the Night (1,500', IV M5 WI5). We climbed up to the hanging glacier that feeds the ice, then descended a snow couloir to the north. We didn't go to the summit.

Kevin Ditzler and I climbed a new line, Darkness Falls (2,500', VI M6 WI6 A2++), on the north side of Nantina Point in mid-February. It is the only route on that side of the mountain. After summiting we descended to the col between Nantina Point and Kiliak, then down the snow gully back to the Kiliak Glacier. The climb took 68 hours round trip from a high camp.

Kevin Ditzler and I climbed a new line— almost—on the west side of Benign Peak in December. It's the obvious couloir to the climber's left of Malignant Gully. We climbed 10 long (70m) pitches then rapped from near the top. I don't care

The west face of Benign Peak: (1) 2010 Ditzler-Kelley attempt, with high point X. (2) Malignant Gully (Mitchell-Sassara, 1987). (3) The Cancer (Ditzler-Kelley, 2011). (4) Grizzly Camel (Kelley-Trocki, 2010). *Kevin Ditzler*

much for excuses but here's mine: I'd been hit in the face by some ice earlier. The climbing was hard, dark, runout, and was scaring the shit out of me. This along with a headache, some blood, heavy spindrift, and the approaching weather knocked the courage out of me. I chickened out of my lead about halfway through pitch 11. So far it goes at M6 WI5 but remains unfinished.

In late December, Ben Trocki and I completed a new line on Benign Peak's west face. Grizzly Camel (V WI4 M4) is 3,200' long and tops out on the south summit of Benign. It took us 36 hours round trip from a high camp. We descended the col between Bellicose Peak and Benign Peak.

Kevin Ditzler and I returned to Benign in early January 2011 and climbed a new line in the center of the west face that we're calling The Cancer. It's 3,200' and goes at VI WI5 M6. The last 800' or so is the same as Grizzly Camel. We descended the col between Bellicose and Benign, taking 48 hours round trip from a high camp.

JOHN KELLEY

Darkness Falls, on the north side of Nantina Point. *John Kelley*

WRANGELL-ST. ELIAS NATIONAL PARK

Mt. Drum, northwest face. On March 17, Dave Johnston and I climbed what we believe to be a new route on the northwest face of 12,010' Mt. Drum in Alaska's Wrangell Mountains. This mountain is well known to anyone who has driven the Richardson or Tok highways, as it is the farthest north-western outlier of the Wrangells. I fell under its spell and felt compelled to plan a trip to come to know a little of this huge massif. We left on March 5, skied from Gakona on the Tok Cutoff Highway for about 35 miles to the northwest glacier of Mt. Drum. We crossed the frozen Copper River and skied up the Sanford River and Northwest Glacier Creek, intersecting the glacier at about 4,600'.

We had hoped to remain on skis all the way up to 10,000', then ascend one of two unclimbed ridges. At 4,600' and up to almost 10,000', we encountered wind-scoured, hard blue ice and heavily crevassed glacier, so we left our skis behind. Crampon work, crevasse avoidance, and running belays were the stuff of several days' work. At just below 10,000' we suddenly transitioned back to snow. The entire basin between our two potential ridge climbs was filled with thigh-deep wind slab. We sadly remembered our skis cached over 5,000' below, as we laboriously broke trail upward.

Dave Johnston below Mt. Drum, with arrows indicating the new route (summit not visible). *Willi Prittie*

We dubbed our 7,280' high camp "Camp Ne'rershine" because of the complete lack of direct sunlight in winter, placed as it was on the Northwest Glacier below the steep north face of Point 8,100'+. We climbed straight up the Northwest Glacier instead of the ridges, and our summit "day" was over 49 hours and included digging a snow cave with a cooking pot and ice axes at 10,600' for a bivy. Our return to Gulkana was by skis and hitching a ride the last 10 miles on snow machines on the Sanford River on March 21.

Good weather predominated the entire time we were high on the mountain, and we enjoyed a balmy (for Alaskan winter) -8° at our snow-cave bivy. On the summit we enjoyed an amazing -2°, with less than 5 mph of wind, and a completely clear day with unlimited views of the Wrangell, Chugach, Talkeetna, and Alaska ranges. The summit block consisted of a 50' cube block of rime ice with a foot-wide crack where it was slowly detaching itself from the rest of the mountain. I wonder if it is still there and if so, how long it will last!

I had originally thought that this was the first winter ascent of Drum, as well as a new route, but we since have found that an Alaskan party consisting of Wayne Kates, Hank Noldon, Berry Kertscher, John Pinamont (and perhaps Gill Todd?) climbed Mt. Drum the first week of January 1975 from a landing at a cabin in the Sanford River valley, and probably via the North Ridge. I believe that this was a previously unreported climb, and this should make our climb the second winter ascent of Mt. Drum.

WILLI PRITTIE, *AAC, Mountaineering Club of Alaska*

Snider Peak, Dicktation to west summit pillar. Growing up in the heart of the Wrangell Mountains in interior Alaska, I have always had a penchant for vertical escape. My friend John Giraldo also shares this interest, and together we spent our teenage years pushing ourselves on little-known peaks in the Wrangell and Chugach mountains. In 2009, at age 19, we mustered the courage to try a new challenge: Snider Peak.

Located within Wrangell-St. Elias National Park and Preserve near Glennallen, AK, this jagged rock pyramid sits between 12,010' Mt. Drum and 14,163' Mt. Wrangell. Snider isn't the tallest summit at 8,200', but its nearly vertical 3,000' north face and the serrated spires on all corners gives this small peak an aggressive stance. Despite standing less than a 15-minute flight from Gulkana airport, Snider had no documented climbs. After our aborted 2009 attempt, we returned to Snider in May 2010.

We did the 10-mile approach, waited out an 18-hour squall, left the tent on the northwest toe at 1 a.m., and scuttled up the snow-loaded flanks with caution. The early Alaskan sunrise found us 1,700' above base camp, inching along the west ridge, which we crested at 6,700'. We then quickly dropped south into a shallow basin below the southwest face, where a couloir runs directly toward the top.

Here, the real climbing began and we simul-climbed quickly up the first half of the narrowing couloir, fighting weak sugary snow, thin ice, and crumbly rock. After 800' we burst out of the gun barrel onto a high step below the summit spire, hanging precariously over half a mile of air. The last pitch tested us with 200' of mixed climbing that swung around directly above the massive north face. Our route, Dicktation, topped-out on the narrow tip of the west summit

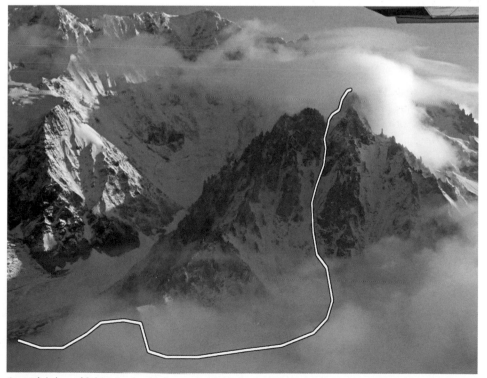

An aerial view of Snider Peak, with the route Dicktation. *Mark Henspeter*

pillar. A razor-thin ridge ran 100' to the east and rose to a slightly higher (~20') spire, but given the exposure and depleted rack, we knew that this was the end of our route.

Mark Henspeter

Peak 10,510', first ascent, West Face. In late July, Jim Beyer and I made the likely first ascent of Peak 10,510', across the glacier northwest of Mt. Hobbs. We landed on an unnamed glacier on the south side of the range, a mile (at most) from the peak, then scrambled up a scree gully and onto the hanging glacier west of the peak. The West Face started around 40° and steepened to 65° at the top. About 3,000' of ice led to the summit block, which was a short pitch of 5.4. We rappelled the route, mostly on V-threads, returning to camp in a 20-hour round trip.

John Kelley

Upper Granite Creek and Jefferies Glacier, probable first ascents. From July 16 – August 6, upon the recommendation of well-known bush pilot and mountaineer Paul Claus, we visited the upper Granite Creek and Jefferies Glacier areas. From our drop-off point (3,014'; N 60°44'16", W 141°57'11") in upper Granite Creek, a lengthy ridge leads up Peak 8,329' (GPS elevation; 8,320' on map; N 60°41'52", W 141°42'32"), which dominates the left flank of the glacier. [Map elevations are from the USGS 1:250,000 Bering Glacier map—Ed.] We gained the undulating west-northwest ridge by loose scrambling through and around a series of low buttresses. At one point we had to drop 180m before resuming the final section toward the summit. This final section—almost one km long—was the most interesting of the route. Several gendarmes offered easy slabs and short walls, though we skirted two on their left. Never difficult (AD) but with extensive scree and boulder debris, the route was interesting and finished with a short snow slope to the top. The route involves 1,100m of ascent and the ridge itself is almost four km long.

Next we headed for the southeast ridge of Peak 7,679' (GPS; 7,656' on map; N 60°39'52", W 141°49'07"), which sits in the upper corner of a branching glacier that connects upper Granite Creek and the Jefferies Glacier. We accessed the peak via snow slopes leading to a col that connects it with a smaller tent-like peak. From here a spur, punctuated by towers and buttresses, leads directly to the summit. Although many of the towers were sound granite, the climbing was consistently loose. But it was an enjoyable and obvious line (AD, ~500m) to a snow-capped summit.

The west-northwest ridge of Peak 8,329'. *Howard-Swinburne collection*

From our camp on the southern edge of the Jefferies Glacier, on skis we ascended Peak 7,178' (GPS; 7,230' on map; N 60°35'10", W 141°45'08") via its easy west face (F) to its rocky summit.

Finally, we attempted the southeast ridge of Peak 7,890' (map elevation), situated near the col by the entrance to the Jefferies Glacier. After weaving through a series of crevasses, we gained a loose and broken rock ridge that we followed to a point 150m below where the ridge appeared to level. But a large wall blocked our way and we descended.

Based upon Paul Claus's extensive knowledge, our research, and Steve Gruhn (who maintains climbing records of many Alaskan peaks), we believe our ascents to be firsts.

STUART HOWARD *AND* DAVID SWINBURNE, *U.K.*

The southeast ridge of Peak 7,679'. *Howard-Swinburne collection*

Mt. St. Elias, summit and sea. At 18,008' and 12 miles from salt water, Mt. St. Elias offers the world's biggest summit to sea drop. Canadians Marcus Warring and Ryan Bougie and I (Telluride, CO) wanted to climb the southwest ridge (Harvard Route) and then ski as much of the mountain as we could. Although parts of this route have been skied and climbed, according to my research, no one has completed the entire route both up and down. Most recently, in 2008, an expedition heavily funded by Red Bull did summit and ski most of the mountain—to within 600' MSL—but it was over the course of two expeditions and they did not ascend from the sea to their base on the Haydon Shoulder.

Overlooking Icy Bay from Mt. St. Elias. *Peter Inglis*

On June 6, pilot Paul Claus dropped us on the Haydon Shoulder (9,750'), where we set-up base camp. On June 10, we summited and descended, two-thirds on skis, to our base. Above our 13,200' high camp we deviated slightly from the Harvard Route by going far to climber's right on the south face, where we found better snow conditions for skiing.Back at base camp, we spent a week waiting for the cloud sandwich to lift. On June 18, we made a break for it. As best we can tell, we followed the Harvard Route, including the loose shale ridge, to a wonderful grassy camp at 3,500'. From there we descended to the Tyndall Glacier. At 2,300' the guidebook shows a base camp and landing area, which was melted out. I had found no descriptions of how to reach Icy Bay from there. We continued along the glacier's edge. At 1,500' the snow ran out and we abandoned our skis. At about 1,000' the route necessitated ugly alder-whacking. At one point we stared over a 750' cliff to the sea below. We continued alder-whacking up and over a small hill and scrambled down steep, rocky slopes to Icy Bay.

With the Tyndall Glacier calving in front of us, bear prints in the sand, and no humans for miles, it was idyllic wilderness at its best. We spent three hours at Icy Bay, making a big fire from an endless supply of driftwood and roasting NY strip steaks and marshmallows. We chose a slightly different route back to our skis, then ascended a gully to a ridge at 2,500', where we cruised across an open glacier and snowfields. This may be a better route with the possibility of skiing to the sea.

On the final ascent back to base camp, while ascending the shale ridge at 6,000', I touched a loose rock and rag-dolled backward for 100'. A flap of skin hung open under my left eye and I sustained a compression fracture of my L2 vertebra. The guys took part of my load and we continued up. Above the shale ridge at 7,800' we made camp and waited for flyable weather. On June 23, the weather improved and we ascended to our base camp and flew out.

PETER INGLIS, *AAC*

Mikey Schaefer on a fantastic pitch of the Witches'
Cleavage (the 2004 Ike-Walsh variation to the 2002
Edwards-Millar route on the West Witches' Tit).
Colin Haley

COAST MOUNTAINS

Devil's Thumb, Diablo Traverse. On August 12, Mikey Schaefer and I flew with Temsco Helicopters from Petersburg, Alaska, to a camp below the southeast face of Devil's Thumb. Our objective was a complete traverse of the Devil's Thumb massif, climbing over the summits of the Witches' Tits, Cat's Ears Spires, and, finally, Devil's Thumb itself. Like the Torres Traverse to Andrea Sarchi, this traverse is originally the dream of Dieter Klose, the Stikine Icecap's most dedicated disciple. The traverse was attempted in 2004 by Jon Walsh and Andre Ike, who became the first to traverse all four spires of the Witches' Tits and Cat's Ears (making the first ascent of the East Witches' Tit in the process), but were stopped at the base of the Thumb by a chopped rope.

On the morning of August 13, we departed our base camp and made a

The west-to-east line of the Diablo Traverse. *Colin Haley*

descending, traversing approach to the base of the Witches' Tits. We climbed to the notch between the two Witches' Tits by the Edwards-Millar route, with the Ike-Walsh Witches' Cleavage variation. The climbing on the upper headwall was absolutely outstanding, and certainly some of the highest-quality alpine rock I've ever touched. The unrepeated Edwards-Millar and Belcourt-Rackliff routes look amazing. We left our packs in the notch between the Tits and quickly tagged the summit of the West Witches' Tit. We then picked up our packs, climbed up to the summit of the East Witches' Tit for its second ascent, and rappelled the east ridge of the East Tit to a tight bivy in the Tits-Ears col. This col had the last snow or ice we encountered before the summit of Devil's Thumb, so we filled our packs with eight liters of water.

On the morning of the 14th, we made one rappel to the north side of the ridge to gain the Elias-McMullen route on the Cat's Ears. We climbed that route to the Cat's Brow (the notch between the ears), then tagged each of the spectacular Cat's Ears summits in single pitches. We knew that Walsh and Ike had rappelled to the south from the Brow, and chopped their rope regaining the ridgecrest in the extremely chossy Ears-Thumb gully. Hoping to avoid a similar fate, we instead rappelled the east face of the East Cat's Ear directly into the Ears-Thumb notch. Our plan avoided the chossy gully, although it was very intimidating to rappel the dead-vertical-to-slightly-overhanging east face of the East Ear. From the Ears-Thumb notch we climbed two pitches up Devil's Thumb's West Buttress to a five-star bivy ledge.

On the 15th we got an early start and continued up the West Buttress of the Thumb. There was one tricky roof that Mikey surmounted with a mix of free and aid climbing, but the majority of the West Buttress was moderate, in the 5.6–5.9 range, on fantastic rock. This is a route worthy of classic status. The West Buttress had been almost climbed in 1990 by Jim Haberl, Mike Down, and Alastair Foreman, who retreated one pitch below the summit ridge in a storm. We found their rappel anchors all the way up, and their last anchor indeed looked like it had been made in haste: a sketchy looking block backed up with a friend.

We continued up the summit ridge, tagged the summit, and kept traversing to the descent of the southeast face. The descent, down a variation of the Beckey Route, was long and tedious (particularly because it was so melted out and there were lots and lots of loose blocks), but we eventually made it into our camp at 10:30 p.m.

This was a fantastic climb in a beautiful area. It is higher in quality than difficulty, and is certainly a traverse that I'd recommend to others. We called it the Diablo Traverse (5.10 A2). Thanks to Jon Walsh and Andre Ike for laying the groundwork, and thanks a ton to Dieter Klose for the original inspiration and logistical help in Petersburg.

COLIN HALEY, *AAC, Seattle*

Mikey Schaefer on the West Buttress of the Devil's Thumb. *Colin Haley*

Canada

The online version of these reports frequently contains additional photos, maps, topos, and extended text. Please visit aaj.americanalpineclub.org

ST. ELIAS RANGE

Mt. Logan, I-TO. Japanese climbers Yasushi Okada and Katsutaka Yokoyama made the first ascent of the enormous south face of Mt. Logan (5,957m), considered by many alpinists to be the greatest unclimbed alpine wall in North America. From May 4–8 they climbed the face, continued to the East Summit, and descended the East Ridge. They named their route I-TO (2,500m, ED+ M6 WI5), meaning "thread, line, relationship," partly in honor of Jack Tackle and Jay Smith, who had attempted and long coveted the route, but willingly shared information with Yokoyama. See Yokoyama's feature article earlier in this *Journal*.

Mt. Augusta, Northeast Pillar, and Mt. Logan. In mid-May we were hanging around Haines Junction, looking for Bill Karman, our helicopter pilot, who was supposed to take us to the Seward Glacier at the base of the Hummingbird Ridge, the main goal of our expedition. We walked into a restaurant, and, to our surprise, a man looked at us and said, "You must be the French guys?" We'd found Bill.

Two days later, thanks to Bill, as well as Andy Williams with his airplane, all seven of us and our gear were at base camp. The south face of Mt. Logan is so massive, it is hard to comprehend its true scale. But 15km away, the north face of Mt. Augusta (4,282m) looked much less daunting. The northeast pillar looked especially attractive, sharp in the evening sun, a natural line drawn by the elements, light, and shadow.

We divided our team into two: Marion Poitevin, Lionel Albrieux, and Jacques Olivier Marie would go for the East Ridge of Logan. The three Sebs (Sebastien Bohin, Sebastien Moati, and Sebastien Ratel) and I would try Augusta by the unclimbed northeast pillar, to acclimatize before attempting the Hummingbird.

On our first attempt, on May 21 at 4 a.m., the temperature was surprisingly warm—around 15°—but we decided to go anyway. After only 150m on the ridge I slipped and was lucky to be

The sit-start attempt to Mt. Logan's Hummingbird Ridge. *GMHM*

Mt. Augusta, with the Northeast Pillar climbing the obvious sun-shade line. *GMHM*

stopped by "my" Seb (Moati), who jumped off the other side of the ridge. My knee was twisted from the crampons, so Seb and I returned to base camp, while Sebs Bohin and Ratel stayed. They started up again at midnight, but nothing had changed—still too warm—and when they reached the rocky ridge, they were disappointed to realize that the rock was just like the snow: soft. So after 500m of climbing, they rappelled down, and in the evening we were all at base camp drinking beer and wondering where the fuck we would climb in the following weeks if this damned global warming continues. We spent some days exploring near base camp, but lots of the climbs had serious objective dangers, with huge seracs on top. Every time we returned to camp, the northeast pillar of Augusta

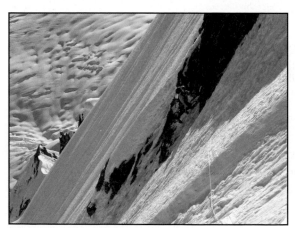

Seb Moati on Mt. Augusta's Northeast Pillar. *Manu Pellissier*

was smiling at us, and, in the end, we could no longer resist.

On May 28, we again crossed the Seward Glacier, but adjusted our tactics. We set up our tent at the base of the ridge, just below a big boulder—a good place with a nice view, until a rock hit the tent. After that, Seb (Moati) slept with his helmet on. We started climbing at midnight. It was still warm but our old tracks helped, and in less than three hours we had reached the Sebs' high point. It was like a race against the sun, and we knew that by 7 a.m. we had to be high enough on the ridge to traverse the north face and stay protected. We climbed in two teams, sharing the same tracks, with a lot of simul-climbing. At 10 a.m., we joined the north ridge at 3,400m, having climbed 1,300m in ten hours. We set up the tent and rested, and at 2 p.m. headed up the 900m-long final snowfield, summiting Mt. Augusta four hours later (Northeast Pillar, 2,300m, TD). The only cloud in the Yukon was with us atop the mountain, hiding the view on the Gulf of Alaska and all the nice beaches we'd been dreaming about: Desolation Bay, Disenchantment Bay, Demolition Bay. Then it was back to the tent for sleep, so we could move early, during the day's coldest hours.

On May 30 we were all back at base camp, our friends having climbed the East Ridge to Mt. Logan's east summit (5,929m), and the good weather was still with us. So, we decided that the three Sebs and I would try the "sit start" to the Hummingbird, by the right branch, and Marion, Lionel, and Jacques would try something they'd heard called the "Dragon Tail Ridge" [believed to be unclimbed start to Hubsew Ridge—Ed.].

On the Hummingbird, the pain in my knee forced me to quit early on. The Sebs, however, climbed two days on the ridge, reaching 3,000m with some hard climbing on poor rock before the weather worsened and forced them to retreat. Team Dragon Tail climbed 600m before turning back as well.

Back in France we were already planning our trip back next year, figuring it will be easier now that we know where to find Bill....

MANU PELLISSIER, *GMHM, France*

LOGAN MOUNTAINS

Mt. Proboscis, Southeast Face Original Route (and variation), free ascent. In late July, with help from American Alpine Club grants, Emily Stifler, Lorna Illingworth, and I helicoptered to the base of Mt. Proboscis in the Cirque of the Unclimbables, Northwest Territories. We spent 25 days in the area and flew out on August 21, after a 20" snowfall ended our climbing. Our objective was to free climb the full Southeast Face (a.k.a. Original Route), first climbed by Jim McCarthy, Royal Robbins, Layton

Madeleine Sorkin freeing the crux eighth pitch of the original Southeast Face route on Mt. Proboscis. *Emily Stifler*

Kor, and Richard McCracken in 1963 (VI 5.8 A4). In 2001 Jonny Copp and Josh Wharton freed the Costa Brava variation (VI 5.12- R) to the Original Route, which takes a detour from pitches 5–8 and 12–16 [confirmed by Wharton; Copp's *AAJ 2002* feature article includes only brief mention of this ascent—Ed.].

After a stymied ground-up effort on the Original Route, we free-climbed the Costa Brava variation to the summit ridge and then, separately, spent four days inspecting, cleaning, bolting and finally freeing pitches 5–8 of the Original Route at 5.12R. To the best of our knowledge, this section had not been repeated since the 1963 first ascent. With permission to add bolts from the first ascensionists, we placed anchor stations above pitches 6 and 7, and added five bolts on the crux pitches: two on pitch 7 (5.11R) and three on pitch 8 (5.12R). We placed a total of nine 3/8" bolts in solid rock. We gave pitch 8 an R rating due to a hollow section of rock and the consequently long distance between the first and second bolts. The climbing is relatively steep and atmospheric with cracks and knobs. I led the crux pitches free on August 17 and the next day the summer weather promptly turned to fall, bringing a deep blanket of snow. It'd be great for someone to free these pitches as part of a continuous ascent of the Original Route.

Since returning from the Cirque we have spoken with Jim McCarthy. We now believe we did not follow the Original Route above pitch 11. Rather, we continued on the Costa Brava line, which traverses leftward along a grassy ledge for pitch 12 and then up a corner system for the remaining four pitches to the summit ridge. Jim's guess is that following their line would add two pitches of 5.10-5.11.

A full expedition report with topo is available in the 2011 *Canadian Alpine Journal*. We also kept this information as well as a journal of stories, photos, and videos at cirqueladies.wordpress.com.

MADALEINE SORKIN, *AAC*

COAST MOUNTAINS

Mt. Endeavor, Arête sans Chaussures and Peak 8,692', Dalestrom. With the help of the McNeill-Nott and Mountain Fellowship grants, Blake Herrington and I spent ten days exploring peaks around the Scud Glacier of the Stikine Region in late July and early August. We flew 50 miles west from the Cassiar Highway to Yehiniko Lake and approached the Scud Glacier via the Quattrin Creek Valley. Somehow,

Nate Farr climbing the Dalestrom, with Mt. Endeavor prominent in the left-center skyline. The left skyline of Endeavor shows the upper one-third of Arête sans Chaussures. *Blake Herrington*

through miscommunication at the dock and improper gear stowing, my climbing boots and trekking pole had disappeared mid-flight, leaving me with rock shoes and a decrepit pair of running shoes that I had found in my garage. With duct tape, some scavenged material, stiff insoles we cut from our pack frame, and several tubes of seam grip we crafted the omnishoes, which allowed me to attach crampons and even lead some steep ice. Our approach through the Quattrin Creek Valley required many waist-deep crossings and a healthy portion of bushwhacking. At the unnamed glacier at the head of Quattrin Creek we suffered another setback: our airdrop had exploded and cost us much of our food supply.

We planned to attempt the north ridge of Mt. Ambition. We climbed steep snow and ice through an icefall to the col between Mt. Ambition and Mt. Endeavor. From the col we climbed the first third of Ambition's north ridge but retreated in the face of horrible rock. After considerable difficulty finding solid anchors for our descent, we changed plans to the south ridge of Mt. Endeavor (9,300'). We climbed a couple of thousand feet up an icefall and then 2,200' of solid, moderate rock to the summit, establishing Arête sans Chaussures (4,000', D 5.6 AI-moderate). From the summit we had a long, loose, and sometimes tense descent along the southeast ridge through the building storm and back to our camp on the Scud Glacier.

After drying our gear we headed toward the west ridge of Peak 8,692', located west of the Quattrin-Scud col. From the base of a broad buttress at the base of the west ridge we climbed through shattered but mostly solid granite in four pitches to the ridge crest, then continued to the summit. We named our route Dalestrom (2,000', D 5.9), in homage of our unforgettable whirlwind of a bush pilot. We descended the east ridge to its base and completed a single rappel to the south back to the Scud Glacier.

NATE FARR, *AAC*

Asperity Mountain, Southwest Face. On July 29, Tony McLane and I flew in to the Plummer Hut in the Waddington Range, and that afternoon we dropped to the Tiedemann Glacier and a bivy at Sunny Knob. The next morning, we negotiated the glacier below the southwest face of Asperity Mountain and mixed climbed past a bergschrund to gain a vague buttress near the center of the face. We climbed this for eight long pitches on generally excellent rock, culminating in a 60m offwidth in a corner that reared to slightly beyond vertical. This gained a lower-angled middle section, where we made fast progress up snow couloirs and low-5th-class rock. Eventually the face steepened again and we followed a ramp leftward to the Northwest Ridge route. A short bit of climbing in a beautiful position brought us to the summit. Southwest Face (950m, ED1 5.10+).

Asperity Mountain: (1) Asperity Couloir-Northwest Ridge (Beckey-King-Magoun-Matthews, 1947). (2) Southeast Ridge (Heselden-Richardson, 1997). (3) Southwest Face (Elson-McLane, 2010). Also shown: Serra 5 and Serra 4. *John Scurlock*

The descent from Asperity to the Tiedemann has a nasty reputation that we found well deserved. We descended the east face toward the col with Serra 5, first with slightly stressful downclimbing and then with some diagonal rappels around a serac once the ice slope became firm enough to make V-threads. We bivied at the col and the next morning set off down the couloir that drops toward the Tiedemann. We soon exited the couloir onto a chossy rib, where at least the majority of the rockfall was self-induced. A long rappel over a bergshrund brought us to a tedious traverse to the top of Carl's Couloir. This proved relatively straightforward, although we still required a rope-stretching rappel over the bergschrund at the bottom. We then downclimbed exposed glacial ice to the Tiedemann Glacier and slogged back up to the comforts of the hut.

NICK ELSON, *Canada*

Squamish Chief, Gravity Bong. After five years of recons, prep work, and keeping my mouth shut, I completed my long-term nemesis. The Prow Wall is one of the last major formations to see development on the Chief, probably

Gravity Bong, on the Squamish Chief. *Colin Moorhead*

Colin Moorhead leading pitch 3 of his new route, Gravity Bong, Squamish Chief. *Rich Wheater*

due to its relatively difficult access and lack of obvious connecting natural lines. Despite this, it is certainly one of the cleanest and most aesthetic walls on the Chief. Numerous solo missions and top-down prep in July resulted in fixing the entire line (on the right side of the dominant "prow" feature, right of Teddy Bear's Picnic) with a 250m static top rope. Tony Richardson and I had a field day whipping-off two-hour micro-ascender laps of this monstrous line. Climbing for this long without racks, belaying, hauling or other such encumbrances of the traditional two-person climbing team is amazing.

It wasn't long before I was climbing the entire line with very few falls on my ascender; it was time to remove the training wheels. On August 23, Tony and I did the first ascent, and I redpointed every pitch first try except the crux changing corners pitch. On August 28, I returned with Jason Kruk and a miserable weather forecast. The weather and my forearms held until pitch 8, when the skies and my fingers opened up. On my third attempt, the rain was blowing sideways, but the leaning, overhanging pitch kept the rock dry. Without much hope of success, I pulled on the starting crimps one more time. Latching the jug hold after the crux amidst hail and lightning was one of my most intense climbing experiences.

The resulting line ranks as one of the most sustained outings on the Chief. The nine-pitch breakdown: 5.10c, 5.11c, 5.12a, 5.12c, 5.12a, 5.12b, 5.11c, 5.13a, 5.12a. Subsequent attempts by Squamish luminaries confirm its quality as one of the best lines in Squamish. Although moderate by today's big wall free standards, Gravity Bong will most likely stand out as the pinnacle of my climbing career.

COLIN MOORHEAD, *Canada*

SELKIRK MOUNTAINS

Turret, Turret's Syndrome. One dark, drunken February night, I cleared off the beer cans from Andrew Boyd's kitchen table to show him a photo I'd seen of the south face of the Turret, in the Adamants. Andrew, a longtime Squamish hardman, was game. We shook on it, and in early August we stood on the glacier beneath the Turret. The face looked even bigger and more monolithic in person— like some unholy stone cathedral. The day the helicopter dropped us off, the weather was absolutely perfect. We spent the afternoon noodling around on the lower pitches and squinting up to see if we could spot the line. That evening we packed our gear and vowed to try the whole shebang the next day. That night clouds filled the tight cirque, but, given the forecast, we thought we had one more day of decent weather to play with.

Turret's Syndrome, on the south face of the Turret. Other routes are thought to exist on the face. *Andrew Boyd*

Will Stanhope approaching the wet offwidth low on Turret's Syndrome. *Andrew Boyd*

We woke at 4 a.m. and bee-lined it for the obvious corner system at the left edge of the face. On pitch 3, I encountered the first major hurdle: a wet, overhanging offwidth. I fell once, lowered to a no-hands stance, and climbed it second try. By early afternoon it became apparent that a storm was coming in. At this point, the climb got much steeper and more exposed, complete with beautiful, lichen-encrusted corner systems, all sandwiched together. We hustled up the corners, snatching glances over our shoulders, worried that we were about to get slammed with some weather. Once a corner would run out, I'd pound a knifeblade, then hopscotch to another one thanks to perfect face holds.

Late in the afternoon I laybacked up a perfect 5.11+ fingercrack in a corner, hoping the route was just about over. To my great disappointment, I realized that I'd butted us into a roof. Loose and steep to the left and blank to the right. The threatening weather had now matured into a full-fledged storm. We were climbing in a cloud.

Andrew, before reaching me at the belay, spied an exit down and left. He bouldered out left from the roof, wrapping his knuckles on the crispy holds, all the while yelling, "I don't like this!" I shivered away at the belay, wishing we had brought more clothes. When Andrew reached the belay, we were out of earshot. Facing an enormous pendulum if I were to fall, I decided to lower-out off a single nut in the roof. I then climbed up to him as a jabbering mess, gear hanging off me in disarray.

From there, the angle tipped back to less than vertical. We snapped a summit picture, then rappelled the backside in our rock shoes. The storm mercifully eased off. By the time we arrived at our packs at the base, the clouds had turned dark again. Turret's Syndrome (600m, V 5.11+ [free for leader]).

WILL STANHOPE, *Canada*

Mt. MacDonald, North Pillar Direct. Mt. MacDonald (2,883m) is an unsung gem of Canadian alpine rock, with clean quartzite walls towering above the Trans-Canada highway in Glacier National Park. On July 8, Jeff Relph and I stood below its north face, with intentions of starting up the North Pillar—mine and Bruce Kay's 2005 route (19 pitches, 5.11 A0)—freeing it, and then continuing up virgin ground for the direct finish. This prominent, direct line stands out, as it follows a steeper prow up high that glistens in the early morning or late afternoon sun. We left the car at 3 a.m., and with prior route knowledge made good time on the first 11 pitches. I freed the first crux at .11b thanks to having the knifeblades already in place for some crimpy face climbing. The next crux came on the sustained seventh pitch, which we solved on second (but not on lead) at 5.11c. As the crux came nearly 50m into the pitch, we didn't bother to lower and try to re-send the pitch, so the original A0 grade remains.

Instead of traversing left to easier simul-climbing terrain on the upper headwall, as Bruce and I had done, Jeff and I continued straight up the pillar staying on or as close to the ridgeline as possible, climbing many more pitches of 5.10 and 5.11. Eventually, the angle relented, but there were moves of 5.9 or harder on every pitch, sometimes on wet rock. After 23–25 pitches, we hit the summit ridge with 200m of 4th-class scrambling remaining between us and the summit. It was nearly 11 p.m. and getting dark, so we used our few remaining minutes of dusk to begin the long descent. Views from Mt. Columbia to the North Howser Tower and the immediate peaks and glaciers of Glacier National Park all lay before us against the alpenglow. Then, under a clear but moonless sky, we downclimbed and rappelled the west ridge, down 50° couloirs into the Herdman Bowl, and enjoyed good boot-skiing below until, at first light, we finally found the log to cross the raging Connaught Creek. We returned to the car 26 hours after leaving it. North Pillar Direct (1,000m, 5.11c A0).

Jon Walsh leading a 5.11a section shared with his 2005 route, en route to establishing the North Pillar Direct, on Mt. MacDonald. *Jeff Relph*

The North Pillar Direct, on Mt. MacDonald. *Jon Walsh*

It is a wild and committing route, with a ton of good rock climbing. The options are there for future repeats: easier on the left or more sustained on the right. We brought a standard double rack with single micro cams, single #3 and #4 Camalots, and one regular set of nuts. We placed one piton, which we left fixed. I'd recommend future parties bring the same, but the pitons are optional. Rappelling from high on the face would be sketchy and dangerous, as chances of getting ropes chopped or stuck and pulling stacked blocks onto you would not be in your favor.

JON WALSH, *Canada*

BUGABOOS

North Howser Tower, Simulator. After two weeks rock climbing and road tripping with my wife, I arrived home to a phone call from Chad Kellogg: "Dude, when are we going to the Bugs! We have two weeks before leaving for China and we have to get in a training climb." I checked the forecast, secretly hoping for bad weather, but…blue skies and 0% chance of precip.

Our original plans to attempt the classic All Along the Watchtower were jeopardized during the drive, as we pored over the maze of unclimbed crack systems visible in the *Alpinist* profile of the Howsers. Looking to simulate our upcoming objective (China's unclimbed Seerdengpu [See China section of this *Journal* for Johnson's report on their first ascent of Seerdengpu—Ed.]), we thought attempting a new line would be more appropriate than reading a topo.

The west face of North Howser Tower, showing: (1) Southwest Face (Jones-Simpson-Woodcock, 1970). (2) Hey Kool-Aid! (Miller-Weidner, 2005). (3) The Simulator (Johnson-Kellogg, 2010). The face has many other routes to the left. *Chris Atkinson*

After a 12-hour drive and a couple hours of sleep beside the car, on August 11 we packed light bags with one rope and no bivy gear and headed toward the west face of North Howser under perfect skies. Our intended route appeared difficult but doable, so we started up without delay.

It starts near the biggest left-facing corner on the far right side of the face. The next major system to the right is the start of Hey Kool-Aid!, which, we later learned, we joined for a pitch or so. The big corner itself is a seam, but the twin finger cracks 15' left of the corner went for 4-5 pitches at 5.10 C2. After pitch 5 we traversed right under a roof, climbed a crux pitch (5.11 C2) on the arête formed by the right side of the giant corner, and entered a prominent chimney system. We stayed in this system—including a four-hour brew-and-shiver stop at 2 a.m.—until one-and-a-half traversing pitches at pitches 11 and 12 took us to the next chimney system to the right. One pitch later we gained the 1970 Southwest Face route.

As the skies illuminated, we encountered wind and low, dark clouds, but we kept climbing, thinking the morning crud would burn off. Then it started snowing. It became clear that our only shot at topping-out was to abandon our plans for an independent line, so we continued on the upper Southwest Face. For the rest of the day the weather deteriorated into snow, thunder, and minimal visibility. Near the top it snowed three inches in less than an hour. We crested the summit ridge at 7 p.m., soaked and cold—we wore tennis shoes and Chad

Some 34 hours into their new rock route, the Simulator, but after joining the original Southwest Face route, Chad Kellogg gets some of the real thing on North Howser Tower. *Dylan Johnson*

had only fingerless gloves. I stumbled around on the summit ridge trying to get oriented in the total whiteout. Neither of us had been to the summit of the North Howser before and I couldn't figure out where the east face was, let alone the rap stations. I nearly rapped off the north face (thinking it was the east face), and then the whiteout thinned for a moment and the glow of the setting sun identified west—we finally got our bearings. Several raps later we barely cleared the 'schrund with our single line and found the boot track below South Howser at dark. We walked back to the car, arriving just under 42 hours after leaving. A short sleep later and we were on the road, returning to Seattle 78 hours after departing. We placed no bolts or pins, and the only gear left was a small piece of tat for a lower-out on pitch 11. The Simulator (19 belayed pitches [12 new], 5.11 C2).

On the way home, looking at photos we realized that in the whiteout we had been standing on the wrong side of the summit gendarme (some 20' shy), so I suppose it was merely an attempt!

DYLAN JOHNSON, *AAC*

CANADIAN ROCKIES

Canadian Rockies, summary. After a promising spring that saw a trio of big new ice lines on Tangle Ridge (see *AAJ 2010*), followed by a new line on the Emperor Face of Mt. Robson (below), the summer was a bit of a disappointment. The lackluster season can be at least partly blamed on the weather. It rained and snowed off and on in the high peaks most of the summer, and as a result the big north faces never really dried off. Dana Ruddy and Eamonn Walsh pulled off one of the more interesting projects of the summer, traversing the southern Ramparts in the backcountry of Jasper National Park over two separate weekends in August. On their first trip, after enduring the 20km approach and a mosquito population of legendary proportions, they traversed the picturesque Amethyst Lake Rockwall. Joined by Raphael Slawinski, they took in the summits of Mt. Redoubt, Dungeon Peak, and Oubliette Mountain in a very long day from camp. The traverse entailed much exposed scrambling over blocky quartzite with the occasional mid-5th-class pitch. A couple of weeks later Ruddy and Walsh returned to traverse the continuation of the ridge over Paragon, Parapet, and Bennington peaks on similar terrain in another long day from their bivy. The next obvious project in a similar vein is the traverse of the northern Ramparts, a rather more serious proposition.

In a similar vein, at the beginning of September, Jay Mills and Walsh took in a horseshoe of rarely visited peaks near the Saskatchewan River Crossing. Over two days, they traversed Mt. Sarbach, both Kauffmann Peaks, and Mt. Epaulette, hiking out the wild Howse River valley on the third. They only belayed one short section, otherwise going ropeless over miles of snowy forth and fifth-class terrain. Interestingly, their traverse was only part of a much longer traverse completed by Don Gardner and Niel Liske back in 1979, again proving that the old guys certainly got after it.

Once it stopped raining and snowing sometime in late September, Indian summer saw fabulous snow and ice conditions on the high north faces. A couple of teams took advantage of this to make rare one-day ascents of the Elzinga-Miller and Robinson-Arbic routes on the north face of Mt. Cromwell in the Columbia Icefield area. It has been said that success in alpine climbing is a matter of timing and hormones. The wisdom of this dictum was nicely illustrated when a team attempting the Elzinga-Miller as the weather window was shutting down retreated just in time to see the whole face avalanche. Unfortunately, the Indian summer dried off much of the moisture from the "real" summer, and, as a

Tsunami, on the northeast face of Mt. Patterson. *Raphael Slawinski*

result, water-ice formation was spotty. Some areas, such as the classic Stanley Headwall, were unusually lean; however, other areas sported some fabulous ice lines. One of these was the intimidating east face of Howse Peak, which last winter made many people driving on the Icefields Parkway stop and stare. However, for whatever reason, it went unattempted. Perhaps the most significant new ice route of the season was completed, surprisingly, on May Day. Joshua Lavigne and Raphael Slawinski climbed Tsunami (300m, M5 WI5+) to the right of the classic (but unformed) Riptide on the northeast face of Mt. Patterson. The route started on scrappy alpine terrain, continued up steep ice, and finished through fortunately benign seracs to end on a glacial bench.

And there you have it, the past year in the grand Canadian Rockies in a nutshell. Perhaps the most remarkable thing about the past winter was the snowpack, which started out horribly unstable, and ended up being the best one in years. The exceptional coverage and stability allowed for a flurry of remarkable ski descents. But that is a different story.

RAPHAEL SLAWINSKI, *Canada, AAC*

Mt. Robson, Emperor Face, new climbing to Emperor Ridge. On Friday June 18, after deejaying the Test of Metal blockparty in Squamish, I hopped in my truck and drove ten hours through the night to meet JR in the Robson parking lot.

Earlier in the year I'd pulled a tendon pulley in my middle finger, and so ice tools were the first things I could reasonably grab. And so if alpine climbing was the only thing in condition for me, there was one guy I knew I needed to contact: Jon Walsh, a.k.a. Jonny Red (JR). He is my total hero. He has climbed the kinds of routes around the globe that people dream of climbing, and usually in an uncompromising, bold style—single push, fast, and free. His response was immediate and positive. At the top of his hit list was a face I had dreamt about since I was a kid: the storied Emperor Face of Mt. Robson. We didn't have to talk tactics for very long to realize we were on the same page. If we climbed fast with small packs, we would only need a couple of good days of weather. JR was adamant that any face in the

The new Kruk-Walsh line on Mt. Robson's Emperor Face, to the junction with the Emperor Ridge. See *AAJ 2008*, p. 184, for other routes on the face. *Jon Walsh*

Jon Walsh on the Emperor Face, with Berg Lake in the background. *Jason Kruk*

Rockies could be climbed in a weekend. "I've realized I can climb continuously for 48 hours before I need to sleep," he said.

We hiked in quickly and established a camp below the face. It was the third time that spring we'd done the long hike (25km one way) in hopes of climbing the face, and the summer solstice seemed a ridiculous time to try to climb a "winter" route. But with a plump snow pack and a mild spring, conditions looked good. Early morning on June 20, we started climbing, and, despite the continuous, cerebral (read: scary) terrain, it was a pure pleasure to climb such entertaining and sustained mixed ground for so long. We climbed quickly, swinging leads the entire way up the face, the climbing never any easier than M5 or M6 and, often, stretching pitches up to 100m with simul-climbing. With a straight face I can call the hardest pitch I led M7. We hit the top of the face at midnight as lightning struck to the north, clouds enveloped around us, and light snow started to fall. At the time the decision to go down the Emperor Ridge, and not continue to the summit, seemed pretty easy. Now I can't help but wonder "what if?"

It always seemed a little silly to argue over the very definitions we climbers make up ourselves. Summit or not, it definitely felt like a new route. In correspondence with a longtime Rockies climber, another hero of mine, his point was clear: "We're not arguing black or white here, rather, different shades of ugly."

Jason Kruk, *Canada*

Baffin Island

Welshman's Peak, Arctic Monkeys. Stu McAleese, Mark Thomas, and I (from Wales, U.K.) spent three weeks in May completing a new big-wall aid route on a previously unclimbed formation in

Arctic Monkeys, the first route on Welshman's Peak. *Twid Turner*

Baffin Island's Stewart Valley. I had spotted the line in 1999 when Jerry Gore, Shaun Hutson, Louise Thomas, and I created The Endless Day (900m, 25 pitches, VI A3+) on the Citadel. I had been itching to return for more than ten years to try this route.

Located on the prominent buttress left of Great Sail Peak, our 1,100m wall was guarded by 300m of tricky mixed terrain. The climbing on the wall proper was difficult aid with most pitches requiring pegs, hooks, and beaks. We generally climbed for 12 hours a day with the two most challenging pitches taking three days each to complete. Life on the wall at that time of year is harsh with temperatures averaging -20° C. Warming water for hot drinks and rehydrating meals took an hour and a half. Belaying required two duvet jackets to combat the extreme cold. We ran out of fuel and food on the last day before we made the summit, but decided to press on. We reached the top at 4 p.m. on May 24, having spent 18 consecutive nights on the wall. We called our new route Arctic Monkeys (1,400m, 31 pitches, VI A4) and dubbed the formation Welshman's Peak.

Climbers typically opt for late spring to tackle the eastern fjord walls because of the generally stable weather and relative ease of access by skidoo across the frozen ocean. Any earlier and it is way colder; later and you risk an early thaw, which can make escape problematic. An early thaw proved the case for us—the skidoo was unable to reach base camp and we had to make a quick exit, wading through freezing slush for 25km to meet our Inuit drivers.

MIKE "TWID" TURNER, *Wales, U.K.*

Greenland

The online version of these reports frequently contains additional photos, maps, topos, and extended text. Please visit aaj.americanalpineclub.org

WEST COAST

Upernavik region, new rock routes. Operating from a yacht skippered by 75-year old Bob Shepton, the four-man American-Belgian team of Ben Ditto, brothers Nicolas and Olivier Favresse, and Sean Villanueva O'Driscoll climbed four new routes huge sea cliffs in or near Sortehul fjord. Their tour de force was the first ascent of the Impossible Wall, where the 850m line of Devil's Brew (5.12+ or E7 6c), climbed in 10 days, is most likely the hardest major rock climb achieved in West Greenland. The team then moved to the Cape Farewell region for five more new routes. For details see Shepton's feature article in this Journal.

Upernavik region, various routes on Qaersorssuaq and Umanaq islands. This was my fourth trip to Greenland. The previous three had been to the East Coast, so I had a good feel for what the land had to offer. The plan was the same as other visits: load the boats with as much food and climbing kit as we could feasibly carry, and have an adventure on sea and in the mountains. This time I persuaded Nigel Robinson and Sin Sinfield to accompany me. Neither had been to Greenland before, but they were experienced paddlers and climbers who could look after themselves in both environments. We shipped the kayaks and food two months prior to our arrival in Upernavik with the idea of circumnavigating two large islands, Qaersorssuaq and Nutarmiut. This would require paddling almost 300km. The trip lasted 21 days, of which five were spent rock climbing.

Northwest face of Sanderson's Hope on the west coast of Qaersorssuaq, a famous navigational headland named in 1587. The first big-wall route on a large sea cliff above the Arctic Circle on the west coast of Greenland was climbed here in 2000, when a three-man UK-Italian team, which sailed to the base on board Bob Shepton's yacht, put up Arctic First Born (800m, British E3 5c A3+). The following year Canadians added a second route Down North (800m, 5.10+ A1). *Olly Sanders Collection*

Any group visiting Greenland has to accept the possibility of becoming a Polar Bear dish, and it is advisable to carry a rifle to ward off, rather than kill, a bear. Our chosen area had minimal chance of bear encounters. Style was important to us: we wanted to maintain the wilderness experience and the essence of self-sufficiency, but in dire emergency felt it prudent to be able to summon help. We therefore decided to take a VHF radio and EPIRB. We kayaked for five or six hours a day in mostly calm, sunny conditions, forced off the water on only one occasion by stormy weather. The west coast of Qaersorssuaq gave exceptional paddling under 900m cliffs broken by waterfalls, and nothing further west until reaching Baffin Island.

Looking south from the head of the Sarqarssuaq Fjord. Large pillar above east bank thought to be unclimbed. *Olly Sanders Collection*

Early in our journey we came across two yachts. The smaller, *Dodo's Delight*, belonged to Bob Shepton, who had earlier in the year provided me with a little information on potential climbing in this region. On board were an American-Belgian team, which had already completed a number of long, free big walls. We spent a brilliant night in the company and generosity of strangers, all together on the

The islands east of Upernavik, showing the circumnavigation paddled by the British trio. White spots indicate the three climbing sites. *Olly Sanders Collection*

second yacht, *Saxon Blue*. We knew that finding new routes to climb would prove interesting, but never envisaged that the hardest aspect would be to find crags small enough for our limited resources. We spent three days at the head of the Sarqarssuag Fjord on the south side of Qaersorssuaq, where the American-Belgian team had recommended we look at a large pillar on the east bank. It was stunning, but obviously a little too ambitious for us and our available kit. Instead, we climbed a number of single pitch lines at around British HVS, and then on the third day a good six-pitch mountain route at E1, with two fine pitches of 5b: Ford Fiesta (200m). Our next climbing was four days later on the small island of Umanaq (290m) at the northeast extremity of our circular tour, overlooking a magnificent carving glacier. Plagued by mosquitoes, we climbed a three-pitch route on poor rock and named it Jigger my Timbers (HVS 5a). According to the map, our campsite here should have been under the ice, showing just how much the ice cap has retreated.

Later, on our way back to Upernavik, we stopped off on the eastern side of Qaersorssuaq, above the Sortehul, and climbed two excellent routes: Get the Shooters George (three pitches, 4a, 4c,

Ummannaq Mountain from the southwest. (1) Black Velvet Band to central (highest) summit. (2) Solid line shows the Chauché-Mackay Route; dashed line, where it differs at points (A) and (B), the Doyle-Leinss Route. Both end on the south summit. *Sean MacKay*

5a, HVS) and Smear or Disappear (four pitches, 4b, 5b, 5b, 4b, E2). Both were ca 160m.

We returned to Upernavik having successfully completed our circumnavigation, stayed friends, met no bears, and saw endless potential for big-wall and alpine rock routes. We would like to thank Greenland Tourism for complementary flights, and the Welsh Sports Council and Gino Watkins Memorial Fund for grants.

OLLY SANDERS, *UK*

Ummannaq region, Pt. 2,280m; Ummannaq south, southeast face. In 2009 the 15m sailing vessel Gambo spent July and August supporting glaciological and oceanographic research on two major outlet glaciers of the Greenland ice sheet. When the skill set of the crew was not in demand for science objectives, it was put to use establishing new routes in the stunning Ummannaq region.

Our most significant mountaineering achievement was the first ascent of the unclimbed 2,280m peak on the south side of Rink's (a.k.a. Kangigdleq) Fjord. This mountain, located at 71°31'51.57" N, 52°19'23.19" W, 1.8 km northeast of Timumanikavsa, appears to be the highest in West Greenland. Gambo's owner, Alun Hubbard, had discovered that due to mapping inaccuracies, previous successful ascents of the "highest mountain" had reached a large (but 35m lower) peak named Snepyramiden, about nine kilometers south-southwest of Pt 2,280m.

On August 10, Jason Box, Nolwenn Chauché, Sam Doyle, Silvan Leinss, and I were deposited by Gambo on the northern flanks of the mountain, planning on a two- or three-day ascent. Previous aerial reconnaissance by Box had shown the east side as having steep glaciers that appeared to provide a nearly continuous route to the ridge, safer than alternative options. From a base camp at ca 800m, we climbed 1,200m up the 40–50° Mighty Mouse Glacier in around 30 technical pitches, the last 400m the most challenging due to reduced visibility and moderate snowfall over variable surfaces.

Once on the summit ridge the weather improved. Apart from an initial, short, steep, knife-edge rock arête, the crest was surprisingly level, and after 1.2km of travel and 200m of elevation we reached the top. It was 2:30 a.m. on the 12th, and we were rewarded with a panoramic view of the Rink Glacier and surrounding relief, illuminated by an almost full moon.

To avoid time-consuming belaying on the upper glacier, we opted to descend a steep and loose rock gully, which required multiple, time-consuming rappels. Finally the gully intersected with the original ascent glacier, and we eventually reached base camp at midday, 27 hours after starting our summit push.

We were now eager to attempt a steeper and more challenging route up one of the many stunning granite faces in the region, and on the 17–18th Chauché, Doyle, Leinss, and I climbed what we believe was a new route to the 1,170m south summit of Ummannaq (70.7152° N, 52.1427° W). Two weeks earlier Doyle, Leinss, and I had climbed two 50m pitches up the 300m southeast face and determined that it was feasible, if not perhaps a little foolish. Our reconnaissance foretold of a variety of rock, ranging from solid faces to chossy and dangerous exfoliating flakes and cracks, an observation confirmed by locals.

Silvan Leinss following pitch five (5.9) of the Doyle-Leinss Route (just lead by Sam Doyle) on Ummannaq. *Sean Mackay*

From a bivouac below the wall at ca 300m, we re-climbed the first two pitches (5.8 and 5.9) and then the two teams diverged, Doyle climbing with Leinss, and Chauché with me. Each rope encountered several pitches of more difficult climbing (up to 5.10a), with Doyle and Leinss overcoming three pitches of beautiful, vertical-to-overhanging crack climbing (5.9), and one difficult traverse (5.9), on solid rock. Chauché and I, on a more westerly line, found lower-angled but poorer quality rock, culminating in a 5.10a R traverse to reach a point where we could downclimb to the more favorable Doyle-Leinss route. We all climbed three more pitches (5.7–5.8) to reach the top of the main shoulder on the ridge above. The remaining 500m up the crest involved short roping, simul-climbing, and the odd pitch up to 5.9. At 11 p.m. we reached the summit.

Nolween Chauché following the difficult traverse over untrustworthy rock on pitch four of the Chau-ché-Mackay Route on Ummannaq. *Sean Mackay*

There, we found a log containing the names of three previous parties: Bill Band and Will Tauber in 1969, Thomas Kopp and Jürg Muller in 1981, and six Italians in 1984 [all three ascents are recorded in the AAJ]. After conversations with locals and further research, we believe these three teams climbed an obvious gully on the southwest flank. Our descent, by a different line, was uneventful, and we reached Ummannaq at 7 a.m. on the 18th.

Our expedition was supported financially (by the seat of its pants) by Alun Hubbard and Jason Box, and the long-in-the-tooth good will shown by a tired and dog-eared crew. In the final hour it was only made possible due to the huge generosity bestowed on Gambo by the many she met, particularly Phinn Sprague and his team at Portland Yacht Services, Maine, who completed a balls-to-the-wall refit in his yard at the height of the season. The spirit of Tilman does live on.

SEAN MACKAY, *USA*

Aerial view of Pt. 2,280m, showing the route of first ascent up the east flank. *Jason Box*

Ummannaq region, various ascents. Sam Doyle, Miles Hill, George Ullrich, and I formed the British Ummannaq Climbing Expedition. After flying to Kangerlussaq on July 27, Miles, George, and I first had to walk 250km (in 70 hours), and then travel 800km aboard the yacht Gambo, to reach the island of Ummannaq. Our first goal was the west buttress on the central summit of Ummannaq Mountain (1,189m, 70°42' N, 52°52' W), which gave 200m of steep ground followed by 50m of overhanging, rounded fins of solid rock that gave the best climbing on the route. The name Black Velvet Band is derived from the bands of extremely soft, black rock that run across the buttress in four lines. With the first four pitches fixed the previous night, Miles and George completed the route on August 8 in 14 hours at British E3 5c. Lesser-angled sections were more serious due to loose rock and spaced protection, and the total amount of climbing to the summit was ca 700m.

We caught up with Sam for our next objective, The Horn (71°17' N, 52°20' W) on the east coast of Upernavik Island above the Inukavsait Fjord (this is Upernavik Ø; not to be confused with the settlement of Upernavik much further north). On August 13 we attempted two lines; George and I followed an apparent crack system up the center, while Miles and Sam opted for the buttress to the right of the main wall. On their first pitch Miles and Sam found signs of previous passage in the shape of old pegs. Above, the rock became progressively steeper and looser, and after eight pitches to E1 5b they decided to retreat.

For us the crux was pitch four. George, in the lead, found himself 10m above the belay, with no gear, the crackline closed, and only smears and underclings for holds. With no possibility of reversing the moves, he tagged the hand drill and precariously placed a bolt while standing in a shallow pod. He then climbed 15m on similar terrain to a ledge, rating the pitch E5 6a. We climbed ca 900m up the face, retreating after 20 hours ca 400m from the top. We'd planned a one-day ascent and were now out of food and water. Most of the climbing was runout British 5b and 5c.

The Island of Ummannaq was the focal point of Gambo's scientific activities, and we attempted to climb all the summits of Ummannaq Mountain. On the 23rd Miles and Sam climbed the central and highest peak via the 800m Benighted in 24 hours Daylight (British S 4b). This route involved a considerable amount of loose rock and easy climbing, and the name reflected their predicament. The following day George and I climbed the west face of the north peak (70°42' N, 52°52' W), which featured some of the best rock on the island. After three pitches I took a fall whilst clipping gear in an insecure position in a sandy pod, breaking my finger. We continued to the summit with George in the lead and named the climb Broken Toblerone (E4 6a, 400m). We also added two shorter new routes to Seven Cairn Crag (70°42' N, 52°52' W): Take it or Leave

The final part of the ascent to the Old Man of Saatut. *Matthew Burdekin*

it Cake (135m, E2 5c, Doyle-Hill) and The Big Tasty One (70m, E3 5c, Burdekin-Ullrich). This formation had been climbed via two routes by the 2009 expedition. We visited the island Agpat, where all four of us made an ascent of The Old Man of Saatut (70°53.9' N, 52°06' W, ca 475m of mostly scrambling, with a section of HVS 5a). Off the southeast corner of Agpat lies the small island of Saatuk. We took time toward the end of the trip to befriend the island community, and while there took the children climbing. We also conducted a public presentation on climbing in the area at the local school. The expedition had received a grant from the Gino Watkins Memorial Fund, and we feel our work on the island captured the essence of this organization. We are extremely grateful to the community for their hospitality and generosity, and especially grateful to the owner of Gambo, Alun Hubbard, glaciologist and mountaineer of kindred spirit, along with his crew, who made the expedition possible. The sail home across the Atlantic in late September was a whole new challenge altogether.

MATTHEW BURDEKIN, *UK*

EAST COAST
PAUL STERN LAND

Paul Stern Land, several first ascents. After a first visit to the area in 2008 (see *AAJ 2009*), Robin Collins (Australia), Geoff Bonney (UK), Paul Walker (UK), my wife Sandy, Willem-B Stern (Netherlands/Switzerland), and I returned to the fine mountains of Paul Stern Land. The combined age of our team was 367 years.

Willem-B is the brother of Paul Stern, after whom the area is named. Like his brother he is also a geologist. He had found my 2008 report, and then made contact, eventually

The Horn, showing the Burdekin-Ullrich attempt (left), and the Doyle-Hill attempt, the latter tried previously, possibly in the 1980s. *Matthew Burdekin*

deciding to join our expedition to see the area firsthand. In 1959 Paul Stern was killed by stonefall in the Swiss Alps, but between 1955 and 1958 he visited Northeast Greenland as a member of Lauge Koch's geological expeditions. In 1958 Stern was on the Gaaseland Peninsula, but with others crossed the Vestfjord Gletscher to access what is now called Paul Stern Land from the south. His party climbed a peak they called Sfinks (Sphinx, 2,295m).

In 2008 we had believed we were the first to climb in Paul Stern Land, but research since revealed two visits by the British military. In 1978 an Army Mountaineering Association team penetrated Vestfjord by boat and climbed Peaks 1,950m, 2,254m, 1,660m, and Rundefjeld, at least two of which were thought to be first ascents. In 1987 a party from the Royal Greenjackets made a similar approach, repeated Peaks 1,950m and 2,295m, and then claimed five first ascents in the eastern end of Paul Stern Land. None of the central peaks were reached. Other names on the map were bestowed by various groups of geologists between w1968 and 1972.

Central peaks of Paul Stern Land seen during the traverse of Ararat. (A) Arken. (B) Pk. 2,260m. (C) Pk. 2,320m. (D) Distant mountains of Gaaseland. (E) Pk. 2,324m. (F) Pk. 2,240m. (G) Sfinks. (H) Snehorn (2,240m). (I) Baendalbjerg with Cloudspotter's Ridge falling toward (CN), Camp Noah. (J) Pk. 2,370m. (K) Pk. 2,377m. (L) Pk. ca 2,350m. (M) Pk. Bruno. (N) Copper Knob. (O) Weisskopf. (P) Vindbjorne (1,830m). (DBG) North branch of Doede Brae Glacier. (ASE) Southeast ridge of Ararat, descended during traverse. (UDB) Upper Doede Brae. (LZ) Landing Zone at 1,540m. Following a straight line in front of the climbers it is ca 150km to the Watkins Mountains and Gunnbjornsfjeld. *Jim Gregson*

Iceland's volcanic ash cloud had blown away northeast as our group flew north to Keflavik. On May 22 we reached Constable Pynt (Nerlerit Inaat) and later the same day flew to Paul Stern Land by twin otter ski plane, now operated by a new company Norlandair. The pilots firmly declined to land at our preferred site in the heart of the mountains, mindful perhaps of several incidents in recent years when aircraft have been stuck in deep, soft snow. We eventually settled for a landing site on the upper Doede Brae (glacier) at 70°27.174' N, 29°52.999' W, at an altitude of 1,540m. This was ca 10km southeast of our 2008 Camp Venturi.

In the evening of May 23, all of us bar Willem traversed a ridge to the south, crossing three tops: Copper Knob (1,890m), Weisskopf (ca 2,000m), and Peak Bruno (2,050m). While these elevations allowed us to look at the surrounding area, the view also revealed numerous crevasse fields in the glaciers, for there was much less snow cover than in 2008.

On the 24th we loaded pulks and tried to move camp to our preferred location. However, we were thwarted by a bad crevasse zone, which barred access to a higher glacier. Somewhat dismayed, we retreated a short distance onto the Doede Brae and made a new camp at 70°26.396' N, 29°47.823' W (1,450m), close to Baendelbjerg. From here we reconnoitred Arken (The Ark) and found a possible line of ascent. On the 26th Geoff, Sandy, and I made an attempt on the west ridge of a 2,300m peak next to Peak Bruno. We were stopped by a 75m rock step of very unstable nature.

On the 28th we all camped at the foot of Arken's south face, crossing numerous crevasses on the way. Soon after midnight, and leaving Stern in camp, the rest of us started up the face and onto the great snow terrace, which runs for more than two kilometers from west to east. At first we made rapid progress but eventually ran into eggshell crust on the terrace and began to plunge crotch-deep into underlying sugar snow. After hours of tediously slow movement, we pulled onto a glacier shelf that would lead up to the main crest, from where we hoped to reach the summit from the east. This shelf was also in poor condition and criss-crossed by crevasses. Eventually, we ground to a halt at well over

Baendelbjerg from the west, showing the 900m line of Cloudspotter's Ridge. (B) Marks the Bonatti Pitch (V-). *Jim Gregson*

Unclimbed rock walls on the north side of upper Vinkeldal. Access to these formations, on the south side of Milne Land, would involve either a long overland trek from the south coast, or approach from the icecap above, where it should be possible to land a twin otter. *Jim Gregson*

2,000m, questioning the safety of continuing. As Geoff remarked, "It's decisions like these that have kept us alive."

On the 30th Collins and Walker took Stern up Copper Knob by a new route, allowing the elderly gentleman to see more of the area. That evening Geoff and I, chomping at the bit, set out for the first ascent of 2,341m Baendelbjerg (Baendel means tape and was so named by geologists for the striped rocks on the west face). In a 15-hour round trip we climbed and descended the northwest ridge, a mixed climb with a notable crux rockband where I led the "Bonatti Pitch," a series of jutting overlaps climbed in crampons and bare hands. Our 900m route was named Cloudspotter's Ridge (D/D+ with a crux of UIAA V-). We rappelled on the descent.

Although tempted by a return to Arken, Geoff and I agreed to go further northwest with the others, and on June 2 made a new camp up glacier at 70°29.113' N, 29°58.896' W (1,640m). Remembering 2008, we soon called this place Camp Katabat, as every evening the familiar,

Arken (Ark) seen from a distance of eight kilometers to the northwest.
The 2010 attempt ran across the south face, out of sight to the right.
Jim Gregson

piercingly cold ice-cap wind-spill battered the tents, only relenting in late morning. From this location all except Stern made the first full traverse of Ararat (2,480m, and the highest summit in Paul Stern Land), Sandy and I having made the first ascent in 2008. We climbed the west ridge and descended the southeast ridge and southwest face. On the 5th Robin, Sandy, and I skied west toward the ice cap, encountering many crevasses, where in 2008 none had been seen. We climbed a high nunatak called Solbjorgs Fjell (2,090m) over rock and ice on its north-northeast ridge. We named the route Cryoconite Ridge (cryoconite is a term coined by the polar explorer Nordenskjold to refer to atmospheric debris, soot, dust, pollen, etc. that is trapped in ice and provides a climate record). We skied quickly back to camp under a hot sun.

By the day of our pick-up we were acutely aware how much depletion had occurred in the snow cover, mostly by sublimation in the warm conditions experienced in 2010. Ten or 12 years ago we always came to Greenland at the end of July. For icecap and glacier trips this would now be very unwise. The summer melt is kicking in earlier, and the air company is unwilling to risk landing its ski-planes so far into the summer. We now come in the late spring, and if 2010 conditions become the norm, knowledge and experience of how to cope with crevasses will become increasingly important.

On our journey out the pilot flew us around Arken's summit. We could clearly see that our attempted route would have led us to the top, if we'd had better luck with conditions. Is this a good reason to return? Yes—but we already have our eyes set on a new area further north.

JIM GREGSON, *UK, Alpine Club*

RENLAND

Grundtvigskirchen (1,977m), east face, Eventyr; Milne Land, Pt. 1,295m, north pillar. An Italian-Swiss team comprising Simon Gietl, Daniel Kopp, Roger Schali, and photographer/climber Thomas Ulrich made the first ascent of the spectacular east face of Grundtvigskirchen, a huge granite wall rising 1,325m from a point not far above the south coast of Renland.

After flying to the airstrip at Constable Point, and crossing Scoresby Sund by Zodiac inflatables, the team established base camp just 50m above the sea. Across the waters of the Ofjord to the south lies the large island of Milne Land. Gielt (Italian) and Schali (Swiss) first crossed Ofjord to a fine granite pillar rising to a 1,295m summit on Milne Land's north coast, more or less directly opposite Grundtvigskirchen. After introductory scrambling the pair started on the upper 850m granite pillar at 6 p.m. They climbed 15 pitches and then took a rest for one-and-a-half hours before climbing the remaining 15 pitches to the top. The ascent took only 15 hours and was easily protected with natural gear. Difficulties were around 6b. They found no evidence of previous passage, not on the pillar nor at its summit.

All four climbers then spent more than a week working their line on Grundtvigskirchen, using a portaledge camp at ca 750m to make a semi-capsule ascent of this superb wall. In a total of 40 pitches, 39 were climbed onsight or redpointed, with difficulties up to 7a+. Although bolts were placed for main belays, only natural gear was used between stances. They reached the summit on August 6 after two days of non-stop climbing (forced by a predicted spell of bad weather). They named the route Eventyr, which means Fairy Tale in Danish.

In 1998 the east face of Grundtvigskirchen was the target for Bengt Flygel Nilsfors, Magnar Osnes, Odd Roar Wiik (all from Norway), and the Swede Micke Sundberg. Heavy rockfall and ice fall forced them to abandon the climb, but Nilsfors, Sundberg, and Wiik returned in 1999 with Patrik Fransson from Sweden to make the first ascent of the south ridge. They accessed the peak by first taking a charter flight to Milne Land and then kayaking across the Ofjord. The ridge, which begins 500m above the fjord and rises almost 1,500m to the summit, gave more than 30 pitches of magnificent roped climbing on superb granite up to 5.11a.

Naming peaks in Greenland has long been a tricky affair, and Grundtvigskirchen has been particularly difficult. The AAJ Online contains two reports on place names in Greenland, including a climbing history of Grundtvigskirchen. One was written by me and the other by geologist and Greenland expert Tony Higgins.

LINDSAY GRIFFIN, *Mountain INFO*

SCHWEIZERLAND

Schweizerland, various ascents. The 2010 Braunschweiger Grönlandexpedition flew to Kulusuk on July 12, and over the next two days traveled northeast by boat and on foot (with pulks) into the mountains between Knud Rasmussen Gletscher and Kangertivartikajik Fjord. Base camp was established northeast of the head of the Kangertivartikajik Fjord at 266m. From there Thorsten Henszelewski, Jens Köhler, Gaby Lappe, Birgit Lehmann, and I were able to climb nearly every day, due to almost continuous sunshine. We reached a number of summits, some of which may not have been climbed before.

Possible first ascents and unofficial names are: Inuuitseerdumud Dunitsud (Birthday Present, 1,325m, UIAA III+, 66°02'22" N, 36°16'47" W); Qaqqardivaq Maluck (Maluck Peak, 1,318m, from northeast at UIAA II, 66°02'33" N, 36°16'27" W); Qaqqardivaq Thorsten (Thorsten Peak, 1,316m, northeast

East face of Grundtvigskirchen, climbed by 2010 Italian-Swiss team. Left skyline (south) ridge is upper section of 1999 Norwegian-Swedish route. *Patrick Huber*

Unnamed Pt. 1,295m on north coast of Milne Land showing 2010 Geitl-Schali Route. blog.tagesanzeiger.ch

ridge, UIAA III, 66°02'06" N, 36°17'13" W); Qaqqardivaq Kohler (Kohler Peak, 1,210m, from northeast, 45° and UIAA II, 66°01'25" N, 36°16'05" W); Emanuelala Neqqisaad (Emanuel's Tooth, 933m, from north, 35-40° and UIAA I, 66°00'08" N, 36°10'18" W); Arpiip Paperngija (Whale's Back), traversed over Pingaarnerdud Qaarpijaa (main summit, ca 515m, 66°00'54" N, 36°14'03" W) and Oqqummud Qaarpijaa (south summit, ca 440m, 66°00'21" N, 36°14'22" W) at UIAA II-; Lehmann Innardaa (Lehmannwand, 466m, 66°02'26" N, 36°12'52" W,) via parallel routes, Pilaadungu (UIAA IV) and Makkariinasud Niimiddiileq (UIAA III-, 120m of climbing); Sarpik (Whale Fluke, ca 270m, from north, ca 66°00'05" N, 36°14'22"W). Repeat ascents were made of the following:

Kunuup Dereqqua (Knud's Corner, 1,326m, from the southwest, 40° and UIAA II-, 66°02'52" N, 36°16'24" W); Qaqqardivaq Emanuela (Cima Emanuela) over Kijammud Qaarpijaa (north summit, 1,006m, 65°59'53" N, 36°10'30" W) and Pingaarnerdud Qaarpijaa (main summit, 1,025m, 65°59'47" N, 36°10'33" W) at 45° and UIAA I (first climbed in 1979 by M. Cotichelli and G. Rupi); Tseriip Isiva (Peaks of the Sun), first to Alaatsimud Qaarpijaa (central summit, 937m, by southwest pillar, III+ on broken terrain, 200m of climbing, 66°01'19" N, 36°08'21" W), and then along the connecting ridge (II+) to Oqqummummud Kimmud Qaarpijaa (southeast summit, 943m, cairns found on both summits, 66°01'13" N, 36°08'09" W); Nartsaamaniip Isiva (Plateau Peak, 915m, by southeast ramp at UIAA I, cairn found on summit, 66°01'34" N, 36°05'57" W); a traverse of Diaavuluup Naddivad (Devil's Horns) over Kijammud Kangimud Qaarpijaa (northwest summit, 794m, 65°58'45" N, 36°14'55" W) and Pingaarnerdud Qaarpijaa (main summit, 910m, UIAA III-, first climbed in 1969 by an Italian Alpine Club expedition, 65°58'20" N, 36°14'25" W); Qaqqardivaq Pyramid (Pyramid Peak, 840m, northwest slope, 35-40° and UIAA I, cairn found on summit, 66°01'04" N, 36°06'19" W); Lappe Innardaa (Lappe Face, 690m, from the west, 66°00'27" N, 36°09'37" W). We arrived back in Kulusuk on the 28th.

A complete expedition report (in German) including maps, photos of the peaks, and route descriptions: hochtourengruppe.davbs.de/download/ExpeditionsberichtGroenland2010.pdf

KAI MALUCK, *Germany*

SOUTH COAST
CAPE FAREWELL REGION

Tasermiut Fjord, Hermelnbjerg, east face, The Corner of Mt. Fayette; Tininnertuup III, Midnight Children. In summer 2009 Calle Martins, Mattias Sellden, Martin Urby, and I from Sweden spent four weeks in the Hermelndal at the head of the Tasermiut Fjord. The best-known climbed features in this valley are the Tininnertuup peaks II to IV. We set up camp below the Hermelnbjerg and on the first day went up to the col at the start of the east-northeast ridge, hoping to climb the peak by the easiest route. Unlike the British party in 2008, who were faced with four pitches of rock to reach the upper valley, we could walk easily on snow and then glacier. From the col we saw the unclimbed east face. We attempted to climb the east-northeast ridge but found it extremely loose, and rappelled after four pitches. This is a wide area with many alternatives from the col, and our route was certainly not that climbed by the 2008 British party.

On July 10 Martins and Sellden attempted a new line on the north face of Hermelnbjerg, starting with a fantastic offwidth splitter. They climbed four pitches up to 6c before it got dark and they rappelled. Four days later Urby and I tried another obvious line on this part of the wall, climbing about half the height of the wall (nine pitches) before finding that we had to traverse ca 15m left via a thin seam to another diedre system. It would have needed skyhooks and

Qaqqardivaq Emanuela from northwest. (A) Emanuelala Neqqisaad. (B) Kijammud Qaarpijaa. (C) Pingaarnerdud Qaarpijaa. (1) Route toward Lappe Innardaa. (2) North face (Henszelewski-Köhler-Lappe-Lehmann-Maluck, 2010). (3) Northwest face (Cotichelli-Ripi, 1979). *Kai Maluck*

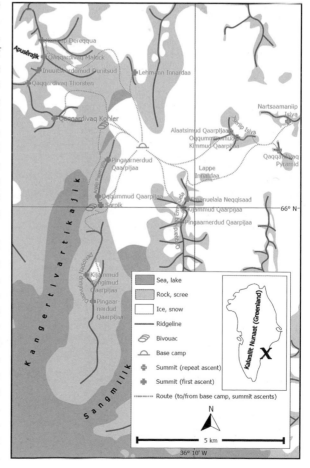

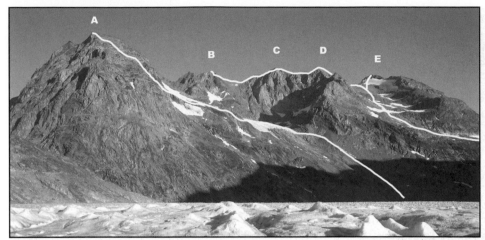

Looking northwest at (A) Qaqqardivaq Kohler. (B) Qaqqardivaq Thorsten. (C) Inuuitseerdumud Dunitsud. (D) Qaqqardivaq Maluck. (E) Kunuup Dereqqua. Routes climbed by the 2010 expedition are marked. *Kai Maluck*

copperheads, which we were not carrying, so we rappelled. To our high point, the difficulties were 6c. In the meantime (13th–14th), Martins and Sellden repeated Rapakavi Road on Tininnertuup IV via

The east face of Hermelnbjerg south summit with the line of Corner of Mt. Fayette. *Henrik Nilsson*

the Freeway start, climbing the route completely free with one bivouac.

Over the 13–14th, with one bivouac, Urby and I climbed variations to the 2008 Grmovsek-Grmovsek route, Nulunaq on the east face of Tininnertuup III. We made a separate start and climbed a few new pitches higher up, naming our 800m line Midnight Children, due to our unplanned freezing bivouac (20 pitches, 6b+). We descended by rappelling the north ridge and then sliding down the long snow gully to the valley.

From the 18–20th Sellden and I made an attempt on the west face of Hermelnbjerg, in an area of previous huge rockfall a long way to the right of the two existing routes on this side of the peak. We estimated the face to be 600m high, but in fact it is probably nearer 1,000m. After climbing 500m (13 pitches, 6c and an A0 pendulum, one bivouac) we realized we had neither enough food nor water to finish, so we rappelled.

The major achievement of our trip was the ascent from 18–21st of Hermelnbjerg's east face by Martins and Urby. This part of the wall falls from the south summit, which was previously unclimbed. The two crossed the col below

West face of Hermelnbjerg from Tininnertuup peaks. The righthand (south) summit was unclimbed before 2009. (1) upper section of Ramblin' Man (1,200m, British E5 6b, McManus-Tresidder, 2007) to west summit only. (2) the 2009 Nilsson-Sellden attempt. *Henrik Nilsson*

the east-northeast ridge at its lowest point and scrabbled down wild and scary loose ground—mud and large blocks—then crossed the glacier to the foot of the wall. From a bivouac at the base they climbed 15 pitches up to 6c+ A0, with a second bivouac on the face. From the top of the wall, scrambling led to the top, where they built a cairn. They made their third bivouac just below the summit and next day rappelled the 600m route, naming it The Corner of Mount Fayette. They highly recommend the climb, and there are other possible lines on this wall.

We found the existing map confusing. There were several occasions when we simply could not get map and reality to match, particularly on the first day when we tried to climb the east-northeast ridge. Also, the highest summit of Hermelnbjerg is marked too far south.

HENRIK NILSSON, *Sweden*

No problem with route finding on this pitch. Mattias Sellden making an unsuccessful attempt on a new route up the north face of Hermelnbjerg. *Calle Martins*

Tasermiut Fjord, Half Dome, Dash-Friday Route, second ascent with variants. Jindrich Mandat and I came to Tasermiut mainly to repeat existing routes. It was only after we had picked the area's most famous jewels that we began contemplating a moderate first ascent. We decided on the east-northeast face of Half Dome, which is something of an outsider here among all the big walls. Our information was rather scant, and we thought there was only one established route, Les Temps sont Durs (500m, 15 pitches, 6c, see *AAJ 1999*), which begins ca 80m left of the edge of the sheer north face and was put up in 1998 by the Swiss Castella, Lehner, Truffer, and Zambetti. However, to the right, the prominent dihedral close to the edge of the face seemed to be unclimbed, and there was no sign of any of the equipped belays that were reported on Les Temps sont Durs. It wasn't until we got home that we discovered the dihedral had been climbed in 2003 by Micah Dash and Thad Friday (500m, 5.10X, see *AAJ 2004*).

We climbed the route in two days, onsighting every pitch. In the afternoon of the first day we fixed the first four pitches; on the second day we jumared and finished the route. The climbing was generally easy, except on pitch four, where a combination of delicate, runout face climbing yielded one interesting section. Jindrich used skyhook runners on this pitch. We completed the route in 12 pitches with the crux fourth pitch at UIAA VII- R.

We rappelled the route, in the upper part using slings for anchors, but further down leaving pegs, nuts, and bolts. The huge dihedral turned out to be a bad rope-eater; be careful here! Altogether we placed seven bolts; five on belays (only one per belay, as there was always a natural gear placement) and two on the slabby first pitch, which we hope is different from the Dash-Friday original. We found no trace of previous passage but did spot a nut with a carabiner to the right of our line on the second pitch. We trust the original route didn't lose any of its X rating.

We also repeated some of the free climbs on Ulamertorssuaq and Nalumasortoq, and hope the following information will prove useful to future

East-northeast face of Half Dome. (1) Les Temps sont Durs. (2) line climbed by Klonfar and Mandat, which approximates to the 2003 Dash-Friday Route. *Martin Klonfar*

parties. Nalumasortoq, Right Pillar, Non C'e Due Senza Tre. We climbed this in a day, with the leader onsighting every pitch. The original topo appears to fake the last two pitches. Instead of climbing upward on terrain indicated as easy, you have to traverse right for two pitches to a wet and icy corner/offwidth, and then climb this in two unpleasant pitches. This finish doesn't remotely share the beauty of the rest of the route. Ulamertorssuaq, Moby Dick. We climbed and descended this with two bivouacs (both on the Black Man). Apart from the two pitches of IX+, which we climbed with rests, the route was led onsight. The belay at the top of pitch 27 comprises three bolts, but only two of them have hangers, and one of these needs a nut to be complete. There is no other possible placement, so bring a nut if you can. Ulamertorssuaq,

On the initial slabs of Half Dome. *Martin Klonfar*

War and Poetry. We climbed this with some rest points and one bivouac. Nalumasortoq, Left Pillar, Life is Beautiful. We climbed this with some rest points in one day. A little before our ascent the route had been repeated using aid by two Americans. Most of the climb is in perfect thin cracks, but unfortunately several loose flakes remain. Surprisingly, the overhang on the sixth pitch was not the crux as expected. This came higher on pitch 12.

MARTIN KLONFAR, *Czech Republic*

Pamiagdluk Island, Baroness, north face, Blue Whale; Camp Peak, South Face Direct. As Sarah Garlick put it, "The dream was to gather a small team of friends and head somewhere unspoiled and far away… and to climb. I chose Greenland for a variety of reasons, but most of them came down to the simple allure of wildness. I knew I could find adventure there." For almost three weeks during late July and August, Dave Nettle, Jim Surette, Sarah, and I explored, climbed, and discovered.

We started our trip on Pamiagdluk Island, reached after a three-and-a-half hour boat ride through the Torssukatat Fjord from Nanortalik—the village where most climbing expeditions launch. We landed on a small beach below the prominent northwest face of the Baroness. Our primary goal was to climb the center of the wall: the large, mostly orange granite face, topped by dark gray corner and crack systems. In 2001 a group of Brits climbed four routes on the right side of this face. After quickly establishing camp, we carried climbing gear to a small meadow at the base of the wall and stared in awe of the project ahead. Our hopes dimmed slightly when we found most of the face running with water.

The next morning we gave the face a good attempt but found our proposed line would require much bolting and likely a substantial bit of aid climbing. This was not the style for which we were prepared. While exploring, Dave and I eyed a line on the sunny Campsite Hill (1,340m) opposite the Baroness. The following day, while Sarah and Jim searched for other potential lines on the Baroness, Dave and I linked corner and crack systems to make a new route: South Face Direct (450m, seven pitches, 5.10-). On the summit we had a great vantage of the Baroness. It was this perspective we needed, and we were able to piece together a possible line up the left side of the face leading to the highest point of the

Danika Gilbert admires rock walls on the far side of the Torssukatak Fjord from a hanging stance on Blue Whale. *Dave Nettle*

North face of Baroness, with 2010 American route Blue Whale. The rock summit immediately behind the top of this line belongs to another formation. *Dave Nettle*

Baroness massif. After an adventurous descent back to camp, we shared the news with Jim and Sarah.

The next morning we set off with renewed enthusiasm. Dave and I launched upward, establishing our route almost as far as two roof sections in an area we dubbed the "gray bands" due to intrusions that promised harder route finding and exciting climbing. The following day Jim and Sarah took over, finding a delicate way where crack systems petered out. Jim pulled around a corner on thin gear to find a hidden splitter finger crack and exclaimed "It's gonna go!" After a few more great pitches, and with daylight waning, Sarah and Jim stopped one pitch shy of the ridge. Early the next day Dave and I set out eagerly and fired the line to the top, summiting the Baroness in a wind storm. We named our route Blue Whale (600m, V 5.11), after our trusty base camp tent that saw us through storms and bugs.

Satisfied with our ascents and eager for new terrain, we headed to Tasermiut Fjord. The 1,000m walls of Nalumasortoq, Ulamertorssuaq, and Ketil were a strong draw. Unfortunately stormy days

Campsite Hill, with 2010 American route South Face Direct. Descent was to the left. *Dave Nettle*

covered peak tops with snow, soaking the crack systems with meltwater for days. Our final week in Greenland was spent mostly reading and hanging out in our base camp tent. When the rain let up, the fog would roll in and re-soak the walls. However, on the last day we rallied for an ascent of Ketil Pyramid, a fine peak, but dwarfed by the surrounding walls. We climbed the South (Swiss) Pillar (5.10) in nine pitches, enjoying a beautiful summit day.

DANIKA GILBERT, *AAC*

Torssukatak Fjord and Quvnerit Island, five new rock routes. After climbing four major new routes on the West Coast (see report from Upernavik region), the Belgian-American team skippered by Bob Shepton climbed five new routes

Dave Nettle on South Face Direct, Campsite Hill, with Torssukatak Fjord beyond. *Danika Gilbert*

in the Cape Farewell region. They generally traversed their summits and descended via a different route. Their feat of climbing such an array of hard, free, big walls during one expedition has probably never previously been achieved in Greenland mountaineering. For details see Shepton's feature article in this Journal.

Venezuela

Carola Perez leading pitch 8 on El Camino del Danto.
Wojciech Wandzel

Adankasima Tepui, El Camino del Danto. The Adankasima Tepui, in the heart of the Bolivar State, is one of 13 tepuis comprising the Chimanta Massif. It is a magical land, where miles and miles of tepuis and sandstone walls make us forget the chores and daily problems of the city. The magic overcomes us. Adankasima had no recorded visits, though domestic and foreign adventurers have visited other parts of the Chimanta Massif—like Acopan, Upuigma, Amuri, and Churi. There is so much to discover and learn.

When we arrived in Yunek, the Pemon community received us warmly; the trip would be simply impossible without them. Our team was comprised of Carola Perez, Daniel Mora, Rafael Bracho, Carlos Pineda, me (all Venezuelan), and Wojciech Wandzel (Polish). For two days we walked through the beautiful Valle del Tirica, between savannas, gallery forests, and streams and rivers with the purest water—a walk among giant peaks: Acopan, Upuigma, and Amuri—and finally to the great Adankasima. We set up camp on the jungled slopes of the mountain and started working on reaching the wall. It took five days before we could begin climbing, and all the way to the tepui, the Pemon called it "El Camino del Danto."

Every day was more special than the one before it, the sights and sounds of the mountain enchanting us—wild fauna, a large anteater with her calf, the sound of two macaws that flew the skies as we were climbing, howlers claiming their places in every corner of the jungle, capuchin

El Camino del Danto, the first route on Adankasima Tepui, rising from the Valle del Tirica.
Cheo García, climtepuyes.com

monkeys that threw stones at Daniel and Carola one day as they walked to the wall, black hens wandering through the forest, large black scorpions trying to intimidate us, forest mice dancing through our supplies, colibris fighting among themselves at the base of the wall, and a guacharo even surprised me on the rappels one evening.

When we started climbing the first day, we saw only a great dihedral overtaking a large section of the wall, so we made that our goal. Some of the climbing was on loose and decomposing rock, while other parts were beautiful. The rock in the "Dihedral of Dreams" was exceptional—clean with cracks of all sizes, simply amazing. The second part of the dihedral had a very hard step, an offwidth, overhangs, and day after day we neared the top…we continued working the route and the adventure, finding our way until, finally, on February 9, 2011, we completed El Camino del Danto (300m, 15 pitches, 5.12a A2 J1), the first route and first recorded visit to the tepui. We finished like we started, in the jungle, shelves and vertical green everywhere, "matatraccion tepuyera," with macaws calling overhead and the expanse of the indescribable Tirico Valley below, extending to a horizon of forests, streams, rivers, tepuis, and savannas as far as we could see.

CHEO GARCÍA, *Venezuela, climtepuyes.com*

Acopan Tepui, Chicatino and Takamajaka. In March, German climbers Jens Richter, Tino Kohbach, Michael Baensch, and I, accompanied by Brits Tony and Sarah Whitehouse, spent two weeks in the Gran Sabana. Inspired by a Stefan Glowacz report from 2007, describing a 700m first ascent, we came prepared for a big wall but instead found the faces and pillars not higher than 300–450m (including the buttress where Glowacz opened his route). Nevertheless, the rock was excellent, providing perfect climbing on steep faces. After two days of jungle experience to explore the base of Acopan, guided by the very friendly local chief Leonardo, we went for a major pillar beside a huge cascade, where, in December 2009, a Polish-Venezuelan team established *Lapa, Yuca y Kachiri*. That route, however, avoided the impressive upper headwall and moved left around half height to a gully to the top. We chose a line starting to the right and continuing directly through the central pillar to the top.

After four days of work and two of rest, we completed and redpointed Chicatino (350m, 8 pitches, 7b/7b+), a route of perfect, sustained, and demanding climbing. The route is mostly very steep face with very few horizontal cracks, so we placed bolts in the blank zones and belays. Bolting itself was limited because the very hard sandstone allowed only 3–4 holes until a drill was dead. Some runouts should be expected.

What makes the route great for Acopan is not only the perfect line and excellent climbing but also the

Some of the routes on one aspect (southeast face) of the massive Acopan Tepui: (1) Hasta Luego Taurepan. (2) Jardieneros de Grandes Paretes. (3) Rey Aruagato. (4) Takamajaka. (5) 10 pounds of Tequila. (6) Lapa, Yuca y Kachiri. (7) Chicatino. (8) El Sendero de los Indigenas. *Ruediger Helling*

200m easy
scrambling
to summit

Chicatino, on Acopan Tepui. See photo above for reference. *Ruediger Helling*

Takamajaka, on Acopan Tepui. See photo above for reference. *Ruediger Helling*

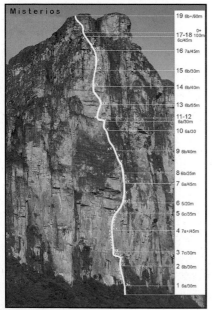

Misterios

19	6b+/60m
17-18	0+ 100m 6c/45m
16	7a/45m
15	6b/30m
14	6b/40m
13	6b/55m
11-12	8a/30m
10	6a/30
9	6b/40m
8	6b/25m
7	6a/45m
6	5/20m
5	6c/35m
4	7a+/45m
3	7c/30m
2	8b/30m
1	6a/30m

Misterios (García-Szczolka-Tomaszewski-Wacko, 2010), on the left side of Acopan Tepui's Gran Torre. We reported the route in *AAJ 2010*, but here we present the line. *Cheo García, climtepuyes.com*

approach: While climbing the jungle to the base of the wall in uncomfortable temperatures, you cross two cascades, each guaranteeing a perfect and very welcome shower. The upper cascade has a pool for bathing in a unique place, high above the jungle with an awesome panorama of the Gran Sabana.

At the end of our trip we left some gear in Yunek for our friends who visited in November. Accompanied by Venezuelan climber Cheo García, they struggled with a rainy season but still opened a new route. Michael Richter and Tilo Waehrich established Takamajaka (310m, 10 pitches, 7a+), on the left of the big buttress where the first route on Acopan Tepui was established (Jardieneros de Grandes Paredes, Botte-Calderón-Gargiter-Obergolser-Obojes-Trenkwalder, 2002) and climbs a more direct line, crossing the Gargitter route and ending near that route.

There is still a lot to explore in the region, including some impressive, unclimbed free-standing towers. The most demanding part is getting to the climbs through the omnipresent jungle. The steep or overhanging rock generally offers very good climbing, whereas lower-angled faces require extensive gardening.

RUEDIGER HELLING, *Germany*

Monte Roraima, Behind the Rainbow. You can still sense the excitement in Stefan Glowacz's voice. During a short phone call last week, the adrenaline in his blood has not calmed down yet and neither has the joy in his voice! Together with his climbing partner Holger Heuber, the pro climber has reached his great goal of conquering a new route, the La Proa wall, located at the Roraima Tepui in Venezuela.

Stefan Glowacz felt the pressure on this expedition. He and Heuber had to reach their goal without their friend, Kurt Albert, who died in a climbing accident earlier this year. Overwhelmed by grief over the loss of Kurt and also aware of the failure on their first attempt in spring 2010, they came prepared this time with a film team and enormous desire to complete the route.

Now the pressure has released. In December, he and Heuber reached their goal. Their prize was their success in establishing Behind the Rainbow. Glowacz and Heuber climbed more than 16 pitches between the 9th and 10th degree of difficulty; which equals 8b on the French scale.

Behind the Rainbow, La Proa wall, Monte Roraima. *Klaus Fengler*

"Behind the Rainbow is the perfect route for me! The higher you get the more difficult it becomes and each pitch has its very own characteristics. The backdrop and scenery you're in is impressive. This adventure was one of a kind for me!" said Stefan Glowacz with an emotional tone in his voice, right after he had touched ground again.

Press release provided by TAKE ONE CONT@CT *for* STEFAN GLOWACZ, *Germany, AAC*

Guyana

Morangma. In mid-September, three other guys and I flew to Georgetown, Guyana. None of us knew each other before leaving. It was for a TV show, and I was asked to join at the 11th hour as a climbing guide. The goal was to find a way through the jungle to a large tepui named Weiassipu, climb its first ascent, and explore its unknown sinkholes. Neither the videographer nor the main character had any climbing experience. I had a gut feeling of disaster before we left home.

The Prime Minister of Guyana arranged a helicopter that we needed to get out of the jungle, given the schedule for the project. A couple of Cessnas flew us to the small village of Phillipai. In dugout canoes, we then traveled to a smaller village called Wayalaleng. With more than 20 local porters, we spent several days walking through the jungle to Weiassipu. Absolute mayhem with our local outfitter turned into continuous drama. I've never experienced anything like it. The

The new route on Morangma. *Mike Libecki*

details are many, but I find them unimportant to list. Patience, acceptance, learning…. Near the tepui, after the porters left, I called our contact on my satellite phone to confirm the helicopter. They told me that the helicopter was no longer available and we were on our own. This meant we would not have enough time to climb the tepui and return for our flight. We immediately hurried back. We left hundreds of pounds gear in the middle of the jungle. I am leaving out a lot of details from the demise of this journey. These notes can help future trips to this area, and I welcome any contact for more information for anyone going there. One level of success: each trip is learning and training for the next. On the way out, I saw a beautiful tepui called Morangma. One of the locals in Phillipai told me that a couple different teams of scientists had been on top before after hiking up from the backside, near Brazil. All our gear was still in the middle of the jungle. I would have to come back for it. Before we left, we paid the locals to retrieve the equipment and bring it to the village.

In early February, I returned to Guyana alone. I took a Cessna to Phillipai, then canoes to Wayalaleng like before. I befriended three of the locals on the first trip, Franklin, Edward, and Harris (local Amerindians living in Phillipai), and they helped me find Morangma. It rained every day after I arrived at Wayalaleng, at least 15 hours a day. As we approached Morangma, cutting a path with machetes, the rain beat me down. We spent four days making our way through the jungle, sleeping in hammocks with rainflys like cocoons. Not *once* could we see out of the trees to the tepui. A compass and gps were of no help; it was not a matter of traveling in a general direction, we had to compromise with the wild terrain. When we reached the base, on the southeast side of the tepui, the jungle fauna and clouds still hid any visuals. My local friends get all the credit for getting to the tepui; it was amazing how they found the way.

After arriving at the tepui, I had two days to reach the top, then two days to meet my plane. The first day was spent climbing about 2,000' of steep jungle, from 70° to vertical, like a prehistoric creature. I had to rope up for about half of it, and then established a camp. The most beautiful part of this journey is that Franklin, Edward, and Harris wanted to come up with me. Because of all the gear we'd left behind on the previous trip, and that we now had, I could accommodate them. The route was mostly jungle, and these guys are strong and smart. I taught Franklin to belay, and all of them how to jumar. The next morning, I started up a huge chimney filled with moss and vines. Everything was soaked. Moss-lined cracks and vines served as holds and protection; I fixed lines and my friends ascended. On the second pitch, the chimney cut back into the wall, and soon I was in a vertical cave, encased in darkness. After a small runout, desperate and slipping, I lunged to a large vine. Ten seconds later it ripped, and I fell 15', Franklin's belay catching me. Back in the darkness of the chimney-cave, about 80' above I could see a small hole of light, about two feet in diameter. In the darkness, I grabbed through spider webs to reach the worm hole. I squeezed through and popped out of the chimney's womb into gray light and rain. I was in a huge corner, the rock covered with moss, but it was easy digging to reach the sandstone. Constant rain. I continued in a crack system on the face, vines and moss offering random purchase but little protection. Some vines were strong enough to hold my weight when I equalized two or three limbs like an insect. At one point, runout 90', I was so pumped I had to wrap my right arm around a vine, and grab my wrist with my left hand. Darkness encroached. I continued up near-vertical vines and trees—so many, I did not even touch stone. I was a spider monkey making my way through the steep web of foliage. Finally, with headlamps, we all climbed wet, slippery 5.5 vines to the top and then sat out the night under a small rock overhang. My feet hurt and throbbed from being wet for several days. When we got down and I finally took off my climbing shoes, I noticed something attached to the bottom of my ankles: foot-shaped clumps of cauliflower, white with a blue hue.

MIKE LIBECKI, *AAC*

Brazil

Pedra do Elefante, Saracura. After three years of attempts, on August 1, Helena Fagundes and Ralf Côrtes established Saracura (6° VII D4 E3 (BR), which could translate to: 540m, 5.11a), on Pedra do Elefante, near the rural village Taquaril in the mountains of Rio de Janeiro. See pictures at www. abrigodoelefante.com. The route is the eighth to the mountain's summit. The best season for climbing in the area is from April to October, when the weather is cooler and drier.

ANA ALVARENGA, *Brazil*

Pedra do Elefante: (1) Pai João (540m, 5.11a X). (2) Sarah Brum (300m, 5.10). (3) Dumbo na Festa do Céu (420m, 5.9). (4) Meleca do Elefante (90m, 5.7). (5) Suvaco de Cobra (130m, 5.11b). (6) Vidas Secas (400m, 5.7 R). (7) Ni'um Homizin (370m, 5.9). (8) Pata de Camelo (480m, 5.11 R/X). (9) Raja (640m, 5.12a). (10) Dona Jararaca (360m, 5.9). (11) Todas as Mulheres do Mundo (400m, 5.10 R). (12) Maria Bonita (125m, 5.12b). (13) A Cerveja do Diabo pro Dono do Céu (475m, 5.13a/A2+). (14) Saracura (540m, 5.11). *Otto Faber Jr.*

Peru

Peru

The online version of these reports frequently contains additional photos, maps, topos, and extended text. Please visit aaj. americanalpineclub.org

CORDILLERA BLANCA

Artesonraju, Southwest Face, variation. On June 13, Michael Sanchez Adams (Chile) made a probable new variation (900m, D+ 70–80° M1/M2), solo, to the classic Southwest Face route. He began at 3 a.m., believing that he was on the classic route but he actually was farther right, on the rock band where there are no known routes. He climbed a 350m 70–75° couloir to reach a rock ridge with hard snow and pitches M1/M2. Then, at 5:30 a.m., he traversed left under the characteristic hanging serac. In the final difficult (80°) section he self-belayed 45m, 50m, and 60m pitches. Finally he reached the summit (6,025m) at 3 p.m. and began the long descent.

SERGIO RAMÍREZ CARRASCAL, *Peru*

El Gran Mono, on the south face of Vallunaraju. *Beto Pinto*

Vallunaraju, El Gran Mono. Peruvian climbers Beto Pinto, Rolando Morales, and Steven Fuentes left Huaraz at midday on July 8. After a two-hour drive to Llaca Valley at 4,300m, they walked toward Vallunaraju's (5,600m) south face. One-and-a-half hours in, they found a small cave under a boulder where they bivouaced. The next morning they set off for the glacier at 2 a.m. The initial ascent included 50–60° sections and was challenging due to an abundance of loose snow. After three hours they reached the wall where they found a difficult section of rock with hard ice in the cracks, which took six hours for two pitches. The first pitch was aid (A2) and the second was rock climbing at 6a, with lots of loose snow that they had to clean in order to place protection. The situation worsened as the clouds descended upon them, reducing visibility, and it began snowing heavily. They then climbed a series of 80° and 90° pitches. Finally, after 17 hours of climbing, at 7 p.m. they reached the summit and then rappelled the normal route on the west face. El Gran Mono (300m, 70–90° 6a A2).

SERGIO RAMÍREZ CARRASCAL, *Peru*

Huantsan West, Les Trois Mousquetaires; Huantsan North, Illusion. From the Rajucolta Valley on July 20, Beto Pinto, Rolando Morales, and I crossed the moraine onto the glacier, navigated extensive crevasses, and camped at approximately 5,100m. The next day, carrying little, we approached the bottom of the face.

Les Trois Mousquetaires, on Huantsan West. *Sophie Denis*

It was a mess. Hip-deep snow made trail-breaking a challenge and increased the crevasse difficulties, but we finally crossed the bergschrund and began climbing the south face of the west ridge of Huantsan's west summit. A nice couloir, 50–60° with deep snow and loose rocks, steepened to 70°, 80°, and 90°. At the end of the last pitch, we tunneled through a hanging mushroom, continued to the summit at 7 p.m., and endured an open bivouac. We called our route Les Trois Mousquetaires.

After resting all day, on July 22 at 8:00 p.m., we started climbing to Huantsan's north summit. We passed some crevasses and climbed three easy (50°) pitches, then continued past some loose rocks and up a couloir of good 70–80° ice to pass a big mushroom on the ridge. We summited Huantsan North after 12 hours of climbing, named our route Illusion, and descended to our previous night's open bivouac.

Illusion, on Huantsan North. *Sophie Denis*

SOPHIE DENIS, *AAC*

Nevado Quillujirca, El Sueño de los Excluidos and La Teoría de la Gota de Agua. In the Rurec Valley, called by many climbers the "Little Yosemite" of the Andes, an Italian expedition opened two new routes on Nevado Quillujirca (5,040m; Quillujirca is the local name, a.k.a. Huantsán Chico or Shaqsha). The team installed base camp on May 6, with a main objective of Punta Numa's west face, where in 1997 a Spanish team opened the first route on the impressive granite wall. Due to unfavorable weather, the Italians decided on Nevado Quillujirca instead. On May 11, Roberto Iannilli and Andrea DiDonato

El Sueño de los Excluidos (right) and La Teoría de la Gota de Agua, with the advanced camp on the vegetated shelf. *Roberto Iannilli*

climbed 300m up to a large shelf where they installed bivouac equipment and then returned to base camp, leaving fixed ropes. The next day, they returned to the bivouac with Ivo Scappatura, but bad weather held until May 15. Scappatura returned to base camp due to health problems, but DiDonato and Iannilli continued climbing the southeast face on muddy and vegetated cracks. After three bivouacs on the ascent and another on the descent, they opened El Sueño de los Excluidos (1,340m, VII/VII+ A2, 25 pitches, May 11–18).

Around the same dates, Luca D'Andrea and Massimo Massimiano climbed the south face of the same mountain, calling their line La Teoría de la Gota de Agua (800m, VII- A2). The route shares the same initial 300m as El Sueño, and does not reach the summit.

SERGIO RAMÍREZ CARRASCAL, *Peru*

CORDILLERA HUAYHUASH

The Spanish climbing on the west face of Mituraju, with Está el Barrio Que da Miedo on the left (ending at the ridge). *Equipo Español de Alpinismo*

Mituraju, west face and other activity. The Equipo Español de Alpinismo (Spanish Alpine Climbing Team) installed base camp at Jahuacocha lake - Gocha Cutan (4,066m) on May 20. From there they crossed a dangerous glacier and carried their equipment to high camp (5,000m) on the plateau beneath Rondoy, Mituraju, Jirishanca, Yerupajá Chico, and El Toro. Conditions in most of the mountains last May were very dry and dangerous, with falling rocks and many crevasses.

The brothers Martín and Simón Elías (director of team) attempted a new route on Yerupaja Grande's (6,634m) southwest face/ridge, reaching 6,200m. Afterward, Alex Corpas, Silvestre Barrientos, Mikel Bonilla, and Simón Elías tried the first repeat of the 1985 Joe Simpson - Simon Yates route the west face of Siula Grande (6,354m), also reaching 6,200m.

On June 5, on the west face of Mituraju (5,750m), Barrientos and Corpas established Está el Barrio Que da Miedo (750m, MD+ 90° M5 V5) to the summit ridge. The next day, Bonilla and Dani Crespo also climbed high on the west face, calling their efforts Pim Pam Toma Cornisazo (MD+ 90° M5 V5). Both attacks were made from the TAM glacier in one day each.

Later in July, in the Cordillera Blanca, Crespo and Bonilla died while attempting a new route on the west face of Chacraraju (6,112m). Beforehand they had climbed the Bouchard route on the same mountain, and also, with David Bautista, made the first almost-free (one pendulum) ascent of Papas Rellenas (650m, 6c A3) on Cerro Parón (a.k.a. La Esfinge, 5,325m), freeing the A3 section at 7b.

SERGIO RAMÍREZ CARRASCAL, *Peru*

CORDILLERA CENTRAL

Huaguruncho, Llama Karma to summit ridge. Tony Barton and I returned to the Quebrada Huaguruncho after a two-year absence. Our objective was the first ascent of the southwest face of Huaguruncho (5,730m), by the same line we had attempted in 2008 with Olly Metherell. Barton had also previously visited on three other occasions between 2003 and 2006.

We initially planned to acclimatize by climbing the S-couloir of Huarancaya Sur, which had appeared icy and viable in 2008. But conditions were far more dry in 2010, so, instead, we acclimatized on an unclimbed ridge on the rock peak Yanacocha (5,150m), on the south side of the valley. On July 27–28, we got most of the way up the ridge, including the likely first ascents of two sub-peaks, until a huge overhanging chasm barred our way and we aborted about 150m below the main summit.

After a couple of days of rest at base camp, we attempted our main objective, the southwest face of Huaguruncho. We were largely successful, climbing the face (but not to the summit), and calling our route Llama Karma (1000m, 24 pitches, ED 90° V[UIAA rock]). We left base camp on July 31, reached the ridge atop the face on August 3, and the next day downclimbed and rappelled the far side, in the direction of the 1956 first ascent ridge and toward the Matthews Glacier until reaching the valley floor. On August 5, we continued hiking down a long valley, up over a high pass next to Huarancaya Sur, and back to the valley of our base camp.

TOM CHAMBERLAIN, *U.K.*

Llama Karma, on the southwest face of Huaguruncho. *Tom Chamberlain*

The new routes on Vicunita, Manon Dos, and Suiricocha. *Sophie Denis*

Suiricocha, Manon Dos, Vicunita, new routes. Over the course of a week in the Cordillera Central in late May, Beto Pinto and I opened three new lines of difficulty MD+. The north face of Suiricocha (5,495m) had nine pitches, finishing with a steep (80°+) pitch of ice and loose rock. The west face of Manon Dos (5,500m) was short, about three pitches of 70–90° ice, but with bad snow, avalanche danger and giant crevasses. Last, we climbed the west face of Vicunita (5,538m), seven pitches including a crux 60m pitch of mixed climbing to 90°.

Sᴏᴘʜɪᴇ Dᴇɴɪs, *AAC*

Bolivia

The start to the new route on the south face of Illimani, by Florian Hill and Robert Rauch. (Inset) Hill traversing low on the route. *florianhill.com*

Cordillera Real, Illimani, Deliver Me. At the end of July, Florian Hill (Austria and Germany) and Robert Rauch (Bolivia and Germany) began climbing new ice, rock, and mixed terrain below the gable-end of the southwest ridge of Illimani. The initial passages were threatened by large, broken seracs and had ice to 90°, difficult mixed climbing, and rotten 5th-class rock. Above, they joined much easier terrain on the Sanchez-Mesili southwest ridge route, and endured an unplanned bivy after 17+ hours and about 1,000m. Four days after beginning their climb they reached the main summit (south summit; Pico Sur, 6,439m). Their route gained approximately 1,600m vertical and 6km length. They descended the normal West Ridge route in another two days. The climbers' individual accounts of the climb differ in many other aspects.

Compiled from correspondence with FLORIAN HILL *and* ROBERT RAUCH

Florian Hill high on Illimani. *florianhill.com*

Cordillera Real, Serkhe Khollu, Chamaka. From our base camp on the glimmering shores of Sirki Khota Lake, Robert Rauch, Stefan Berger, and I spotted a logical line on the southwest face of 5,546m Serkhe Khollu, which is the main summit of the Serranias Serkhe and Murillo, situated between Mururata and Chacaltaya. On June 10, in total darkness and sub-zero temperatures, we searched for access to its base. Not even three meters wide, the icefall soared vertically upward. We sorted our gear, racked up, and stepped into unknown terrain. On the second pitch, the ice surprised us with poor quality, and every swing of our picks at that altitude felt like hard work. On the fourth pitch, the ice tube unexpectedly ended, forcing us onto sparsely protected mixed terrain with brittle ice. Happiness lit-up our faces as we reached the next ice tube, and we climbed faster—a good thing, as the sun illuminated seracs overhead. But we managed to escape the danger zone. Pitches of 75–85° glacier ice followed, and we climbed quickly. In the last two pitches leading to the summit ridge, the glacier steepened again but Stefan led us through with confidence, and we crested the ridge after ten hours of climbing 600m of ice and mixed terrain.

Chamaka, on the southwest face of Serkhe Khollu. Another route, Durch das Nasenloch, by Austrian climbers, has been climbed on the face, but it largely disappeared with glacial retreat. *florianhill.com*

Robert Rauch leading off on Chamaka, Serkhe Khollu. *florianhill.com*

The descent, not technically challenging but littered with crevasses, led down to a scree field that again called for surefootedness and concentration. We donned our head torches and continued back to base camp. So near the equator, the transition from day to night happens without twilight. Our new route, Chamaka (Aymara for darkness), began and ended in moonless darkness.

FLORIAN HILL, *Austria-Germany*

Saturno from the west: (1) Camino de la Luna y del Sol (Calisaya-Pratt). (2) Plaza Alonso de Mendoza (Garrison-Phillips). *Everett Phillips*

Josh Garrison climbing Plaza Alonso de Mendoza, Saturno. *Everett Phillips*

Cordillera Quimsa Cruz, Monte Rosa, Minute Men, and Saturno, Plaza Alonso de Mendoza. The northern fringe of the Quimsa Cruz comprises Bolivia's stash of alpine granite. North of the mining town of Villoco, spires and gendarme-protected ridges occupy the sky between 4,000m and 5,000m. Josh Garrison and I visited this area twice between May 1–10. The information we'd collected online and around La Paz before our trip suggested that some of the best climbing was located one ridge north of Villoco in the Mocoya Valley. We completed two new routes there. In our first stay we climbed Minute Men (350m, III 5.8) to the top of Monte Rosa's (4,710m) south face. The route begins on slabs rising from Laguna Blanca's northern edge. It trends right on mossy splitters (mostly 5.4/5.5) before moving back left to the ridge at the top. After that, weather closed in so we returned to La Paz to recharge.

We returned three days later to climb the west buttress of Saturno. The sketchy guidebook I got in La Paz lists Saturno at 5,011m, though the seemingly more reliable report from the 2007 Imperial College group [*AAJ 2008*, pp. 238–239; their full report can be found online—Ed.] puts it at 5,340m. It is obviously the tallest peak around. From the base of the formation, we easily followed parallel crack systems (5.7/5.8) to the top of the buttress in seven pitches. Though we were unable to find any record of previous climbs on the buttress, we found two pitons with slings on pitch one, and a sling on pitch six. Many route possibilities exist on the features we were climbing, though we thought it unlikely that our line had been taken to the summit before. From the top of the buttress we traversed down a narrow bridge of loose rock to the summit pyramid. The final 150m consisted of vertical rubble, taking us five more pitches to finish Plaza Alonso de Mendoza (580m, IV 5.9) at the summit. We reached the talus at midnight after six hours spent rappelling the mountain's north face, and were back in camp two hours later.

EVERETT PHILLIPS, *Intervale, NH*

Argentina and Chile

The online version of these reports frequently contains additional photos, maps, topos, and extended text. Please visit aaj.americanalpineclub.org

CENTRAL ANDES

Ansilta 4, Seis Hermanos. On September 19, during Argentina's dry 2010 winter, in the remote and little-visited Cordillera Ansilta, located 250km north of Mendoza and 50km from Barreal, Gabriel Fava (Argentina) and I climbed a new route on Ansilta 4 (5,116m).

Seis Hermanos, on Ansilta 4. *Henry Bizot*

From base camp (3,950m) we hiked along a moraine toward the mountain; early in the walk, in the Morillos hills, we found fantastic caves with ancient paintings. We continued to the base and climbed the 750m southeast ridge (French D in these dry conditions, 55° max), beginning with a 400m ice face and followed by 350m of mixed terrain to the summit. In the absence of previous known ascents, we named the route Seis Hermanos, dedicated to my six boys.

HENRY BIZOT, *France, AAC*

Ramada Range, Pico Polaco North, Cheto Alpino. On Tuesday, October 5, with the great enthusiasm and motivation of Ivan "Topo" Rocamora, we left his flat in Mendoza for the mountains, and with 23kg on our backs—no mules in our low budget—and three hours of daylight remaining, we started up the Rio Colorado gorge. The next day we continued the remaining 30km to the icy and very windy Santana Base Camp, "Pirca Polaco," at 3,600m.

Thursday started sunny and windless, so with some food and one sleeping bag we went to the base of the northeast face of Pico Polaco (6,000m), and shivered through a windy night at 4,700m. At 6 a.m. on October 8, we began climbing, first on easy rock and then into an ice runnel between rock towers, leading to a 40m ice cascade at 5,400m. We bypassed the ice with 55m of hard-to-protect rock to the left, then reconnected with the ice, which led to about 150m of 50° snow, another step of rock, and

Ivan Rocamora leading on Cheto Alpino, Pico Polaco. *Gabriel Fava*

Cheto Alpino, the new route to the north summit of Pico Polaco. *Gabriel Fava*

more ice and snow finishing in some large towers. We navigated the towers via some rock on the right leading to a couloir that took us back left with a narrow strip of 70° ice. We continued connecting snow and ice gullies to the summit ridge, where we climbed some rotten rock and, after 18 hours of climbing, gained the North Summit and reveled in the colorful beauty of the desolate landscape.

It was a nice evening with some clouds rolling in, and we descended the route of first ascent, climbed by Antonio De Nigris and Edgardo Beorchia Yacante in 1958, carrying firewood with them up the mountain. We carefully descended the couloir, with some ice steps to 60° and excellent snow taking us to the glacier and the awkward moraines, where we could feel water running, and we spent a dark and quiet night with our one sleeping bag and no food. But still we were happy, having climbed a new route on a beautiful mountain. Cheto Alpino (1,000m, D+ 70° 4+(UIAA rock)).

We continued down on Saturday, and on Sunday we enjoyed a day of cragging by Los Colorados, with maté, food, and more food....

GABRIEL FAVA, *Argentina*

Note: Soon after this ascent, Ivan Rocamora fell and died while he and Fava were climbing on the south face of Cerro Mercedario.

Aconcagua (6,962m), 2010–2011 overview. This season fewer people visited Aconcagua and the weather was bad, with many days of snowfall. Unfortunately, there were six casualties (only one climber died last year). There were 197 rescues (46 of them complex), which is a decrease from recent years. The cost of rescue operations, however, has gone up, specifically due to the use of helicopters, and the climbing fee has increased. The cleaning of the park was completed and two new huts were constructed, one at 3,800m in the Quebrada de las Vacas and another at 6,000m. On another positive note, more climbers and trekkers are accessing the mountain by the Quebrada de las Vacas, leaving the Plaza de Mulas and the normal route less crowded.

Of 2,800 trekkers and 3,498 climbers, 85% were non-Argentinian. Compared to last season, this was 600 fewer trekkers and 300 fewer climbers. On February 3, Peruvian guide Holmes Pantoja Bayona broke Aconcagua's speed record, going from Laguna Horcones (2,850m) to the summit in 13 hours, and round-trip in 20:35.

MARCELO SCANU, *Buenos Aires, Argentina*

The remote Chimbote (5,489m) from the south, with dots representing the initial climbing on the north face. The peak on the left is Polleras (5,993m). Inset: close-up of the summit pyramid. *Fernando Fainberg*

Chimbote, first ascent. Chimbote sits about 100km east of Santiago, near Mt. Polleras and the Tupungato Volcano. Despite many attempts since 1944, it remained unclimbed. It is guarded by a difficult approach, flanked by big mountains and deep valleys. Access is via the Olivares River to Las Pircas Pass and the Las Toscas Valley, then the main ridge to high camp. This approach took Waldo Farias and me four-days, starting at 3,000m, then crossing the 5,000m pass, dropping into the valley at 3,700m, and then hiking back up to 5,000m and high camp—all with 30kg packs.

Chimbote from the north, with the route of first ascent. Dots indicate where the route switched to the south face to the summit. *Fernando Fainberg*

The mountain has two 1,500m faces with bad rock (one on the El Perdido Valley, and the other in the El Quebrado Valley), and a third that's less steep, but still with 120m of bad rock. We started to the side of this third wall, from the north, climbing 300m of 50° ice and free rock climbing, then rappelled 200m to the glaciated part of the south face and made a 100m ice traverse to a 200m ice headwall (65°–70°) that reached the summit pyramid. Another 130m of rock climbing (very bad rock with almost no protection, but no harder than 5.8) brought us to the 5,489m summit (my GPS read 5,498m) on April 1, 2011, at 6 p.m. We returned the same way, the adventure taking 11 days.

Fernando Fainberg, *Chile*

The line of Pico Navarro Norte's first winter ascent, the east face and north ridge. *Pablo David González*

The Southwest Ridge route on Cerro Palo Plantado. *Elvis Acevedo*

Pico Navarro Norte, first winter ascent and possible new route. Named after a famous miner from the 19th century who discovered gold and copper, the beautiful Navarro Valley is situated south of Las Cuevas Village. A group of four peaks stands on the west side of the valley. The name of the northern peak is Santa Elena, a classic training summit for Chilean and Argentinean climbers. Santa Elena can be climbed in one day from Cristo Redentor Pass. The second peak is difficult, unnamed and with no recorded ascents. The last two peaks are usually called Navarro. Javier Gutiérrez and I climbed northern Navarro (4,660m) on September 14 by the east face and north ridge (50° snow and UIAA III/IV rock steps near the summit). The last climbers known to reach its summit were Carlos Sansoni and Jorge Crescitelli on April 14, 1977. Ours was the fourth ascent and the first in winter.

PABLO DAVID GONZÁLEZ, *Mendoza, Argentina*

Cerro Palo Plantado, Southwest Ridge. The weekend of June 4–5, the G.A.M (Grupo de Alta Montaña) de los Perros Alpinos went to the sector Queltehues – Las Melosas, near Santiago but very seldom visited by climbers, mostly due to private companies prohibiting access.

On the map we had found an interesting summit in Cerro Palo Plantado (3,497m)—low compared to others, but without recorded ascents—and we decided to try its southwest ridge. We wanted to try an unclimbed peak, and open a much neglected sector for mountaineers to visit more frequently.

On Saturday, Roberto Toro, Jaime Wastavino, Juan Carlos Caro, and I ascended easy terrain to install base camp at the base of the ridge. The next morning we started climbing, advancing on easy terrain along the narrow ridge, traversing a stretch of gendarmes (El Filo de las Jorobas) and a section of mixed with some rockfall, and powder on slopes of 70° that seemed ready to collapse at any time. We overcame the mixed stretches and were soon on summit.

The difficulty of the 1,000m route seemed to be D-, with grade IV rock, ice, verglas and unstable snow slopes.

ELVIS ACEVEDO, *Chile*

NORTHERN PATAGONIA

Cerro Tronador, Pico Internacional, Finito Sur. In October, Argentines Tomy Aguiló and Luciano Fiorenza ascended this ca 3,500m mountain near Bariloche, Argentina, by a new route they named Finito Sur (550m, 80° mixed, 5th class rock). Their route climbs to the highest of Tronador's three summits (Pico Internacional, a.k.a. Anón). In 2009 Fiorenza, Jorge Ackermann, and José Bonacalza made a variation to the Clausen (normal) Route, calling it Generación Descartable (300m, 85°).

MARCELO SCANU, *Buenos Aires, Argentina*

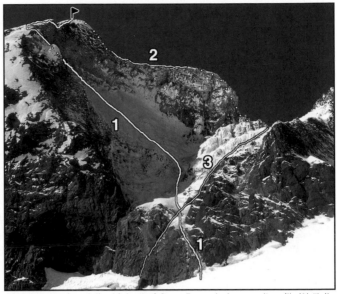

Pico Internacional, the highest of Cerro Tronador's summits, with (1) Finito Sur. (2) Clausen (normal) Route. (3) Jeneración Descartable variation. *Luciano Fiorenza*

Cochamó, Pared de Profetas, Prophecy. Stefan Brunner and I, spent three weeks together in the Cochamó Valley at the end of January and beginning of February. We found a great line on the far right side of the Profetas Wall, which is on the opposite side of the valley from Mt. Trinidad. Initially, we aided the 420m wall. The first half of the route was mostly thin cracks, so we used a lot of peckers and bird beaks. The upper part widened to better cracks and then widened further to off-widths and a two-pitch dihedral system. The last pitches to the top are on slabs. After aiding the first ascent, we rappelled in, adding bolts where necessary to make it a free climb. Because it rained almost every day, the route took six days to complete. It's called The Prophecy and has grades up to French 7b. It's a beautiful crack system to free climb, with only one part of aid, on a slab, where we did a five-meter leftward pendulum. But even the slab is probably possible to climb free.

GERDA RAFFETSEDER, *Austria*

Cochamó, Pared de Profetas, Las Venas Cerradas de America Latina. Escaping from Torres del Paine's awful weather, German Kevin Bartke and I landed in Valle Cochamó in late February, seeking some dry, sunny granite walls. After repeating some routes in the Anfiteatro, La Zebra, and Valle de Paloma, we teamed up with North American Erik Kinsley to open a new route that Kevin and Erik had seen on the Profetas Wall, up the Valle de Paloma. On our first push we climbed the first three pitches of Otro Dia Otro Largo (*AAJ 2009*, pp. 197-199), and then turned

Routes on the right side of Pared de Profetas: (1) Genesis (Deering-Estep-Stember, 2009). (2) Otro Dia Otro Largo (Laramie-Parada, 2009). (3) Las Venas Cerradas de America Latina (Bartke-Bonilla Rau, 2010). (4) The Prophecy (Brunner-Raffetseder, 2010). *Gerda Raffetseder*

left to the crack system in the center of the wall, just above the characteristic roof. After two high-quality pitches (the second being the hardest), the wall steepened and the cracks flared, making free climbing almost impossible. We traversed back right and shared some meters with Otro Dia Otro Largo, until the wall allowed us to return to our original crack system. In the end, we spent about five full days working on the route (Las Venas Cerradas de America Latina, 330m, 5.11+), cleaning, freeing, and bolting some of the pitches and the belays. The first two pitches, which we added after our initial push, were rap-bolted, and we believe they bring an easier and nicer alternative to the C1 roof of Otro Dia Otro Largo. We would like to thank Daniel Seeliger for his support and his unending kindness.

ALEJANDRO BONILLA RAU, *Spain*

Valle Pirita, Pirita Right, Under a Southern Star; Valle Mariposa, various activity. Leeches, carnivorous bees, hacking through thick bamboo jungle on the approach: these are not what come to mind when you talk about Patagonia. But the mystery and secrecy surrounding the many hidden granite walls of the Turbio IV valley (which I also have heard called Valle Oscuro) piqued my interest, and in late January 2011 I found myself in Bariloche, Argentina, with Josh Garrison, preparing to go in with directions from a decade-old, hand-drawn map.

After waiting several days for the river to go down from recent flooding, we began a difficult 60km horse ride with our gear to the junction of the Turbio tributaries. We made our first trip into the Mariposa Valley. The trail finding was desperate, through dense forests of cane colihue jungle and over sketchy Tyrolean

Josh Garrison attempting a new route on El Diente, in the Mariposa Valley. *Ryan Huetter*

crossings, but, after a mid-approach bivy while hopelessly lost, we reached the open Mariposa meadow, which became our base camp for the next 14 days. We had lots of heavy rain, but in between did the second ascent of the Brazilian route, El Palito (550m, 5.10+), on La Oreja, and simul-soled a Royal Arches type feature we named the Earlobe (900m, 5.6), to the east of La Oreja. We attempted a new route on a feature

Valle Pirita, with routes on Pirita Right: (1) Voces en la Noche (Anderson-Beckner-Spaulding, 2009). (2) Under a Southern Star (Garrison-Huetter, 2011). (3) Todos los Caballos Lindos (Stanhope-Querner, 2009). *Ryan Huetter.* Inset: *Dave Anderson.*

we called El Diente (200m, 5 new pitches), and another on the northeast pillar of La Oreja (400m, 9 pitches), but were thwarted on both by closed-out, vegetated cracks. While we found the rumor of "10 Half Domes" to be true, most of the walls are capped by large glaciers that sweep the faces.

After a final resupply at the Turbio junction, we moved camp into the Pirita Valley. Pirita Right has seen action from two different teams in recent years (*AAJ 2009*, pp. 200–202), and for good reason: it has the cleanest and most spectacular granite in either of the valleys. Days on end of heavy rain confined us to our tarp-shanty, as we grew anxious and began slimming down our rations.

At last, with four days left, our window arrived. We left camp under a cold and clear sky, and reached the bottom of the approach slabs by daybreak. The approach to the main wall is long and involved, kind of like the Death Slabs with pitches up to 5.10. By late morning, we reached the bottom of our intended route in the center of the face, and climbed pitch-after-pitch of clean, rope-stretching, laser-cut cracks, sometimes connected with heady slabs and traverses. We topped out at dusk to a brilliant orange sunset, sweeping from the Pacific Ocean (only 30 miles away!) to the snowy flanks of Monte Tronodor, before settling in for a very cold, full-moon-lit, open bivy. In the morning we descended for seven hours down the shoulder and slabs, for a camp-to-camp time of 33 hours, having established Under a Southern Star (460m, V 5.11).

On February 22, we loaded all of our gear into two lightweight packrafts and descended the Rio Turbio to Lago Puelo in a long, relaxing day, finally able to let the river do its share of the work after 34 days in the alpine.

This was by far one of the most rewarding and enriching experiences of my life, and Josh and I would like to thank the American Alpine Club Mountain Fellowship Grant, Sterling Rope, Alpacka Rafts, Montbell, and our gauchos Cholo and Mikol for helping turn this trip from pipe dream to reality.

Ryan Huetter, *AAC*

SOUTHERN PATAGONIA

Chalten massif, summary. The biggest news of the 2010–11 season, not in the individual reports below, was the "fair-means" attempt to climb the Southeast Ridge of Cerro Torre (a.k.a. Compressor Route) by Canadians Chris Geisler and Jason Kruk. They had hoped to climb the Southeast Ridge without using any of Maestri's bolts for progression. They reached the headwall following the Mabboni-Salvaterra and Wharton-Smith variations to the Compressor Route, and then climbed four pitches weaving around Maestri's bolts to 40m below the summit snowfield, from where they retreated in bad weather. Hats off for such a great effort!

Elsewhere in the Torre Range, early in the season American Colin Haley made the first solo ascent of Aguja Standhardt, which he climbed via Exocet.

During the same good weather window, Swiss Michi Lerjen and Simon Anthamatten made an impressive one-day outing with ascents of Punta Herron and Torre Egger. They climbed across the snow ramps of Standhardt to reach the Col dei Sogni, summited Herron after midday and Egger around 4 p.m., before descending to the Egger-Torre col and down the east face of Torre. Also on Egger, during the austral winter a few months earlier, Swiss Dani Arnold, Thomas Senf, and Stefan Siegrist made the peak's first winter ascent. They followed the Martin-O'Neill link-up (lower part of the Italian route to the upper part of Titanic), taking three days round trip.

Toward the end of December, Mikey Schaefer, Jens Holsten, and Colin Haley climbed 350m of new terrain on the right side of the east face of Mermoz to reach the Argentine Route, which they followed to the summit. They called their line Jardines Japoneses (600m, AI4 M5 6b A1).

On the west face of Aguja Guillaumet, Czech Michal Pitelka and German Carsten Von Birckhahn climbed their third new route on the face, an obvious crack system between Padrijo and Rayo de Luz. Just to the left, between Padrijo and Disfrute la Vida, Americans Blake Herrington and Scott Bennett climbed a new route that they called Las Venturas. On the nearby Aguja Mermoz, Herrington and Bennett did the first free ascent of Cosas Patagonicas (5.11).

On Cerro Piergiorgio Brits Jonathan Griffith and Will Sim made the second ascent of the first ascent route (Jorge and Pedro Skvarca, 1963, 350m, 5[UIAA rock] A1 70°).

On Desmochada, Belgian Sean Villanueva made the first free ascent of Golden Eagle (5.11+).

On Cerro Fitz Roy, Slovenes Matjaz Dusic and Lovro Vrsnik made the first integral ascent (to the summit; the route originally ended atop the Goretta (north) Pillar) of Mate, Porro y Todo lo Demas, climbing the route to the summit in two days. Just to the right, between Mate-Porro and the Polish Route, Argentines Luciano Fiorenza and Jimmy Heredia, with Brazilian Sergio Tartari, climbed a new route on the Goretta Pillar over three days. The called their line Al Abordaje (900m, 6c A2+).

Fitz Roy was the site of a dramatic accident that resulted in the death of Brazilian climber Bernardo Collares. Collares and Kika Bradford were descending from an attempt on the Afanassieff Route when the rap anchor pulled. Collares suffered multiple injuries and was unable to move. Bradford descended to get help but because of Collares's location, 1,200m above the glacier, and the absence of helicopter rescue, it was impossible to reach him. The accident should serve as a reminder to all climbers that, despite the area's growing popularity and the apparent ease with which some climbers ascend these big peaks today, it is still a serious and remote area. Carry strong painkillers, rely on only yourself, and climb with no illusions of rescue.

ROLANDO GARIBOTTI, *AAC*

Editor's note: As most of the obvious lines in the Chalten massif have been climbed, refinement ascents and variations are, naturally, increasing. Many of these don't meet the AAJ's criteria for inclusion, but Garibotti provides more comprehensive information than we present here, as well as an authoritative source on Patagonia climbing and its ongoing history at www.pataclimb.com.

Scott Bennett negotiates a gendarme between the summits of Cerro Pollone. *Blake Herrington*

Cerro Pollone, A Fine Piece variation to summit, and first traverse. In February 2011, Scott Bennett and I started 45m up and left from the toe of Cerro Pollone's west pillar, climbing a "scoop" and series of left-facing corners and overlaps. This was a four-pitch variant start to A Fine Piece (5.10 A2, Crouch-Donini, 1999), which starts a couple of pitches lower and 50m or more to the right of the toe of the west pillar. Our first four pitches involved discontinuous cracks and flakes/overlaps, and we joined A Fine Piece at the end of their seventh pitch. After the initial four or five pitches, we saw a single bolt at each belay (left on Swiss Michel Piola and Daniel Anker's 1988 attempt, which ended about two-thirds up the pillar). We also found occasional cams and slings left by Crouch and Donini, as they descended from atop the pillar. We bivied at pitch 12 (of 14 or so) on the pillar, then continued to the top of the pillar and for another five more pitches to the summit via good rock and mostly easy climbing (one short bit of 5.10). The rock is fantastic, and many of the middle pitches feature interesting knobs and pockets. The freeclimbing crux was a well-protected rightward crack switch on the 4th pitch that was about 5.11d/7a. The leader freed every pitch, with the follower sometimes A0-ing, pulling on gear, or doing poor-man's jugging.

The climbing from atop the pillar to the summit was in the vicinity of the 1949 first ascent route, some likely on new ground. Between the summit of Pollone and the (lower) east summit, we rappelled off of two gendarmes and finally found some bad rock on the final gendarme before the east summit. Here we used a point of A0 to surmount an overhang. From the east summit we found some of the anchors left by Neil and Jim [see below], and generally copied their descent onto the Fitz Norte Glacier.

Blake Herrington, AAC

Cerro Pollone East, first ascent, Re Puesto! Foregoing Chalten's legendary New Year's Eve fiesta, Neil Kauffman and I launched into the hills. We caught a few hours of sleep at the Piedra Negra bivouac, grabbed our previously-cached gear, and headed over Paso Cuadrado and down onto the North Fitz

Neil Kauffman on pitch 4 of Re Puesto!, Cerro Pollone East. *Jim Toman*

Re Puesto!, the route of first ascent on Cerro Pollone's eastern summit. *Jim Toman*

Roy Glacier. As first light hit our objective, we sat back and studied our anticipated line to Cerro Pollone's untouched eastern summit. We would begin on the right side of a low rock buttress, try to avoid imposing seracs, then cross a high snowfield and try to access the unclimbed northeast ridge to the summit.

Neil launched off on the first lead block, weaving through 250m of mostly high-quality rock. At the top of the buttress we switched to ice gear and simul-climbed past an upper bergschrund to access the ridge. Leading off this second block in rock shoes and with a single tool, I delicately climbed a frozen water groove to a large flake and then onto the ridge proper. A few pitches of thin ridge climbing later we found ourselves at a crux. A steep, slabby gendarme blocked further ridge climbing. We found a great hand and fingers crack until it ended in a seam, then pounded some iron and pendulumed into another crack system. Exposed free climbing then led to easy, clean aid in a wet, dirty crack that brought us back to the ridge. Another few pitches of great 5.10 crack systems led to just below the ridge, where we romped to the summit block.

After an exaggerated summit photo session and several minutes scoping the wonder-land of alpine rock around us, we started our descent. Three 60m drops landed us on the high snowfield where most of Cerro Pollone's eastern routes end or transition. We decided to bivy at the top of the Mastica e Sputa buttress and finish the anticipated walk-off in the morning.

Fitz Roy's south face: (1) California Route (with variations; Chouinard-Dorworth-Tejada Flores-Jones-Tomp-kins, 1968). (2) Washington Route (Rutherford-Schaefer, 2011). (3) Canadian Route (McSorley-Walsh, 2005). (4) Boris Simoncic (Biscak-Fadjan-Lenarcic, 1985). (5) Anglo-American (Anthonie-Birch-Derby-Lee-Nicol-Wade, 1972). Dots and dashes represent hidden portions. *Mikey Schaefer*

The night passed slowly in our one-man sleeping bag cover, switching alpine spoon positions until dawn. After a short walk down the glacier, we made two quick raps and were back to the North Fitz Roy Glacier.

"Re puesto" has many meanings, but in Argentine slang is understood as "totally buggered" or "wasted," which matched our dehydrated physical state. Re Puesto! (600m, 5.10 A1 65°).

JIM TOMAN, *AAC*

Fitz Roy, Washington Route. Like so many good missions in Patagonia, it started with the painful task of changing our plane tickets. A possible good weather window was coming, so it was go-big-or-go-home time. A day and a thousand bucks later we were committed to trying a new route on Fitz Roy.

On the morning of February 8, 2011, Kate Rutherford and I packed up, caught a taxi to the trailhead, and made the pleasant five-hour walk to Piedra Negras. In a light rain we headed to Paso

Kate Rutherford starting the first new pitch of the Washington Route. The route continues up the obvious open corner/gully above. *Mikey Schaefer*

Guillaumet and continued to the base of Fitz Roy's southeast face and the Brecha de los Italianos.

In improving weather, we found deteriorating conditions in the couloir, and were sopping wet when we reached the ridge. We looked over to our objective, the shaded south face, and spent the next few hours soaking up the sun and drying out. Around midday we put the boots back on and slowly traversed beneath the south face. Conditions on the traverse were much harder than expected, and we regretted our choice of aluminum crampons, lightweight boots, one set of tools, and only two screws. After some sketchy traversing and rappels we reached easier terrain but once again were slowed by hard, blue ice. The day had grown late and we hadn't even started any of the new climbing. We traversed farther west, past the start of our proposed line, hoping to find a bivy spot near the start of the California Route.

After a cold night sans sleeping bag, we were doubting our tactics: light, lucky, and slow. But with no reason to turn back we continued on, making one long rappel from the top of the ice slope at the base of the California Route. This deposited us back at the base of huge gulley/corner system. Kate took over the lead and navigated thin, ice-filled cracks via 5.10 and C1. Thankfully, the ice soon disappeared and we were rewarded with beautiful splitter cracks in a huge corner. A couple pitches of mostly hands led to a stout wide pitch, which was challenging to protect with only one #4 Camalot. We stayed in this corner system for many pitches, climbing mostly good splitters at 5.10 C1. I followed in boots and gloves and found myself bat-manning the rope more than I care to admit. After a cool alcove and a layback off-width through a bulge, we trended right for easier terrain.

I took over as the angle eased and the sun slipped toward the horizon. Fun, moderate climbing led us up and right to the large 50° ice slope shared by the other routes on the southeast face. We continued up in fading light, past descending teams. Not wanting to join the inevitable rappelling junk show, we found a sheltered spot on the summit, moved some rocks, put on our shiver sack, and stayed warm with the stoke of having just done a new route on Fitz Roy.

MIKEY SCHAEFER, *AAC*

Fitz Roy, east face, onsight free ascent. In a 36-hour roundtrip push from base camp on February 19–20, 2011, Sean Villanueva and I made an onsight free ascent of the east face of Fitz Roy. We mostly followed El Corazon, but to avoid some wet rock we started with the closest good-looking dry line, which was the Ferrari Route. We followed it for about five pitches before traversing horizontally to join El Corazon, along with a couple pitches of Royal Flush, and a couple new variation pitches, to connect it all together. From pitch 12 of El Corazon, we stayed on that route to a pitch before its A4 pitch (pitch 21)—from a free-climbing perspective it looked easier and more logical to traverse left into the cracks of Royal Flush. After a few pitches on Royal Flush, it then joins El Corazon to the top.

We climbed the entire route switching leads, with both of us free-climbing each pitch (no jumars). Our strategy was to climb nonstop to the summit so that the climbing would keep us warm through the night and we would not need to bring bivy gear. At 3 a.m. we stopped on a little ledge for a couple hours to melt some snow, down some warm liquids, and refuel.

The whole route is amazing, with mostly perfect cracks on a beautiful piece of rock. We were quite surprised that the ascent went as smoothly as it did. The route is very sustained in the 5.10–5.11 range, with a couple of 5.12 cruxes.

We encountered hundreds upon hundreds of meters of steel ladders on the Ferrari Route. It's a real mess and it was not enjoyable to climb around them. We tried to remove them but you would need cutters to cut through the steel cables. I got a small cut on my thumb while trying to remove them, and 24 hours later it got badly infected and swollen, requiring hard antibiotics and a week of rest. These ladders are ugly, they're garbage, and they really need to be removed!

NICOLAS FAVRESSE,
Belgium, AAC

Sean Villanueva (belaying) and Nico Favresse (seconding) on pitch 19 of El Corazon, during the team's onsight free ascent of the east face of Fitz Roy. *Paula Jones Volonte*

Aguja Desmochada, Circus Pets. At the beginning of February 2011, Peter Fasoldt, Carsten von Birckhahn, and I began a new route on the southeast face of Aguja Desmochada. Due to the bitter cold and our general slowness we only made it up six pitches before bailing. The climbing was great and we were psyched to give it another go when weather permitted.

About a week later, the weather cleared, and on February 9, we gave it another shot. Unfortunately, Carsten had to return home with his family, so Pete and I began the complicated approach from Camp Polacos at 1:00 a.m. This approach involves a lot of scrambling, a pitch of 5.10, and travel under a big, scary serac. Just before dawn, Pete started leading the 5.10 pitch in the dark. About halfway up, while mantling around a bulge, he pulled out a huge, loose block and both Pete and the stone came tumbling down. Pete smashed his head, broke his headlamp, and took some chunks out of his hand, elbow, knee, and butt. He was pretty shaken, but some Percocets helped him continue.

Aguja Desmochada from the east: (1) The Sound and the Fury (Sharratt-Wilkinson, 2006). (2) El Facón (Bowers-Bransby-Tresch, 2004). (3) CoDa (Kauffman-Wharton, 2011). (4) Circus Pets (Fasoldt-Simon, 2011). (5) Puerta Blanca (Huber-Walder, 2007) and (v) Haley-von Birckhahn variation. *Colin Haley*

The sun rose and we began climbing under blue skies. The route starts at a snow ledge about 30m below the huge, horizontal ledge that splits the first third of the tower's south face, and follows a major crack system for 13 long pitches. The climbing is great, on clean rock, and mostly in the mid-5.10 range. We climbed the entire route free except for two meters of ice-filled off-width on the last pitch. I'm sure it would easily go free at 5.11.

After a few summit shots, we descended the route. About halfway down, the wind picked up, and, in typical Patagonian style, our ropes got continuously stuck. After a cut rope and a bunch of gear left behind, we reached the base 12 hours after leaving the ground. We named the

Never mind the butt shot, look at those hand cracks! Peter Fasoldt on pitch 7 of Circus Pets. *Eli Simon*

route Circus Pets (600m, 5.10 A0), a play on the word Percocets.Those little pills proved to be the key to our success.

ELI SIMON, *AAC*

Aguja Desmochada, CoDa. In mid-February 2011, Neil Kauffman and I climbed a new route on Aguja Desmochada. After climbing the first five pitches of Golden Eagle we traversed right for 500', below the south face, to a point just right of the obvious overhanging pillar that flanks the wall's right side. From here we climbed seven new pitches in mostly steep, right-facing corners, before gaining the lower-angled slabs above, and traversing back left to Golden Eagle's finish. The route is relatively high quality (all routes on Desmochada have a bit of "ball-bearing rock"), and would be a worthy candidate for repeat ascents. I named the climb CoDa (V 5.12- A0), which means the end of a musical movement, and honors my dear friends Jonny Copp and Micah Dash.

JOSH WHARTON, *AAC*

The Wave Effect (Desmochada, De la Silla, Fitz Roy enchainment). One tower at a time, Nate Opp, Josh Wharton, and I wanted to do it right. The Wave Effect started with Aguja Desmochada. We linked parts of two different routes: the original Bridwell line, El Condor, and the Huber route, Golden Eagle. The key was freeing the A2 pitch on El Condor, which went at 5.12+, using the rivet and bolt Bridwell placed on the original ascent. We called our free line The Brass Parrot.

Atop Desmochada, as with every summit, the bivy was the main concern. With some work we'd carve little spots for the three of us to cram into our two-man tent with one sleeping bag. We compromised comfort for the ability to travel extremely light. Also, between every tower was extremely exposed ice and snow. We had crampons, and the leader took our single ice tool, while the two followers carried sharp rocks—not ideal, but light.

Next was the rarely climbed Aguja de la Silla. Not totally sure where we were going, we picked the path of least resistance and established an independent new line, Vertical Current, that climbed to the notch between Silla and Fitz Roy. From the notch we followed the original East Ridge route to the summit. Major clouds had built up, making for poor visibility that would stay with us for the remainder of our enchainment. Ours was the fourth ascent of the tower.

After the summit of de la Silla we crossed the notch to the shoulder of Fitz Roy and bivied below the California Route. Spirits were high as we finished the last of our dinners and left just enough gas to make water in the morning.

We woke in a total white out, but thankfully dead still—in Patagonia, a rare and fair trade for visibility. Following our noses and old piton anchors, we made a five-hour ascent of the California Route. We were climbing together on one rope, moving fast, with no idea where we were, when suddenly Josh yelled, "Cumbre!" We had just completed The Wave Effect (1,900m, 5.12+ (leader freeing every pitch), February 20–22, 2011).

On the final morning, we had been without real food for 24 hours; nobody complained. It was one of the most beautiful mornings I have ever seen. An inversion left a blanket of clouds below

Josh Wharton leading the upper pitches of Golden Eagle, on Aguja Desmochada, during the Wave Effect. Whit Magro belaying. *Nate Opp*

us and only giant towers poking up all around. Before starting up Fitz Roy we just stood there, warming in the sun like lizards.

WHIT MAGRO, *Bozeman, Montana*

Cerro Moyano, correction. In the 2009 *AAJ*, pp. 209–210, Robert Koschitzki reported our climbing what we thought was a new variation on Cerro Moyano. Now, after personal contact with Héctor Cuiñas, a member of the Argentine 1976 first ascent party, we have learned that our route is not a variation of the Argentine Route, but a completely independent one. [The Argentine Route ascends a gully on the left side of the north face (barely visible on the shaded north face in the inset photo in *AAJ 2009*), then the northeast ridge to the summit—Ed.]

MARKUS KAUTZ, *Germany*

Francisco Parada climbing the third pitch of the east face of Torre Norte. *Felipe Gonzalez Donoso*

TORRES DEL PAINE

Torre Norte, east face, attempt. Felipe Gonzalez Donoso and I, both from Chile, climbed on the east face of Torre Norte in Torres del Paine National Park in January and February 2009. We climbed all new territory, following three main dihedrals and then through a large overhanging section in the upper wall. We climbed for 11 days with one three-day stop for bad weather. Most of the climbing was icy, forcing us to aid a lot of pitches. Atop pitch 5 we camped for ten nights, as this was the only natural refuge on the wall, protecting us from frequent rockfall. One day we fixed ropes to the top of pitch 8, with plans to try an alpine attack from there to the summit. The next day we climbed for 15 hours in bad weather and darkness, with snow on our climbing shoes and cold in our bones. We opened another seven pitches before stopping, almost at dawn, perhaps 150m or 200m below the summit. We descended, not knowing if we would have time or the conditions for another attempt.

We returned in summer 2010 with the same plan in mind, but I was sick on the only day it didn't rain. Felipe tried alone, but was turned back by constant ice and rockfall. Afterward, during bad weather, we retrieved our gear. We had climbed about 800m, up to 5.11 and A2+, and left bolt anchors until pitch 13. It was a great learning experience, not only of making a big wall route in Patagonia, but how to survive it.

FRANCISCO PARADA, *Chile, AAC*

The Chilean attempt on the east face of Torre Norte. A 1993 French route (Bernard-Cayrol-Fabre-Giot-Petitjean) runs fairly parallel and just right of this line, continuing to the summit. *Francisco Parada*

Antarctica

The online version of these reports frequently contains additional photos, maps, topos, and extended text. Please visit aaj.americanalpineclub.org

All ascents reported took place in the 2010–11 season, unless otherwise stated. In the summaries, Damien Gildea acknowledges contributions from Alex Abramov, Dana Coffield, Kip Garre, Bob Headland, Rajiv Joshi, Gary Kuehn, Colin Monteath, Victor Saunders, Phil Wickens, and Scott Woolums.

ELLSWORTH MOUNTAINS

Vinson Massif summary. It was another busy season on Vinson (4,892 m) with 183 people successfully climbing the mountain. Repeat ascents took the total number of summits to exactly 200. Among those successful were two 16-year-olds: George Atkinson (UK) and Crina Popescu (Romania). After descending to Base Camp a number of climbers were stuck for several days due to bad weather; their February 1 flight out was the latest that climbers have left the mountain for many years.

There were several notable ascents. The first was by Dana Coffield, Jocelyn Dufour, and Brent Manning. This group went up the right-hand side of the West Face Ice Stream, a repeat of a combination of three existing routes that had first been linked by Slovenians in 1997. The three initially climbed the route taken in 1995 by Spanish climbers, who made the first ascent of the rocky shoulder now known as Asturias Peak. They then crossed up and left to join Heavenly Father, climbed in 1993 by Jo Bentley and Jay Smith, before continuing across flat terrain at the top of the ice stream, and finally up to the summit of Vinson. The trio placed two camps on the route before finishing up the southwest ridge of the summit pyramid. This last section had been climbed in 1999 by Conrad Anker after his solo, single-push first ascent of the full west ridge.

Another interesting ascent, in the dying days of the season, was a new route on the northern section of the west face by climbers from France's Groupe Militaire de Haute Montagne (GMHM). The main rocky part of this face was first climbed in December 2007 by Maria "Pachi" Ibarra and Jarmila Tyrril via a 1,200m line on steep snow and rock that they named the Chilena-Slovak Route. On January 28 Sébastian Bohin and Marion Poitevin put up a new line left of the Chilena-Slovak Route. Their climb involved steep snow, moderate mixed terrain, and was named Tack-Tack, in tribute to a friend who had helped with the expedition.

A further piece of new climbing was the first full ascent of the north ridge of Branscomb Peak. This summit sits at the apex of the main west face of Vinson, overlooking the Branscomb Glacier. It was named in 2006 by the USGS during publication of the Omega Foundation's map *Vinson Massif & The Sentinel Range*. It was first traversed in 1992 by Roger Mear and Martin Hood on their descent from Vinson's summit, and in 2004 was climbed via a couple of different routes on its eastern and southern sides, by diverting from the normal route to Vinson's main summit. In recent years ALE personnel had ventured up its north ridge from High Camp, but none had continued all the way to the summit. On January 13 a British military group comprising Gordon Clark, Simon Hall, Rajiv Joshi,

(A) Mt. Shinn (4,660m). (B) Mt. Farrel. (C) Mt. Waldron (3,217m). (D) Mt. Havener. (E) Mt. Tuck (3,588m). (F) Schoening Peak (4,743m). (G) Mt. Vinson (4,892m). (H) Clinch Peak (4,841m). (I) Wahlstrom Peak (4,677m). (J) Hollister Peak (4,729m). (K) Silverstein Peak (4,790m). (L) Fukushima Peak (4,634m). (M) Asturias Peak. (N) Branscomb Peak (4,520m). (O) Knutzen Peak (3,373m). (HC) High Camp (2007–). (SC) Shinn Camp (formerly High Camp until 2007). (1) Vinson Normal Route (2007). (1a) Vinson Headwall Route (1966–2007). (2) Vinson West Ridge Integral (Anker, 1997). (3) Asturias Route (Alvarez-Huez, 1995). (3a) Slovenian Connection (Boi-Groselj-Klemenc-Voduake, 1997), repeated in 2011. (4) Heavenly Father (Bentley-Smith, 1993). (5) Ice Stream Right Side (Anker, 1998). (6) Rudi's Runway (Lang, 1991). (7) Banana Friendship Gully (Vidal, 2004). (8) Purple Haze (Morton-Passy, 2005). (9) Conjugant Gradients (Brown, 2006). (10) Linear Accelerator (Smith, 1993). (11) Chilena-Slovak Route (Paz Ibarra-Tyrril, 2007). (12) Smith descent route from 10. (13) Gildea Route (Gildea, 2006). (14) Ruta Galfria (Lagos-Vidal, 2004). (15) Vinson Original Route (1966–1993, variants to col). (16) Hahn Route (Hahn, mid 1990s). (17) Sol de Media Noche (Paz Ibarra-Rada, 2006). (18) Shinn Normal Route (Corbet-Hollister-Silverstein-Wahlstrom, 1966). (19) Shinn southwest face (unknown). (20) Chouinard Route (Chouinard, 1985). (21) Shinn southeast ridge (Monteath-Mortimer, 1988). (22) Pt. 3,692m from Goodge Col. (23) Hubert Route (Garcia-Hubert-Joris, 2003). (24) Knutzen Normal Route (unknown). (25) Knutzen north face (unknown but climbed ca 2007 by Paz Ibarra and Tyrril). (26) Tack-Tack (Bohin-Poitevin, 2011). *USGS/Damien Gildea*

and James Lancashire pushed up the ridge and reached the summit, finding the edge quite corniced in places.

Mount Shinn (4,660m), the continent's third highest mountain, also saw a significant repeat this year, when two ALE guides made the second ascent of the elegant southeast ridge. This narrow line forms the right-hand skyline of Shinn as commonly seen from Vinson, rising above Goodge Col. It was first climbed in 1988 by the New Zealand-Australian team of Colin Monteath and Greg Mortimer.

Damien Gildea, *Australia*

HERITAGE RANGE

Union Glacier, various ascents. This was the first full season of operations at ALE's new camp on the south side of the Union Glacier. Situated in the southern Heritage Range, itself the southern section of the Ellsworth Mountains, the camp is much closer to a multitude of climbing objectives than the old camp at Patriot Hills, 60km further south. This section of the Heritage was first visited in the summer of 1962–63 by various U.S. personnel, exploring and surveying the entire Ellsworth Mountains. Very little mountaineering was done in these early years, but in subsequent seasons some minor ascents were made during the course of work. The area was visited again in the mid-1970s by a Norwegian geological expedition with USAP support, and it is believed that members probably climbed a number of peaks.

ALE undertook a lengthy process to establish the suitability of the Union Glacier's blue ice for large

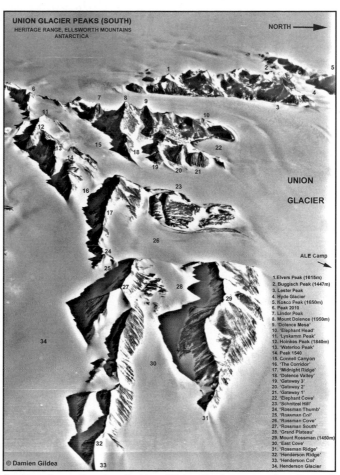

UNION GLACIER PEAKS (SOUTH)
HERITAGE RANGE, ELLSWORTH MOUNTAINS
ANTARCTICA

NORTH ⟶

UNION GLACIER

ALE Camp

1. Elvers Peak (1,615m)
2. Buggisch Peak (1447m)
3. Lester Peak
4. Hyde Glacier
5. Kosco Peak (1650m)
6. Peak 2010
7. Linder Peak
8. Mount Dolence (1950m)
9. 'Dolence Mesa'
10. 'Elephant Head'
11. 'Lyskamm Peak'
12. Hoinkes Peak (1840m)
13. 'Waterloo Peak'
14. Peak 1540
15. Connell Canyon
16. 'The Corridor'
17. 'Midnight Ridge'
18. 'Dolence Valley'
19. 'Gateway 3'
20. 'Gateway 2'
21. 'Gateway 1'
22. 'Elephant Cove'
23. 'Schnitzel Hill'
24. 'Rossman Thumb'
25. 'Rossman Col'
26. 'Rossman Cove'
27. 'Rossman South'
28. 'Grand Plateau'
29. Mount Rossman (1460m)
30. 'East Cove'
31. 'Rossman Ridge'
32. 'Henderson Ridge'
33. 'Henderson Col'
34. Henderson Glacier

© Damien Gildea

Peaks on the west and south sides of Union Glacier, as seen from the east. (1) Elvers Peak (1,615m). (2) Buggisch Peak (1,447m). (3) Lester Peak. (4) Hyde Glacier. (5) Kosco Peak (1,650m). (6) Peak 2010m. (7) Linder Peak. (8) Mount Dolence (1,950m). (9) Dolence Mesa. (10) Elephant Head. (11) Lyskamm Peak. (12) Hoinkes Peak (1,840m). (13) Waterloo Peak. (14) Peak 1540m. (15) Connell Canyon. (16) The Corridor. (17) Midnight Ridge. (18) Dolence Valley. (19) Gateway III. (20) Gateway II. (21) Gateway I. (22) Elephant Cove. (23) Schnitzel Hill. (24) Rossman Thumb. (25) Rossman Col. (26) Rossman Cove. (27) Rossman South. (28) Grand Plateau. (29) Mt. Rossman (1,450m). (30) East Cove. (31) Rossman Ridge. (32) Henderson Ridge. (33) Henderson Col. (34) Henderson Glacier. Many of these names are unofficial. *Supplied by Damien Gildea*

aircraft landing and ground operations. This required permissions and inspections from various governmental authorities. Some clients operated from the base in the 2009–10 season, but in the recent summer all clients and expeditions used the new facilities, which are reportedly a significant upgrade over the Patriot Hills camp, versions of which ran every summer from 1986–2010. At the new camp,

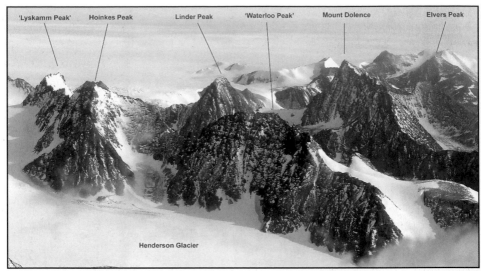

'Lyskamm Peak'   Hoinkes Peak   Linder Peak   'Waterloo Peak'   Mount Dolence   Elvers Peak

Henderson Glacier

Looking west-northwest at the Hoinkes and Dolence groups. Peaks behind Elvers remain unnamed and unclimbed. *Damien Gildea*

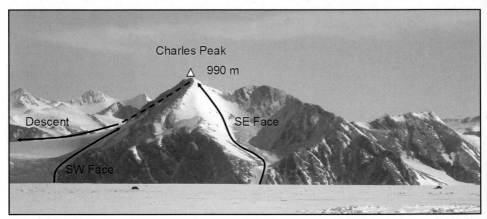

Charles Peak
△ 990 m

Descent   SE Face

SW Face

Charles Peak from the south. Southwest face was climbed on January 15, 2011 by Dufour and Manning following a 50° snow/ice line on the right side of the icefall. Southeast face was soloed on the 19th by Dana Coffield (50° snow). Neither route is necessarily new. *Dana Coffield*

tracked vehicles are used more extensively for client transportation, including access to nearby peaks, thereby enabling enjoyable day climbs.

The peaks on the south side of the glacier had been visited by ALE guides and clients in the 2009–10 season, but last summer teams made more substantial climbs. The main feature is Mt. Dolence (1,950m), a large peak on the western side of Connell Canyon, a southern tributary of the Union Glacier. On January 7 the Swiss guide Kaus Tscherrig and client Markus Ineichen made its first ascent. In a 16-hour round trip from a drop-off point near the feature unofficially known as Elephant Head, this pair climbed a 1,200m mixed route on the rocky north face.

Just to the south of Dolence is a shorter but very impressive rocky spire, Linder Peak. Prolific British guide Victor Saunders and client Nick Wilkinson bagged the first ascent on January 11,

North face of Lyskamm with Hoinkes off picture to left. Dana Coffield and Jocelyn Dufour took the direct route to the summit to make the first ascent. Their descent route traversed the ridge left as marked. *Dana Coffield*

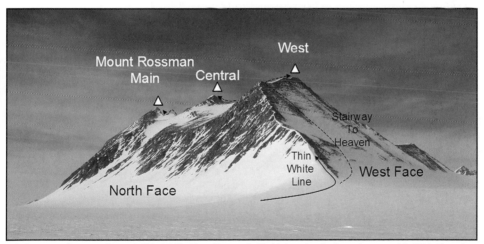

Mt. Rossman from northwest. Thin White Line (Dana Coffield-Jocelyn Dufour, January 14, 2011. They traversed all three peaks of Rossman). Stairway to Heaven (Browning-Chapman-Herschke-Jewell-Sahney-Snyder-Tejas, January 10, 2011). *Dana Coffield*

climbing easy but loose rock on the north ridge before passing through a steeper rock band and out onto the west face to reach the top (Tower of Winds, AD).

East across Connell Canyon lies a chain of summits, the highest being the unclimbed Hoinkes Peak (1,890m). Northeast of Hoinkes is a slightly lower summit of 1,850m that Saunders and Wilkinson climbed on the 14th via the north face (AD) in a round trip of nine hours from their tent, giving it the unofficial name Waterloo Peak. West of Hoinkes, jutting into the head of Connell Canyon, is an attractive snow face leading to a rocky summit. On the 17th, during a three-day round-trip from the ALE camp, Dana Coffield

Rossman West from the north. All routes marked were climbed during January 2011, but some were not necessarily first ascents. (1) Thin White Line (Dana Coffield-Jocelyn Dufour, January 14). (2) Gratitude (PD, Caroline George-Dominic Jude-Richard Parks-Victor Saunders-Nick Wilkinson, January 21). (3) Route du Jour (PD, Caroline George-Gavin Melgaard-Victor Saunders-Nick Wilkinson, January 23). (4) White Spider (Morgan Bati-Jim Diani-Aaron Mainer-Paul Niel, January 19). (5) Swiss Couloir (Mark Ineichen-Klaus Tscherrig, January 18). (6) Let's Strike (Mark Incichen-Klaus Tscherrig, January 13). (7) The Ilyusionist (AD, Dominic Jude-Victor Saunders-Nick Wilkinson, January 20). (8) Diagon Alley (AD, Caroline George-Victor Saunders-Nick Wilkinson, January 22). (9) Blind Faith (Lisa Amatangel-Aaron Mainer-Paul Niel, January 13). (10) The Triangle Route (PD, Dominic Jude-Victor Saunders-Nick Wilkinson, January 7). *Victor Saunders*

and Jocelyn Dufour made its first ascent via a direct route up the north face (snow and ice to 60°). The duo named it Lyskamm Peak after its more famous Swiss likeness. They descended by traversing the spectacular rocky ridge back east to below Hoinkes Peak, then going north down an intervening gully.

However, this season it was Mt. Rossman that received the most attention. Rossman is an elongated massif with three obvious summits, the eastern one being the highest. The north face of Rossman overlooks the new ALE camp and provides an accessible venue for short, moderate climbs. Due to weather and flight delays this season, an unusually large number of climbers were stuck in camp for some time. They generally made the most of the situation. Many ascents of Rossman were completed, including several new routes. Most of the lines were a combination of steep couloirs and slopes of snow and ice, though on occasions there were sections of moderate climbing on poor-quality rock. The western buttress of Rossman forms a triangular rock face less than an hour on foot from the camp. This aspect of the peak was particularly popular (see accompanying photodiagram); five different lines were climbed by the Saunders party alone.

Charles Peak (990m) is an obvious objective on the north side of the Union Glacier. It gives good views of the surrounding area, is easily accessed by vehicles from the ALE camp, and has an ALE VHF repeater unit on the summit. The smaller summit west of Charles was used as a USGS

North Face of Central Summit of Mt. Rossman. Marked routes were climbed during the 2010-11 season, but were not all necessarily first ascents. (1) Unnamed (Lisa Amatangel-Jim Diani-Aaron Mainer-Paul Niel, January 12). (2) Warm Up (Mark Ineichen-Klaus Tscherrig, December 30). (3) Rockafella (Philip Herschke-Vik Sahney, January 12). (4) Moonwalker (Philippe Herschke-Vik Sahney, January 17). (5) Ilyushin Fields (Kent Harvey-Jake Norton, January 23) Unmarked central couloir used for descent. *Victor Saunders*

survey station in the mid-1960s, and there is a good chance the main summit of Charles was reached in the 1960s and/or '70s. The peak received dozens of ascents this season, mostly via easy routes, though with some variations.

On the south side of the Union Glacier, west of Rossman, and north of Mt. Dolence at the mouth of Connell Canyon, three small summits, named the Gateway peaks, also received their first ascents this season. Gateway I (by the Lily Couloir, PD) and II (by the north ridge, F) were climbed on January 9 by Dominic Jude, Saunders, and Wilkinson in a five-hour round trip from the so-called Elephant Cove. On the 15th, Saunders and Wilkinson climbed Gateway III by the KFC Couloir at AD.

In behind the Rossman massif are a number of lower peaks that were visited in 2009–10, but last season one notable feature received its first ascent. On the 17th, American guide Caroline George, along with Jude, Saunders, and Wilkinson, made a 10-hour round trip from the Union Glacier camp to climb the east ridge of Midnight Peak at AD.

Early in the season a team from the UK-based Fuchs Foundation hauled sleds northeast across the Union Glacier toward the Nimbus Hills, where they planned to conduct scientific studies and ascend small peaks. On November 27, partway through this journey, they climbed the highest point of Buchanan Hills (ca 1,100m), and two days later a slightly lower peak. On December 1 they reported climbing a peak of 1,494m, and then reaching another summit, before continuing north through a pass west of Mt. Capley (1,830m) the next day. Poor weather, then high winds, kept them tent-bound for several days in the upper Flanagan Glacier.

Eventually they were able to cross back south via a high pass between Mt. Sporli and Ronald Ridge. The team encountered bad sastrugi on the lower Driscoll Glacier but climbed Charles Peak on December 13 before returning to the ALE camp next day.

DAMIEN GILDEA, *Australia*

MARIE BYRD LAND
EXECUTIVE COMMITTEE RANGE

Mt. Sidley (4,285m). Nowadays, any climbing expedition to inland Antarctica, outside the Ellsworths, is significant. Mt. Sidley, highest peak in the Executive Committee Range, and highest volcano in Antarctica, was first climbed on January 11, 1990 by Bill Atkinson (NZ), who worked as field assistant for a team of vulcanologists studying the area. They also ascended nearby Mt. Waesche, mostly on snowmobiles. Atkinson climbed from a camp at 2,380m on the west side of Sidley, reaching, in poor visibility, what he ascertained to be the highest point on the crater rim.

In January 2011 an ALE team made the first non-government ascent. Mike Sharp and Scott Woolums, with Alex Abramov, Mario Trimeri, and Crina Popescu, flew from Union Glacier to the flat ice near Sidley, landing ca 16km from the summit. They then skied for seven hours and made camp on the mountain. The next day, January 24, all but Sharp climbed over sections of soft snow and blue ice to the crater rim. It turned out to be a 13-hour day, as the party continued around the rim, first crossing one top, which they thought was the highest, but later discovering another a few meters higher. They found the terrain quite unusual and ephemeral with snow features along the rim seemingly formed by the mountain's thermal activity and then sculpted by the wind. Popescu and Trimeri became the first climbers to attain what they have termed the Seven Volcanic Summits: the highest volcano on each continent.

DAMIEN GILDEA, *Australia*

ANTARCTIC PENINSULA

Overview. The first team to visit the Peninsula during the season comprised Sergy Baranov, Rissa Bullock Ivory, Kris Erickson, Kip Garre, Nickolay Veselovskiy, Doug Stoop and Ilyas Mukhtarov. Traveling aboard *Australis*, skippered by Roger Wallis, their first successes were the summits of both Delaite and Emma islands, which they climbed and skied. On the latter, an attractively steep, small island peak, their initial route was up the short, steep north face; but afterward, while skiing couloirs on the eastern flank, they saw that sea ice had come in, forcing the yacht to move. Though they were able to reach the boat by Zodiac, it is a reminder of one of the unique objective hazards of climbing in this region.

After spending three days skiing lines on and around the popular Jabet Peak, and being stopped from entering Lemaire Channel due to thick ice conditions, they headed back to Paradise Harbor and skied lines on the north side of Bryde Island, above Alvaro Cove. Later, they headed to Lemaire Island, where they climbed and skied Rojas Peak—at first down the east side, and then south, right down to the water. From here they moved to the western side of Wiencke Island, where they repeated the steep, north-facing line on Noble Peak (720m) skied once previously by Erickson. Noble Peak was first climbed in 1948, six months after Jabet, and has been visited a number of times since. On November 27 they were forced to abandon attempts at skiing on Lion Island, but this resulted in one of the best descents of their trip, when as an alternative they climbed and skied a large couloir on the east side of Ronge Island, between Sherlac and Kerr points. Later that same day they skied more lines on Sable Pinnacle, up the coast of Ronge Island opposite Cuverville Island. Unfortunately, Garre was killed skiing in California's Sierra Nevada in late April 2011.

The season on the Peninsula continued with the ambitious Alpine Club Antarctic Expedition sailing aboard Spirit of Sydney (see below). This expedition brought to light one of the significant errors on the 1:250,000 British Antarctic Survey (BAS) map *Brabant Island to Argentine Islands,* published in 2009. The obvious and popular Mt. Shackleton is unnamed, and instead the name "Mt Shackleton 1300" is placed on another peak to the northeast, further up the Wiggins Glacier. Recent visitors to the area have taken to calling this latter peak "False Shackleton." Ludovic Challeat's French team made its first known ascent in January 2010. On December 4 the AC team made the second known ascent. Their GPS showed 1,475m on the summit of this peak, for which they have proposed the name Mt. Faraday. A little later, finding good conditions, Jim Blyth's party ascended and descended this peak on skis—three times (see Blyth report below).

Despite the increase and success in recent years of yacht-based expeditions to Antarctica, sailing remains a serious mode of transport for these regions. In February 2011 the Norwegian yacht Berserk was lost with its three crew during a severe storm in the Ross Sea. Some weeks previously the owner, Norwegian adventurer Jarle Andhøy, had been put ashore with 18-year-old Briton Samuel Massie, reportedly to attempt a crossing to the South Pole by quad-bike. February is extremely late in the season to be doing anything in inland Antarctica, much less anything near the South Pole. Ships usually aim to leave the Ross Sea by the third week in February due to ice conditions, and yachts generally do not go there at all, deeming it too dangerous.

Other private operators had advised Andhøy against this plan, but he chose to ignore them. He obtained no permits, despite needing to transfer quantities of fuel in a hazardous and sensitive environment, and he had no search and rescue logistics in place. Most nations are signatories to the Antarctic Treaty and its associated Environmental Protocol, and most of those nations have domestic legislation that applies to their citizens in Antarctica.

Andhøy and Massie had to be evacuated to Christchurch on a U.S. government flight. Private expeditions to Antarctica have long walked a delicate line, drawn and monitored by the relevant governments operating in the area. On occasion, relations between the two have been severely tested. Poorly planned and executed ventures, such as Andhøy's, jeopardize access to Antarctica for all non-government people, and provide authorities with easy examples of why private expeditions, including those of climbers, should be banned. Most adventurers applaud risk-taking, rule-bending, and plans that seem a little crazy, and we all want to think we can venture into the wild without government interference. But when we court publicity, involve media, and activate rescue beacons, we bring others into our plans, and we should act accordingly.

2010 saw the passing of Lieutenant Commander Malcolm Burley, who died aged 82. In 1964 he made the first ascent of South Georgia's highest summit, Mt. Paget, one of the world's most elusive peaks.

DAMIEN GILDEA, *Australia*

Various ascents. The 2010 Alpine Club expedition set sail on November 25 from Tierra del Fuego aboard the Australian yacht *Spirit of Sydney,* skippered by Darrel Day and Cath Hew. On board were seven climbers: Derek Buckle, Mike Fletcher, Stu Gallagher, Richard MacIntyre, Olly Metherell, Dave Wynne-Jones, and me as leader.

Derek Buckle on the summit of Cloos with (A) False Shackleton, (B) Mt. Peary, and (C) Mt. Shackleton.
Phil Wickens

False Shackleton from the northwest, showing the route up the north face and east ridge. *Phil Wickens*

During the course of my work I had become very familiar with the mountains of the Peninsula, and had come to suspect that several were significantly higher than marked on official maps. The most prominent of these, named Mt. Matin by Charcot after the Swiss newspaper, dominates the southern skyline of Flandres Bay and appears much higher than all other peaks to the east of Lemaire Channel. We made landfall at the southern tip of Anvers Island and, after making a quick ascent of the popular Jabet Peak (552m) above Port Lockroy (southwest face and south ridge, PD), sailed into the Lemaire Channel. Immediately to the north of its narrowest point is Deloncle Bay, where we landed and followed steep but relatively crevasse-free slopes to the Hotine Glacier. We established our main camp at 850m, below the pyramidal Mt. Nygren, and the rumbling southwest face of Mt. Matin.

December 3 was overcast, and we headed up the east ridge of Nygren (1,454m, all altitudes in this report are the average of readings recorded by two GPS and one altimeter), which was not threatened by seracs. A broad snow slope gradually steepened and narrowed to form an elegant snaking ridge, which we followed past several large cornices to reach the small conical summit (AD-). Next morning the clouds were more broken, so we skied southward across Leay Glacier to reach the north face of what is erroneously marked on the map as Mt. Shackleton. Starting up the face, we crossed several large crevasses before the slope steepened to 60° and led to the broad east ridge, a giant whale-back rising to the summit. There the clouds occasionally parted to reveal amazing views of Nygren, Matin, and the Wiggins Glacier. This was the probable second ascent of "False Shackleton" (1,476m, AD+), but by a new line. We have submitted a new name, Mt. Faraday, to the UK Antarctic Place-names Committee, to commemorate the former British base (where the ozone hole was first discovered).

Matin from Flandres Bay to the north. The line of first ascent came from the far side to reach the right-hand ridge. *Phil Wickens*

Cloos from the Lemaire Channel to the northwest, showing the main summit (left) and south summit (far right). The first ascensionists approached from the opposite side and followed snow slopes to the snow shoulder on left, then up the left skyline ridge. *Phil Wickens*

From our camp, Matin seemed to rise in two distinct steps. An early foray up the south-west ridge, just after we first arrived, had taken us to a slightly higher altitude than the summit height as marked on the map. However, the peak had continued far above. On the 5th, with skies now devoid of both wind and cloud, we headed back up the southwest ridge, quickly reaching our previous high point. The rounded summit looked deceptively close, but the broad ridge continued on. What seemed like another 300m became 1,000m. When the ridge ended, we headed up the summit dome, which was frosted with rime ice. From the 2,415m top, in bitter cold, the view was breathtaking, with the mountains of the Peninsula extending in all directions. All but the highest peaks of Brabant and Anvers Islands were below us. The route was PD, and the descent back to camp gave over 1,400m of sensational skiing. The next day we relocated camp five miles to the west at the base of Mt. Cloos. This twin-sum-mited peak forms the dramatic east wall of the

Fletcher and Metherell preparing to pass the serac on the steep, upper east face of Cloos. *Phil Wickens*

Fletcher, MacIntyre, and Wynne-Jones high on the north face of Mt. Inverleith, with Dallmeyer Peak behind. In the far distance is Mt. Francais on Anvers Island. *Phil Wickens*

West side of Nygren from Deloncle Bay. On the first ascent the climbers crossed the Hotine Glacier from right to left immediately in front of the peak, placed a camp at the end of the east ridge (left skyline), and the next day followed the ridge to the summit. This peak was named after Rear Admiral Nygren, who in 1970 was Director of the National Oceanic and Atmospheric Administration Corps. *Phil Wickens*

Inverleith from the east, showing the line of first ascent. Inverleith was first charted and named Inverleith Hill by a Scottish geologist in 1913–14. *Phil Wickens*

Lemaire Channel and had dominated our view since we arrived. The east side appeared straightforward, except for the top 300m, where a line of very steep and active seracs blocked access to the main top.

After a day of poor weather the sky again cleared and, although strong katabatic winds buffeted the tents, we headed out on the 8th and were soon above the wind. We reached the lower, south summit (935m, F) without difficulty, but the main top was blocked from this direction by large crevasses and ice cliffs. After climbing another high point between south and main tops, we headed east of the summit mass. Between the cliffs and the north face was an ice slope that led past the seracs. Although it was initially threatened, we were soon to the side of the seracs, and the climbing was enjoyable. A large wall of gently overhanging ice capped the slope, but a narrow ice chimney led around the steep terrain and onto gentler summit slopes (D+). We reached the 1,200m main top in afternoon sunlight and were visible to Cath and Darrel on the yacht in Pleneau Bay.

Having climbed all the major summits surrounding the Hotine Glacier, we arranged a pick-up the following morning. During our second night in Pleneau Bay, heavy brash-ice moved in from the south, and we had an exciting few hours working our way out to open water. Since it was too risky to remain near the ice, we sailed to Paradise Harbor to sit out bad weather.

High above Paradise Harbor stands the huge mass of Mt. Inverleith. Marked at 2,038m on maps, it is one of the highest Peninsula peaks north of the Antarctic Circle and remained unclimbed. It is difficult and dangerous to access from Paradise Harbor, so as the weather started to clear, we sailed into Andvord Bay and were set ashore in high winds at Steinheil Point. After weaving through a broken icefall, four of us skied up snow slopes in search of somewhere sheltered to camp. We eventually tucked ourselves behind a sharp spur at 600m, protected from katabatic blasts.

Thankfully the winds dwindled overnight, allowing us to start early on the 14th. We zig-zagged around enormous crevasses to a col, from which there was a direct descent to Paradise Harbor. The slope above was broken with crevasses and seracs, but a safe line led through them all and gave interesting climbing that included steep steps and tenuous snow bridges. We reached a shoulder high on the north ridge of Inverleith, the main difficulties below us but the summit still several kilometers away across endless slopes of breakable crust. It took forever, but we finally stood on top (AD+). Beyond lay the rolling tops of the Peninsula and Forbidden Plateau, the dramatic granite cliffs of Mt. Theodore, and a sea of mountains all the way to Deception Island. Beyond them all stretched the Drake Passage, across which, after a day's rest, we would return to Argentina.

PHIL WICKENS, *Alpine Club, UK*

Various ski descents. We demanded a lot from Stephen Wilkins, Australian owner and skipper of the yacht *Xplore*, which delivered us to the Peninsula. It was not just the quantities of food and drink we consumed, but also the number of drop-offs and pick-ups we requested. The weather proved so good that we had several days with multiple ski objectives.

The "we" were Dave Baldwin, Trevor Craig, Steve Day, and Martin Vince from England, Bethan Davies from Wales, Scott Stephenson from the U.S., and IFMGA guides Gary Kuehn, an American living in New Zealand, and me, a Scot living in France.

I mention the people first, as our experience in Antarctica was above all a human one; an experience shared by a group of exceptional people. The memories we took with us are as much about our friends as the place itself. We set off with no fixed objectives, and little idea as to what we wanted to do. Our idea was to discover the place with our own eyes and ski what was good. We couldn't have had it better.

Our first tracks were made just after New Year on Wiencke Island in the murk. We then made a 26km approach to establish base camp for an attempt on Mt. Français (2,825m) over Mt. Agamemnon, a superb ski mountaineering objective. Our high point was around 1,100m on Agamemnon. We turned back because the weather was slowly deteriorating and we were "only another six-eight hours from the top." Striking camp, we returned along our tracks in a whiteout. Reaching Francais over Agamemnon is long. Parties should count on 30km each way with pulks, a rest day, and then will need one or preferably two more days of good weather. We saw no crevassing after we left the shore.

From January 9 until we left on the 20th, the weather was generally sunny with clear skies and no wind. So many people have since commented on our luck. We skied lines on Booth Island, Mt. Scott in 30cm of fresh powder, and False Shackleton three times (and to both summits; 1,354m and

Gary Kuehn skiing Demaria, with Mt. Peary in the background. *Jim Blyth*

On the approach to Mt. Shackleton, with Mt. Cloos behind. Marked is the route followed to both south and main summits by the Alpine Club party a month prior to this photo being taken. *Jim Blyth*

Southwest face of Agamemnon. Skiing this face would need care, but descending the left skyline ridge would be easier and safer. *Jim Blyth*

1,336m. Measured heights in this report were taken from an altimeter set at sea level. BAS map height of False Shackleton is 1,300m). The highlight of the trip was arguably Demaria, followed by a traverse of Hovgaard Island. Sailing close to Bruce Island (320m) we simply had to ski it, and from the summit spotted that afternoon's fun: an ascent of 675m Mt. Banck. We later skied Rojas Peak (670m) on Lemaire Island, and a wonderful short run in the evening light on the south side of the main peak. Champagne on deck rounded off the day nicely.

The west summit of Mt. Hoegh (603m) gave a great run in rather flat light, and Nansen Island provided a nice little trip after a day motoring around looking for suitable objectives. There were lots of them; we just couldn't find acceptable drop-off points. Mt. Harris (1,030m) took three and a half hours to ascend and eight and a half minutes to ski. We then called *Xplore* for beers, which were delivered onshore by Zodiac along with two full-sized, home-made pizzas.

Setting foot on our last objective, Emma Island (465m), proved a challenge, as did its north face, ca 150m of 45° on snow that needed care. We set off that evening for home, with the Southern Ocean like a millpond, and whales putting on one final show. I am planning to return. If you would like details, visit jimblyth.com

JIM BLYTH, *France*

Turkey

The online version of these reports frequently contains additional photos, maps, topos, and extended text Please visit aaj.americanalpineclub.org

ALA DAGLAR

Cappadocia, Kizilin Baci (2,944m) northwest face, Red, Moon, and Star. Rolando had talked about Ala Daglar for a couple of years, both for its rock faces and his friends Recep and Zeynep Ince. This husband and wife team, engineers and climbers from Istanbul, were so in love with the place and its tranquility that they left everything behind and came to the Ala Daglar to climb and run a campsite. A couple of photos had captured my attention, so, slowly but surely, the idea to explore a new route up Kizilin Basi's northwest face began to form.

Accompanied by Recep, we reached the base of Kizilin Basi on October 1. The northwest face is a 400m, yellow, limestone wall, totally overhanging and extremely impressive from below. With so many smooth sections, there are few obvious lines. We looked for the easy within the difficult. Right from the outset, it was obvious that we understood each other; independently we picked the same line. Without wasting a minute we set off that same afternoon and before nightfall had finished the first two pitches: a 55m 7b followed by a 20m 6c. The latter was to become the easiest pitch on the entire route. Unfortunately, during the next days the temperatures plummeted to 3–4°C, and gusty winds forced us to climb with numerous layers of clothing.

Northwest face of Kizilin Baci and line of Red, Moon, and Star. *Rolando Larcher*

Our daily program began with the 5 a.m. alarm. This was followed by breakfast, a one-and-a-half hour approach to the wall, and then continuous climbing until the stars came out. We then rappelled the fixed ropes by headlamp, returned to camp, and ate a Turkish dinner of Kebab and Pide until we were stuffed. During those days the route name sprung to mind: Red for the color of the rock face, Moon that we saw as we set off each morning, and Star for the stars that accompanied us during our descent. All three are found on the Turkish flag. I have fond memories of those intense days, with their long immersions into climbing, and the exploration of friendship, wild nature, and endless landscapes. Eagles flew freely above us, and I vividly remember the voice of the muezzin who, from afar, called for prayer.

After Rolando established the difficult 9th pitch, the angle eased to vertical, and we realized that the greatest difficulties lay behind. We scrambled up another 60m and then reached the top of the pillar, exhausted and cold. We

Luca Giupponi on pitch six (50m, 7b+) of Red, Moon, and Star.
Recep Ince

took shelter behind a rock and stopped to listen to, and observe, the world around us. We were happy with life, and happy to have discovered all those holds to free climb such an overhanging face.

It then rained for several days, but we used the time for resting, and to visit Recep's crag, four kilometers along a dirt track from the campsite. We parked on a plain with no crag in sight, but after walking no more than five meters, a beautiful canyon unfolded beneath our feet. This was the Kazikli Valley, which now boasts 230 perfectly bolted routes, all put up by Recep.

When we returned to the route it was cold; one day it snowed, and we felt we were carrying out a winter ascent. On our penultimate day we set off, determined to play our last hand. Rolando had trouble at the start, but after warming up, his engine was able to climb well all the way to the summit. I began much better, sent the first pitches immediately, but used all my reserves rather quickly. Just before nightfall, in light rain, Rolando redpointed the final pitch first try, a terrible slab with a hard obligatory section of 7b. I failed to redpoint this pitch; time had run out for a second attempt, as had my energy.

Recep followed us up the entire route with his jumars, camera and video camera. By the time we all dragged ourselves to the car for the last time, we were exhausted yet warmed by an immense inner joy for having achieved, in extremis, our goal. Red, Moon, and Star (established ground-up, then redpointed in a day) gave nine pitches up to 8a/8a+, 7b obl.

We owe our success to the unconditional support given by Recep and Zeynep, and their fantastic, nourishing meals. The area has great rock faces, and peaks that reach an altitude of 3,800m. It is ideal for ski mountaineering too. I promised myself I'd return with my family.

LUCA GIUPPONI, *Italy, supplied by Rolando Larcher CAAI*

Rolando Larcher on pitch three (30m, 7c) of Red, Moon, and Star. *Recep Ince*

Northwest face of East Al Hamra tower. (1) Zizanie Chez les Fransaouis. (2) En attendant les Lents. (3) Les Becs de Gaz pissaient leur Flamme au clair de lune. *Christian Ravier*

Oman

Al Hamra Towers. On February 8, 2010, Philippe Hourcle, Luc Pauget, and I put up Les Becs de Gaz pissaient leur Flamme au clair de lune (180m, TD+, 6b+) on the East Al Hamra Tower. The towers lie in northeast Oman above the old town of Al Hamra and are reached by a steep 40-minute ascent (two kilometers) up scree slopes. The East and West towers are about one kilometer apart. Our new line is a fine little route on excellent rock to the right of Zizanie Chez les Fransaouis (230m, seven pitches, TD, mainly 5, 6b+ on 5th pitch, Bruzy-Salle, 2004), and crosses the "classic" of the tower, En attendant les Lents (275m, seven pitches, TD-, 6a with a final pitch crux, Thierry Renault, free solo, 2004. Renault came back a year later, repeated the route with Nathalie Hanriot, and equipped the belays).

CHRISTIAN RAVIER, *France*

Various ascents. In January 2009 Olivier Cantet, Régine Lemaire, and Emmanuel Ratouis put up five new routes, and made two new canyon descents, in various parts of Oman.

They first visited Tahab Canyon in the northeast of the country. Access is via the road to the coastal town of Fins. Just before Tiwi when coming from Qurayyat, leave the road and follow a piste across the Salmah Plateau toward Qurran. After 5.7km there is a piste on the left, which stops after 250m. This is a good bivouac spot. From here it is an awkward descent via an old Bedouin route into the canyon. On the 9th Lemaire and Ratouis put up the 200m Pancréatite Aigue, a fine route on excellent rock with an airy fifth pitch, traversing left above overhangs. The route is equipped and has six pitches (5b, 5a, 5a, 5c, 6a, and 5c), followed by 80m of 3+ to the top.

The team returned on the 18th, and all three climbers added Sans Foie, ni rate (280m), another fine climb on excellent rock, save for the start of the seventh pitch. Anchors are equipped for a rappel descent, a set of Friends is necessary, and the pitch grades are: 4c, 5b, 5a, 5a, 5a, 6a+, 5b, 6b, and 5a.

On the 13th the three French visited Wadi el Hemia (south of Sint) in the Western Hajar, not far from the well-known Jebel Kawr. The team climbed highly sculptured rock in an area of orange and gray slabs, completing the 180m L'esprit Ludique at 5c obl. Two bolts are visible at the start of the first ropelength, and pitch grades are 5c, 5c/6a, 5b, 5a, and 5a. Belays are equipped

High above the waters of Wadi Tiwi during the first ascent of En Attendant Allah. *Emmanuel Ratouis*

Sculptured rock architecture on the first pitch (5c) of En Attendant Allah in Wadi Tiwi. *Emmanuel Ratouis*

for a rappel descent, but it is easily possible to walk off left from the top. Take a good rack of Friends, as there are only a few bolts on each pitch.

On the 16th the team put up En Attendant Allah in Wadi Tiwi, approached from Mibam, again in the northeast of the country. This is a magnificent and varied route on excellent sculptured limestone, with the belays equipped for rappels, and one or two protection bolts per pitch (take full rack of Friends). There are nine pitches: 5c, 5c/6a, 4c, 5a, 5a, 5c, 5c, 4c in a tube then 6b, and 5c. Descend in eight ca 50m rappels.

Further northwest, and close to the border, lies Wadi Surwayh and the natural baths of As Suwayh. After parking in this village, it is a 30-minute walk via the aquaduct to the foot of Révélation (200m, five pitches, 5a, 5b, 5a, 5b, and 5c), put up by all three climbers on the 20th. The last two pitches are simply brilliant. Again, the belays are equipped but only a few protection bolts were placed.

In January 2010 Lamaire, Ratouis, and friends returned, but a serious car accident, which resulted in the vehicle exploding, equipment burnt, and one member seriously injured, curtailed activity. Later, Lemaire and Ratouis were generously lent gear by a British climber, which allowed them to complete one new route (and a new canyon descent). The new route was established in the Cirque d'Umq, 40 minutes approach (including three rappels) from the village of Umq and Al Majin cave, well west of Fins. Together with local Ali (upper pitches only), the two climbed Providence (250m, 10 pitches: 6a, 6b, 5a, 4c, 5b, 3c, 3c, 4c, 4c and 5a; 5c obl.). While not sustained, this is a very worthwhile route on excellent sculptured limestone in a wild cirque, and the first line climbed by Ali.

LINDSAY GRIFFIN, *Mountain INFO, from information provided by Emmanuel Ratouis*

Jabal Yiti, Hassal Hidn Pillar, Jabal Kawr-Kawr Tower, Mawal Needle, Jabal Awi, various ascents. Drawn by an exotic fascination with the Arabian Peninsula, Roberto Masia and I left Sardinia on December 23. Our idea was to explore the central part of the Hajar and look at Jabal Misht's interesting walls. Unfortunately, Alitalia lost one of our rucksacks, which included two ropes, a hammer and pitons, some bolts, part of our rack, climbing shoes, a harness, and helmet. While waiting for this to arrive, we looked at areas closer to Muscat, and 50km south along the coast, near the village of Yiti, we found an interesting formation with an altitude of 140m, situated between two wadis. We tried to find its name by asking locals, but in return we only received big smiles, so we named it Jabal Yiti. In the wadi below the west face (23°31.2007' N, 58°39.7108' E), only accessible to 4X4 vehicles, there is a hot spring, in which

Hassal Hidn Pillar, with Pioneers Route (left) and No Wings to Fly. *Marco Marrosu*

Jabal Yiti east face. From left to right; South Ridge, Quattro Mori, and Cercatori d'oro. *Marco Marrosu*

Jabal Yiti west face. From left to right; descent route, Spigolo Ovest, La Fessurona, and South Ridge. *Marco Marrosu*

we swam after our climbs. Low on gear but with a lot of enthusiasm, we climbed on a single rope, used a sling for a harness, a stone from the river as a hammer, a bandana stuffed with clothes and an empty carton as a helmet, and the second climbed in trekking shoes. We found no sign of previous passage on all the routes we completed during our stay, and painted a small red arrow at the start of each. The total amount of climbing, rather than vertical interval, is quoted for each route.

On the west face of Jabal Yiti we climbed Spigolo Ovest (200m, four pitches, UIAA V+), and La Fessurona (120m, V-), both on December 29. The same day we also added South Ridge (105m, two pitches, V+). On the east face, above Wadi Yiti, we climbed Quattro Mori (150m, three pitches, V+) on the 30th, and Cercatori d'oro (145m, four pitches, V-) on the 31st.

Prior to these ascents we had climbed two routes on a pillar that lies on the left side of the unnamed wadi used to access the west face of Jabal Yiti. We named this formation Hassal Hidn Pillar (23°31.0674' N, 58°39.1483' E). On the 26th we climbed Pioneers Route (200m, four pitches,

Kawr Tower, west-northwest face. (1) Sardinian Shortcut. (2) Queen of Sheba (incorrectly marked in AAJ 2010). (3) Wadi Girls (500m, VI, Barlow-Nonis, 1999). Sardinian Shortcut has at least 450m of independent climbing, differing from Queen of Sheba in the first four and at least the last four pitches. *Marco Marrosu*

IV+), and the following day added No Wings to Fly (195m, four pitches, VI-), which starts 50m to the right. The rock in this area is reasonably good (it looks like dolomite), and the east face of Jabal Yiti is particularly fine, offering middle-grade routes of rare beauty.

On January 1, 2011, we were reunited with our missing rucksack and able to head for the Hajar mountains. From the road we saw Jabal Kawr; the west-northwest face of Kawr Tower immediately exerted its magnetism. We slept the night near it. The next day we set off for what we thought would be 300–400m of climbing, taking only three-quarters of a liter of water each. This was a big mistake. It took two hours to reach the base of the wall, and we had to spend one night on the face, only reaching the top on the 3rd. We built a big cairn (no paint arrow) at the start (1,235m, 23°0.5124' N, 57°5.2583' E) and on the route left three slings, a peg, and, inadvertently, a pair of trekking shoes, which meant one of us had to walk all the way back in rock shoes. The descent was long, and we only got back to the car by headlamp. We named the route Sardinian Shortcut (900m, 18 pitches, VI+); it initially climbs left of the 1999 British route Queen of Sheba (British E1 5a, Hornby-Ramsden) to meet it in the lower section of the face, but then takes a more direct finish.

After a rest day we noticed a needle inside a gorge, and concentrated our efforts in finding a way to reach it. We discovered a crossroads between Nadan gorge and Nadan village, where a road sign indicated "Mawal 6km." Following it, we soon had a clear view of our goal. A dirt road led into the gorge, and after parking the car at its end (23°5.7009' N, 56°56.6394' E), we walked one hour to reach the needle. Three pitches, the first in an offwidth on the south face, and the following two on the west face, led to the summit (135m, VII-). The route was hard due to loose rock in the first 30m, and we named the formation Mawal Needle (Guglia di Mawal, 915m).

On January 7 we discovered a gray marble tower with white crystalline veins, situated between Wadi Bani Awf and Wadi Sahaten, near Al Basawi village. It resembles a big dark horn.

Next morning we reached the foot of the 200m northeast ridge (23°15.0052' N, 57°25.56' E), constructing cairns on our approach. We climbed the crest to the final spur, where, from a notch, we moved to the right of a long chimney and climbed the crux pitches (VI+) to the top, placing a bolt for rappel at the last belay. We named the climb Black Horn's Ridge (260m, five pitches), and after a big effort trying to communicate with a goatherder, found—if we understood correctly—that the name of the summit was Jabal Awi (1,155m).

In all we climbed 10 new routes and came away with the impression that the locals are kind and hospitable. There is huge potential in Oman for discovering unclimbed walls and putting up new routes.

MARCO MARROSU, *Italy,*
marcomarrosu@tiscali.it

Mawal Needle from west, showing Marrosu-Masia route. *Marco Marrosu*

Roberto Masia on Black Horn's Ridge of Jabal Awi. *Marco Marrosu*

Canary Islands

The online version of these reports frequently contains additional photos, maps, topos, and extended text. Please visit aaj.americanalpineclub.org

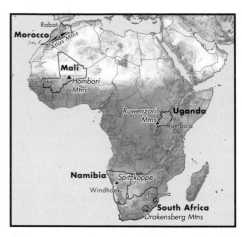

GRAN CANERIA

Los Quemados, El Cardonal. Geographically in Africa, but politically in Spain, the island of Gran Canaria is home to a "mature" climbing area that has failed to get onto the radar of most climbers due to lack of information. Most of Gran Canaria is a beautiful and mountainous national park, rising in its center to almost 2,000m. There, volcanic cores of several mountains give rock scenery that is a cross between the Dolomites and the canyons of Arizona.

Mountaineers have climbed on this Canary island since the 1930s, and in the early days

El Cardonal on Los Quemados. *Pat Littlejohn*

alpinists used pitons for protection and occasionally aid. In the early '80s, climbers in Gran Canaria were still making hard traditional ascents, comparable with the adventurous sea cliff climbs being done in Britain at that time. Topos for these routes can be found in the central café/bar in Ayacata. They make impressive reading. The routes are big—up to eight or nine pitches—and hard, with naturally protected free pitches up to F7a. The topos still seem to be the only written information but are not easy to interpret. Apparently a guidebook is in preparation, but my feeling is this will principally cover the sport climbing that took off in the late '80s.

There are now many pure sport crags (probably the best in the Canaries), and many of the harder trad routes are being retro-bolted. At first only the lower sections of trad routes were bolted, but even this is changing. It would be a real shame if these routes were lost, as they are very impressive, and big, adventurous, full-day outings. It is a similar situation to many areas of mainland Spain, where trad climbs going back many decades are now being claimed by bolters. The rock on the island is variable, but perfect at Roque Nublo, where most trad routes are now bolted, and on most other sport crags.

For a good visual impression, try an Internet picture search of Gran Canaria rock climbing, or Escalada en Gran Canaria.

The best climbing season is probably October-April inclusive, but Steve Sustad and I visited in February. Our main objective was a big, southwest-facing mountain escarpment on the south side of a peak called Montaña de Ojeda, towards the south of the island, where it forms a massive tiered cliff called Los Quemados. We had no idea whether anything had been climbed there, so we went up for a look with all the gear. With bolts many things would have been possible, but for us the challenge was to find a line that would go in our preferred style, i.e. no bolts, pegs, or hammers—just a British rack of nuts and Friends.

The first pitch on the impressive main tier turned out to be the crux of the route at British E3 5c.

Stephen Sustad on the sculptured rock of El Cardonal's fifth pitch. *Pat Littlejohn*

After sustained bridging up a long groove, we had to break right to reach more grooves, which gave really good climbing on perfect rock for two further pitches. We then realized we were in no shape to continue: we'd made too late a start on a baking hot day, and had not brought enough water.

The next day we approached the crag at dawn with six liters of water between us. Above our high point the line linked a series of scoops and caves before landing us below another steep and imposing tier. By now the sun was beating down again and the crag felt truly African—we had hit some unusually hot days. Another technical groove, with memorable finger-tip layback moves, was followed by a narrow chimney, after which we broke right through wind-eroded scoops to reach the final 50m wall. There was a possible direct line, but after 15m it was blocked by a rotten overhang. Luckily, a groove 20m to the right turned out to have better rock and better gear than

The excellent rock of Roque Nublo is now largely bolted. *Pat Littlejohn*

expected from below. It led past an overhang to a cave stance and one final pitch to the great shelf, where the cliff terminates. The result of our efforts was El Cardonal, a 13-pitch route that was sustained but nowhere too hard. It is definitely a worthy objective for people wanting to experience a long, adventurous trad climb on Gran Canaria.

PAT LITTLEJOHN, *UK, Alpine Club*

Mali

HOMBORI MOUNTAINS

The southeast face of Suri Tondo with the line of Black and White. *Jens Richter*

The crux pitch of Black and White. *Jens Richter*

Hand of Fatima, Suri Tondo, southeast face, Black and White. Black and White is a great new route on solid rock typical of the remarkable Hand of Fatima. The first time we studied the line from the desert below, it was around mid-day and the temperature felt like 60°C. Our eyes followed the shadow of Kaga Tondo as it bisected the yellow southeast face of its smaller brother, Suri Tondo. The line looked magic, and also impossible to climb. Some days later we were following black and red stripes on this wall. These ended at a headwall with obvious white "slabs" of guano, produced by the huge vultures that encircled the summit.

For the first 180m the route offers excellent, hard, exposed climbing on a steep, technical, yellow face. It is mainly bolt protected, though small and medium cams will prove useful. Above, the route follows a broken crack system, where a full rack is required. The last two pitches are shared with the Spanish route Txa-txa Punk (6c+, Miguel Alegre-Joan Olivé-Marta R-Edu Sanchez, 1996), which comes in from the right. Padlo Madl and I climbed our 420m line in nine pitches, from December 18-22. The first pitch is the crux at 7c+, the second is 7b+, and from then on it is sustained at 6b+ to 6c+ before reaching the easier final pitches. Obligatory difficulties are 6c, and all belay anchors are equipped, except on the last two pitches. Climbing on this face offers spectacular views toward the desert, and of huge vultures, which live in close proximity. Future parties will see many bats, falcons, and maybe snakes, and should carry plenty of chalk and water.

JENS RICHTER, *Germany*

Chad

Driving toward the Citadel, Ennedi Desert. *Jimmy Chin*

Ennedi Desert, various ascents. On November 14 Jimmy Chin, Tim Kemple, Alex Honnold, Renan Ozturk, James Pearson (UK), and I arrived in N'Djamena, the capital of Chad. Our goal was to explore and climb in the Ennedi Desert, which lies in eastern Chad near the border with Sudan. The expedition was outfitted by an Italian company called Spazzi D'Avventura and our guide, the company's owner, 66-year-old Piero Rava.

We spent one night in N'Djamena and the next morning loaded all of our supplies into two Land Cruisers and a Range Rover for the ca 800km journey to the Ennedi. Piero's crew included four Chadians: a cook, cook's helper, mechanic, and a driver. For the first 100km we followed the only paved road in the country, which led us northeast out of the city. The landscape was desolate: a flat, gray expanse of sand that stretched as far as we could see in every direction. We were only on the road for an hour before Piero drove over a sand bank on the side and began punching buttons on his GPS. We thought we were stopping for lunch, but Piero simply said, "this is the way to the Ennedi."

We spent the next three-and-a-half days questing, mostly off-road, across nearly the entire country of Chad. One whole day was spent crossing a particularly bleak expanse of hardpan sand flats that Piero called his "short-cut." Along the way we saw many Chadian nomads, who eke a living out of this barren environment by raising

Photographed by Chin, Pearson follows the top pitch of the Wine Bottle, belayed by Synnott on the summit. *Renan Ozturk*

Synnott and Pearson on the final pitch of the Arch of Bashikele. *Jimmy Chin*

James Pearson stands atop the Citadel after an onsight first ascent using only trad gear. *Jimmy Chin*

camels, donkeys, and goats. There are ancient wells spaced periodically across the desert, and life for these people revolves around trips to their local watering hole. We stopped at many of these wells to resupply our own water, and it was fascinating to observe the local Chadians and their herds of livestock. November-December is their winter and the dry season, and we hardly saw a cloud during our trip. High temperatures during the day were in the low 90s F. At night they fell into the 50s. The air was very dry, and it was always comfortable in the shade.

I had first heard about the possibility of rock climbing in Chad back in the late 1990s on a climbing expedition to the Mandara Mountains in Cameroon. I knew that climbers had visited the Tibesti Mountains in northern Chad, but I wondered if there were other areas worth exploring. After studying Google Earth, I found the Ennedi, and an Internet search brought up amazing photos of beautiful rock towers and arches.

As we entered the Ennedi, we could

A Chadian nomad family crosses the Ennedi Desert. Unclimbed formations behind. *Jimmy Chin*

have been in Utah's Canyonlands desert. Sandstone buttes, towers, and arches covered an area that Piero said was about 60,000 km². Piero had been to the Ennedi many times and was the first person regularly to start leading adventure tours to the area. He is also a climber, but a modest one, as it was only after Tim pulled out a book on Patagonia that Piero casually mentioned he had almost made the first ascent of Cerro Torre with Casimiro Ferrari back in the early '70s. Piero is THE authority on the Ennedi, and he assured us that we were the first group of technical rock climbers to visit the area. Every time we turned a corner and a new landscape was unveiled, we had to up our estimates as to how many towers there may be in the Ennedi. By the end of our first day in this African canyonland we were debating whether there were thousands or tens of thousands of unclimbed towers.

Over the next two weeks we drove around the Ennedi establishing different camps, venturing out to climb as many towers and arches as we could get our hands on. All told I estimate that we made first ascents of about 20 different towers, ranging from 50-300 feet tall. Many of these were onsight free-solos (up to 5.10), completed by Honnold. Alex also made an impressive ascent of an offwidth splitter, which incised the underside of an 80'-tall freestanding arch. His ascent involved upside-down levitation and foot camming, as well as exploding choss holds, and a section dripping in guano. Protection consisted of a toprope that Kemple lowered down through the crack from the top of the formation: The Rainbow

The Arch of Bashikele. *Mark Synnott*

Arch 5.12+ (a.k.a. The Hardest Route in Chad). Other highlights of the trip include the first ascents of three of the most impressive towers in the Ennedi: The Citadel (5.11d/5.12a R, 200', Honnold-Pearson-Synnott, no bolts); The Wine Bottle (5.11d R/X, 300', Chin-Pearson-Synnott, three bolts); The Arch of Bashikele (a.k.a. Delicate Arch of the Ennedi, 5.10c R/X, 200', Chin-Honnold-Ozturk-Pearson-Synnott, one bolt).

The rock varied considerably, much like it does in other desert climbing areas. Some of the towers were encased in a dark varnish or patina that made for solid holds and protection. Other towers that lacked the varnish were sandy and dangerously loose. All told, we were pleasantly surprised by the quality of the climbing. Truly, the Ennedi contains a lifetime's worth of unclimbed sandstone towers, and I look forward to getting back there some day.

Our team would like to thank The North Face, without whose generous support this trip would not have been possible.

MARK SYNNOTT, *AAC*

James Pearson making the first ascent of the Citadel. *Jimmy Chin*

Norway

The online version of these reports frequently contains additional photos, maps, topos, and extended text. Please visit aaj.americanalpineclub.org

Norway

Lofoten Islands/ Vagakallen

Troll Wall

Oslo

Stockholm

TROMSO REGION

Kvaloya Island, Blammanen (861m), north face, Luna. In late August Ole Ivar Lied and I climbed a new route toward the right side of Blammanen's north face. Luna (430m, Nor 5+ A3) starts 15-20m right of Frost (M5 A3, Bo-Nebell, 2007) and in the first section follows a well-defined line. Above, the route becomes more complex, with thin seams connected by exciting aid climbing. We climbed five pitches largely on aid before reaching easier ground and connecting into Frost below its final pitch. We spent two days fixing the first three pitches, then completed the route in a long day. The route needs everything from hooks to a Camalot 5. Peckers/Birdbeaks were particularly useful on every aid pitch. Overall, the line provides nice climbing, although some sections are often wet. We didn't stay on the wall; for that we would have needed a portaledge, as there is no real ledge before the top of pitch five.

ODD-ROAR WIIK, *provided by Marten Blixt, AlpinKlatring, Norway*

Kvaloya Island, Blammanen (861m), Tingeling. In 2007, on a visit with Markus Haid, I managed the first one-day ascent of Arctandria on the north face of Blamannen. I was so impressed that I decided to return in July with Much Mayr. During the first trip my eyes continually strayed left across the wall to Bongo Bar, a 400m line climbed in July 1998 by Marten Blixt, Thomas Ekefalk, and Erik Massih. This six-pitch route has difficulties up to A3 and Norwegian 7 (F6c+). While I was certain the rock quality wasn't as good as Arctandria, I could see that this section of face held immense potential for difficult, free, multi-pitch routes. After two days on the wall we started to feel a little downhearted. The third, steeply overhanging pitch of Bongo Bar was completely wet. Free climbing it was impossible. But why not try traversing left onto virgin territory? What about a link-up of the routes Bongo Bar and Atlantis? The latter was one of the original routes to breach the north face and climbed in June 1980 by Frode Guldal, Havard Nesheim, and Sjur Nesheim (400m, eight pitches, A1). It was freed in July 1990 by Per Hustad and Johan Nilsson at Norwegian 8 /8.

North face of Blammanen. (1) Atlantis. (2) Lost and Found. (3) Tingeling connection. (4) Bongo Bar. (5) Arctandria. (6) Luna. *Marten Blixt*

Auer and Mayr gaze at the north face of Blammanen. Their new route Tingeling, and the top section of Atlantis, are marked. *Reinhard Fichtinger*

On day three we were successful in linking into Atlantis, but I had to place a bolt because the loose flake, which enabled us to climb the pitch free, fell into space after a couple of hammer blows as I tried to place a peg. We couldn't have done it without the bolt. Unfortunately the corners and cracks above were extremely dirty and often wet. Climbing in these conditions was very demanding, and we needed a further two days to complete the ascent and then redpoint the remaining pitches. We used copperheads, pegs, nuts, cams, and the one bolt for protection, and our new line, Tingeling, now the fourth completely free route on the wall, goes at 7c+.

Unfortunately, almost uninterrupted rain then stopped us from making a one-day, continuous free ascent. But that's Norway.

HANSJÖRG AUER, *Austria*

Editor's note: the Austrians spent five days working on the route over a period of two weeks. On the last day they reached the junction with Atlantis, having climbed the first two pitches of Bongo Bar, plus four new pitches. However, the upper four pitches of Atlantis were too wet to climb, and the pair descended. Given the weather during their visit, Auer and Mayr were more than happy to have opened the free link, but a complete one-day ascent to the top of the wall remains. Auer's single protection bolt was drilled by hand.

Much Mayr on the lower section of the second pitch of Bongo Bar, now free at 7c+. *Reinhard Fichtinger*

(A) Breidskardtinden, (B) Rundtinden, and (C) Eidetind. The new Czech routes on the south face of Rundtinden are marked: Mispule (left) and Stay Cool. The right skyline ridge of Rundtinden is the 1978 Soderin-Sundberg route. There are several Norwegian routes on 845m Eidetind, notably on the north face, which has 15-pitch lines. *Ondrej Svihalek*

Rundtinden, south face, Stay Cool. In 2009 I climbed new routes in Lofoten (see *AAJ 2010*) and promised to return to Norway the following year. We did, but unfortunately this time we experienced really bad weather, with long periods of rain. Even when the weather improved for a couple of days, the big walls

remained desperately wet. We had to amuse ourselves fishing, trekking, kayaking, and scoping new lines.

My younger brother Ondrej and I spent a whole month in the wonderful landscape of northern Norway and finally, on one sunny day, July 1, were rewarded with the opportunity to climb the first ascent of Rundtinden's south face. This 798m peak is located between Tysfjord and Efjord in Nordland, on the mainland southeast of Lofoten. It forms the east side of a broad massif (with Breidskartinden to the west) and looks like a needle when viewed from the east. The area is surprisingly deserted despite being close to the main E6 highway. Our route is the first on the true south face and possibly the only one climbable without bolts—our most important consideration when climbing in Norway. The southeast ridge was climbed in 1978 (six pitches, 5+, Soderin-Sundberg).

Jiri Svihalek high on the unprotected slabs of Stay Cool. *Ondrej Svihalek*

In common with our other new routes in Norway, this line was extremely compact and slabby, and even after studying with binoculars we were uncertain we could climb it without bolts. We encountered huge monolithic slabs of solid but almost protectionless rock. The crux sections of 6+ and 6+/7- were protected by single pitons, often less than perfectly placed. Runouts above were more than six meters. Most of the easier pitches afforded only two or three points of protection in a full 50m. Therefore, the ascent was more demanding mentally than physically, and discovering a way through the vertical wall on pitch 9 (the crux) was a small miracle. However, all the crux sections appear to be more difficult than they are, so... Stay Cool (450m, 10 pitches, 6+/7-). It is a bold climb and requires a committed party, but offers much fine friction climbing. Pitches 8-10 have some vegetation.

We had a great time in Norway, and it's highly likely we'll return to the wild and (from a climber's perspective) unexplored Nordland.

JIRI SVIHALEK, *Czech Republic*

Rundtinden, south face, Mispule. On July 1, the same day that the Svihalek brothers put up Stay Cool, Filip Zaoral and I climbed the huge corner system on the left side of the south face of Rundtinden. This nine-pitch (400m) route, climbed in four hours using only nuts and cams for protection, was named Mispule after my girlfriend. Most of the climbing is UIAA IV to V+, but the crux (pitch seven) is VI, and requires a few powerful moves between two large roofs. The belay at the end of the eighth pitch is poor.

The area is beautiful (when the weather is good), and the rock on our route solid and clean. However, despite being in this region for six weeks, the weather was so poor we could only climb six routes.

LUKAS MARECEK, *Czech Republic*

Stay cool! 6+/7-, 450m

Mispule 6, 400 m

South face of Rundtinden. Mispule (left) and Stay Cool, with belay points marked. *Ondrej Svihalek*

ROMSDAL

Trollryggen, Trollveggen, Arch Wall, first free ascent. The highlight of climbing activity in Norway during 2010 was undoubtedly the free ascent of Arch Wall on Romsdal's iconic Trollveggen, the Troll Wall. For some, this ascent was perhaps the most impressive in the history of summer climbing in Norway, on arguably the most notorious route in the country.

Arch Wall climbs the left and highest part of the 1,200m Trollveggen, at first to the right, and then left of the 1967 French Direct, passing through the conspicuous "arch" above half height. When first climbed in 1972 by Brits Ed and Hugh Drummond, it was one of the most demanding big-wall climbs in the world. Completely unrelated, the two Drummonds were contemporaries at Bristol University, putting up new routes and making notable repeats. But in 1972, while Ed was in his prime, Hugh spent some time away from hard climbing, teaching in Mexico City.

Once committed to the wall, typical Norwegian harsh summer storms plagued the pair so badly that they topped out 21 days later, dangerously hypothermic and with Hugh's feet frostbitten. They had taken food for only 12 days and, although they conserved supplies during delays on the route, they still had to climb the last three days without food or water. The ordeal required inspired leading by Ed and involved bold and extensive skyhooking. Completing the route in 41 pitches, they assessed the technical difficulties at A5, with some free climbing to British 5b.

Since then the route has received only two ascents. In 1989 it was repeated by Norwegian Aslak Aastrop and American Thomas Cosgriff (resident in Norway), both highly experienced big-wall climbers, who confirmed a grade of 5.11a and A4+, and completed the route in 37 pitches after nine days on the wall. The third ascent was an impressive "tour de force" by the strong Polish trio of Jacek Fluder, Janusz Golab, and Stanislaw Piecuch. These three made the first winter ascent over 12 days in February-March 1994. They found numerous difficult sections of blank rock, and overhanging grooves that could only be climbed on RURPs and skyhooks. The highly accomplished and experienced Poles found the climb incomparable with any other big-wall route in Europe. The

Troll Wall in late winter, with the line of Arch Wall. *Lindsay Griffin*

visionary Cosgriff is reported to have said that a free ascent might be possible but would require a lot of cleaning and an extremely bold climber.

Enter Sindre Saether, a young Norwegian from Andalsnes. In 2008, partnered as usual on big climbs by his father Ole Johan, Saether made the first free ascent of the Norwegian Route further left on the face (originally UIAA VI and A2/3, later climbed at about 5.11a, 30 pitches, Eliassen-Emersen-Patterson-Teigland, 1965). Saether followed this in 2009 with an astonishing first free ascent of the French Direct, which has seen few repeats since its ascent in 1967 by Yves Boussard, Jerome Brunet, Patrick Cordier, Claude Deck, and Jean Frehel. Current topos rate this 37-pitch route 5.10c and A4, but the Saethers climbed it in two days on their second attempt at 5.12b/c.

The Saethers studied Arch Wall in detail, taking many pictures in different light and from different angles, with and without snow, until they knew exactly where to climb and what sort of gear they might need. They found the existing descriptions accurate, though with a few anomalous pitch grades (a section rated 5.8 turned out to be one of the hardest on the climb). While the French Direct follows obvious features and has many crack and corner systems, Arch Wall is more devious, finding a way up large blank walls. The climbing is very sustained, steep and exposed, though on mostly sound rock with little vegetation. However, some sections remain wet. Maximum difficulty was about the same as the French Route: 5.12b/c (though Sindre is known for being modest with his assessment of grades).

The French route has plenty of old in-situ gear, but Arch Wall has little: mostly ageing belay anchors, a few original bolts, and a few newer bolts in the lower section. The Saethers feel it must have been a highly difficult first ascent for the era, given the compact nature of the rock. The two first climbed the initial four pitches and left two ropes on the first three. They returned in good weather two weeks later and, after jumaring the ropes, completed the route in two days, with a bivouac on the Great Flake Ledges. Sindre led all pitches, with Ole Johan following free or on jumars.

The most dangerous part from rockfall is reaching the foot of the route, and the first pitch features much damaged rock. Above, the line is relatively protected from stonefall. Pitch 3, previously A4+, proved relatively straightforward technically until the last few moves, which formed one of the climb's cruxes. They found protection only with Birdbeaks and small blades. Pitch 4 (previously 5.11a and A2) provided much dirty, muddy climbing at 5.11d. There were three crux pitches to the Great Flake Ledges, and most of the climbing to that point was 11a and above. The impending wall above the Ledges (A2-A4+) was "not too bad."

They made three variants: to pitch 5, which proved difficult and more messy than expected; to pitch 21 (previously A4), which was very poorly protected with hardly any gear in the entire pitch that would hold a fall; and through the Arch, where they climbed about five meters right of the original line. In fact the most significant feature of this ascent was the bold climbing, which involved making hard moves up to 15m above poor protection from Birdbeaks. This seriousness, combined with the great rock falls that still occur on the wall during the summer, and the Norwegian weather, which prevents a route like this being tackled on more than a few days a year, will ensure continued unpopularity. On one reconnaissance, the Saethers witnessed a huge rock avalanche from the wall end up in the river.

Lindsay Griffin, *Mountain INFO,*
from material provided by Marten Blixt and Bjorn-Eivind Artun

SOGNEFJORD

Lady Momo. Outer Sognefjord and Hoyanger provide a spectacular destination for ice climbing (Sognefjord is the largest fjord in Norway). In some winters, when the ice conditions are good, you can climb with a view over the open sea. There is a 600m line towering over the center of Hoyanger that rarely reaches the bottom for any length of time. I've dreamt of climbing this magnificent icefall for many years. Growing up in Hoyanger, the waterfall was part of my daily view, as I looked out from the kitchen window.

One day in January I phoned my mother, and she mentioned she could see the entire icefall. Hmmm.... Was this a desperate attempt to get visitors? Or was it really there? Sigurd Felde and I had to find out, so we packed the car and headed from Andalsnes to Hoyanger. When we stood below the climb at 8 a.m., the temperature was -15°C. This would later cause four frozen toes, though the compensation was a fantastic meal on the table provided by my parents, who had followed our progress that day.

We belayed three pitches and then moved together for 150m. Another pitch, followed by ca 100m of moving together, led to the headwall, which gave three sustained ropelengths to the top of the ice. Here, there are plenty of trees for belays. Two descents are possible: rappel the icefall, or follow an indistinct path to the left (red marks on trees). The latter is steep in parts, and it's probably best to keep roped for some sections. We named the climb Lady Momo (WI5).

HEGE NORDEIDE, *provided by Marten Blixt, AlpinKlatring, Norway*

Russia

The online version of these reports frequently contains additional photos, maps, topos, and extended text. Please visit aaj.americanalpineclub.org

ALTAI

North face of Russian Tent, showing new Czech route. *Michal Kleslo*

Taban Bogdo Range, Russian Tent (4,117m), northeast couloir; Ak Alakha Range, Ak Alakha (3,650m), east ridge. In September our Czech-Slovak expedition visited two areas of the southern Altai. We first traveled to the Taban Bogdo on the border with northwest Mongolia. Immediately north of Huiten, which forms the triple border point of Russia, Mongolia, and China, stands Russian Tent (a.k.a. Russkiy Shator), which had been climbed several times by its frontier ridges (east and southwest) and by easy glaciated slopes on the Mongolian side. Libor Kejr, Tomas Lakpa, and I made the first known ascent of the northeast couloir. This was an icy slope of 45° with several crevasses. One, above a flat section at around mid-height, was rather large.

Forty kilometers west, close to the triple border point of Russia, Kazakhstan, and China, lies the Ak Alakha, south of the Ukok Plateau. Only scientists and military had visited this area prior to our expedition. Due to its proximity to China, the region was closed to the public until 1991. Until recently access to the land within 20km of the border was restricted. Today there is a military base on the Ukok Plateau, and although access within five kilometers of the border is still officially denied, controls are rare and not strict. Unfortunately all peaks lie within three kilometers of the border. The mountains are either snow/ice or composed of very poor rock. There are three main glacier systems on the Russian side: Ukok to the west, Ak Alakha in the center, and Kanas to the east. All were unexplored prior to our visit.

We reached the military base on the Plateau in one day's drive from Kosh Agach. Beyond the base it was possible to progress a few kilometers with 4WD, but after that we needed to walk about five hours over swampy permafrost to the glaciers. From there it took one day to ascend the eastern side of the Ak Alakha Glacier, climb a 200m section of 60° ice to the China-Russia border, then follow the east ridge of Ak Alakha, the highest peak in the range, to its summit. The first part of the ridge was flat and wide. After this we climbed the east face on 45° snow/ice and the final section of sharp north ridge to the top. The ascent was made by Vladimir Bures, Libor Kejr, Tomas Lapka, Martin Pes, and I (Czech), and Jan Dolezal, Jan Krchnavy, and Viliam Murcek (Slovak). Two days later we returned to Kosh Agach.

During the descent from Ak Alakha, showing route taken on final section of ascent. *Michal Kleslo*

The bureaucracy required to visit this region is complex. First you need a Russian visa and an invitation letter, then registration for temporary stay in Russia (only available through a local agent—and don't forget to cancel it when leaving), then registration with a local rescue team (can be obtained on the spot but is compulsory for border visits), then a border permit (in fact only issued for greater than five kilometers from the border and needs to be applied for at least 60 days in advance), and finally you have to pass through two or three border controls on the Ukok Plateau (be sure to have all your documents in order). This is a nature reserve, and you may find problems with "rangers" asking for a fee. Feel free to contact me for more details.

Looking east from the summit of Ak Alakha along the Russian-China border toward the distant Tabun Bogdo. *Michal Kleslo*

Looking west from the summit of Ak Alakha along the China-Kazakhstan border. All peaks visible in this photo are unclimbed. *Michal Kleslo*

MICHAL KLESLO, *Czech Republic, kleslo@pamir7000.cz.*

DAGESTAN
EASTERN CAUCASUS

Erydag Northwest (3,887m), northwest face, Voronin Route, first free ascent. In 2010 the Russian Championships were to be held in the Karavshin, but the events in Kyrgyzstan forced them to be moved to Erydag. Michael Borich and Sergey Dashkevich attended because Borich needed another 6B to become a Master of Sport. But Dashkevich had little interest in climbing a route of this high grade by normal means. So they compromised: they would try a free ascent. After a week of poor weather they attempted a new line between the Polyakov and Samodeda routes. But around half-height they were forced down after climbing sections of poor rock, enduring a rainstorm, and witnessing a bad accident to a party on a nearby route. On July 26 they started up the Voronin Route (1,200m, A3) hoping for a free ascent. If successful, this would set a benchmark in Russian alpine rock climbing.

After two-and-a-half days, with bivouacs at the top of pitches 11 and 21, they arrived on the summit having free-climbed all 29 pitches, four at 7a. There were sections of friable sandstone, with the sting in the tail being the final ca 20m corner, which was covered in wet clay from one to five centimeters thick. It took Borich an hour to lead. The pair believe that with previous knowledge of the terrain, a fast party could free-climb the route in a day.

Erydag (main summit 3,925m) lies at the eastern end of the Caucasus chain. Its huge, alpine, northwest face boasts over 20 difficult rock routes from 5B to 6B, one of the most famous being the Mirror, a competition-winning climb on the left side of the wall put up in 1981 by Sergey Efimov and partners. The Voronin Route, put up in the winter of 2001 by a team from Dagestan led by Sergey Voronin, climbs the central buttress of the face. Blinov, Kofanov, Novoseltsev, and Yarunov from Ekateringburg made the second ascent in 2002 during the Russian Championships. The third ascent took place in the winter of 2006, and then four parties climbed the route during the summer of 2010 as part of the Championships, before Borich and Dashkevich made their first free ascent. Subsequently, three more parties climbed the route, though not free.

From information supplied by ANNA PIUNOVA, *mountain.ru*

Georgia

Chaukhi Mountains, Javakishvili (3650m), Perseverance. During April, while Graham Dudley was making a ski ascent of Kazbek (Kasbegi, or more properly Mkinvartsveri, 5,034m) in the Eastern Caucasus, he noticed an attractive range of lightly glaciated peaks ca 30km to the southeast and was determined to come back for a look. I joined him for a seven-day visit in September.

Research revealed these were the Chaukhi mountains, close to the Russian border and known as the Dolomites of Georgia, boasting fine alpine rock routes. The massif consists of a ridge of unusual, metamorphic, volcanic rock with four separate summits, the highest, Asatiani, 3,820m. It is surrounded by grassy hills rising to 3,500m, although to the southwest a steep peak holds a big wall that typically takes three days to aid climb and is rarely ascended. The area is attractive and can be reached in a three-hour 4WD from Tbilisi (local bus or normal taxi is much cheaper but slower), and a two-hour walk with horses (cheap and easy to arrange). We established base camp at 42°33.256' N, 44°46.321' E.

Our stay caused a little local excitement. Apparently we were the first foreigner visitors to climb technical routes. The area is popular with trekkers. We saw a couple of parties each day, and

The north face of the Chaukhi Group. (A) Asatiani, (B) Kameruni, (C) Leonidze, and (D) Javakhishvili. (1) Russian 6A, (2) 4B, (3) 5A, (4) 4A, (5) 5B, (6) 4A, (7) 5A, (8) 5A, and (9) 5B. *Simon Richardson*

invariably they proved to be from Israel. Non-local climbing parties, for example from Estonia, have either hill walked or made simple Grade I scrambles. However, we were certainly not the first overseas party, as it is possible that Asatiani was first climbed by the Scottish female, Una Cameron, in 1932. Russians must certainly have climbed here, and there was mention of a Czechoslovakian team in the 1980s.

Since we knew nothing of the area, we spent our first day climbing the Normal Route on Javakishvili (3,650m), Chaukhi's second highest summit, with Georgian guide Tito Nadiratze. Graded 3A, this was about Alpine PD, following an easy snow/scree couloir, and then British VD rock to the summit. The next day we climbed the Normal Route on Asatiani. This took a long

couloir, then climbed four, long, protectionless pitches up slabs at British Hard Severe. Graded 4A, the route equated to Alpine D-, and descending our line proved quite serious. The first ascent of this peak was made via the southwest ridge at 2, but is apparently rarely repeated these days.

We then took a rest day, and our run of good weather ended. I think we were unlucky because the previous eight weeks had been perfect. Thereafter we made three attempts to climb a 5A on the north face of Javakishvili, but on every occasion the cold and

Asatiani south face showing the Normal Route. *Simon Richardson*

South face of Javakhishvili with (1) Guiabidez-Nadiradez Route, (2) Perseverance, and (3) Standard Route from south. *Simon Richardson*

rain beat us down. However, we managed a route on the south face, which Nadiratze had pointed out to us as unclimbed. On September 10, starting midway between the Nadiradze-Gujabidze route and the ridge of the Normal Route, we followed weaknesses up the face at British VS (not sustained) to join the Normal Route a little before the summit. Our line, named Perseverance, was 320m (around six pitches) and grade 4A.

Despite the weather we managed to do something every day. After our various failed attempts we would go off walking in the rain, eventually reaching the tops of almost all the surrounding 3,500m peaks.

The Chaukhi region is breathtakingly beautiful and very much unknown outside Georgia. The best rock is on the north face of Javakishvili, where routes reached 600m in length. In my opinion a one-week visit to Chaukhi, followed by an ascent of Kazbek, would make an excellent two-week mountaineering holiday.

SIMON RICHARDSON, *Alpine Club*

Tajikistan

ZERAVSHIN RANGE
FANSKIY GORY

Parandas (4,250m), Odessa Route; Bodhona (5,138m), west face, Odessa Route. The main mountaineering development of the Fanskiy Mountains took place in the 1970s and early '80s. After that, attention turned to the newly discovered areas of Karavshin and Laylak. It appeared that all good lines in the Fanskiy had been climbed. However, looking at the walls with a fresh eye, climbers have recently discovered several new and logical lines. Our team for Parandas comprised Alexander Khomenko, Maxim Polyakov, Taras Tsushko, and I.

Parandas is rather small by Fanskiy standards with an official altitude of 4,250m. However, our GPS registered 4,600m on the summit. It is not an independent summit but more a wall on the ridge leading to Zamok (Castle). In the old days climbs on Parandas were only considered complete if they finished up the very long crest to the main summit of Zamok. However, times change, and nowadays a route on Parandas alone is acceptable. The main face is 800m high and two kilometers wide with marble-like dolomitic limestone. After the two ascents in 2010 there are only five routes on this wall and still plenty of scope for others.

We climbed a prominent line up the center of the face, characterized by a big C-shaped overhang at mid-height, above which a deep-red corner rises to large overhangs that can be turned via a system of corners to the left. In general the wall is compact with only a few loose sections; we only had to drill bat-hooks in the section around the C-shaped overhang. Climbing was often hampered by streaks of water or ice, but I think we chose the optimal time for an ascent—the first half of July—because warmer weather could pose the problem of rockfall from the summit ridge. We were able to climb without a portaledge, bivouacking each night on ledges. One night we had to sleep sitting. Similarly, there was no need to carry water, as there was plenty of snow and ice on ledges. We climbed 28 pitches to the summit ridge and from there scrambled several hundred meters to the top. Named Odessa Route, the difficulties were Russian VI 6B, A3.

The west face of Bodhona with (1) Mogila Route (5B), (2) Moshnikov Route (6B), (3) Zhitenev Route (6B), (4) Volodarchik Route (6B), (5) Kolchin Route (6B), (6) Senchina Route (6B), (7) Odessa Route (2010), and (8) Maximenja Route (2010). *Alexander Lavrinenko*

From the top we examined closely the west face of Bodhona, particularly the right side. There are seven routes on this wall, some of which provided their first ascensionists with Championship prizes in the former Soviet Union. However, no one had attempted the buttress on the right. We took several days rest at Alaudin base camp and then started up a system of corners in the lower buttress. It took two days to climb the first six pitches. Here, a small ledge allowed us to bivouac in a semi-prone position. On the third day we committed to the wall and managed to reach a big outward sloping, snow-covered terrace below the second step. It was not a good place to spend the night.

The step has a number of large overhangs, but we managed to find a logical route through, though we made slow progress in bad weather and had to sit out a night beneath roofs. The weather improved the following day. We finished the second step and began on the third, which was easier. On the snow-covered terrace below this, we met Maximenja, who had been soloing a route to the right. On our eighth day we arrived at a snow and rock ridge leading to the summit tower. A 40m rock step festooned with huge icicles proved an unexpected obstacle. We climbed the thickest and most stable of these and then continued to the summit over relatively easy snow and rock. The vertical interval of the route was 1,188m (840m on the west face) and gave us 1,552m of climbing (26 pitches plus some moving together) at Russian VI 6B, A4 70–75° ice.

ALEXANDER LAVRINENKO, *Ukraine*
(provided by Anna Piunova, mountain.ru, and translated by Ekaterina Vorotnikova)

Parandas (4,250m) and Bodhana (5,138m), Maximenja routes. From July 13–18 Alexander Maxi-

Parandas with (1) Tischenko Route (5B), (2) Maximenja Route (2010), (3) Odessa Route (2010), (4) Arkhipova Route (6A A2), and (5) Mogila Route (VI 5B A3). *Alexander Lavrinenko*

menja from Minsk, Belarus, climbed a new route on Parandas. His route is situated to the left of the line put up by the Odessa climbers, who were operating on the wall at the same time and who he met on the descent. Maximenja's route crosses the Tischenko route in the upper half of the face. Meltwater affected the climbing in the lower section, beginning between 10–12 a.m. and reaching its worst between 3–5 p.m. The overall grade was 6A, with technical difficulties of 6c and A3. Substantial sections of the route could be free climbed, and more would have been possible were it not for the wetness of the wall.

After resting, and then some days of rain, he set off for the west face of Bodhana, and from July 25–August 2 made a solo ascent of a new route on the far right side of the wall. He had to contend with cold, wet weather; as with his climb on Parandas, he used a hammock for bivouacs. As usual, he took neither sleeping bag nor down jacket, which as a rule he finds get wet on these climbs and become a burden. His line was parallel to but right of the Odessa team, whom he met at the snow terrace at the base of the upper section of the wall, and who generously left chocolate for him on the summit. The route had an overall grade of 6A with technical difficulties up to 6c and A4.

ANNA PIUNOVA, *mountain.ru, from information provided by Alexander Maximenja*

Kazakhstan

TIEN SHAN
ZAILISKIY ALATAU

Talgar (4,973m), northwest face; South Talgar (4,950m), southwest face. For Almaty (Kazakhstan) climbers, the Zailiskiy Alatau in the northern Tien Shan is our most accessible mountain range and the foundation of our mountaineering. Even though roads reach 3,000m, climbing routes can be long and difficult; they allow climbers to gain the first level in our sports program. Talgar is the highest peak in the range, but access is relatively difficult. Roads are cracked and have not been repaired for a long time, approaches to the mountains are long and have not been maintained, there is a fee for parking, and base camps are at a shockingly low altitude. For the last 20 years it has been easier and cheaper for us to climb in neighboring Kyrgyzstan. However, in 2010 there was a revolution in Kyrgyzstan. If something else were to happen while we were climbing there, the return home could be extremely difficult. So this year we stayed in our home country.

The main development of the Talgar group took place in the 1970s when computers were not widely available. Nobody considered documenting climbing information on punch cards, because there would not have been enough cards to describe all the routes. There were no photos from that period, but I did discover more recent helicopter footage. Incidentally, I first went there with the Army in 1993, in my early climbing days, setting up base in the area of the former Soviet climbing camp.

Our 2010 trip into the Middle Talgar involved Boris Dedeshko, Andrei Kolbin, Vladimir Kolmagorov, Vitali Komarov, Vadim Trofimov, Ellina Vasilyeva, and me. We carried heavy sacks to above the tree line at 2,800m and made base camp next to a ruined building, which we covered with a tarp in order to have a good communal spot to spend gloomy, hopeless days. In poor weather Andrei and I climbed a rock route on the west face of Aktau, while Boris, Vadim, and Vitali succeeded on the north face of Karaulchitau. Andrei and I then tried the northwest face of Talgar, but after spending a night on the upper North Talgar Glacier surrounded by rockfall, we realized it was too risky in the prevailing warm temperatures and incessant rain. We descended, only to have the weather improve that evening.

Vitali and I rushed back up the next morning at 3 a.m. We ascended an ice couloir to the right of Pelevin's Route. The rock section on the latter looked discouraging, but in the old days no one climbed ice in preference to rock. Using a 57m rope we climbed 23 pitches and reached the summit at 5 p.m. on August 8, just as it started to snow. We started down the southeast ridge immediately, followed by the Korzhenevsky Glacier and Surovyi Pass, regaining base camp at 3 a.m. Our new route was nearly 1,200m, graded 5A, and close to the top reached an angle of 75-85°.

Taking advantage of clear weather, on the 10th Boris, Vadim, and I set off for the southwest face of South Talgar. Unfortunately, the weather began to deteriorate rapidly as soon as we started up an ice couloir between the Snesarev and Meshkov routes. We climbed 10 pitches before being forced to shelter on a rock ledge left of the couloir. After a night of snow and wind, we were greeted by clear skies, and we continued up icefalls for another eight pitches, eventually reaching the snow plateau on Baranowski's route, not far below the summit. We pitched the tent and climbed up ice and rock (50°) to the top. We returned to the tent and early next morning, while the slopes were still well consolidated, descended Baranowski's route, reaching base camp by 1 p.m. We graded our route 5B and there were two narrow sections of 80°.

Southwest face of South Talgar showing 2010 Dedeshko-Trofimov-Urubko route and bivouacs. *Denis Urubko*

Sometimes I feel the best days of my life are disappearing. Although still young and with plenty of strength, I can see what is happening. However, all's well that ends well, and I was pleased with my 2010 ascents in Talgar, compared to my first 5A in the region during 1993. On the 12th, after having robbed the local bears of several plots of their wild raspberries, we started our return to Almaty.

DENIS URUBKO, *Central Sport Club of Kazakhstan Army, translated by Ekaterina Vorotnikova*

Northwest face of Talgar main summit showing 2010 Komarov-Urubko route right of the rock buttress of Pelevin's route. *Denis Urubko*

Kyrgyzstan

The online version of these reports frequently contains additional photos, maps, topos, and extended text. Please visit aaj.americanalpineclub.org

TIEN SHAN

ALA ARCHA

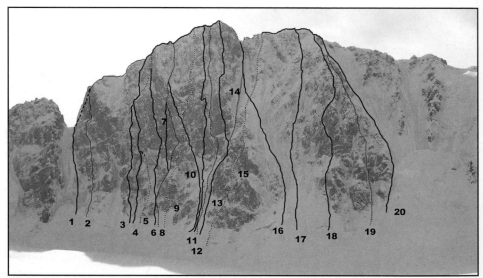

The north face of Svobodnaya Korea. (1) Kocherga Agafonova (Agafonov's Poker), (2) 5B, Balezin, 1991, (3) 5B, Svab, 1982, (4) 5B, Balezin, 2000, (5) 6A, Studenin, 1966, (6) 6A, Kustovskiy, 1969, (7) 6A, Mikhaylov, 1999, (8) 6A, Semiletkin, 1988, (9) 6A, Popenko, 1975, (10) Narodnyj (People's Route), 6A, Ruchkin, 2001, (11) 6A, Bezzubkin, 1969, (12) 6A, Ruchkin, 1997, (13) 5B, Myshlyayev, 1961, (14) Samarskij Variant (Samara's Variant), 5B, (15) 5B, Bagaev, 1974, (16) 5B, Barber, 1976, (17) Akimov-Gutnik, 5B, (18) 5B, Balezin, 1994, (19) 5A, Andreev, 1959, and (20) 5A, Lowe, 1976. *Sergey Dashkevich*

Pik 4,300m, northwest face, Discovery; Pik Svobodnaya Korea (4,778 m), north face, Balezin Route, first alpine-style and first free ascent; Pik Baylyan Bashi (4,720m), west face, Long Way Home. These days I'm interested in making single push, alpine mixed climbs without using aid or fixed rope. Last winter Gennadiy Kabalin, Boris Tretjakov, and I had an unforgettable adventure in Ala Archa, one of my favorite places for winter climbing.

To aid acclimatization we first made a new route on the northwest face of an unnamed 4,300m summit that lies on the west ridge of Korona (4,860m). We climbed more or less up the center of the face and then left along the ridge to the summit. We named our 860m line Discovery (M5-).

A few days later we were below the incredible north face of Svobodnaya Korea (Free Korea peak). In my opinion the finest and most logical lines are situated toward the left side of the wall. The Balezin route was put up in 2000 over a six-day period, largely using aid (A3). We made our attempt in light alpine style. We wanted to climb as fast as possible, so took little gear and no bivouac

Looking southeast up the Uchitel Glacier at (A) Korona and (B) Pik 4,300m, with new route Discovery. *Sergey Dashkevich*

equipment. All that day and through the following night we progressed by mixed climbing and dry tooling. We completed the 1,070m route entirely free—the second overall ascent—at M6+. We were exhausted when we reached the summit.

During our few remaining days the weather got worse, but we wanted to climb one last route. We chose the northwest face of Baylyan Bashi, which lies on the ridge between Svobodnaya Korea and Korona at the head of the Ak-Sai Glacier. Our new line, which we called Long Way Home (700m, M5+), wasn't so hard and took the right flank of the buttress followed by the 1985 Kuzmenko route (6A). It proved a fine end to the trip.

SERGEY DASHKEVICH, *Russia, supplied by Anna Piunova, mountain.ru, photo captions translated by Luca Calvi*

Sergey Dashkevich starting an ice pitch on the first ascent of Discovery. *Boris Tretjakov*

The northwest face of (A) Baylyan Bashi and north face of (B) Simagina. Svobodnaya Korea is just off picture right. (1) Kuzmenko route, 6A, 1985. (2) Long Way Home (Dashkevich-Kabalin-Tretjakov, 2010). (3) Mansurov route (includes traverse of peak), 5B, 1961. *Lindsay Griffin*

TORUGART-TOO

Various peaks above the Karakol and Arpa valleys. In July I returned to Kyrgyzstan for the third time, my main goal being to explore more of the Torugart-too and in

The steep ice runnel splitting the upper tower on Long Way Home. *Sergey Dashkevich*

particular to push further along the Fergana range, an extension of the Torugart-too running northwest along the divide between the regions of Osh and Naryn. In this, Misha Sukhorukov, Glenn Wilks, and I were highly successful.

We began by again visiting the Naryn Tal to acclimatize. The wooded valleys make for beautiful camping and the clear streams pleasant fording. We climbed a prominent peak at the head of the Kandi Valley. A steep moraine led to a long snow bowl and onto the flank of the northeast ridge. Crossing below a prominent gendarme, we roped up for a steep, loose step. This was fortunate as Misha took a fall. A direct ascent of the headwall led to the summit of Pik 4,450m (41°21'28" N, 76°28'38" E, all GPS readings). To the west we could see the mountain I climbed in 2008 (*AAJ 2009*). There was no evidence that any human had been here before, but ibex tracks crossed the summit.

We then moved south to the Torugart-too, driving across trackless country in 4WD. We stopped at the last civilization; a collection of yurts hard up against an impassable Karakol River, but with a way open to the target valleys we had identified in the UK. The resident families were most friendly, and like so many people who have little, they were generous and hospitable.

We first headed southwest and camped just below a glacier at 3,500m, surrounded by unclimbed peaks of 4,400–4,700m. Our ascent of Pik 4,470m (40°37'58" N, 74°31'45" E) took place in full Scottish conditions: wind, rain, snow, and cloud. In a whiteout I drifted over a cornice in the final section, fortunately having just put on the rope. Dropping down from the summit, an intense tingling in the rear warned us of the thunder clap that was shortly to follow.

The inner ranges of the Fergana, with summit of Peak 4,318m up to the right. *Mark Weeding*

Our next ascent took us west to the peak at the head of the glacier above base camp. The summit was 4,510m (40°38'41" N, 74°30'04" E) and gave views of a huge horseshoe with a higher peak on the other side. How could we resist the temptation of a long ridge traverse on such a great day? Going up and down repeatedly at over 4,500m was hard, but the views, south to the Pamir, east to the Kokshaal-too, and north to the endless inner ranges of Kyrgyzstan, were wonderful. Soon, we arrived at the main top: 4,616m (40°39'10" N, 74°28'54" E), as marked on the Russian Military map.

Enigmatic peaks of the Torugart-too rise above the Arpa Valley. *Mark Weeding*

Our plan was now to head south along the Karakol River and up to the snout of a long glacier marked on the map. The range is relatively deep here, and a score of peaks appeared unclimbed. We camped next to a torrent disgorging the fastest flowing milk chocolate yet discovered, and the following morning, at 5 a.m., Misha and I forded it in our underpants (Glenn was ill). Moving east on a

Peak 4,450m in the Naryn Tal. The route of first ascent crossed the basin and then climbed the snow slope on the far side of the rocky rib that comes down from the squat rock gendarme. Above, the crest was followed easily to the summit. *Mark Weeding*

narrowing ridge, we ascended the loosest and steepest scree in my memory. We reached a top of 4,318m (40°36'41" N, 74°34'35" E) but were denied a further summit by my lack of crampons, which had been left at camp. One thousand meters of perfectly padded descent on soft shattered slate had us down in minutes.

Next day, while Glenn headed down to summon the horses, Misha and I traversed another horseshoe ridge culminating in a massive, overhanging cornice on the final summit, which had been visible far down the access valley: Pik 4,378m, 40°34'28" N, 74°37' E. This appears to be just north of the 4,848m peak climbed in 2007 by Dmitry Shapovalov (*AAJ 2008*).

Deep in the broad basin of the Arpa Valley, the Fergana peaks have a remote and isolated feel, and the Karakol Valley provides access to a pass over the range known to locals. While probably visited by adventurous trekkers, the yurt families had seen only one group of trekkers (French) in 10 summers. There is opportunity to climb an almost unlimited number of peaks with no recorded ascents, although the presence of the Russian military makes it likely that some may have received the attention of enthusiastic Red Army alpinists if they were allowed to escape the clutches of their organized climbing camps, none of which were in this area.

Mark Weeding, *UK*

Mur Samir (5,035m), northeast ridge; Pik Karyshkyr (4,836m), Ten Pin; False Pik (4,801m), west face. The Torugart-Too is a range of glaciated peaks rising to 5,000m on the border between Kyrgyzstan and China. There have been few expeditions, but the highest peak, Mustyr (5,108m), was first climbed in 2007 by Barney Harford and Pat Littlejohn. From July 22–August 12, John Proctor, Robert Taylor, and I from Edinburgh University Mountaineering Club visited Kyrgyzstan, spending 12 days in the range and making three first ascents.

We knew that the recent revolution and riots in Kyrgyzstan might cause problems, and when we boarded the flight to Bishkek in July, it was suspiciously empty. On our first day in the capital we were picked up by local police and taken to the station, but they only wanted to check our paperwork and search us for knives. Soon, with the help of our agency, ITMC, we were driving south. A few days later we established base camp in the Mustyr Valley opposite Middle Sister.

While two of us climbed, the third would remain at base camp the entire time to guard against inquisitive locals, who showed a keen interest in our gear. I took the first shift while John and Robert headed up the Three Sisters, first climbed in 2008 (*AAJ 2009*), for a reconnaissance of the unnamed glacier east of Mustyr. Next day I made a quick ascent of the Sisters while John and Robert packed for a bivouac below their objective at the head of the glacier.

John writes: "Mur Samir was climbed by the northeast ridge. Prior to the ascent the only information we had about the mountain was the map, and a few glimpses through partial breaks in the cloud while acclimatising on Big Sister. We observed that the main north face had a number of séracs, so opted to climb a broad couloir at the eastern edge, and then follow the ridge above to the summit. Easy ground in the couloir led to the ridge, and in the mist we chose the wrong couloir, resulting in a long traverse to reach the summit. Most of the crest was pleasant and spectacular, but in places we had to negotiate thin and rotten (but thankfully not steep) ice, and scramble over rock like Weetabix. By the time we neared the summit the weather had cleared, and we could see down the north face. It was obvious that there was ample space toward the eastern end to climb the face while staying clear of the séracs, so we descended this way over easy ground. With a GPS we recorded an altitude of 4,419m at the base of our route, and 5,035m (slightly higher than the 5,008m recorded on the

West face of False Pik with line of ascent. Pik Helen to the left. *Adam Russell*

Peaks at head of unnamed glacier east of Mustyr. (A) Torolok (4,870m) climbed by Leach, Moneypenny, and Nichols from the UK via the central north face ice slope (D). (B) Mur Samir. (1) Proctor-Taylor (first) ascent via northeast ridge, and (2) their descent. (3) Diligent Epiphany (TD-, Moneypenny-Nichols, descended via 2). *Adam Russell*

Russian Military Map) on the summit." The ascent was AD and Scottish II, while the easier descent PD and Scottish I.

Mur is a Kyrghyz word for marmot (the range is overrun by these rodents), while the full name is a play on words; Mir Samir is a peak in the Nuristan region of Afghanistan, made famous by Eric Newby in his classic book, *A Short Walk in the Hindu Kush.*

On the next day, I walked with Robert to the foot of a fine northwest face on a peak immediately north of Mustyr. There, we watched sizeable rockfall sweep the entire lower section of the route. We changed plans and the following day attempted a couloir on the eastern side of the mountain. This gave several hundred meters of technically easy but tiring climbing through wet snow. Rocks bounced down frequently as we "ran" from one sheltering rock to the next, eventually skirting the cornice and landing on

John Proctor high on the west face of False Pik. *Adam Russell*

the col. At first we moved north, climbing on thin ice over scree, but then decided to attempt the south summit instead. We climbed up snow slopes and ice runnels, and past chossy towers, to reach the top. With the cloud closing, we raced back down the now very slushy gully, and wandered back to the tent for a brew before walking out. We named the summit Pik Karyshkyr (Kyrgyz for wolf), and the route Ten Pin (PD+ and Scottish I).

For our final climb John and I wanted to try the unclimbed 5,000m peak northeast of Mur Samir, but the river had risen significantly, forcing a rethink. Instead, we moved up the Teke-Lutor Glacier, looking for an objective. On the east rim an ice field swept up to a summit south of Pik Helen. It looked promising. After a night on the moraine, an alpine start saw us trudging up the lower snow slope for what we thought would be a quick route. The early sun soon turned the surface ice to slush as we moved together for another 550m (Scottish II) to the ridge. We skirted a melting cornice to reach

Pik Karyshkyr from the west. Mustyr just off picture to right. Russell and Taylor climbed to col (C) from far side, then ascended ridge right (south) to pointed summit. *Adam Russell*

the "summit," but then saw the ridge continuing to a slightly but definitely higher point (Pik 4,850m on the Russian map). Without adequate gear to bivouac, we made the tough decision and headed down—a time consuming, cold, and tiring affair, given our lightweight approach. We named the summit False Pik and graded our route on the west face AD. We walked out the next day, planning to look at a possible 300–600m rock route on the west face of Big Sister, but the weather closed in, and we were left to develop the limestone boulders at base camp instead.

Locals converged to celebrate our departure, determined to get us to hand over kit. Despite our friendly but firm refusal, we woke next morning to find that seven meters had been cut from the end of my rope. Photographs from the British expedition [see next report], gave evidence that it had been recycled into horse reins. We were supported by a Mountaineering Council of Scotland Bursary from Sport Scotland, and the Scottish Mountaineering Trust/Sang Award. They made this expedition possible.

ADAM RUSSELL, *UK*

Torolok (4,870m), north face; Mur Samir (5,035m), north face, Diligent Epiphany; Free Tibet (4,700m); Pik Abu (4,495m). After landing in Bishkek on August 19, Tom Nichols, James Moneypenny, and I reached the Mustyr Valley on the 22nd, well after the Edinburgh University Expedition had left for home. We made base camp by our vehicle, just below the grass line. We first acclimatized by attempting a new line on Pik Kumay (4,830m) that followed a couloir onto the northwest ridge. Unfortunately, a deep gap in the crest, poor rock, and bad weather turned us back.

We then took five days' food and established an advanced base on what we dubbed the John Charles Glacier, immediately east of the Mustyr Glacier. This flows down from the north face of Mur Samir, the 5,035m peak climbed by the Edinburgh University team. Our goal was the peak to its left, which we named Torolok after its similarity to the Tour Ronde in the Mont Blanc Massif (Torolok is the nearest Kyrgyz translation of "tour ronde"). The following day we climbed the peak via the north face at D (60°). It gave a superb climb on hard ice. We climbed eight or nine pitches from the rimaye to the summit ridge and then followed this to the chossy rocky top. We reversed the route in seven long rappels using Abalakov anchors.

Two days later Nichols and Moneypenny climbed Diligent Epiphany on the right side of the north face of Mur Samir, I returned to base camp unacclimatized and unwell. This route featured immaculate alpine ice filling a four-meter-wide couloir with a section of 85°, and was graded TD- [the face is 600–700m in height].

After a brief period of bad weather, and the slaughter of our sheep, we headed up again to establish another advanced base, this time in the next glacier basin east of the John Charles Glacier. More bad weather kept us tentbound, but on a beautiful morning we quickly climbed two virgin peaks, Free Tibet (4,700m) and Pik Abu (4,495m); we graded both F. Views to the east were tantalizing, so we decided to explore there during our last few days. I remained at base camp with bad knees, while Nichols and Moneypenny made an abortive attempt on shapely Peak 4,788m, Nichols's bowels eventually getting the better of him.

We returned to Bishkek via Tash Rabat and then spent a few days sunning ourselves on the shores of Issyk-Kul before flying home. Our gratitude goes to the Mount Everest Foundation and British Mountaineering Council for their generous grants.

SAM LEACH, *UK*

The north face of Torolok. *Sam Leach*

At Bashi Range

Mustabbes and Kensu Valleys, various ascents. Two International School of Mountaineering (ISM) expeditions, both led by me, visited the Tien Shan in 2010 with the aim of exploring the At Bashi Range, a 100km-long spine of alpine peaks up to 4,788m in height. I had twice previously visited this range (*AAJ 2003* and *AAJ 2008*), which is very accessible from the north, being just two hours' drive from Naryn. At least three previous expeditions had approached from this side, where many valleys remain to be explored. This time both ISM teams approached from the south, necessitating an extra day's driving to get around the range, but opening up a wealth of new possibilities.

The east face of Kensu (right) rises above the Kensu Glacier. The route of ascent followed the left-hand skyline. *Paul Wellicome*

On the east ridge of Dom Byely. *Pat Littlejohn*

On the summit of Beersh Berkut in the Mustabbes Valley. The fine rock pyramid in the left distance is Topoz (4,600m), climbed in 2007 from the far valley by Max Gough, Barney Harford, and Pat Littlejohn (AD). *Pat Littlejohn*

In August the first group, comprising Ed Brown, David McMeeking, Mat Piaseki, Steve Taylor, and I approached up the Mustabbes River, establishing base camp where the river divides, each branch flowing from two different glaciers. Advanced base camp was set up at 3,950m on the eastern glacier, and after acclimatizing on Pik Stefan (4,480m, PD), the team climbed the striking tower of Pik Bashnya (4,690m) on the east side of the glacier. We reached the summit via the north ridge at AD. Our next objective was a domed peak of light-colored rock at the head of the glacier. Its east ridge gave another varied and enjoyable AD, with a compact rock tower providing the crux.

Lower down on the west side of the glacier are several forbidding rock spires, and further north various summits approachable by steep snow faces. The most attractive of these was traversed from north to south and featured exposed climbing over the rock tower of Pik Darshana (4,570m, AD). Near the top of the main peak, five huge eagles circled the climbers, providing a memorable moment and a name for this summit: Beersh Berkut (4,600m).

After this the weather broke, precluding an attempt on the rock spires. However, the trip had shown the potential of the range for very enjoyable mountaineering, which is technically interesting but generally less serious than the neighboring Kokshaal peaks to the south.

In September a larger team consisting of Patrick Cadell, Adam Dickins, Mark Dillon, Tim Evans, Laura Fletcher, Tom Fox, and Paul Wellicome, with guides Adrian Nelhams, Vladimir Komissarov, and I, began the trip in the limestone valley of Tash Rabat on the northern flank of the range. Famous for its thousand-year-old Caravanserai/fortress, the valley also had good climbing potential. We climbed five routes up to 500m in length and British HVS over two days. We then drove around the range and up the Kensu River valley to a group of glaciers below the second highest peak of the At Bashi: Kensu (4,757m). This had been climbed via its glaciated west flank by Soviet cartographers mapping this part of range. Their metal tripod still sits on top after 50 years.

Climbing from a base camp at 3,780m, and from an advanced base at 4,120m, three climbing teams managed 11 new peaks/routes over seven days. Grades ranged from F to D+, and highlights included the long, pinnacled rock ridge overlooking base camp (Sumashedshaya south ridge, 4,510m, D+), the east Ridge of Pik Ara (4,595m, AD), the north ridge of twin-summited Ekilik (4,496m, AD-), and the long and demanding south ridge of Kensu itself (AD). Unseasonable heavy snows then hit the range, forcing a retreat to Naryn, where we waited out two further days of snowfall before heading to Son Kul Canyon. Aside from the "big-wall" climbing of the Aksu and Karavshin valleys, Son Kul is currently Kyrgyzstan's premier rock climbing destination, having "alpine rock routes" up to 900m, as well as many shorter but adventurous crag climbs. Here we added several new routes up to eight pitches long and British E2, giving a total of around 20 routes in the canyon to date. As usual, Son Kul granted superb weather and was a perfect conclusion to a very enjoyable trip.

PAT LITTLEJOHN, *UK, Alpine Club*

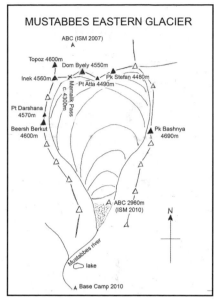

Mustabbes Map. *Pat Littlejohn*

Beyyt Kashka-Suu and Oshairak valleys, various ascents. In late July, Ann Piersall and I explored several drainages in the northeastern section of the At Bashi. A recipient of AAC research grants, Piersall was living in Kyrgyzstan and studying local perceptions of glacial retreat in the rural communities surrounding the At Bashi Range. From the small village of Ak-Muz, we hired a local horseman to take us a day's walk into the Taldy-Suu Valley (this area is more or less due south of Naryn).

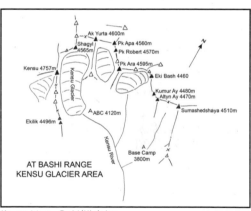

Kensu Map. *Pat Littlejohn*

The following day we proceeded south unsupported, crossed a 4,000m pass, and set up camp in the Beyyt Kashka-Suu drainage. From there we climbed four peaks. The first (4,390m, GPS) we climbed in deteriorating weather via its rocky northeast arête at PD (400m, II). The following day, under clear skies, we made our way south across a large glaciated basin that rose to a col between two prominent peaks. We climbed the corniced western peak first (4,561m, GPS), before returning to the col and linking two additional summits to the east (4,535m and 4,546m, GPS) via a high ridge (800m, PD III). On the summit of the middle peak (41°03.172' N, 76°08.935' E, GPS) we were surprised to find a large weathered tripod made of aluminum and wood. The location of the tripod corresponded with a triangular mark on our 1:100,000 Soviet map, supporting our belief that it was an instrument of Soviet geodetic survey.

After a week we exited the range via the Djol-Bozoshty Valley, tagging Pk. 4,340m (300m,

Looking into the Oshairak Valley. On the left is Pk. 4,530m, climbed to within 30m of the summit. The distant summit to the right is ca 4,700m. *Ben Logan*

Looking westward from Pk. 4,546m above the Bayyt Kashka-suu. The large snowy foreground summit is Pk. 4,535m, on which the Americans found a Soviet tripod. The distant snow peak at the far end of the continuation ridge is Pk. 4,561m. *Ben Logan*

F) along the way. We later confirmed that survey tripods, used in producing Soviet topographic maps, were installed by professional climbers and engineers in mountain ranges throughout Kyrgyzstan. Conversations with Valeri Kuzmichenok, the former head of the Kyrgyzstan Geodetic Survey, suggest that At Bashi's numerous historic survey points contradict assertions that the range was unexplored until recently.

A month later we made a trip into the southwestern At Bashi. Hiring a bemused local herder outside the village of Kazylbek, we rode to the head of the Oshairak drainage, where we took leave of our guide and camped at the tongue of a large glacier. The following day we ascended the glacier, negotiating large crevasses and snow bridges, to make camp on a moraine (40°56.001' N, 75°41.000' E; 4,001m, GPS). From there we attempted Pk. 4,530m, climbing east on steep, hard snow to gain a low-angle ridge, which took us to the summit pyramid. Thirty meters from the top we abandoned the attempt, lacking sufficient rock protection to proceed. From our high point we descended to the southwest via a snow couloir that was icy in sections, eventually returning to the glacier, and then skirting the base of the mountain to regain our tent (500m, PD III).

Over the course of the next few days we moved camp west across the glacier and onto a high ridge, putting us in position to attempt a group of attractive 4,700m peaks. However, foul weather and dwindling food and fuel forced us to abandon our exposed location. We did so via a short scramble over a small peak to our west, then descended the Chet-Keltebek Valley.

BEN LOGAN, *AAC*

WESTERN KOKSHAAL-TOO

Dzhirnagaktu Valley, first ascents and new routes.
Oktawian Ciez, Jakub Galka, Mariusz Norwecki,
Piotr Picheta, Jakub Wrona, and I formed the
Krakow High Mountain Club expedition to the
Western Kokshaal-too. We wanted to explore
Dzhirnagaktu Valley, which lies immediately west
of the Kyzyl Asker Glacier basin, and between it
and the Ak-Bai-Tal. Before we left we couldn't find
any record of previous visits by mountaineers.

Pk. 4,530m from the west. The attempt from the
Oshairak Valley stopped within 30m of the summit.
Ben Logan

On August 3, after crossing three glacial
runoffs, we established base camp at 3,800m.
From here it took five days to transport all
our gear up to an advanced base at 4,271m.
During this period we discovered our satellite
phone was not working, so on the 6th, in an
attempt to find a signal,
we climbed onto a nearby
ridge, in the process
reaching the top of two
summits that we named
Sputnik Hope (4,371m)
and Long Spire (4,564m).

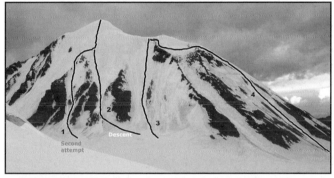

Night Butterfly from the south, showing (1) south face ascent and (2)
descent. (3) is the descent used after the failed attempt (4) by the east
ridge. *Tomasz Owerko*

On the 9th we made
an unsuccessful attempt
on what was unanimously
agreed to be the focal
point of the entire valley,
a peak we named Night
Butterfly (5,056m). We
tried the icy east ridge and
got as far as a false summit, but big cornices prevented us from continu-
ing. As we had made a late
start, and the temperature
was high, snow conditions
became quite dangerous.
A few days later Norwecki,
Picheta, Rowna, and I
tried again, this time from
the south. We reached the
top at 8 a.m. after eight
hours climbing.

The north side of Night Butterfly (right) and Pik Uigur from advanced base
on the Dzhirnagaktu Glacier. *Tomasz Owerko*

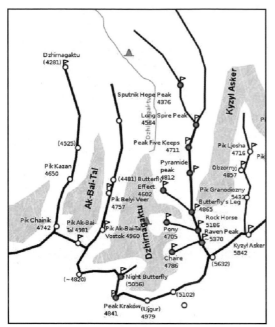

Map of Dzhirnagaktu. *Tomasz Owerko*

On the 12th Ciez, Galka, and Picheta tried Pik ca 5,370m on the east rim of the upper glacier basin. The west ridge looked the logical line, but thin ice, poor protection, and fragile rock turned them back not far from the summit. The rope got stuck on the first rappel, and they were only able to retrieve a short section. This later saved Ciez, who was tied to it when he fell into a crevasse. The round trip from camp lasted 27 hours. A few days later Ciez and Galka returned, and in a 24-hour continuous round trip from camp climbed and rappelled (from Abalakovs) the 700m north face. The summit was named Raven Peak.

During the expedition we reached 12 summits: three above 5,000m; four high 4,000ers, and five low 4,000ers. However, the main goal, and the highest

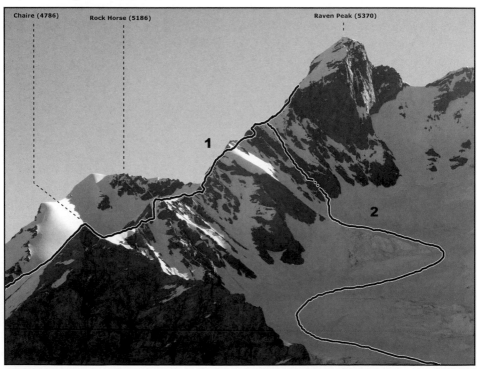

Raven Peak from southwest with (1) attempted route on west ridge and (2) descent. *Tomasz Owerko*

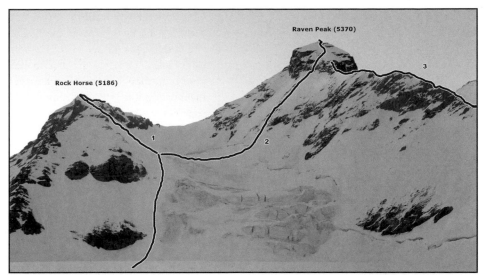

Rock Horse with (1) Norwecki-Picheta route from west, (2) north face direct of Raven Peak, and (3) attempted route on west ridge. These peaks were first climbed by Soviets, most likely in 1985, along the skyline ridge. *Tomasz Owerko*

mountain in the valley, Pik 5,632m, was not reached. *[Editor's note: although there is no evidence that climbers operated in the Dzhirnagaku prior to this expedition, archive Soviet documents show that Pik 5,632m was climbed in the 1980s from the Kyzyl Asker Glacier via the ridge over Rock Horse and Raven Peak. It seems likely this was in 1985, when a large Kazakh expedition led by Kazbek Valiev climbed the west face of Kyzyl Asker over eight days in August. It also seems likely that other peaks climbed on the Kyzyl Asker-Dzhirnagaku divide by the Krakow team were previously climbed by Soviets.]*

Apart from peaks mentioned above, we climbed: Rock Horse (5,186m, west ridge, Norwecki-Picheta); Butterfly's Leg (4,865m, west ridge, Galka-Norwecki-Picheta, a cairn was found on the summit); Pik Krakow (4,841m, Galka-Owerko-Picheta); Pyramide (4,812m, Picheta, but thought to have been climbed before); Chaire (4,786m, the top of the west face of Raven Peak leading to the latter's west ridge, Ciez-Galka-Picheta); Pik Five Keeps (4,711m, Picheta, thought to have been climbed before); Pony (4,705m, south couloir, Owerka-Picheta); and Butterfly Effect (4,602m, west ridge, Galka). We also reached the Uigur Pass (4,631m) on the frontier ridge between Pik 5,102m and Uigur (4,979m). There are still four good virgin peaks left, two above 5,000m.

Throughout our stay the weather was unstable and the temperature often too high for safe climbing conditions. We also experienced an annoying föhn wind, which not only warmed the air dramatically, but also kept breaking the Chinese tents we'd bought in Bishkek. We often started out in the middle of the night. Ice was often very thin and buried under loose snow. The rock is mainly schist and quartzite, very fractured and folded. Finding a good belay on this was almost impossible. We also found the glaciers tricky, especially higher up where there were moderately sized crevasses concealed by a thin layer of snow. For more information visit kw.krakow.pl/kokshal2010.

TOMASZ OWERKO, *Poland*

Pik Vernyi (ca 5,250m), northwest face, No Shachlik. In July Julien Christe, Alexandre Gal, Jérôme Gottofrey, and I headed for Kyrgyzstan to attempt the northwest face of Pik Vernyi above the Kyzyl Asker Glacier. We had climbed in this region during 2004 and seen the face, but we didn't have the equipment to make an attempt. This 700m wall of vertical, compact granite, split by few cracks and characterized by enormous tafoni (cave-like features in the rock formed by wind, or salt erosion), has been attempted around seven times since the early 1980s but was not climbed until 2009, when Nikolai Bandalet's five-man team spent four days climbing a line close to the left edge (*AAJ 2010*).

Looking south-southeast over the Kyzyl Asker Glacier at (A) Pik Unmarked Soldier (5,352m), (B) Pik Vernyi (ca 5,250m), and (C) Pik Panfilovski Division (5,290m). (1) 2009 Belorussian-Russian Route. (2) No Shachlik. (3) Original 1988 Soviet Route—northwest face and south ridge. The left skyline of Vernyi is the difficult north ridge, climbed in 2002 by a British team. *Maria Gal*

We reached the area in an old Soviet vehicle. Though not inspiring on first acquaintance, it proved remarkably efficient. To access base camp we had to drive 15km across a marshy delta. We bogged down four times and had to use jacks to lift the wheels, then put boards and stones on the ground to start moving. We were lucky that our driver, Sasha, was bold and experienced. Two days later we reached base camp, exhausted. A French team, which also planned to operate from this valley, never made it, the driver being less adventurous.

After establishing an advanced camp at the foot of the face, we watched a meteorological parade. A night of bad weather plastered the face with snow, making it impossible to climb. Spindrift and sloughing snow cascaded down the face that day after the storm, and it was another day before fine weather returned, melting the snow and soaking the rock. We realized that we shouldn't fret but instead

Starting pitch 14 (A2) from the second portaledge camp in the giant tafone. *Maria Gal*

Pitch 21 (A1 M6) on No Shachlik. *Maria Gal*

make progress, whatever the conditions. Our beautiful dream of free climbing had to be forgotten; we were forced into an aided ascent.

The wall can be divided into three parts: first a sort of compact shield with thin cracks; second the main section of wall, which features large crack systems; and finally a section of ice. Progress was slow, but after five days we'd climbed the initial buttress. Then it was time to haul the portaledges to the top of pitch six and set off in capsule style.

The first night the ledges proved uncomfortable; we were not well protected from the snow and ice that drummed on the fabric of our precarious habitat. Shelling the next day was intense, and we found it impossible to go out. Eventually, we were able to start moving, only to find the cracks chocked with ice. Wet snow on the rock didn't help either, making the climbing more difficult and progress even slower.

We placed our second camp in one of nature's peculiarities: an enormous tafone, large enough to give complete shelter, at the top of pitch 13. In fact the cave was formed by a large flake, completely separated from the rock. There was a drop of 600m below our feet and a long arch over our heads. The ground above proved the most trying on the nerves. A large snowpatch, 200m above, was melting. It was the start of the summer season, and the cold temperatures predicted by the Russians were now beginning to rise uncomfortably. Streams turned into torrents down the wall. We became soaked to the skin, and while one pair was climbing, the other was drying shoes, jackets, and outerwear over three gas stoves, which burned non-stop inside our ledges. Morale was low, but over the next two days we managed to make it to the snowpatch.

The final pitches leading to the top were mixed, and we were able to climb faster. On the summit, in the slanting rays of the setting sun, we were euphoric, and celebrated by clinking glasses of smuggled brandy, carried up the route for this occasion. Below our feet lay 900m of climbing and the new route No Shachlik (No Barbeque in Russian, 23 pitches, VI 6c A3 M6).

MARIA GAL, *Switzerland*

CENTRAL KOKSHAAL-TOO

Djangart Range, Pik Howard-Bury (4,766m), Horseman's Horror; Pik Sutherland (5,080m), Will your anchor hold?; Pik Illumination (5,040m), Postcard for the Chief. Matt Traver (UK), Chris Parenteau, and I (both American) arrived in Bishkek on July 1. We were accompanied by Jamie Maddison (UK), who was investigating the bouldering potential of the area while reporting on the trip for a UK magazine. We spent two days sorting logistics before spending the weekend working as volunteers for the Alpine Fund, climbing with Kyrghyz children at the sport-climbing venue of Chon-Kurchak. Our last member, Dan Clark (UK), arrived on the 5th, and the following day we left for Djangart on a 6WD truck, accompanied by Abdybek, an Alpine Fund intern who we intended to employ as a translator and expedition cook.

After two days' travel we reached the military border post of Uch-Koshkon, where Abdybek, lacking photo identification to go with his border permit, was denied passage and had to return to Bishkek.

Due to impassable conditions on the track over the Djangart Pass (4,158m, 41°40.678' N, 78°48.951'E), we were dropped in the Kaichi Valley. On his way home to Bishkek, our driver arranged for local nomads to help us, and over the next two days four horses transported all our equipment over the pass to a base camp alongside the Djangart River, near the outflow of the Akoguz Glacier.

Pik Illumination with the line of Postcard for the Chief. *Mike Royer*

We spent several days on acclimatization and reconnaissance before Clark, Traver, and I (Parenteau was ill and remained in camp) set off for the Djangartynbashi Glacier, one of four glacial valleys that rises south of the main Djangart Valley. It took a day and a half to reach the foot of Pt. 4,766m (41°37' N, 78°51' E), and on the following day, in a snowstorm, we made a 22½-hour round-trip ascent of the peak via the northwest face. We climbed an elegant 700m icy couloir leading directly to the summit, and we named our line Horseman's Horror (D+ 80°) after discovering that nomads had cut 20m from one of our ropes. We propose calling the summit Pik Howard-Bury, after the British explorer who visited the Tien Shan in the early 20th Century.

After a day's rest at base, Traver and I set off for the N2 glacier, with Clark and Parenteau heading for the N1. After a perilous ford of the Djangart River, Traver and I made a

The highest summit in the Djangart, Pik 5,312m, remains unclimbed. The upper east face is seen here from Djangart Pass. *Mike Royer*

lengthy approach up the broken glacier to the east face of Pt. 5,080m (41°39' N, 78°59' E). Delayed by morning snow squalls, we began our ascent at mid-day, climbing the southernmost couloir on the face, then following the broad shoulder above to the summit block. As night fell, heavy winds scoured the shoulder, and just meters from the true summit we elected to descend to avoid traversing into the full force of the wind. We have proposed naming the summit Pik Sutherland, after Traver's great uncle, Robbie L Sutherland, a prominent Orcadean sailor and author, who recently passed away. The route was aptly christened, Will Your Anchor Hold? (700m, TD-), which is also the title of one of his books.

Pik Howard-Bury with the line of Horseman's Horror. *Mike Royer*

Clark and Parenteau were less fortunate. During their approach, Clark collapsed and suffered serious concussion. Parenteau escorted Clark back to base camp, where a day later Clark collapsed again. Unable to make a medical diagnosis, the team arranged evacuation with the assistance of Global Rescue. Accompanied by Maddison, Clark reached the Kaichi valley and went by vehicle to Bishkek for medical consultation. Back home, Clark has been diagnosed with a heart arrhythmia.

Pik Sutherland with the line of Will your Anchor Hold? *Mike Royer*

Rain and snow, which were a daily occurrence throughout the expedition, now intensified, but determined to make one more climb, Parenteau, Traver, and I again headed to the Djangartynbashi to attempt Pt. 5,048m (41°35' N, 78°52' E). On July 26, after

A challenging bridge crossing during Clark's evacuation to Bishkek. *Jamie Maddison*

a full day of post-holing up the glacier, we pitched camp at the base of the mountain. The following day, with Parenteau forced to remain in camp due to wet boots, Traver and I climbed the north ridge and northeast face under sunny skies, one of only a couple such days during the entire expedition. We named the route Postcard for the Chief (650m, AD+) as a tribute to the soldiers, in a nearby military post, who were unable to receive mail. Due to the good weather we propose the name Pik Illumination for the summit.

We left the valley on the 31st, but a washed out bridge forced us to walk to Uch-Koshkon before meeting our truck, assisted in hauling gear and crossing a river by a horse and soldier sent from the post. Unable to carry all our gear, and unable to make a second trip because of the truck's schedule, we paid the soldiers to make a second trip after our departure for Bishkek and offered them our equipment. We were supported by an AAC Mountain Fellowship, a WL Gore Shipton-Tilman Grant, the Mount Everest Foundation, British Mountaineering Council, Welsh Sports Council, and the Jeremy Willson Charitable Trust.

Considerable additional information about this expedition can be found at its website: kyrgyzstan2010.com.

MIKE ROYER, *AAC*

Editor's Note: Lying 95km south of Karakol city, the Djangart region was first explored by Russians in 1932, though little documentation is available on their activities. The peaks had to wait over 70 years for their next visit by mountaineers. In 2004 British climbers Ingrid Crossland and Graham Sutton made two unsuccessful attempts on the highest summit, Pik 5,318m.

In 2008 a team from Moscow climbed Pik 5,291m, the first known ascent of any summit in the range. They also climbed two lower peaks from the Kaichi Valley. This leaves the area offering enormous potential for first ascents and new routes, and there is at least one glacier system still completely unexplored. On some granite ridges and shorter walls the rock quality appears high.

ADYRTOR MOUNTAINS

Piks Kongsberg (4,468m), Resilience (4,447m), Majulah (5,152m). From August 2–19, 2009, David Lim, Mohd Rozani bin Maarof, and Grant Rawlinson, forming the "Spirit of Singapore Climbing Expedition," traveled to an area loosely known as the Adyrtor Mountains, just north of the famous Inylchek glaciers. We drove from Almaty in Kazakhstan to Karakara Base Camp (2,000m) and were then helicoptered 90km by a Kyrgyz Army MI-8 to the Mushketova Glacier, where we established our own base camp at 3,950m.

After two-and-a-half days of reconnaissance and acclimatization, we chose our first objective, an unnamed and unclimbed peak on the watershed ridge north of the glacier, marked as 4,468m on our large scale map to the region. On the 7th we climbed seven hours up rock and scree to a broad, snowy ridge, which we followed to the top. We named it Kongsberg Peak (42°18'47.2" N, 79°57'45.0" E, 4,551m GPS, Alpine F) in honor of our premier expedition partner. The Kazakhstan Mountaineering Federation believes this peak to be unclimbed, as were all the peaks we shortlisted in the upper Mushketova. The exception was Pk. 5,153m, which had been heli-skied but not actually climbed. No evidence of any previous parties was found except for a few candy wrappers on the moraine.

Looking south from Kongsberg Pk. over the Mushketova Glacier to high peaks on the Inylchek watershed. The route up Majulah is marked; the rest are unclimbed. The pointed fourth peak from the left was dubbed the Razor (ca 5,500m), originally one of the main objectives of the Singapore team. Close inspection revealed serious crevassing and avalanche risk. *David Lim*

Three–five km east and northeast of Kongsberg lie three peaks first climbed in 2005 by the Singapore Maccoffee Expedition and also led by David Lim: Ong Teng Cheong Peak on the Kyrgyz-Kazakh border (4,763m), Temasek, and Singapura I (4,550m).

On the 9th we made an attempt on Pk. 5,153m but turned back at ca 4,250m due to avalanche danger. The next day Lim and Rawlinson climbed for seven hours to a previously virgin summit (PD-, 42°18'57.7" N, 79°56'08.1" E, 4,447m map, 4,457m GPS), west of Kongsberg.

Looking east from Resilience Pk. at Kongsberg Pk. The glacier below and to the right is the upper Mushketova, while the high peaks behind form the watershed with the Inylchek, or the Semenova (a parallel glacier to the Mushketova immediately north). *David Lim*

The ascent was particularly satisfying due to the extreme weather and exposed third-class scrambling over steep, loose rock. It was energy sapping and very difficult for Lim, who is partially disabled by Guillain-Barre Syndrome. His right leg no longer works below the knee, but it hasn't stopped him from making more than 32 climbs since his disability in 1998. The summit was named Resilience Peak in respect of the determination Lim needed to reach the top.

Finally, on the 13th and in gradually worsening weather, we made a last attempt to climb a mountain over 5,000m. Shown on the map as 5,152m, and lying between the Mushketova and North Inylchek, it required three days of reconnaissance and much "discussion" before we agreed on a relatively safe route up the northeast face and onto the long north ridge. After a cold 3:30 a.m. start, we climbed strongly up the glacial headwall and onto the ridge, where the snow was heart-breaking soft. At times we sunk to our waists. It took seven hours in high wind to reach the summit. This was definitely the hardest ascent of the trip, with strong winds and a snowstorm reducing visibility (sometimes to 20m), and wiping out our tracks for the four-hour descent. We picked our way carefully down the long ridge and rappelled some sections before winding through a mass of crevasses along the Mushketova glacier to regain base camp, 13 hours after leaving. We recovered after many brews of tea, mouthfuls of dried Kazakh horse meat, and muesli bars. We named the peak Majulah (PD+, 42°16'19.9" N, 79°56'52.2" E, 5,174m GPS), a Malay word meaning "onward," or "forge ahead." All GPS heights are uncorrected, and we estimate errors of between +/- 20m.

DAVID LIM AND GRANT RAWLINSON, *Republic of Singapore*

TENGRI TAG

Khan Tengri, second ascent of Ukrainian Route. In early August Alexander Kirikov and I completed what we believed at the time to be a new route on Khan Tengri. It began from the standard site of Camp 2 (5,300m) on the classic route from the south up the Semenovsky Glacier and then followed a beautiful, logical, and relatively easy line up the southwest face, between the Normal Route (Russian 5A, Pogrebetskogo, 1931) up the west ridge, and the 1964 Romanov Route up the south-south-

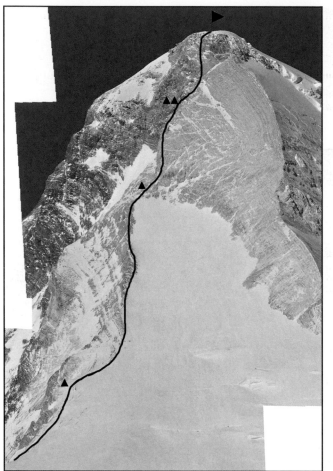

The upper section of the 1982 Ukrainian Route on the southwest face of Khan Tengri with the Kirikov-Sokolov bivouacs. *Gleb Sokolov*

west or Marble Rib (6A). We named our line Zmeyka (little snake) due to its sinuous nature and graded it 5B. I felt that it was generally safe and could be recommended to soloists. However, only later we discovered it was not new.

Historically, Soviet mountaineering was a highly structured affair, with climbers progressing through "categories" towards gaining their Master of Sport. More experienced alpinists participated in Soviet Championships. Ascents were recorded, and new routes, particularly at high altitude, were recorded in great detail and submitted to the USSR Classification Committee of the Federation of Alpinism. So it is strange that a report of a new route on Khan Tengri climbed in 1982 by Eugeniy Kondakov and his Ukrainian team was either not completed or it was lost. A description of their line appears in the standard Putevoditel guide by Solomatin, and in several other sources, but it is vague to say the least.

There was a lot of snow on the slopes of Khan Tengri this August, and it quickly became soft in the calm weather and hot sun we experienced. This forced us to camp early and spend a comfortable night enjoying a little cognac and making long philosophical discussions about the meaning of life. The second day on the face saw us moving on or alongside the twisting rock rib. The large snow slope to the right looked tempting, but who knows what could have been in store for us: A gigantic ride on an avalanche, melting out 1,000 years later as objects of research studies and to the astonishment of our descendants? We only roped up for the upper part of the ridge, and even there moved together.

Camp 4 was pitched between two large boulders and again provided a comfortable site. However, during the night the wind picked up, and it started to snow. By morning there was no change.

We continued climbing. Crampons held perfectly on the rock, and we found Peckers, angle pins, Friends, and nuts very useful for protection. The upper wall is a huge chunk of marble, but in

Alexander Kirikov during the second ascent of the 1982 Kondakov Route on Khan Tengri. *Gleb Sokolov*

the bad weather was covered in ice crystals, which appeared as though someone had spilled a sea of acid down the slope.

We spent two nights at Camp 5, located on the ridge beneath a rock. The wind was so strong that we spent the whole time inside the tent fully dressed with our boots on, scared that our home would be blown away. It was extremely cold.

On August 8 we left late for the summit, the wind having only begun to decrease at 10 a.m. We wore down jackets and insulated pants on top of our Goretex suits. Close to the top the rock became steeper, but it was always possible to set up a good belay. The wind froze whimsical patterns on the slope; leaves and needles protruded from boulders. At 5:30 p.m. we reached the summit in blue sky, the rays of the setting sun, and relative calmness, while below is was still total shit. The entire summit area was covered in ice fronds, like millions of frozen children, or maybe little devils, trying to reach us with their glistening hands. It was enchanting but also a little terrifying. We tried to tread carefully as we descended to the fixed ropes of the west ridge, the maelstrom, and home.

GLEB SOKOLOV, *Russia. Supplied by Anna Piunova, mountain.ru,*

translated by Ekaterina Vorotnikova

Editor's note: Kirikov and Sokolov, the latter with intimate knowledge of the mountain having climbed it more than 20 times, followed the little-known 1982 Ukrainian route, though it now appears as though a similar line may have been climbed in 1936 during the third ascent of Khan Tengri by Eugeniy and Vitaly Abalakov, Michael Dadiomova, Leon Gutman, and Lorenz Saladin. These five were ostensibly repeating the west ridge but there was much snow on the mountain and they had only a photo from above 6,000m given to them by Pogrebetskiy. They ended up taking the easiest way at the time. Their descent from the summit proved something of an epic. All suffered frostbite and the great Swiss explorer Saladin died of his injuries less than two weeks later.

Afghanistan

The online version of these reports frequently contains additional photos, maps, topos, and extended text. Please visit aaj.americanalpineclub.org

KOH-I-BABA MOUNTAINS

Koh-i-Baba towers from the south. (A) First tower attempted, by line (1). (B) Second, highest, tower (ca 15,400'), climbed by the couloir (2) and face on far side. (C) Third tower, climbed by traverse (3) from second tower. *Mike Libecki*

Koh-i-Baba towers. In early July I arrived in Kabul alone and took a chartered flight to Bamiyan Province. Here I hired a 4x4 and local guide/translator and drove to the Koh-e-Baba Mountains, a western extension of the Hindu Kush 170km west of Kabul. I had photos of some towers, but no one I met recognized them. After several hours of driving, I spotted them from the road. Locals agreed to hire a horse and mule to take me to the towers. At first the locals were concerned that helping an American might cause political trouble in their village, but as I had official documents, they allowed me to continue. Next day we established base camp close to the towers. The photo had made them look like granite, but now I could see they were loose, crumbly limestone. Rain and wet snow settled in, part of the same system that caused horrific floods in Pakistan at that time.

A week later the weather stabilized, and I fixed a pitch through snow and ice (rock climbing shoes with crampons) and up into the gray-white limestone. The stone was so loose and sandy that most cam placements slid out under bodyweight. Next morning I started pitch two. After 175' the system I was following led to a questionable, chunky flake, about eight feet wide, five feet tall, and just over a foot thick. I tapped it lightly with my hammer. I had to pass through this section or retreat. I put in a cam on the very right edge of the flake, weighted it, and it pulled out. The limestone seemed to be all mudded together, so I decided not to touch the flake again. I drilled a couple of holes underneath it and hooked past the flake. Ten feet above and left of the flake, I started to drill an anchor. As I hammered the bolt, ckckrrrhhhupulchch. The entire flake exploded down the face. Frightening is an understatement. My main thought was that the ropes could be cut. I finished building my anchor, then, with two back-ups on my tag line, slowly lowered. The tag line was hit badly in two places; I tied double knots and passed them. My lead line was cut, exposing white cord. This was the worse rock I had come across in my life, and, tail between my legs, I went back to camp.

Next morning I swapped my lead line for a spare and continued. But 100' up the fourth pitch I finally accepted the message that the rock, lubricated by rain, was giving me. At that moment huge stonefall came down to my right. The lead rope was hit in two places. I had to go down now, finally limping away from the base of the tower after a grapefruit-sized stone connected with my foot.

I had a few days left before catching the plane home, so I focused on the remaining two summits. Several couloirs led to a ridge that would get me to the backside of the towers. I climbed one that was enjoyable: easy enough to climb fast with crampons, steep enough for a long fall. After about 1,500' I was on a ridge of dragon-back peaks and fins, again composed of the shittiest rock. I had come upon a self-born rating system, which I reference as Russian Roulette Rating to quantify the looseness of the rock. On a 1 to 5 RRR system, the first climb I attempted had to be RRR4 (am I sugar coating this, some kind of denial?), while this second tower was RRR3. The rock crumbled every few moves. Downclimbing would be scary. Twenty feet below the top I thought of turning back. I moved s-l-o-w-l-y, to the summit, touched it with my hand (tag, you're it) and downclimbed.

It was now late afternoon, and I still had one more summit I wanted to climb. I scrambled through gullies and along ridges to reach its base. Although loose, the climbing was straightforward, and the ascent quick. I arrived back at camp as a manzanita-maroon sky and jagged black horizon became one.

MIKE LIBECKI. *AAC*

HINDU KUSH

Noshaq (7,492m). From 2007-2010 there were four ascents of Noshaq, the highest mountain in Afghanistan and second highest in the Hindu Kush. In the autumn of 2007 Iranians Mehdi Amidi and Azim Qeychi-Saz became only the second group of climbers to reach the summit in nearly 30 years. In 2003, Carlo Alberto Pinelli, gained official permission to visit the Wakhan Corridor with his expedition 'Oxus, Mountains for Peace in Afghanistan'. His team successfully made the first ascent of Noshaq for 25 years, though they had deal with unexpected objective danger in the approach valley, which they discovered had been planted three years previously with over 600 anti-personnel mines (*AAJ 2004*).

In mid-July 2009 Amruddin and Malang, Afghans from the Wakhan who had trained in Chamonix, reached the summit with French guides Jean Annequin and Simon Destombes. In 2010 there were two ascents. James Bingham (UK), Bill Lyden (US), and Mark Wynne (UK) reached the summit on July 21 from a high camp at 7,100m. On August 29 it was the turn of Iranians Husain Asghari, Amin Moein, Gholam Nodehi, Mohammad Rafiei, H.Reza Sanjari, and Iraj Taheri, who topped out just 17 days after arrival at base camp. All climbed via the "standard" west ridge.

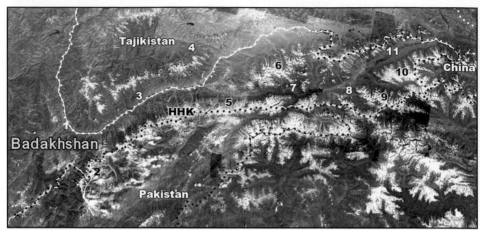

Afghanistan's Wakhan Corridor lies in the province of Badakhshan and is surrounded by Tajikistan, Pakistan, and China. This map serves to locate reports in the 2011 *AAJ*, along with various geographical
features. (1) Ishkashim. (2) Noshaq. (3) Oxus River. (4) Pik Karl Marx (6,723m) in Tajik Southwest Pamir. (HHK)
High Hindu Kush. (5) Qala-i-Hurst. (6) Big Pamir. (7) Roadhead at Sarhad-e-Boroghil, south of which lies
Koh-e-SuzAnna. (8) Little Pamir. (9) Koh-i-Iskander. (10) Koh-e-Ak Su, the sector of the Little Pamir explored
by the Polish expedition. (11) Lake Chaqmaqtin (4,000m), reached by Madge and Torretta. *Compiled by
Lindsay Griffin on a Google Earth map*

The expansive upper Qala-i-Hurst Glacier basin. (A) Koh-e-Beefy. (B) Koh-e-Baffa. (C) Koh-e-Forot Zorman.
(D) Top of unnamed peak attempted by Dutch. (E) Koh-e-Yakhi. Low rocky ridge in right foreground is
southern end of Pt. 5,200m, climbed in 2008. *Bart Klein*

In 1978 a coup d'etat and the Soviet invasion the following year put the Hindu
Kush off-limits. Otherwise, Noshaq's west ridge would probably be one of the world's
most popular objectives for commercially organized expeditions attempting a high but
technically moderate ascent. If access to this region (via Tajikistan) continues to be relatively straightforward and safe, the mountain could see a strong resurgence in popularity.

LINDSAY GRIFFIN, *Mountain INFO*

Qala-i-Hurst (valley), Koh-e-Hoppa, Koh-e-Baffa, and Koh-e-Forot Zorman. Roeland Bom, Bart
Klein, Daniel Kuipers (leader), and I wanted to travel to an adventurous part of the world, without

many climbers, within our limited budget, and with mountains below 6,000m. Our gaze had already turned towards the stan countries of Central Asia, when we discovered the strange strip of land between Tajikistan and Pakistan, known as the Wakhan Corridor. After some internet research, we decided this would be our goal: an area untouched by the war in the rest of Afghanistan, with friendly people, and many beautiful, unclimbed mountains.

Koh-e-Hoppa on east side of Qala-i-Hurst Glacier, showing route of first ascent. The mountain was traversed from right to left. *Bart Klein*

We arrived at the Tajikistan-Afghanistan border with 200kg of luggage. It felt strange to be entering voluntarily a country that makes headlines daily with stories of war and terrorism. Nervous due to our satellite phone, supply of strong medicines, and video camera, we approached the check point. Our worries turned out to be groundless.

Koh-e-Forot Zorman. From col camp on frontier ridge, west ridge was followed to summit. Photograph taken low on east face of unnamed peak, attempted by Dutch. *Bart Klein*

The Afghan border guards were happy and friendly and only took interest in our Netherlands candy.

After four days of increasingly remote travel, we arrived at Qala-i-Hurst, a village 150km into the Corridor, from which the glacial valley of the same name rises south to the Pakistan border. We arranged for 10 porters for the final trek to base camp at 4,800m, which we reached in two days. The glacier here is more than 10km wide, and rimmed by many imposing north faces. On our first day we made an acclimatization climb on a small mountain in the middle of the glacier, from which we had a good view of the surrounding peaks. Our preparation at home had consisted of looking at Google Earth maps and a few photos from a previous expedition, so it felt good to view the mountains for real. We decided to try four mountains that looked feasible, all previously unclimbed, as far as we knew.

The first peak quickly gave us a lesson in estimating scale. We thought we would run up and down it in a morning, but we needed a full day to summit, panting because of the lack of oxygen. A rocky couloir, followed by steep snow and a short ridge, led to the 5,300m top, which we named Koh-e-Hoppa, after the word most frequently used by our porters. The route was AD and mostly

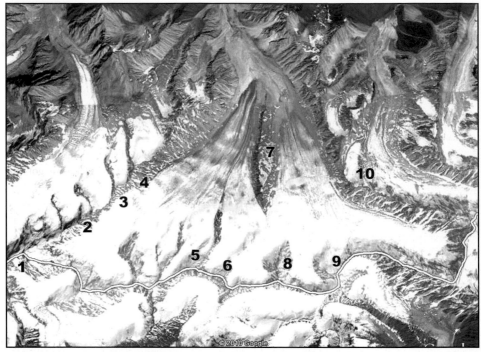

Qala-i-Hurst. Named peaks and ascents, where known, are indicated. (1) Koh-e-Yakhi (Koh-e-Goldar, 5,974m), (2) Sakh-e-Kucek (5,408m), (3) Sakh-e-Sangi (5,237m), (4) Koh-e-Awal (5,299m), (5) Koh-e-Forot Zorman (5,500m, Dutch 2010), (6) Koh-e-Baffa (5,300m, Dutch 2010), (7) Pt. 5,200m (Gorg Ali, Amruddin, Lucia Foppoli, Elisabetta Galli, Afiat Khan, Giorgio Mallucci, and Angelo Quattrini, 2008), (8) Koh-e-Beefy (5,410m, Joe Fiddes and Chris Philipson, 2009), (9) Pt. 5,600m (Elisabetta Galli, Afiat Khan, Giorgio Mallucci, 2008), and (10) Koh-e-Hoppa (5,300m, Dutch 2010).

Koh-e-Baffa. Peak was traversed from right to left: up north ridge, down southeast ridge and east flank. *Bart Klein*

snow to 70°, with a chimney of UIAA III.

Our second objective lay at the head of the glacier, and we first had to establish an advanced base. Heavily loaded, we certainly felt the altitude at 5,000m and again underestimated the distance. After a night of little sleep, we were greeted the following morning by a beautiful, steep, snowy ridge rising to the summit. Deadmen and snowstakes proved most useful, and we named the 5,300m peak Koh-e-Baffa: the good mountain. We traversed the mountain, descending an ice couloir. The ascent of the exposed ridge was AD+.

Three days later we prepared for the most beautiful mountain so far by establishing a camp in a col on the frontier ridge. To our knowledge this pass had not been crossed by humans, but that night we dreamed of carpet-smuggling Taliban. The next day we woke to a glorious morning. We climbed a snowy ridge, then made a steep traverse around a rock tower, and finally followed another ridge to the top. Superb! We called it Koh-e-Forot Zorman (5,500m), after Roeland's newborn nephew. Our route was AD+, with snow to 60° and one short mixed gully of 80°.

We spent another night at the border camp and then tackled our fourth peak. Again, we had problems estimating scale. A couloir led to a ridge. We thought the couloir looked rather difficult and delicate, but the ridge seemed to pose no problem. How wrong we were. Climbing the couloir on the east face was effortless, but the ridge turned out to be steep, unconsolidated snow alongside equally steep rock. Two hundred meters below the top we had no choice but to retreat. As far as we got, the grade was D-, with loose snow to 70° and rock to UIAA V. We were a little disappointed by this failure but, overall, very satisfied with our journey through a wonderful country, and our three new peaks.

MARIAN MICHIELSEN, *The Netherlands, with additional information by Daniel Kuipers*

PAMIR

Hindu Kush, Koh-e-SuzAnna (4,660m); Little Pamir, Koh-e-Ski (4,760m) and Koh-e-Grivel (4,800m).
On May 25 Anna Torretta, from Italy, and I arrived in Dushanbe, Tajikistan, and traveled southeast for two days by 4WD to Ishkashim, where we crossed into Afghanistan. This sensitive border is renowned for opium and people smuggling, so imagine my astonishment when I stepped outside the smoky wooden passport hut and spotted Anna filming with her video camera. Was she mad? A shriek from a border guard told me that someone certainly was. My nostril got nervous as a gun was poked up it. Not good. Anna took out the tape and offered it to the police. I wanted to snatch it from her, stamp on it with my mountaineering boot, and attack it with my ice axe. Slowly, slowly, the matter was settled with cigarettes, cash, and diplomacy, and my nostril breathed again.

Anna had visited the Wakhan in 2008 (*AAJ 2009*) and was keen to go farther east. But the valleys of the Hindu Kush south of the Wakhan Corridor were loaded with snow, and the weather did not seem good, so we decided to stay low and attempt smaller peaks with less avalanche risk.

Our aim was to complete a journey on horse and foot along the Oxus River to Lake Chaqmaqtin, stopping along the way to ski anything that tickled our fancy. We had no maps or photos, but knew there was one difficult snowy pass to cross. We didn't even know whether we would get to ski. And I had never ridden a horse.

After two days of bureaucracy we boarded another 4WD and traveled a further two days along the Corridor to the roadhead at Sarad-e-Boroghil (3,300m), where we stopped for a day, May 31. It was time for some skiing.

"I think the peak is about 4,000m" said Anna. By the time we reached 4,500m, I was fried. My feet were on fire, and my throat as dry as the Sahara, from six hours of ascent in ski boots. We had started the day bumping south across the Oxus on horseback—my triumphant first ride. We then scrambled for two hours on scree, followed by skinning for four hours. It was a bold acclimatization day, but every sweaty painful step was worth it for the final, astonishing views into Pakistan from the top of what we named Koh-e-SuzAnna. After the first ascent came a magical ski descent on spring snow.

Suzy Madge (left) and Anna Torretta near Sarad-e-Boroghil. Behind and to the south is Koh-e-SuzAnna. *Suzy Madge*

Next day we reached the Daliz Pass (4,173m), but deep snow prevented the horses from crossing. We tried again next morning, having to unload the horses and drag the loads ourselves. Incredibly, there was a dry path on the far side, and the horses merrily trotted beside us as we skied east from the pass.

For the next three days we walked and rode spellbound into the Little Pamir, occasionally crossing paths with Kyrghiz nomads driving yak herds. Eventually we reached Bozai Gumbaz (4,000m), a Kyrghiz nomad spring village, where we paid our horsemen. Poor weather encouraged us to stop here and climb/ski two small mountains: Koh-e-Ski, via an ascent of the southwest flank and descent of the northeast, and Koh-e-Grivel, up and down the southeast flank. Unstable weather kept us from bigger ascents.

On June 7 we reached Lake Chaqmaqtin (4,000m) and two days later made an attempt on a 4,800m peak via the north ridge. Not far from the summit the weather turned and we retreated, skiing the northeast slope (35-40°).

All too early, we were forced to start heading back to Sarhad; the Kyrghiz were returning to collect supplies from the World Food Programme and we needed their horse transport. The four-day journey was arduous, with 13,000m of ascent and descent on narrow paths above 1,000m drops, which provided huge motivation for a novice to cling to her horse. Poor weather in Sarhad spoiled our plans to ski in the Big Pamir to the north, but we did get to walk into the unexplored Kharej Valley in the Hindu Kush and look at three terrific unclimbed peaks of about 5,500m.

We found the locals welcoming and hospitable, and felt we were probably treated no differently from men visiting this region; foreign travelers are simply considered a different (and rich) species, irrespective of gender. In fact, the people who expressed the most surprise were German soldiers, whose path we crossed the day we left. They were utterly shocked to see us, asked for photos with us, and were intrigued to know how two women had fared. We never felt in any danger, nor did we feel we were doing anything unacceptable. I would recommend this region to any man, or woman.

SUZY MADGE, *UK*

Neil Gwynne on first ascent of Koh-e-Khar, twin rock peaks toward right side of photo. *Alan Halewood*

Pamir-i-Wakhan, Koh-e-Iskander (5,561m), Koh-e-Khar (5,327m). Despite some effects from the much-publicized, devastating monsoon rain just south in Pakistan, in July and August Neil Gwynne and I, both from Scotland, were able to make first ascents in the Little and Big Pamir at the eastern end of the Wakhan Corridor. We were inspired to make this trip by a simple Japanese map that I had bought 20 years ago in a Glasgow climbing shop.

Like other recent visitors, we accessed the area from Tajikistan, via the town of Ishkashim. After a day buying supplies and arranging permits, we made a two-day drive by 4WD to the road-head at Sarhad-e-Boroghil, the vehicles becoming stuck in recent mud slides and deep rivers on several occasions. From there we made an eight-day approach on foot, in unusually wet conditions, to become the first mountaineers for many years to reach the interior of a mountain group west of the Wakhjir River. *[Editor's Note: The Wakhjir is the upper Oxus River. The Scots originally thought they were the first to reach these peaks, but Steffan Graupner, who traveled along this river in 2008, points out*

that in 1964 a German expedition climbed 5,424m Koh-e-Bay Qara, and 10 years later a Polish team climbed a 5,548m peak, both in this same mountain group; see below.] We followed a side valley south from the Wakhjir, starting from the point where the latter turns from southeast to east. Often we were forced to unload the horses and ferry loads up steep muddy slopes.

Finally, we left our horsemen in the valley and established a high camp, from which we subsequently reached a col at the valley head. This involved some of the loosest rock I have ever encountered and a brutal wade up a glacier, which would have been significantly worse were it not for snowshoes loaned to us by the Anglo-American team that climbed Noshaq. From the col I continued alone to make the first ascent of Koh-e-Iskander (5,561m), named after both Alexander the Great, whose armies passed nearby in 326 BC, and my two-year old son, Sandy. There was one section of Scottish

Neil Gwynne during first ascent of Koh-e-Khar. *Alan Halewood*

Koh-e-Iskander. Route of first ascent took left skyline. Glaciated slopes behind form northern flanks of an eastern summit of Qara Jilga I. *Alan Halewood*

3 on loose rock. Carefully descending avalanche-prone slopes, we regained our high camp after a 12-hour day. *[Editor's note: This peak lies northeast of 6,094m Qara Jilga I—see AAJ 2010. Qara Jilga I, named by the 1974 Polish expedition after the glacier and river at its foot, remains unclimbed. The German Koh-e-Bay Qara is nine kilometers to the west, while the Polish 5,548m peak, named by them Awal-Wakhjir Sar, lies within a four kilometers of Koh-e-Iskander].*

Time lost on the approach meant we were forced to leave the area almost immediately, but on the way out we did manage one more ascent. While crossing the Uween-e-Sar (a 4,887m pass), we traversed a ridge north and, finding relatively solid granodiorite, continued along the crest to a twin-summited mountain, which we named Koh-e-Khar (5,327m, Peak of the Donkey, the twin towers resembling donkey's ears). This involved another pitch of loose Scottish 3 and an eventual 1,000m descent straight to the valley floor to reunite with our

Koh-e-Khar from vicinity of Uween-e-Sar to the south. Route of ascent followed skyline ridge from right to left to reach twin summits directly above tent. *Alan Halewood*

horsemen at nightfall. On our return to Sarhad-e-Boroghil we found the road had been washed away, so we had to hire more horses and spend two long days riding 80km to regain our vehicle.

A local agency named Wakhan Tourism helps visitors secure permits, interpreters (some local guides have undergone training with Italian alpine guides in recent years), and vehicles. Throughout our trip we met with nothing but kindness, respect, and incredible hospitality.

The security situation east of Ishkashim remained stable in 2010, with no threats to the 70 or so western tourists who visited the Wakhan. However, this means that in 2011 the region might be considered a tempting "soft target" for insurgent or criminal gangs, so it will be important to get local advice before visiting. There is certainly enormous potential for first ascents at a wide range of technical difficulty in the area east of Sarhad. Thanks to the Mount Everest Foundation, British Mountaineering Council, and Mountaineering Council of Scotland for their support.

Alan Halewood, *Scotland*

Looking south up the Polish Glacier to (A) Koh-e-Wawel - the highest point of the Dragon Ridge, (B) Koh-e-Ikiv East, and (C) Koh-e-Ikiv West. Marked is the route followed by Kłosowicz and Rojek. *Bartek Tofel, tofel.eu*

Koh-e-Ak Su range, various ascents. In July and August our 14-member Polish expedition climbed eight new peaks from what we believe to be a previously unexplored valley in the Koh-e-Ak Su mountains of the Little Pamir, immediately east of the lower Wakhjir Valley. Half the expedition members travelled overland from Poland, a distance of ca 5,000km to the roadhead at Sarhad-e-Boroghil in the Wakhan

Corridor. From here we trekked east for five days, and on July 21 established base camp at ca 4,400m at the foot of the glacier (later named the Polish Glacier) in the Uchjilga Valley, close to the entrance of which lies a Kyrghiz summer settlement of the same name.

On the 24th Jacek Kierzkowski and Tomek Klimczak climbed our first peak, Koh-e-Atram (5,321m). They ascended a steep snow slope on the west side of the north face to a small saddle on the ridge above, and then followed the crest over mixed terrain to the summit (AD, 700m). They named the route Simple Solution.

Next day Piotr Kłosowicz and Tomek Rojek reached the summit of Bordze Polandi (Polish Tower, 5,566m). The pair climbed 800m up the east face by a system of couloirs. Despite three avalanches (two of snow and one rockfall) and an unplanned bivouac the previous night, they managed to return

Tomek Klimczak following a rock section during the ascent of Ursa Major to the summit ridge of Peak 5,625m. *Maciek Ostrowski, maciekostrowski.pl*

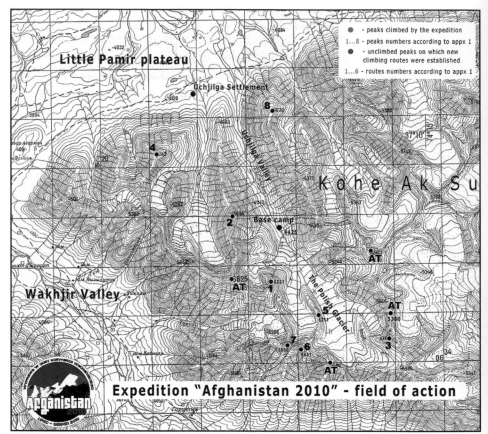

Polish activity in Uchjilga Valley. Peaks climbed: (1) Koh-e-Atram; (2) Bordze Polandi; (3) Koh-e-Se Zeboi; (4) Darwaza-ye Oqabi; (5) Koh-e-Wawel; (6) Koh-e-Ikiv East; (7) Koh-e-Ikiv West, and (8) Miz-e-Sangin. Other attempts marked (AT).

safely to base camp the same day. They named the route Polish Minger (AD+). On the 26th Michał Karbowski, Sławek Korytkowski and Rafał Sieradzki climbed Koh-e-Se Zeboi (peak of three beauties, 5,735m), which had been tried unsuccessfully on the 24th by Justyna Leszczuk, Maciek Ostrowski, and I. They climbed a snowy rib on the north face (Three Beauties, Russian 3B). On the same day Mirosław Łabuz attempted nearby Peak 5,613m but retreated 10 vertical meters below the top when confronted with approaching darkness and a seemingly endless summit ridge. On the 27th Jakub Gajda hiked up to the rocky summit of Darwaza-ye Oqabi (Eagle Gate, 5,142m, Russian 1B) at the entrance to the valley.

The weather now deteriorated markedly and thereafter most parties leaving base camp came back without success. The most interesting attempt was made by Ostrowski and Klimczak. On the morning of the 28th they climbed the 700m east face of Peak 5,625m but were stopped from continuing up the summit ridge by bad weather. Although the route terminated on the crest at 5,550m, the pair named it White Surf (AD)

On the 31st the weather improved enough for three teams make the best use of the remaining time: we were scheduled to leave on August 5.

On August 2 Kłosowicz and Rojek climbed three virgin peaks in a 15-hour round trip from camp. The first, named Koh-e-Wawel (5,211m, PD+) is the highest point of the so called Dragon Ridge. This continues to a higher snow-and-ice ridge with two summits, Koh-e-Ikiv East (5,551m, PD+) and Koh-e-Ikiv West (5,560m, PD+), which were both climbed.

On the same day Ostrowski and Klimczak made another attempt on Peak 5,625m. They again climbed the 700m east face, this time via a different line, but were stopped by loose rock covered with fresh snow on the ridge above. They named their route Ursa Major. It finished 25m below the summit and had difficulties of 750m, D AI3 M5. It was the hardest technical climbing on the trip.

Also on the same day, Gajda reached the summit of Miz-e-Sangin (Heavy Table, 5,030m, Russian 1B). This hiking peak lies at the entrance to the valley opposite Darwaza-ye Oqabi.

Meanwhile Elzbieta Kaminska, Korytkowski, Kierzkowski, and Sieradzki joined forces to attempt Peak 5,420m. After a rough night at the base, they climbed the northeast face to the crest of the ridge at 5,310m but deep, loose snow made it impossible for them to continue. Before returning to base camp, Kaminska and Sieradzki made an attempt on Peak 5,613m (almost climbed on the 26th by Labuz). They climbed the west face but retreated below the summit due to lack of time.

It was a difficult return to Sarhad due to high water levels and we had to take the longer and more strenuous "high route," which crosses three passes between 4,200m and 4,900m. Once at Sarhad our troubles were far from over,

Koh-e-Atram from the Polish Glacier showing first ascent via north face and northwest ridge. *Bartek Tofel, tofel.eu*

Koh-e-Se Zeboi showing the line of Three Beauties on north face and north-northeast ridge. *Maciek Ostrowski, maciekostrowski.pl*

East face of Peak 5,625m. (1) Ursa Major and (2) White Surf. *Tomek Klimczak*

The view west-southwest from Kotale Tasznob, a 5,350m pass on the north-northeast ridge of Koh-e-Se Zeboi. Nearer peaks are the Pamir-i-Wakhan, but the three pyramidal summits in the distance lie in the Karakoram, on the northwestern fringes of the Batura Muztagh, and are ca 6,000m. Every peak in this photograph is unclimbed. *Bartek Tofel, tofel.eu*

as the heavy rain had severely damaged the road along the Corridor. While the rest left Afghanistan on the 16th, I remained and explored the Wakhjir Valley and Big Pamir Plateau.

Conditions in the Koh-e-Ak Su were poor: even the glacier was hard to cross due soft surface snow one meter deep. Alpine ice was scare and the rock was very poor. However, at least 200 peaks in this group remain unclimbed and probably around 600 in the entire eastern Wakhan Corridor. The expedition would not have been possible without the financial support of the Polish Alpine Association (PZA). A detailed map of this area, on which peaks climbed and attempted are marked, can be seen on the AAJ website. On Google Earth 37°06'35.19" N, 74°10'41.97" E positions you on the summit of Koh-e-Atram.

BARTEK TOFEL, *Poland*

Pakistan

The online version of these reports frequently contains additional photos, maps, topos, and extended text. Please visit aaj.americanalpineclub.org

Peaks above 6,500m; overview. The year 2010 proved extremely bleak for mountaineering tourism in Pakistan. Only 26 expeditions comprising a total of 234 climbers took up permits for 6,500+m peaks (summits below this altitude require no royalty fee). This is nearly half the number of 2009, a year that was also considered very poor. Of the 26, three were attempting 8,000m peaks in winter: K2, Broad Peak, Gasherbrum I and II, all during December 2010–January 2011. Six teams attempted both Gasherbrum I and II, while four tried both K2 and Broad Peak. One team attempted four of the Gasherbrums: I, II, V, and VI. This raised the total number of attempts on various summits to 40.

Twelve expeditions were successful on Broad Peak, Nanga Parbat, Gasherbrum I, or Gasherbrum II, with a total of 53 people reaching these summits. No one climbed K2. Gasherbrum II was climbed the most, including an historic ascent on February 2, 2011, by Simone Moro, Cory Richards, and Denis Urubko, who made the first winter ascent of any 8,000er in Pakistan. Other than this, an expedition to Spantik, one to Latok I, and another to Tahu Ratum were all unsuccessful.

As in 2009 the reduction on royalty fees was continued for 2010, with a 90% reduction for all peaks except Spantik in Chitral, Gilgit, and Ghizar (peaks above 6,500m outside these areas receive a 60% reduction), and a 95% reduction on all peaks during the winter season. These reductions will continue in 2011.

KARRAR HAIDRI, *Alpine Club of Pakistan*

WESTERN HIMALAYA
NANGA PARBAT RANGE

Chiche Peak, showing line of first ascent up northeast face and southeast ridge. Dot marks camp on crest of ridge. *Christian Walter*

Chiche Peak (5,860m) and other first ascents. During our 2009 climb of Schlagintweit Peak (5,979m, *AAJ 2010*), I spotted an impressive summit in the neighboring Chiche Valley. Back home I did some research. I found a sketch map, on which it was named Chiche Peak. Later, I was told that the famous British mountaineers Collie and Mummery had tried it in 1895 while preparing for their Nanga

Nilo Peak (left) and Gerd Markert Peak. *Christian Walter*

Shalmuki Peak, showing line of first ascent; Breathless (UIAA VII-). *Christian Walter*

Parbat attempt. There is no other report of any mountaineering action in this valley since Mummery's visit.

Stefan Wolf and I arrived in the valley during July. Bad weather accompanied us. Heavy rains had swept away bridges, so even reaching base camp proved difficult. We established base camp at 3,700m. Although we could barely see the peaks, we had selected this site previously using Google Earth.

When the clouds parted that evening, we could hardly believe our eyes: in front of our tent rose a superb piece of granite. It was not Chiche Peak, but it was a beautiful objective. We checked our gear: three Friends, five nuts, and four pegs. Not much, but in the main we'd expected to be ice climbing.

We started the next morning at 4:30 and climbed the first 900m of easy ground in three hours. Then, following fine cracks, chimneys, and diedres through steep granite (UIAA VII-), we reached the 5,086m summit. It was 3 p.m., and the vertical rise of our climb had been 460m.

Rappelling and downclimbing the route took a further four hours. Locals told us that the name of the peak was Shalmuki, which means "a hundred faces."

Over the next three days we climbed two more peaks: Nilo Peak (4,986m, GPS), and Gerd-Markert Peak (4,966m, ice at 45°, and two pitches on rock at UIAA IV). We named the latter after a German climber, who died in April 2010.

The weather now turned bad, and we had heavy rain for one week. In our remote valley we were unaware of the devastation this was causing throughout Pakistan. Then, a short window of three days allowed us to make the first ascent of Chiche Peak, our principle objective. We first followed the Chuchuel Glacier to the rimaye, which we found difficult to cross. Above, 600m of excellent névé of increasing steepness brought us to the southeast ridge, where we found a nice tent site at 5,200m.

On August 11 we set out late due to poor visibility. Apart from two crevasses, there were no major difficulties, and the névé was good, rising to 60° just below the summit. We only needed to belay part of the route, and we reached the top at 3 p.m.

The weather now turned bad again, and we were brought news of disastrous floods. This forced us to leave base camp early. Travel back to Islamabad was a real adventure, with every road

Stefan Wolf about to tackle the curving crack on the first ascent of Breathless, Shalmuki Peak. *Christian Walter*

blocked and most bridges damaged. We were lucky to reach the capital within two days, having changed vehicles 11 times.

Back home I got a reprint of Norman Collie's *Climbing on the Himalaya and Other Mountain Ranges*. It clearly shows their Chiche Peak to be different than ours, as they began their attempt from the Rupal Valley. It might possibly be Shaigiri Peak (6,245m, *AAJ 2010* map, p. 261), which was climbed in 1988 from the north by Canadians Barry Blanchard, Kevin Doyle, and Ward Robinson.

CHRISTIAN WALTER, *Alpinclub Sachsen, Germany*

WEST KARAKORAM
SHIMSHAL REGION — GHUJERAB MOUNTAINS

Chashkin Sar. In September Samina Baig from Shimshal Village made what is reported to be the first ascent of Chashkin Sar (quoted as 6,400m but according to some sources more likely to be ca 6,000m; a similarly named peak close to Shimshal was climbed in winter during 1997). Baig, an 18-year-old from Shimshal Village, climbed with her brother Mirza Ali, Yahya Baig, Arshad Karim, Salamat Khan, Tafat Shah, and Romanian film-maker, Stelian Pavalache. The expedition was organized by Pakistan Youth Outreach, an educational youth mountaineering program (founded by Mirza Ali) that also promotes women adventurers. The mountain has been renamed Samina Peak.

In early December Baig attempted a quasi-winter ascent of Mingligh Sar (6,050m) but retreated 150m below the summit due to extreme cold and insufficient clothing (mostly due to the expedition's financial constraints). This previously climbed peak close to the Shimshal Pass was ascended again on January 3, 2011 by eight girls from Shimshal and their four instructors from the Shimshal Mountaineering School, including the renowned Qudrat Ali. One of the successful female summiteers, Hafiza Bano, was 16 years old. Summit temperatures were recorded as -38°C.

LINDSAY GRIFFIN, *Mountain INFO*

KARAKORAM
BALTORO MUZTAGH

Broad Peak North (7,750m), west face and south ridge, then traverse over Broad Peak Central (8,011m) to Broad Peak Main (8,051m). On July 9 Alberto Iñurrategi, Juan Vallejo, and Mikel Zabalza reached the summit of Broad Peak North after climbing a new line up the west-facing glaciated slopes leading directly to the 7,350m col between the north and central summits. The weather was very windy, and after the short ascent of the south ridge to North Peak, they spent a rough night back at the col. Their goal was to continue to the Main summit and the next day they would face the hardest section of this traverse: the ascent of the north ridge of Central peak. Receiving a weather forecast that confirmed strong winds continuing for the next two days, the three decided to return to base camp.

The Basque trio set out again on the 16th and regained the col on the 17th after a bivouac at ca 6,300m. The same day Iñurrategi repeated their previous ascent of the south ridge to the summit of Broad Peak North. All three left the col at 3 a.m. the next day, expecting it to take 11–12 hours to reach the summit of Broad Peak Central and descend to a bivouac on the 7,800m col before the Main summit. They were wrong. Although they climbed the first 400m of the ridge in two hours, it took another 10 to finish the remaining 300m and then two more to negotiate the summit ridge. Snow conditions were abysmal, and at one point they took five hours to gain only 50m of elevation. All declared it was the worst snow they had ever experienced.

By the time they arrived at the 7,800m col, they had been on the go for 17 hours, were exhausted, and—having traveled very light—were completely out of food. As it was nearly dark, they decided to descend to Camp 3 at 7,100m on the Normal Route.

After just seven hours rest, only Iñurrategi felt like getting up at 3 a.m. and going for the main summit. In an exhausted state and suffering from stomach pains it still took him only six hours to reach the top via the upper section of the Normal Route, a faster time than most fresh and well-provisioned mountaineers would clock for this section. The saving grace was that he was able to follow a track opened by other climbers several days previously. He regained camp in just over four hours, from where all three descended the Normal Route.

The traverse of the three Broad Peaks summits had only been achieved on two previous occasions. In 1984 Kukuczka and Kurtyka started via the northwest ridge of Broad Peak North, and this same line was repeated again in 1995 by Toru Hattori, Toshiyuki Kitamura, and Masafumi Todaka from Japan. All three traverses have been made alpine-style.

LINDSAY GRIFFIN, *Mountain INFO*

Gasherbrum II (8,035m), first winter ascent. On February 2, 2011, Simone Moro (Italian) Cory Richards (American), and Denis Urubko (Kazakh) reached the summit of Gasherbrum II via the Normal Route up the southwest ridge. The team made the summit in a three-day push, after having been helicoptered to base camp only 22 days previously. Prior to their attempt they had established Camp 1 at 5,900m, and Camp 2 at 6,500m. Their top camp was at 6,900m. The descent proved arduous. On the 3rd they had to contend with a raging storm as they climbed down from camps 3 to 1. The following day, crossing below Gasherbrum V on the way to base camp, they were hit by an avalanche and swept ca 150m. All three were mostly buried, though Moro only slightly. He was able to unrope and excavate the other two.

This was the first winter ascent of any of the main 8,000m peaks in Pakistan. On March 6, 1988, in a remarkable effort, Maciej Berberka, a member of the Polish winter K2 expedition, reached the ca 8,030m foresummit (rocky summit) of Broad Peak. At the time the visibility was poor, and he believed he had reached the highest point of the mountain. It was only later, on examination of photographs, that he realized he had stopped short.

LINDSAY GRIFFIN, *Mountain INFO*

Gasherbrum I (8,068m), south face, winter attempt. In 2011, together with Alex Txikon from Spain, we spent more than 50 days making the first attempt to climb Gasherbrum I in winter. The approach to this mountain had never been done on foot in winter; we took seven days to walk from Askole to base camp at 5,100m, arriving on January 31. During the previous autumn we had employed a caravan of porters to take all our equipment to base camp. Now, we discovered some of the equipment had either been stolen or broken—but not enough to put our project in jeopardy. Base camp temperatures were similar to Quebec, between -20 and -30°C at night, and our spirits were high, particularly after Simone Moro, Cory Richards, and Denis Urubko made their historic first winter ascent of Gasherbrum II [see previous report].

We planned to climb the mountain by a partial new route, following the couloir and ridge close to the right edge of the triangular rock face that forms the left side of the west-southwest face of Hidden Sud (a.k.a. Gasherbrum South, 7,069m). The left bounding (west) ridge of the triangle was ascended in 1983 by Spanish climbers, while further to the right a prominent spur on the

Gasherbrum I from southwest. (1) Upper southwest ridge (Stremfelj-Zaplotnik, 1977). (2) Southwest face and southwest ridge (Afanasiev-Babanov, 2008). (3) Southwest face (Kukuczka-Kurtyka, 1983). (4) Hidden Sud west ridge and southeast ridge (Arnal-Cinto- Escartin-Lopez-Ortas-Ubieto, 1983). (5) Southeast ridge (Kauffman-Schoening, 1958). (6) Winter attempt with camp marked. The line followed by French climbers in 1980 lies just off picture to right. *Louis Rousseau*

south-southwest face, leading directly to the top of Hidden Sud, was climbed by Frenchmen in 1980. At the top of the triangle (ca 6,800m) we would cross to the upper section of the southeast ridge, where we would join the original 1958 American Route at 7,500m.

We started opening the route on February 4, and from then till early March experienced nothing but clouds and poor weather. We worked hard to establish a camp at 6,300m on the crest of a rock spur. To that point the climbing had involved difficult rotten rock and hard ice to 70°. On March 9 we reached 6,650m, having climbed 1,500m of new ground, but the final 200m of ice rising to 70° was not climbable for us. The ice was like marble, and we simply were unable to place any ice screws for protection.

Back at base camp, weather forecaster Karl Gabl in Austria gave us a second chance. We decided to use the weather window to make an alpine-style attempt on the Standard Route up the Japanese Couloir. We spent our first night at 6,200m, and the second above the exit of the couloir at 7,050m. However, at this altitude the northeast wind was blowing more than 80km/hour, and showed no sign of abating next morning. Realizing to continue would be suicidal, we retreated and reached base camp on the 15th. We left the mountain on the 21st, the first day of spring.

LOUIS ROUSSEAU, *Canada and* GERFRIED GÖSCHL, *Austria*

Gasherbrum V (7,147m/7,133m), west face, attempt. Only six Korean teams have successfully put up first ascents on 7,000m peaks. Nearly all of these have been made in either capsule or expedition style. Kim Hyung-il, who in 2009 climbed a new route in alpine style on the northwest face of Spantik (*AAJ 2010*), planned to attempt the untouched west face of Gasherbrum V. With him were Im Il-jin, Jang Ji-myung, and Lee Sang-woo.

Gasherbrum V has no recorded ascent. In August 1978 three Japanese reached the east summit (7,006m Polish Satellite Map, ca 6,900m on others). The following day the expedition leader, Ryuichi Babaguchi, set off ahead of another pair for a second summit attempt. After reaching the top of the east peak, the pair found Babaguchi had fallen into a crevasse and died. A French team also made an unsuccessful attempt in 1980. Both attempts were made from the South Gasherbrum Glacier.

From a base camp at ca 4,800m on the Baltoro Glacier, all Koreans except Im set off on July 7. A difficult crevassed section took them to their first bivouac, and the following morning more glaciated terrain led them to the rimaye. Deep snow had put them behind schedule, and they climbed the first few hundred meters of the face (50°) without protection. Above, they climbed two pitches of 80° before cutting a tent platform at 6,100m. Continuous front pointing on the 9th exhausted them, and there were sections of delicate thin ice over rock. At 4 p.m. they reached the base of a couloir. The warmth of the sun was melting the upper section and causing rock fall, so the team took shelter until the sun set and then climbed ca 100m to below a steep rock wall, where at 10:30 p.m. they finally settled down for a (barely) sitting bivouac at 6,550m. During the night snow and spindrift covered them, and the gaz stove malfunctioned. At 4 a.m. Kim made the decision to retreat. They had already been on the wall four days, the stove was now faulty, they were low on gaz, and the team had expended much energy on the approach. They also felt the objective danger was higher than they had expected. At around 4:30 a.m. they set their first Abalakov; 15 hours later they arrived safely in base camp.

CHRISTINE PAE, *Director Korean Alpine Federation, and* LINDSAY GRIFFIN, *Mountain INFO*

MASHERBRUM RANGE

Hushe District, Las Damas Primero; Baush-ul, Spanish System – Very Good System; Cholon, second ascent but first to highest point. Under the direction of mountain guide Simon Elias, a female national climbing team from FEDME (Spanish mountaineering and climbing federation) made three ascents from the Hushe Valley. Maider Fraile, Miriam Marco, Maialen Ojer, Patty Trespando, and Asuncion Yanguas spent a month living with the women of Hushe, getting to know their personal needs. In the area at the time were paragliders Thomas de Dordolot and Ramón Morillas, who were helpful with aerial exploration of potential access to the peaks. And then there was the well-known mountaineer and film maker Sebastien Alvaro, creator of the series *Al file de lo Imposible,* who with his film crew, Mariano Izquierdo and Esther Sabadell, were responsible for documenting the expedition. The main objective was a fine spire west of the lower Chogolisa Glacier; locals had dubbed this Sebas Tower as a tribute to Alvaro for his help with bettering the lot of Hushe people through an NGO project. Alvaro had noted this peak as an attractive objective on previous visits.

In order to acclimatize, Elias, Fraile, Ojer, Trespando, and Yanguas first made the ascent of a rock needle immediately northeast of Hushe Village. The 850m ascent took place over three days, June 28, 29, and 31, was graded 6c+, 6b obl., and named Las Damas Primero (Ladies First). On August 3, and from a camp at 4,550m, Elias, Fraile, Marco, Ojer, Yanguas, and Sabadell, with local porter Hassan Jan, made the possible first ascent of Baush-ul

Las Damas Primero on an unnamed rock spike on the west flank of Baush-ul. Below is the junction of the Hushe Valley with lower Aling and Masherbrum glaciers. *FEDME*

West ridge of Cholon. The 1993 team failed to surmount the cornice onto the final crest at a point estimated to be 15m below the summit. *FEDME*

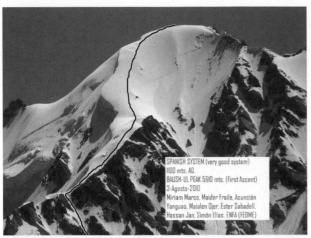

SPANISH SYSTEM (very good system)
1100 mts. AD.
BAUSH-UL PEAK 5610 mts. (First Ascent)
3-Agosto-2010
Miriam Marco, Maider Fraile, Asunción
Yanguas, Maialen Ojer, Ester Sabadell.
Hassan Jan, Simón Elías. ENFA (FEDME)

The Spanish ascent of Baush-ul. *FEDME*

Four members of the female climbing team at Hushe. From left to right: Asuncion Yanguas, 33; Maider Fraile, 33; Miriam Marco, 29; and Maialen Ojer, 39. *FEDME*

(5,810m) via a 1,100m snow route at AD named Spanish System – Very Good System. Las Damas Primero lies on the west flank of this peak, which forms the (southern) cornerstone at the Hushe-Charakusa junction.

Elias and all five members of the climbing team now turned to "Sebas Tower," unaware at the time that this peak had been climbed in 1993 during a UIAA International Camp led by the Dutch guide Edward Bekker, who had named it Cholon. Bekker, Evelyne Binsack, Jorg Witz (all guides), plus Andreas Daffner and Julian Neumeyer climbed the west ridge at D/TD but were stopped by a huge cornice 15m below the summit. The Spanish team repeated the west ridge on August 13, approaching from the lower Gondokoro Glacier, camping at 4,900m, and then climbing for a continuous 19 hours to reach the top. They managed to climb through the cornice, which they found difficult, and then on for a further pitch to the highest point. The 900m route was graded D+ (IV and 75°).

The Spanish climbers' map marks this peak as 6,050m, and the recent Polish sketch map by the famous cartographer Jerzy Wala gives the height 6,294m. The UIAA team felt they reached an altitude of ca 6,000m. However, the Spanish climbers carried an altimeter that they matched several times during the trip with GPS readings, and recorded a height of 5,860m on the summit, an altitude the paragliders also confirmed as more likely.

Elias felt that the expedition exceeded expectations due to the great enthusiasm of the participants. One year had been spent in preparation—improving technique by winter climbing in the Alps and Pyrenees. The three-year women's climbing project will end in 2011, hopefully with another trip to Pakistan.

FRANCESC ESTORACH, *Director de Comunicación, FEDME, Spain*

Farol West from the southwest with (1) Telegraph Road, and (2) Open Eyes to the summit of Margherita's Peak. *Daniele Nardi*

CHARAKUSA VALLEY

Margherita's Peak (5,400m), south ridge, Open Eyes; K7 West (6,615m), southwest pillar, attempt; Farol West (6,370m), west face, Telegraph Road. Bad weather thwarted our plans to attempt unclimbed Hassan Peak. Instead, Lorenzo Angelozzi and I looked elsewhere and attempted three other summits, on two of which we were successful. Our first ascent was Margherita's Peak, a previously unclimbed rock tower at the end of the south ridge of Farol West. It makes a good acclimatization ascent after arriving in the Charakusa, with an approach that involves a night's sleep at the end of the glacier moraine. We climbed the south ridge. An ice slope led into a goulotte, where the climbing became steeper and more mixed. Finally, two rock pitches led to the top. We named the route Open Eyes (400m, UIAA V M5 WI5) because it

Daniele Nardi starting the UIAA VI crack at 5,900m on Farol West. *Lorenzo Angelozzi*

A Dead Man protects Daniele Nardi as he traverses the summit ridge of Farol West. *Lorenzo Angelozzi*

Badal Wall on the southwest pillar of K7 West. The 2007 attempt, Badal, more or less climbs the center of the face visible, stopping several hundred meters below the right-hand of the two summit spires (AAJ 2008, p. 81). The Italian attempt was further left, aiming toward the light-colored walls, but is invisible in this photo, hidden by the foreground ridge. The fine pillar up and to the left was dubbed the Chandelle. *Daniele Nardi*

opened our own eyes to the possibilities on Farol West, which would subsequently become our goal.

We then attempted a new line on the southwest pillar of K7 West [*dubbed the Badal Wall in 2007 by the Belgian-Polish team that nearly climbed it*] in capsule style. We started up the west face left of Badal (1,200m, 5.12+ A1, Favresse-Favresse-Pustelnik-Villanueva, 2007, to ca 5,900m, *AAJ 2008*). Getting started was difficult; we had to make several attempts due to poor weather, with rain rather than snow falling at altitudes of ca 6,000m. On the sixth pitch we had to overcome a fantastic offwidth, which was hard to protect without Friends 5 and 6. Instead we were compelled to make a 25m runout above Friends 3.5 and 4. We descended in more rain, returning on our ninth day to move the portaledge and equipment to the top of pitch five. We finished the sixth pitch, climbed a seventh, and then part of the eighth, where we were forced to make a pendulum from a tied-off blade peg only in two centimeters. Then, a large rockfall narrowly missed us but destroyed our portaledge. Water cascading down the face had loosened large blocks, but fortunately, while climbing, we had been protected by the steep rock above. That night we tried to repair the badly damaged ledge, but on the next day, our 11th, we realized that continuing was futile, so we removed our gear from the eighth pitch and descended. To our high point, about one quarter height on the wall, the difficulties were UIAA VII+ and A2/3.

A short break in the weather prompted us to try a fast ascent of Farol West, though at the time we were unaware that this peak had a name and had been climbed in 1991 by Ian Stewart and Neil

Wilson via the south-southeast face. Lorenzo and I opted for a probable new line on the west face. We left base camp at 1 p.m. with 14kg rucksacks, and we bivouacked on the edge of the glacier when the snow became too soft to continue. We started up the face during the night, after the ground had re-frozen. Occasionally it snowed, and the darkness made route finding difficult. The middle section of the climb presented several challenging pitches, and at ca 5,900m we found one pitch up a granite crack stuffed with ice that was almost impossible. We graded it UIAA VI but climbed with axe and crampons. Once above it, we realized we were past the worst. Continuing up 55–60° slopes, we eventually arrived on the summit ridge, which we followed to the highest point in swirling cloud. We made 20 rappels down the face on a more direct line, which will provide a good route to another party in the future. We climbed our route, Telegraph Road (900m, UIAA VI M4 WI4), in 32 hours round trip from base camp, with 21 hours needed for the ascent (including five hours of rest at the bivouac).

Angelozzi stands below the lower southwest pillar of K7 West. (1) Italian attempt with (L) the site of the portaledge hit by rockfall, (P6) the hard offwidth on pitch six, and (H) the high point. (2) the approximate line of Badal. *Daniele Nardi*

Bad weather had compelled us to change our goals many times, but the situation for the rest of Pakistan was far worse, with thousands dead and millions displaced from their homes. We felt deeply sorry for them, and rather guilty, as we were there simply to focus on our climbing.

DANIELE NARDI, *Italy, danielenardi.eu*

K7 West (6,615m), southwest pillar, attempt. Miguel Anta, Ruben Calvo, and I spent 35 days from mid-June to the end of July on the Charakusa Glacier with a plan to attempt a new line on the southwest pillar of K7 West.

For the first 10 days base camp was covered with snow. As temperatures were low we were able start the line up a couloir that normally would be dangerous and rocky but was now snow and ice up to 65°. We established a camp here and then climbed above until we reached the rock wall (the last few meters were 80°). We then climbed a pitch of A3, left our ropes, and descended in bad weather.

Returning when it was much warmer, we saw a huge ice avalanche cascade down the upper part of our line. We decided to alter track to a safer line on the right. From the base of our A3 pitch we traversed up and right for five pitches (up to 5.10a), until we reached a large ledge at 4,900m where we established a second camp. Conditions above were bad. There was much ice fall, and snow covered the lower-angled sections. We climbed one pitch on the face above and, coming across an in-situ anchor, realized we had joined an existing route. Again,

Southwest pillar of K7 West. (1) Variante de Sol. (2) Luna. Spanish team's high point was just before the hidden top section. The pillar on the right was climbed in 2007 by Marko Prezelj and Maxime Turgeon (900m, 5.11 A0). *Matt McCormick*

Cecilia Buil above Camp 2 on southwest pillar of K7 West. *Cecilia Buil collection*

bad weather arrived, so we left our two portaledges and descended.

When we returned, it was with the knowledge that we were going to continue up the Slovenian route Luna (1,400m, UIAA VII+ A2, Cesen-Sisernik-Hrastelj, 2008). We spent six days on the wall repeating a line that could be climbed much faster, as on the first ascent. Conditions were bad, with copious running water, muddy cracks on the lower part of the route, and melting snow and ice in the upper. We moved slowly, established another portaledge camp at ca 5,100m, and after 20 pitches and ca 1,200m of climbing reached lower-angled terrain just below the ridge, where granite slabs were covered with rivers of flowing water. Four to five pitches below the point where Luna finishes, we retreated. We have called our variation start Variante de Sol (250m, 5.10 70–80°).
CECILIA BUIL, SPAIN

Editor's note: The southwest pillar of K7 West is a rock wall that terminates at a distinct rock tower (ca 6,300m) to the southwest of K7 West. The tower lies at the start of the long snow ridge leading northeast to the summit and has not been climbed, although three named routes, Badal, Luna, and Children of Hushe have been established on the wall below, all terminating between ca 5,500m and ca 5,900m. The Slovenian team that climbed Luna in 2008 reached the end of the rock difficulties at ca 5,700m—a little more than halfway between base of rock wall and top of K7 West—but estimated it would take three days to climb the intervening ice and mixed ground to the summit of K7 West and descend to their high point.

The altitude of K7 West has previously been quoted as 6,858m. However, the 2005 sketch map compiled by the famous Polish cartographer Jerzy Wala attributes this height to unclimbed K7 Middle, and an altitude of 6,615m to K7 West. Photographic study seems to confirm this.

Pathan Brakk (ca 5,410m), southwest flank, second ascent; K7 West (6,615m), southwest pillar, attempt. In April 2010, Tim DeRoehn and I were awarded one of the inaugural Copp-Dash Inspire Awards. It would be our first trip to Asia. We had big goals, specifically to make the first complete ascent of the southwest pillar of K7 West and to explore the endless rock spires ringing the Charakusa Valley.

After settling into base camp (ca 4,500m) along with our friend and cook Fida Hussain and his assistant Abbas, we acclimatized by climbing on beautiful granite boulders a minute's walk from camp and hiking the area, scoping almost limitless objectives.

After a week in camp Tim was floored with altitude sickness, resulting in a resting heart rate of ca 100. After keeping an eye on him for a day, I left for a solo mission near Farol Peak. Several days previously a group of Swiss climbers had made the first ascent of a peak they named Pathan Brakk, a ca 5,410m summit on the watershed ridge running south-southeast from Farol Far East. They described enjoyable mixed climbing and a beautiful granite top. For me it sounded like perfect acclimatization and an opportunity to scope a still-unclimbed mixed line on the south face of Farol Far East.

After ascending the South Farol Glacier immediately north of camp, and seemingly endless snow slopes, I bivouacked several hundred meters below the summit on a shoulder overlooking the

Pathan Brakk from southwest showing the route soloed by Matt McCormick. *Matt McCormick*

entire valley. The next morning I awoke at 4 a.m. and climbed steep snow (up to 65°) and moderate mixed terrain (up to M4) to the spectacular granite spire. Straddling the summit spire I took in a view of K2, Chogolisa, and Broad Peak. After a rappel and much downclimbing I headed back to base camp in time for dinner. There are many small unclimbed peaks similar to Pathan Brakk in the Charakusa Valley.

Naisa Brakk (ca 5,200m) stands over the entrance to the valley and has Egyptian Pyramid-like architecture. With Tim feeling better, we bivouacked below the start of Tasty Talking (300m, 5.10+, House-Prezelj-Swenson, 2005) on the upper southeast ridge. Earlier in the trip we had bailed from a point around a pitch-and-a-half from the summit after underestimating the route, thinking it would be a good warm-up.

Despite its relatively moderate grade, this route served a full course of excitement, complete with pitch after pitch of what felt more like run-out 5.11 than 10+. True to form last season, it began to rain a couple pitches below the summit, but we were not going to bail this time. I led the last two pitches, including a particularly fun and exposed final pitch in the pouring rain. This may have been the third complete ascent. Dirty rainwater spurted from our belay devices and soaked us to the bone as we rapped down. This would become the norm for the rest of the trip.

Our remaining time in the Charakusa was highlighted by two attempts on our main objective, the southwest pillar of K7 West. On every attempt we would dubiously eye dark clouds coming up the valley, stubbornly press upward, and eventually get soaked by heavy rain. We were attempting to climb the first five or six pitches of Badal and then break left onto the west face, where a line of ramps and corners led to mixed climbing just below the top. A direct start to this line was attempted by Italians [see above report by Daniele Nardi]. The initial corners of Badal are 5.11+, but they were wet, making free climbing difficult. The southwest pillar is an amazing objective, which in my opinion has not had a true ascent. The Belgian-Polish team came closest, but Luna appears to end very far from the summit.

The summer of 2010 brought one of the wettest monsoons in Pakistan's history. Thousands of people were killed and even more displaced by the devastating flooding that followed. Each day we would hear more bad news on Fida's radio; our qualms about the weather from a climbing perspective seemed trivial.

Pakistan is the subject of endless bad press in Western media. Many of our friends and family expressed concern about us traveling to this country, which in their eyes was overrun with anti-American sentiment. Right from our arrival in Islamabad we found only kind and generous people, who often went out of their way to have a conversation with us.

MATT MCCORMICK, *AAC*

Tim DeRoehn on Tasty Talking. *Matt McCormick*

Looking north at K7 group; K7 (6,934m) highest summit on right. (A) Pt. ca 6,300m. (B) K7 West (6,615m). (C) Pt. 6,736m. (D) K7 Middle (6,858m). (1) Luna (UIAA VII+ A2, 1,400m, Cesen Sisernik-Hrastelj, 2008), with its high point at just over 5,700m. (2) Southeast face (2,000m, 5.11a WI5, Anderson-House-Prezelj, 2007). (3) Southeast Buttress - Russian Route and high point. *Marek Holecek*

K7 West (6,615m), southeast buttress, not to summit. We arrived in the Charakusa with no single plan, but were quickly captivated by the beautiful southeast buttress of K7 West. We saw that this sheer wall, which begins at 5,000m, could be logically divided into three sections. The first third is very smooth and capped by a snow-covered, outward-sloping terrace. Consequently, it is wet. Leading to the center of the terrace is a long slanting crack, breaching a series of overhangs. In the middle third we could clearly see a series of wide cracks, most of which looked possible to free climb. The upper third of the buttress has a large, icy corner-chimney, overhanging in the lower part. We felt this would probably be the crux of the climb.

Our main goal was to climb to the top of the buttress, which we estimated to be 1,000-1,100m high. Above, a long mixed ridge with gendarmes led to snow slopes below the summit. Climbing this is practically a separate ascent, and, for us, did not seem a logical option. We made our first attempt on August 6, climbing the first three pitches on aid. They were extremely wet due to high rainfall, which we weren't expecting at this altitude. That night, at the foot of the wall in our portaledge, we were nearly washed away by a torrential downpour. Water came through the fly and we were soon flooded. Eventually, we took a knife and made several extra holes in the floor, to let out the water. A falling stone ripped through the fabric, injuring an arm. Next morning we retreated.

On the 12th, having proved ourselves fit by playing an international soccer match with Americans and Italians, we started again, with an extra flysheet from one of our tents. On the 15th we reached the terrace at 5,370m, having climbed eight pitches up to A3.

The first two pitches in the wide cracks of the wall above were almost as difficult; vertical,

with a large overhang in the middle. Then the wall became less steep and much drier, so we were able to free climb sections. Six pitches above the terrace we reached the icy overhanging corner. It was cold, damp work inside the chimneys, and when a large cam popped and hit me hard in the cheek, it was too painful to smile again until the end of the climb. On a five-meter section, bypassing a chockstone, we had to hand drill a few holes, the only time on the route we used drilled aid. Four days and eight pitches took us to the top of the wall.

We were now rewarded with two fine days, and spent the first studying the upper part of the face and a descent route, after which we moved onto the left flank of the ridge, and placed our portaledge at 6,020m. Next day we set off with only the fly, a stove, and three-days food. We climbed the left flank of the ridge, overcoming sections of difficult mixed terrain, until reaching

Russian Route and high point, southeast buttress K7 West. (inset) On the upper section of K7 southeast buttress, above the big wall section. *Supplied by Anna Piunova, mountain.ru*

the crest at 6,260m, where we bivouacked. The following morning the weather began to deteriorate. We climbed to a big gendarme at ca 6,300m, and decided to call it a day. It was the 22nd and this was our summit. We made a difficult descent to the portaledge, and then took a further two days to reach the base of the mountain. On the first we made 18 rappels west into a big glacial amphitheatre and bivouacked in a rimaye. On the second we climbed down to the bottom of the amphitheatre and then made nine rappels to the glacier. Our emancipated bodies barely carried our rucksacks, but fortunately we were met by our sirdar and his son, who helped us down to base camp.

VJACHESLAV IVANOV *and* OLEG KOLTUNOV, *Russia,*
provided by ANNA PIUNOVA, *mountain.ru*

India

The online version of these reports frequently contains additional photos, maps, topos, and extended text. Please visit aaj.americanalpineclub.org

Indian Himalaya, overview. If you pardon the cliché, whenever God closes a door, he opens a window. This adage truly described experiences in the Indian Himalaya during 2010. There were not many expeditions, and few high peaks were climbed. This could be a reflection of higher peak fees and, more significantly, hindrances caused by the bureaucracy. However, there was much activity on small peaks, in new regions, and by smaller teams. This may be indicative of the future, as these expeditions are cost-effective. Many climbers did not mind meeting serious challenges below 5,500m, as above this height peak fees are required.

There were 40 foreign expeditions to India, a steep drop from the normal figure of around 65. There were 63 Indian expeditions, but many were on standard peaks or washed out by weather.

In early August a flash flood hit the lower areas of Ladakh. Rivers of mud flowed, destroying houses, roads and fields, and causing long-term damage. Aid from the army and government agencies has poured in but is never sufficient. Various organizations, including the Himalayan Club, raised funds to help projects. More work on rebuilding and damage repair will commence this summer, once the harsh winter is over.

HARISH KAPADIA, *AAC Honorary Member, India*

LADAKH

Thanglasgo Valley, Big Rock Candy Mountain, first ascent; Dawa Peak, Kangsaimathung and Peak 2, new routes. Sheltered in the rain shadow of higher Himalayan peaks, the Nubra Valley is almost high-altitude desert, often expedition-friendly when other areas are drenched by monsoon. It was opened to foreign expeditions as recently as 1994 and remains relatively

View down Sniamo Valley from Kangsaimathung. Shabib Chasser (6,050m) is peak on far right. Geshi lies at far end of the ridge on left, Dawa Peak behind it in far distance. South face of Peak 6,060m and Samgyal are visible beyond the entrance to valley. *Matt Bridgestock*

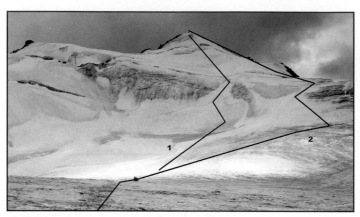

North face of Dawa Peak. (1) 2008 BSES Route. (2) Northwest ridge–route of previous ascents. *Matt Bridgestock*

unfrequented. Previous ascents in this region have largely been made by Indian teams and visiting Sherpas, dating from the late 1990s. However, in 2007 a commercially organized Jagged Globe expedition picked off several new peaks.

In 2008 the British Schools Exploring Society (BSES), a London-based charity aiming to develop the next generation of leaders and scientists through the underlying principle of "adventure with purpose," organized its first expedition to the Thanglasgo Valley, a deep natural thoroughfare that bisects the Nubra region from north to south.

We took 38 young explorers, novices between the ages of 16 and 18, and trekked south from Hundar (3,150m, close to the military road to the Siachen Glacier) as far as Wachen (ca 4,000m). There we split into two groups, one moving southwest for a day up the Palzampiu Valley to establish a base camp at 4,400m, while the other trekked for longer, up the Sniamo Valley to the south, eventually making camp at ca 4,750m.

After a long period of training and acclimatization, the expedition sped to a fast-paced finale. In the Palzampiu Valley a team repeated Samgyal (5,810m, first climbed by Samgyal Sherpa in the late 90s) via the northeast ridge, and William Ames, Will Blackshaw, and Simon Fowler climbed a new direct route up the north face of Dawa Peak (5,890m, ice up to 55°). This peak was first climbed in the late 90s by Dawa Sherpa, probably by the northwest ridge, which has now received several ascents.

East of base camp a summit of nearly 6,000m had no previously recorded ascent. It was guarded

Peak 2 (5,717m, possibly Yanchen Kangri) with new route up south gully and east ridge. *Matt Bridgestock*

by an extensive rubble pile, which was deemed unsafe to attempt with the whole group, so we opted for a one-to-one ratio of leaders to youngsters. Leaders Simon Fowler, Chris Horobin, Liz Yeates, and I, with Will Anderson, Harry Eaton, and Luke Havers, summited via the north ridge—crevassed slopes up to 30°. At 2 p.m., in white-out conditions, a disappointing yet unanimous decision had been taken to turn around, to avoid re-crossing the boulder field in the dark. However, with masterful timing the cloud parted just enough to reveal the summit no more than 50m away. A final burst of energy came from somewhere, and minutes later we were posing on the mist-enshrouded top and recording a GPS altitude of 5,980m. We dubbed the peak a distinctly non-Ladakhi name, the Big Rock Candy Mountain.

Over in the Sniamu Valley, Kangsaimathung (5,770m) and what is still known simply as Peak 2 (5,717m) lay within striking distance of advanced base. Both had been climbed in 2007, but our group was able to establish new routes on each.

A large group climbed Kangsaimathung from the northeast at PD+. (The mountain had previously been climbed from the south.) Leaders Matt Bridgestock, Andy Cowan, Sarah Lewis, and Sarah Major, with Harry Andrews, James Couzens, Luke Daly, Amy Forrest, Livvy Hampsher-Monk, Sarah Keane, Naill McLoughlin, Debbie Morgan, Henry Renninson, James Richardson, James Wood, and Yuan Yang took a diagonal line from the glacier to a point 80m from the summit, then climbed a final 50° snow slope to the top. They were accompanied by two Sherpas and a member of the cook team, who had

Big Rock Candy Mountain (5,980m GPS) from east, with route of ascent up north ridge. 2008 base camp was close to river at bottom of picture. *Matt Bridgestock*

never climbed a mountain before. On top these three celebrated with a chorus of beautiful Tibetan chants.

Peak 2 is probably the same as Yanchan Kangri, summited by the Jagged Globe expedition. Bridgestock and Lewis, this time with fellow leader Katherine Baldock, took Andrews, Couzens, Daly, Forrest, Hampsher-Monk, Morgan, Richardson, Wood, and Yuan Yang across a moraine field to a gully filled with loose snow yet liberally scattered with crampon-scratching scree, leading onto the east ridge. Once the cornice had been passed with care, the crest provided a gently angled ascent over snow to the top (F).

The expedition finished with a five-day trek south to Leh over the Lasirmou La (5,500m), from where we noticed a ca 5,600m peak to the east that would provide an easy but worthwhile goal for future parties.

ANDY RUCK, *UK*

Thanglasgo Valley, Peak 5,850m, northwest face and northeast ridge; Peak 5,995m, southeast ridge. From 2007 to 2009 I led expeditions to the Nubra Valley for the British Schools Exploring Society (BSES), picking off a few previously climbed and unclimbed peaks in the Thanglasgo Valley south of Hundar.

Lying north of Leh in the rain shadow of the Himalaya, this region has seen few parties outside the main trekking routes; because of its proximity to the Pakistan border, it is regarded by the Indian military as being particularly sensitive. During the 2009 expedition plans were laid to attempt unclimbed Telthop (6,010m), which lies at the head of the Khalsar Dag Valley.

In 2010 our primarily British group arrived at the IMF offices in Delhi to discover that our intended approach from Hundar was impractical due to washed out bridges. After three days acclimatizing in Leh, we crossed the Kardung La to Desket, where we attempted to reach the mountain

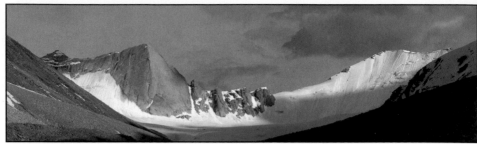

Peak 5,850m (right) from northwest. First ascent climbed short snow face right of rock pillars, then up left skyline ridge. Rock summit to left is a little lower, unclimbed, but has easy access on hidden side. *Chris Horobin*

Looking west at Peak 5,995m, right of center. First ascent climbed ridge that slants down left toward camera. Shabib Chasser (6,050m) is peak on far left. *Chris Horobin*

over a high pass south of Desket Gompa. Although this would have worked, we retreated when we realized our horses could not follow through the steep rocky terrain.

Reaching Hundar, we shelved our disappointment and made alternative plans to access the mountain via the main Thanglasgo Valley. A three-day trek took us to Thanglasgo hamlet (ca 4,600m) and the mouth of an unexplored valley to the east that we hoped would lead to our peak. A reconnaissance next day showed this approach to be long and difficult, with much moraine and a steep glacier. Although we could access the mountain via this route, we realized we would not have time to make a realistic attempt. However, we caught sight of a peak at the head of the initial valley. It is marked on the map as 5,850m and was confirmed by our Sherpas to be unclimbed. We were also rewarded with views of a possible route to another reportedly unclimbed peak lying immediately to the north of Shabib Chasser (a summit climbed by the 2007 Jagged Globe expedition).

From a base camp at Thanglasgo hamlet we established a high camp in the valley leading to 5,850m, and the day after crossed incredibly unstable moraine and a long glacier to reach the northwest face. This gave 300m of climbing up to 60° and led to the snowy, sometimes knife-edge, northeast ridge. Andrea Bainbridge, Sarah Reynolds, Bob Shiels, and I climbed rapidly in deteriorating weather to reach the rocky summit, where a GPS reading gave the altitude as 5,870m. The ascent was graded F.

In the few days remaining we attempted the peak north of Shabib Chasser. Given the warm weather and poor snow conditions, we decided to reconnoiter the southeast ridge, which was mainly rocky. We placed another high camp, and after a few hours sleep the mandatory alpine start saw us scrambling in the dark up a loose scree/boulder slope to gain the ridge. The crest gave climbing up to British Severe, and after nine hours Reynolds, Shiels, and I reached the summit, on which we recorded a GPS altitude of 5,995m. The overall grade was AD+.

We descended steep and alarmingly soft snow on the northeast ridge, regained high camp, dismantled it, and returned to base, crossing a cold, unpleasantly high and fast-flowing river.

We ended the trip by reaching Leh via a two-day trek south over the Lassermola La (Lasirmou La, 5,550m). Soft snow prevented the horses from making the crossing, providing us with an unforeseen forced march, while they took the long way round. On our first night back in Leh, the unseasonable weather culminated in a cloudburst that devastated the city and surrounding area. Expedition members were unscathed, and after a 24-hour delay while the airport was cleared of debris, we were able to make our way to Delhi and connecting flights home.

Other members of the expedition were Colin Bainbridge, Henry Latti (Finland), David Moseley. and Matt Powell (US). Special thanks to Mr. J. K. Sharma, First Secretary of the Indian Consulate in London, for helping with the X Visa process, and support staff and Sherpas at RIMO expeditions in Leh for making the impossible possible.

CHRIS HOROBIN, *UK*

Ibsti Kangri (6,340m), southeast face; Dzo Jongo, east (6,200m) and west (6,265m) summits. We had initially hoped to attempt a peak in Ladakh's Angtung Valley, but due to bureaucratic difficulties in obtaining mountaineering visas for our American members, we decided to try one of the newly opened peaks that did not require the X Mountaineering Visa. We zeroed in on Pk. 6,340m in the Nimaling Topko region, southeast of Leh.

We flew to Leh and drove the Leh-Manali road as far as Lato, from where we trekked across the Puja La (4,930m) and a second, 5,354m, pass (sometimes referred to as Lalung La) to a 5,200m base camp at Nimaling Topko. During this approach we experienced fierce thunderstorms

Southeast face of Ibsti Kangri. *Dave Adams*

Connecting ridge leading to Dzo Jongo West. *Divyesh Muni*

and torrential rain but had no inkling of the tragedy that had struck elsewhere in Ladakh. Later on the radio we heard the magnitude of the calamity. Initial estimates listed 140 people dead and 600 missing. Roads were damaged, entire villages swept away, and there was chaos everywhere. We immediately sent a message to friends and family that we were safe.

We moved to advanced base camp at 5,620m on August 10, our peak still hidden from view. After reconnaissance and deliberation, we decided to attempt the southeast face and placed a high camp near the foot. On the 14th Dave Adams, Don Goodman, Dawa Sherpa, and I set off up easy soft snow and rock to a gully. Keeping to the edge of the gully, we weaved around rock outcrops on snow and ice. It was a fairly steady 45-50°, and the weather remained cloudy, keeping the snow firm and allowing unroped progress. We fixed one rope on the final slope before reaching the east ridge. Carefully climbing 100m along the crest, we reached the summit, in low visibility at 9:30 a.m., where we were surprised to find a small cairn toward the west ridge of the peak. The summit had been reached before, though the IMF has no record of a previous ascent. Mountaineering history in this region is vague, but it is likely the previous party took a more direct approach from the Nimaling Valley to the west. We decided to refer to this summit as Ibsti Kangri.

Next day the weather seemed more settled, and we decided to capitalize on it by attempting the twin peaks of Dzo Jongo, which lay above our camp. My wife Vineeta and I established a high camp at 5,800m, while Dave, Don, his wife Natala, Dawa Sherpa, and Phujung Bote climbed directly from advanced base. We met on the 16th at 6,000m on the east ridge and continued together to the east summit (6,200m), which we reached at 9:30 a.m.

The higher west summit (6,265m) lay one kilometer along a connecting ridge. It proved too tempting, so Dave, Don, and I made the traverse. The rock was surprisingly solid, allowing us to move unroped, and after an hour and a half we reached the top, which showed no sign of previous visitation. After our return home, research showed that while the east summit has been climbed several times (as witnessed by various flags and cairns on top), there is no record of any attempt on the west peak.

Contacting Leh, we learned that 15km of road between Upshi and Lato had been washed away, forcing us to return across the Kongmaru La (5,250m) and descend to Shyam Sumdo, where vehicles could meet us. Most of the track had been washed away, but we were found a passable route for horses. We arrived in a deserted Leh on the 22nd; only those involved in rescue and rehabilitation, army personnel, and a few trekkers and climbers on their way home, were present. We were saddened to see the effect on those that were hit and determined to do our bit to help Ladakh recover.

DIVYESH MUNI, *Himalayan Club, India*

Barma Kangri (ca 6,500m), southeast ridge; Kangju Kangri (6,725m), attempt. On July 12 Rentaro Nishijima and the Indian guide Kumchuk Thines made the first ascent of Barma Kangri. High-altitude porter Pemba Norbu, Thines, and I (75 years old) repeated the route on the 17th. We were the first non-Indian party to climb in this area.

On southern slopes of Kangju Kangri East, with main summit ahead. On 2001 ascent of main summit, as probably on all previous ascents, party climbed obvious south-facing snow slope rising directly to summit. *Kumchuk Thines/Masato Oki Collection*

After several days spent obtaining our Inner Line Permit, we left Leh and over two days drove the Tangtse-Chushul military road (only possible by Jeep in fair weather) to a roadside base camp at 4,800m, close to an area known locally as Barma. On July 5 we established Camp 1 (5,400m) on a grassy plateau east of base camp in the Tastra Lungpa Valley. We then followed the plateau north for four kilometers and placed Camp 2 at 6,000m, on moraine near

Virgin 6,000m peaks on right bank of Kangju Glacier. Peaks rise to 6,489m. *Masato Oki*

the source of the river, due south of our mountain.

On the 12th the first summit party left at 6 a.m. and climbed rock and snow to reach a ca 6,200m col on the main divide of the Pangong Range. From here they followed the ridge northwest to arrive on the huge rock summit at 9 a.m. They fixed 200 meters of rope on the final snow slope. After talking with local people, we decided to call our previously unnamed summit Barma Kangri. The name was later ratified by our LO and the IMF. Barma means intermediate in Ladakhi. The altitude is an estimate from Google Earth.

Two kilometers to the northwest stands the highest peak in the range, Kangju Kangri. The ridge connecting it to Barma Kangri appears steep, rocky, and difficult. Kangju Kangri was first climbed in 1983 by members of an Indo-Tibet Border Police and local army expedition. It has subsequently been climbed at least three times; in 1987 by the ITBP, in 1995 again by the ITBP, and in 2001 by the Indian Army. Other 6,000m peaks in the range that have been climbed are Peak 6,580m, Kakstet Kangri (6,461m), and Peak 6,134m. However, there are several unclimbed 6,000ers remaining, the highest probably 6,670m.

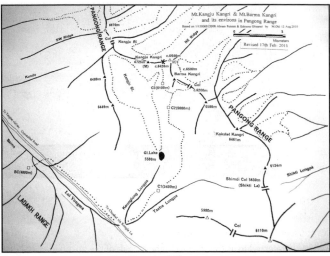

Pangong map, supplied by *Masato Oki*

On the 18th we made Camp 3 at 6,100m under the virgin east summit (ca 6,600m) of Kangju Kangri and climbed to the ridge between the east and main summits. At this point (ca 6,420m) we could see a sharp notch in the summit ridge, and, as continuing looked difficult and dangerous, we gave up, returned to base camp with all our equipment, and departed for Leh on the 24th.

MASATO OKI, *Chukyo Alpine Club, Japan*

ZANSKAR

Returning from southwest ridge of Langsarmo. *Alison Criscitiello*

South Suru Group, Lingsarmo, southwest ridge. Kate Harris, Rebecca Haspel (both Canada), and I, as leader, formed an all-female, unsupported expedition that visited the Nun Kun Massif with the goal of climbing Lingsarmo (formerly known as Pinnacle Peak, 6,955m). We used the standard Kun base camp, approaching from Shafat Village, and made Camp 1 (5,490m) just under Rabbit Rock, a little higher than the normal site used for an ascent of Kun. We climbed the Swiss Face, bivouacking part way up, before fixing six ropes on the steep section. Above the face we established Camp 2 at 6,130m. After traversing the plateau north, we placed Camp 3 (6,270m) closer to the high peaks. After one attempt, aborted due to heavy snow and wind, Rebecca and I reached the Kun - Lingsarmo col (34°01.166 'N, 76°04.180' E) and followed the southwest ridge of Lingsarmo toward the summit. Where the crest steepened, we made a rising traverse across the south flank, reaching the top at 6:30 a.m. on August 16. It took two hours to regain Camp 3. Research at the Indian Mountaineering Foundation shows that no permitted expedition had summited Lingsarmo since records were first kept, starting around 1958.

ALISON CRISCITIELLO, *US*

Harish Kapadia adds: The historic first ascent of Pinnacle Peak was made in 1906 via the southeast ridge by American Fanny Bullock Workman, Savoye (her guide), and a porter. At the time it was the highest summit reached by a woman, and close to the human altitude record. The ascent is well recorded in the Workmans' 1909 book, *Peaks and Glaciers of Nun Kun.* The first editor of the *Himalayan Journal,* Kenneth Mason, created doubts about this ascent, although he never wrote explicitly that he doubted it: "Mrs.

Looking south from near Gelmothungos. From left to right, Pk. 5,780, Rungofarka (6,495m), Lingsarmo. *Harish Kapadia*

Bullock Workman claimed to have ascended to 23,300', to the summit of a peak which she named Pinnacle Peak, and which she persistently referred to as the second highest peak of the group. Her heights and this statement were at variance with previously triangulated values." This was published in *A note on the topography of the Nun Kun Massif in Ladakh,* and later repeated in Mason's scholarly work, *Abode of Snow.* The use of "claimed" fueled controversy, though it is not clear whether Mason doubted Workman's ascent or whether he, as a surveyor, was only discussing the height she gave.

Other teams have also reached this summit, particularly in the 1980s, and referred to it as Pinnacle Peak. These ascents have been recorded in various journals, and photos taken of the summit show it to be the same as that which appears on the front cover of the Workmans' book, confirming Fanny Bullock Workman's claim. Modern maps name it Lingsarmo and quote both Nun and Kun as 7,135m, making Workman's peak the third highest in the group. It appears on the official list of new peaks opened for climbing in 2009.

Gulmatonga Valley, rock climbing. The branch valleys that rise south of the Zanskar road to Padam over the Pensi La hold many possible rock-climbing objectives. These small valleys offer potentially good climbing without the need for much bureaucracy or advanced planning. The large Shafat Valley, leading to Nun and Kun, is one, and its rock-climbing potential has been explored during the last 10 years by Italians and Americans. Another is the shorter Gulmatonga valley across the Suru River from the check post at Gulmatonga. Here are a variety of possible rock climbs. A team of young American rock climbers, led by Rushad Nanavatty, spent an enjoyable three weeks here in the summer, climbing challenging routes.

HARISH KAPADIA, *AAC Honorary Member, India*

Unclimbed rock peak of 5,926m on east rim of Shafat Glacier. *Harish Kapadia*

HIMACHAL PRADESH

Shiva Shankar West (left) and Shiva Shankar from Tarundi Valley.
Bruno Moretti

Shiva Shankar West, west face. The Pangi straddles the Himachal Pradesh–Jammu and Kashmir borders and is isolated for more than seven months of the year. The road into the area crosses 4,000m passes and is a difficult and adventurous journey even in summer. During winter the climate is arctic and the land blanketed with snow, making it impossible to enter or exit this region from November until May or June.

From mid-August to mid-September Lynn Iacobini De Fazio, Massimo Marcheggiani, and I, all instructors with the Italian Alpine Club, explored the Saichu Valley, the first of the Pangi's sub-valleys right of the Chenab. After reaching Udaipur via the Rothang Pass, we had to deal with the devastating consequences of the huge storm that days before had hit southern Asia and produced tragic flooding in Leh. The 65km road to Pangi, built in the 1990s along a narrow terrace suspended above the swirling Chenab River, had become a series of dangerous fords caused by an almost unbroken succession of landslides. Two of these forced us early into trekking mode, ferrying our loads from jeep to horses. We eventually reached the lush Saichu Valley, inhabited by hospitable Pangwali and Tibetan Buddhists. Two days' trekking took us to the narrow entrance to the Tarundi Valley, leading to the east side of Shiva (6,142). Horses were unable to go beyond this point, so we established base camp (3,535m), much lower than we wanted. Several days' bad weather intervened before we could establish advanced base at 3,830m (33°05'57.8" N, 76°36'59.8" E).

Taking advantage of a good weather window, we continued north up-valley, camping at 4,165m, 4,600m, and 5,080m, the last 20m above a col overlooking Sural Valley and dominated to the west by Peak 5,860m. Visible to the southwest was the huge northeast face and magic east pillar of Shiva. On September 1 we started up the face immediately east of the col, first climbing a 200m wall of very crumbly shale in huge unstable blocks, with difficulties up to UIAA V. Some of this was verglassed, and we had to climb in crampons. We then climbed a steep ice slope, followed by a snow shoulder that led to the 5,510m rounded dome of Shiva Shankar West (33°09'19.5" N, 76°36'48.9" E). This summit was first reached in 2005 by Italian Diego Stefani, who named it Zero Point. Continuing east would lead to the summit of Shiva Shankar (6,011m)—the Horn of Shiva. All information suggests that the two Italian expeditions are the only ones to have climbed from the Tarundi Valley. Two days of exhausting descent took us to base camp.

BRUNO MORETTI, *CAI, Italy*

Pangi Valley, mountaineering history; unclimbed objectives from the Saichu Valley. Early history in the Pangi was made by Japanese Junko Tabei, the first woman to summit Everest, who in 1988 made the first ascent of Shiva by the southwest face from the Parmar Valley (*AAJ 1989*). In 2001 a Japanese team climbed Baihali Jot (6,290m) by the north ridge (*AAJ 2002*). In 2002 an Indian expedition made the second ascent of Shiva, following the 1988 route (*AAJ 2003*). In 2004 Chris Bonington, Harish Kapadia, and friends trekked north up the Saichu as far as the confluence of the Tarundi and Paphita valleys, then continued east up the latter to climb Jot Mund (5,130), Jambu Peak (5,105) and Pimu Peak (5,480) on the watershed between the Miyar and Paphita valleys. The following year Diego Stefani's expedition climbed Shiva Shankar West, as mentioned in the previous report.

Unclimbed northwest face of Menthosa. *Bruno Moretti*

In 2007 Bonington returned, this time going up the Sural Valley from the administrative capital, Killar. While he and Raj Kumar climbed Peak 5,027m, the other three members of his British team, Rob Ferguson, Graham Little, and Jim Lowther, attempted the northwest face of unclimbed Shiva Shankar (6,011m), failing due to rotten rock.

East face of unclimbed Peak 5,860m, seen from rock band on west buttress of Shiva Shankar West. *Bruno Moretti*

It was left to Japanese Kazuo Kozu, Hidetaka Lizuka, and Reiko Maruyama, with three Indian porters, to make the first ascent of Shiva Shankar (Sersank Peak, because it dominates the Sersank Pass to the north) the following year, via the route attempted by the British trio.

Many challenges remain, the most notable being the eastern and northern aspects of Shiva [attempted by Russians, see below]. Equally interesting are the unclimbed icy northwestern faces of Menthosa (6,443m), Baihali Jot (6,290m), and its satellites, the latter with elegant ice faces above the Saichu Valley. No less intriguing is the south face of Shiva Shankar, though it has a disturbing array of seracs that get the sun most of the day. East of our base camp lay the confusingly named Baheli Jot (5,600m), a miniature Everest. The southwest ridge would provide good acclimatization and an interesting exploratory climb. Most of the history of climbing in the Pangi region is yet to be written.

BRUNO MORETTI, *CAI, Italy*

Spectacular upper east ridge of Shiva. However, unlike nearby Miyar Valley, most rock in the Pangi is very poor. *Bruno Moretti*

Shiva. Central spur attempted by Russians separates east-northeast face, on left, from shorter north face seen almost in profile to right. Andrey Muryshev

Shiva (6,142m), north face, attempt. In 2008, while climbing a new route on Mahindra in the Miyar Valley (*AAJ 2009*), we were captivated by a mysterious peak to the northwest. I later discovered it was Shiva, first climbed in 1988 by Junko Tabei. I explored the mountain on Google Earth and found that it had a huge north face, which I estimated to be ca 1,800m. I could find no further photographs but went in September 2010 with fellow climbers Evgeny Korol and Alexander Kornilov and snowboarder Natalia Lapina to see and climb it. Only the seeing part of the plan was successful.

Climbing the north side of Shiva is problematic. It is divided into two parts by a central spur. On the lower section of the east-northeast face, huge hanging glaciers constantly discharge avalanches. Two fine ice couloirs rise almost to the summit, but accessing them is difficult, and due to poor weather during our stay, they were avalanching. The north face is only 50° and shorter, because it starts from an easily accessible ice terrace at ca 5,000m. However, even here a route will be dangerous due to a large serac barrier in the middle of the face. There are only three lines that can be considered objectively safe: the arêtes bounding the face to the left (east) and right (north) and the central (northeast) spur.

We tried the central line, starting at 5,000m. Although it looked simple at first, the 45-50°snow was wet, deep, and unstable. Evgeny spent an hour climbing one ropelength with no protection. We gained rock, only to find slabs under 10cm of wet snow. In good conditions it would have been a walk. We had provisions for five days but quickly realized we could not climb this terrain in that time. More importantly, we didn't have enough pegs for a rappel descent, and unprotected down-climbing was unthinkable. We retreated, leaving a stash of gear below the ridge.

For four days the weather was bad, and when we returned, we found our equipment had been buried by a huge ice avalanche. Our climbing was over. I was in fact relieved, as the whole experience had seemed too dangerous. I wonder if this ridge is justifiable, as the top is capped by an overhanging serac barrier that may prove insurmountable. From about September 20 to the 30th, the weather was good, but it was too late for us. We hope this information will help future parties climb this magnificent objective.

ANDREY MURYSHEV, *Russia*

Miyar Valley, Dome Peak (5,650m), Lopez-Pfaff Direct; Point JAMES (4,965m), Southeast Ridge. At the end of August, after a three-day trek, Anna Pfaff and I established base camp in the Miyar, at the spot we had used for our 2008 visit, the grassy meadow below Castle Peak. Taking advantage of an eight-day weather window we had enjoyed during the approach, we set off on September 1 for the southeast face of unnamed Peak 5,650m on the north side of the Chhudong Valley [immediately southwest of Veneto Peak and northeast of Premsingh Peak]. Accessing the face via steep talus and a dry gully proved the most dangerous part of the climb. Apart from a few loose sections, the climbing above was good and generally 5.8-5.9 until we reached three-quarters height, where we could either continue direct to the headwall or traverse right to a gully. We opted for the headwall. I led a steep 5.10 face, then Anna led two pitches of 5.10+, overcoming a loose section, before I continued up moderate 5.8 terrain to the summit, arriving in twilight. We slung the most prominent section of the summit with our cordalette, and then began the first of 14 rappels through the night. Along the way we lost one of our ropes, ran out of slings, and almost lost our bivouac gear, but eventually made it down in one piece. We named the route Lopez-Pfaff Direct (IV 5.10+, 800m), and the previously virgin summit, Dome Peak.

The weather then turned bad for 10 days, forcing us to play the waiting game. Carrying no communication technology, we could only assess the weather by looking at cloud and wind movement. However, it wasn't difficult to figure out that winter had arrived. With that in mind, we decided to retrieve our gear cache left on the Chhudong moraine.

When we reached our gear, the weather began to improve, and we wondered whether we might snatch another route over the next couple of days. We stopped for the night, opting to try a fast ascent next day. The fine pyramid of Point JAMES was close at hand, and we thought the southeast ridge was unclimbed.

Next morning we awoke to a rainstorm. Fortunately, our tent was watertight, so we decided to stay another night, just in case. On the morning of the 11th we woke to perfect blue skies. Simul-climbing moderate terrain on an exciting ridge, we reached a point where it ended below a headwall. On a good ledge we changed into rock shoes and contemplated the weather. We were close to the top, so decided to go for it. I led a full 70m pitch up a 5.10 finger crack through exposed, solid rock, and then Anna took over the lead and reached a roof, which she bypassed by a

Lopez-Pfaff Direct on southeast face of Dome Peak. *Camilo Lopez*

rightward traverse that proved to be the crux of the entire route. I followed, to find her on a hanging belay just a couple of meters below the summit. To reach the top involved crossing an exposed overhang with no protection. My lead was only a few minutes but felt like hours. Soon we were both hugging each other on the very top, having completed the 600m Southeast Ridge at III 5.10c. There were no other climbers in this region at the time; in fact, we barely saw any trekkers.

CAMILO LOPEZ, *Colombia and US*

Southeast ridge, Lopez-Pfaff route on Point JAMES. Other routes on peak lie on far side of ridge. *Camilo Lopez*

On summit of Tribulation Point. Sentinel Peak is rock summit immediately above head of foreground climber (Derek Buckle). Directly behind is broad-topped Snow Leopard Peak. South wall, facing camera, is split by an obvious broad couloir system. Route of ascent started right of this and slanted left up a ramp to its top. Rock on splendid "aiguille" looked superb, though it is a long approach for a short climb. *Mike Cocker*

Jiwa Nala, Snow Leopard Peak (5,365m), Sentinel Peak (5,140m), Tribulation Point (5,125m), Snowcock Point (4,890m). In September and October Derek Buckle, Drew Cook, John Hudson, Laura Millichamp, and I, all members of the Alpine Club, visited the Jiwa Nala region of the Great Himalayan National Park. The Jiwa drains west toward the Beas River, south of the famous tourist resort of Manali. It lies in Banjar region, approximately 70km east-southeast of the large regional town of Kullu. The area had been recommended by the Himalayan authority, Harish Kapadia, and as far as is known had not previously been visited by mountaineers. The valley can only be accessed by two difficult passes, and although shepherds have occasionally grazed their flocks there, it has never seen any permanent settlement.

Glacial cirque at head of Jiwa Valley. High peak left of center is 5,445m. Snow Leopard Peak is just out of frame to left. *Derek Buckle*

We established base camp at 3,725m, beyond which the valley terminated in a glacial cirque of unclimbed peaks rising to 5,445m. From a high camp just below the glacial snout, Buckle, Cook, and I accessed an upper glacier via a steep snow couloir and from there made the first ascent of Snow Leopard Peak by a mixed route on the south face (AD). From the same camp various members of the team made ascents of Tribulation Point and Sentinel Peak in the crenulated cirque and from a separate high camp ascended Snowcock Point, at the head of the southern valley. The rock in this area is mostly coarse mica-schist but, surprisingly, the little that we climbed (a five-meter chimney on Sentinel Peak and on our mixed line up Snow Leopard) was reasonably solid.

We frequently came across bear scat (our porters saw a Himalayan bear) and saw snow leopard tracks on the glacier. Thanks to the AC Climbing Fund for supporting the expedition.

MIKE COCKER, *Alpine Club*

Kinnaur, Naufragi. From August 15 to September 8 I soloed a big wall south of the Kinnaur-Kailash Range. The wall lies roughly northeast of Sangla in the Baspa Valley, on the southern flanks of Raldang (5,499m). Before I left for India, the only information I had was a picture of the wall, which had appeared on John Middendorf's big-wall web page, and its Google Earth coordinates.

I had no idea how to start the approach, but once in the valley I showed the picture to locals. I hired porters, and we set off in heavy rain. In thick mist, they left my haul bags at 3,800m and returned to the valley. I made this spot my base camp. As usual, I took neither phone, internet, GPS, nor other communication device.

Last summer the monsoon was strong, and in the seven days I spent at base camp I never saw the whole wall. In fact, it took two days to find the foot of the wall, in almost zero visibility. Access was like trying to climb a river ravine, complicated and slippery. I had to fix several ropes and employ three porters to help carry for part of the approach.

A 950m wall on southern flanks of Raldang. Marked is line of Naufragi. *Marc Martin*

My advanced base at the foot of the wall was a portaledge hanging from a boulder at 4,300m, because there was no flat place for a tent above base camp. I fixed the first three pitches (150m) and then spent 25 days alone on the face in horrible weather. (A local newspaper reported that last summer this area received 156% more rain than normal.) There was rain and mist every day, and once, while jumaring, I lost consciousness due to hypothermia. I had only taken 18 days food and water and more than once thought about abandoning the climb. However, my motivation and desire to stay up there were stronger.

Against my principles, above the 10th pitch, 14 days into the route, I resorted to drilling bathooks to overcome monolithic sections where there was no natural line, even for extreme aid. I didn't have enough bolts. At one point, deciding that I should retreat, I downclimbed part of a pitch but then realized I didn't want to give up; I'd made such a big effort already that, despite the constant bad weather, my motivation carried me upward. Eventually, I

Home for the night. Camp 1 on Naufragi. *Silvia Vidal*

reached the top of the wall at ca 5,250m. The summit of the mountain was still far away—I never saw it. I had climbed 1,050m at A4+ and 6a+, and had tried not to use bathooks to increase the grade; the sections of A4 and A4+ are natural. I've named the route Naufragi, which means Shipwreck in Catalan.

SÍLVIA VIDAL, *Catalonia*

Head of Singekang Valley. Snow and rock pyramid center is northwestern outlier (Singekang Minor) of Singekang. Summit of Singekang is just visible immediately behind. *Jeremy Windsor*

Seen from north-northwest, Snaght Kang (left), and in distant right unclimbed Peak 6,091m. *Jeremy Windsor*

Spiti, Singekang Valley, Singekang (6,008m), attempt; Snaght Kang (5,500m), north ridge. In October and November six mountaineers from Ireland and the UK (Martin Boner, George Carlton, Sandra Kennedy, Alan Tees, Andrew Tees, and I) made an attempt on Singekang (Lion Peak), an unclimbed mountain situated at the head of the Singekang Valley. In doing so, we became the first mountaineers to explore this remote Spiti valley.

From Delhi we traveled overnight by bus to Manali, and then by 4WD to Kaza. After two days spent acclimatizing and gathering supplies, we continued east, first by road to Poh and then by foot, across the Spiti River, to the small settlement of Pomrang. Situated close to the valley entrance, Pomrang proved to be an ideal starting point. We spent the next eight days establishing three camps along the valley and within two weeks of leaving home were ready to make an attempt on the mountain.

From high camp we made a long traverse south around Singekang's subsidiary northwestern peak, before turning sharply east into a sheltered snowy bowl. Ahead lay a steep and rather intimidating slope, covered in loose scree and featuring a tall rock tooth. However, using a fixed rope, we quickly overcame these difficulties and emerged on a narrow col that overlooked the glacier beside which we had camped and the mountains of Tibet beyond. Ahead lay the northwest ridge of Singekang and our proposed route. However, unconsolidated snow, low temperatures, and steep ice towers halted progress, and we eventually abandoned the attempt at 5,600m.

On returning to advanced base, we identified a potential route up a peak north of Peak 6,091m, a high unclimbed summit on the southern rim of the valley. Two days later we placed a high camp at 4,800m on a snow platform. This site provided excellent views south to Manirang (6,593m), the highest peak in Spiti. The north ridge of our peak was complicated by deep snow and steep ice gullies, but we made excellent progress, and after outflanking several obstacles on the crest, reached the summit in less than five hours. We subsequently named the mountain Snaght Kang.

Exploration of the valley also revealed other potential objectives. To the north we photographed an elegant rocky pinnacle (Peak 5,796m), which lay directly across from Snaght Kang. From beneath its northern face, a narrow valley appeared to give straightforward access to a snowy col and the summit slopes above. On the south side of the valley we identified Peaks 6,091m and 5,882m, which form part of the ridge connecting Singekang with Snaght Kang. Although steep and complicated in places, these two appeared to be excellent objectives. We also found a potential crossing from the head of the valley toward the east, and we hope that our visit will encourage others to enjoy this stunning area.

Without the generous assistance of the Mount Everest Foundation, Mountaineering Ireland, Indian Mountaineering Foundation, and Adventuremania this expedition would not have been possible.

JEREMY WINDSOR, *UK, Alpine Club*

WESTERN GARHWAL

Obra Valley, Peak 5,480m, southwest ridge; Dauru (5,877m), northwest ridge; Ranglana (5,554m), south ridge. Boris Korzh, Philip Leadbeater, Kunal Masania, Andrew McLellan, and I, all from Imperial College, London, spent the latter part of September exploring the Obra Valley. The rainfall had been significantly higher than normal for the time of year, and roads were blocked by a number of landslides. Rather than the expected six-seven hours, it took three days from the hilltop tourist resort of Mussoorie to reach the roadhead at Jakhol. We planned a three-day walk to base camp, because the height gain was 1,700m, and this schedule would allow porters to use huts located in the valley. The weather took a turn for the worse toward the end of the trek, with persistent rain throughout the last day. Our porters became disheartened and deposited loads at 3,867m, farther down valley than we had intended. We spent two days there in persistent rain before clear weather arrived on September 20. Over the next four days we established tents at our originally planned site (4,100m) and a high cache at 4,900m. Our initial trips were through snow and slush, but the snowline gradually rose from 3,900m to 4,300m, just after we had post-holed and load-ferried our way through it.

From our high cache we were intending to make a single push to the summit of Peak 5,877m, referred to by locals as Dauru. However, we were moving slowly due to the altitude, and so changed our objective to nearby Peak 5,480m, which we climbed on the 24th by the southwest ridge (500m, AD-). We were unable to get a good fix on the summit from our GPS, so we settled for the nearest contour on the map. On our return we noticed another peak labelled 5,480m slightly north of what we climbed. It is unidentifiable on Google Earth, so maybe the peak we ascended is positioned wrongly on the map.

To climb Dauru we realized we would need to move our camp as close to the headwall at the top of the glacier as possible, to allow us to get on Dauru while the snow was still frozen early in the morning. We descended to base camp and spent the 26th resting, but as the weather remained stable we returned with more supplies the following day, collected what remained of our cache, and moved camp up to 5,100m

An early start on the 28th saw Phil lead up to the col at 5,400m, after which we climbed the northwest ridge of Dauru, alternating leads to the summit (700m, AD). After enjoying an excellent panorama, we returned to our camp, packed, and descended to base camp with all our equipment.

On the 30th, in continuing stable weather, we decided to make an attempt on Ranglana (5,554m) by placing a camp on its western col. (Phil had reconnoitered this during a rest day and thought it a feasible route.) With the aid of three porters, we carried to the snowline at 4,300m, then continued on our own to camp at 4,687m, on the glacier descending from the col. Following a chilly night we crossed the 4,950m col and descended a little way toward the Maninda Valley, before joining the south ridge of Ranglana and following it to the summit (900m, D-). We descended by the

Looking southwest across upper Obra Valley. (A) Andurko, (B) Ranglana , (C) Dhodhu (5,418m), and (D) Dhodhu Kha Guncha (5,135m). Ascent of Ranglana crossed saddle between it and Dhodhu, then climbed hidden south ridge. *Jonathan Phillips*

Peak 5,480m (left) and Dharu (5,877m) from southwest, showing lines of first ascents. *Jonathan Phillips*

same route and returned to our high camp for a night, before descending to base.

We left the area on October 4, earlier than planned, as we had received reports of further landslides near the roadhead and needed to make sure we could reach Delhi for our flights on the 9th. We arrived in the capital on the 8th and spent our final day buying souvenirs and watching track cycling and athletics at the XIXth Commonwealth Games, which were being held in the city. We thank the Imperial College Exploration Board, Mount Everest Foundation, British Mountaineering Council, Welsh Sports Association, and the Lyon Equipment Award for their generous support.

JONATHAN PHILLIPS, *UK*

Gangotri, Bhagirathi III-IV col, west face. A team of six young French alpinists, under the guidance of Frederic Gentet and Christophe Moulin, hoped to repeat classic rock routes on Bhagirathi III. Snowfall of one and a half meters at base camp prevented any attempt on these objectives, but several members of the group, including Thomas Arfi and Simon Duverney, took advantage of a short weather window toward the end of September to climb a 900m ice line on the west face, leading to the 6,100m col between Bhagirathis III and IV. The crux, early on the route, was a 60m pitch of maximum angle 90°. The exit, on soft snow, was difficult, and, as the continuation to the summit of Bhagirathi III was considered too dangerous under the conditions, the team descended from the col. La Fée Clochette (ED) was a tribute to team member Chloé Graftiaux, a young Franco-Belgian who was killed in a fall on the Aiguille Noire de Peuterey that summer.

LINDSAY GRIFFIN, *Mountain INFO*

Gangotri, Vasuki Parbat (6,792m), west face. Attempted once before, by Mick Fowler and Paul Ramsden, the 1,600m west face of the rarely-visited Vasuki Parbat gives sustained mixed difficulties of Scottish VI, 7 (or approximately M6). British alpinists Malcolm Bass and Paul Figg reached the summit ridge after nine days on the face, and traversed the serpentine crest over the top and down the northwest ridge, returning to base camp in a round trip of 10 days. There are only two previous claimed ascents of this mountain, but the first does not seem to be recognized by Indian authorities. For details, see Bass's feature article in this Journal.

CENTRAL GARHWAL

Ekdant (6,128m), north spur and northeast ridge; Kartik (5,113m), north face. Ashes from the Iceland volcano threatened our flight, but Paulo Roxo and I arrived in Delhi as planned, on May 11. Our goal was the virgin Parvati Parbat (6,257m) above the Satopanth Glacier, and something more if we had time. We had little information: a few pictures we found on the Internet and the best available map (1:125,000). Our aim was to explore and enjoy all the inevitable surprises.

We established base camp on the glacier at 4,179m, 30°45'18.47" N, 79°22'46.57" E (GPS). Our choice of route was an elegant spur leading to a plateau, from which we hoped to reach the summit of Parvati Parbat. We pitched a tent at 4,750m, hoping the following day to make an acclimatization climb. However, in the night we were hit by a huge thunderstorm and snowfall. Deciding that perhaps we were not in the safest place, we dressed hurriedly and headed down to base camp.

Deeming that we were now acclimatized, we decided to try our luck with the spur over a two-day weather window. On May 21 we left base camp at 3 a.m. and climbed the more gently angled, lower

Kartik, with route of first ascent marked, lies to the right of the serac torn north face of Peak 5,812m. In the right distance is Chaukamba (7,138m). *Daniela Teixeira*

section of spur and pitched our tent on a col 5,450m. After 7 a.m. the snow became soft and deep and, with the heat from the sun, started to sap our energies. An easy rock scramble, followed by a 15m rappel, brought us close to the col, which we reached at midday.

Upper section of the new Portuguese route on the north spur of Ekdant. The main summit of Parvati Parvat is just off picture to the right. *Daniela Teixeira*

Paulo Roxo on the north spur of Ekdant (taken during the descent). (C) marks the high camp at 5,450m. Satopanth Glacier below. *Daniela Teixeira*

Next day we began at 1 a.m., hoping to reach the summit by midday at the latest. Even at night the snow was far from perfect, and we protected an increasingly steep ascent with snow stakes and ice screws. At 5 a.m. we reached the crest and saw that the plateau marked on the map was in fact 100m down the far side. We closely followed the crest toward a prominent triangular peak not marked on the map. We traversed 30m below its summit and then descended to the plateau, following it monotonously southwest, thinking it would lead directly to the main summit of Parvati. Two previous attempts on this ridge had stopped at a "dome-like foresummit," and at 7:30 a.m. we indeed reached a snow dome at ca 6,150m. To our horror, between us and the main summit was another sharp peak. "What's this f... ing mountain doing here?" I exclaimed to Paulo.

The main summit was still an estimated three hours distant, and the snow was becoming increasingly poor. We had to be realistic. If we went on, our return would be dangerous, with no reliable protection in the softening snow. Our spur was original, the first Portuguese new line in the Himalaya, but we hadn't reached the summit.

Then, turning back, we saw the triangular peak we had passed. "Let's go for it." We climbed to the summit, now pleased that our new route had a logical conclusion (1,900m, D+ 65°). At base camp we discovered that this peak was called Ekdant and had a previous ascent. [*Editor's Note: this was in 1980, by Shashank Kulkarni and high-altitude porter Narayan Singh, who were part of an Indian expedition attempting Parvati Parbat via the northeast ridge, from the ca 5,500m col between it and Nilkanth. They named it Ekdant, meaning "one tooth"*]. The descent of course was epic, with many 25m rappels from Abalakovs, as we had only climbed on a single 50m rope.

A few days of bad weather intervened before we again tried Parvati, by a more direct line on the north face. This time huge avalanche danger turned us back at 5,100m. On the last day of good weather, June 2, we opted for a beautiful, triangular peak farther east, immediately south of Lake Satopanth. We took minimal gear and reached the top by the north face at 10 a.m., the crux being the last seven meters, where we had to climb rock (UIAA IV). We named the route Directa Lusitana (D+, 55-60°) and the peak Kartik (30°43'52.93" N, 79°21'9.96" E, GPS), to maintain the Hindu spirit of the area. Kartik was the smaller brother of Ekdant and warrior son of Lord Shiva and his consort Parvati. It is the first virgin Himalayan summit reached by Portuguese.

DANIELA TEIXEIRA, *Portugal*

EASTERN GARHWAL

Nanda Khat (6,611m), east spur and north ridge. Situated immediately west of Traill's Pass, Nanda Khat has been a much-attempted peak, though few have reached the main summit. In pre-monsoon, a team of seven male and five female climbers, organized by the Indian Mountaineering Foundation and led by Anil Ghurtoo, established base camp on the Pindari Glacier at 4,482m. The team then ascended north to the vicinity of Traill's Pass, and after establishing two high camps, Bharat Bhushan, Dhruv Joshi, Takpa Norbu, and Cheten Pandey reached the summit via a partial new route up the east spur to the north summit, then back along the sharp north-northeast ridge to main summit. The date was June 22, and the final ascent made in a 22-hour roundtrip from their highest camp. They employed no high-altitude support.

HARISH KAPADIA, *AAC Honorary Member, India*

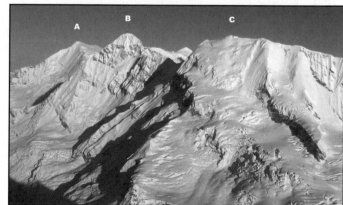

Looking southwest from northwest ridge of Changuch. In foreground are crevassed slopes of Traill's Pass, while Pindari Glacier lies down to left. (A) Maiktoli (6,803m), (B) Panwali Dwar (6,663m), and (C) Nanda Khat, with north-northeast ridge forming right skyline. *Martin Moran*

Northwest from west ridge of Nital Thaur. (A) Hardeol. (B) Tirsuli West. (C) Tirsuli. (1) Southwest ridge. (2) South ridge. (3) East ridge. (4) Northeast ridge. Attempted route and bivouac site marked. First ascensionists of Hardeol probably climbed one of spurs toward right edge of picture, then crossed obvious glacier plateau to reach col between Hardeol and Tirsuli, before finishing up northeast ridge. *Boris Lorencic*

Ikualari (6,059m), southwest ridge; Nital Thaur (6,236m), southwest spur and west ridge; Hardeol (7,151m), south ridge attempt. In autumn Urban Golob, Boris Lorencic, Karel Zavrsnik, and I visited the mountains at the head of the Milam Glacier, a relatively little-visited area. After the border closure with China in the 1960s, only Indians were allowed here for many years. There have been few ascents; many summits are virgin, and most faces untouched.

Just a few foreign expeditions have climbed from the upper Milam Glacier, so we were surprised to arrive at our base camp and find a Swiss commercial expedition in place and attempting Tirsuli (7,074m), the immediate neighbor of our main goal, Hardeol, the highest summit of this area. [*Editor's note: The nine-member German-Swiss team abandoned its attempt at 5,700m, when time ran out.*]

Tirsuli West (7,035m) remains unclimbed. Most peaks on the west side of the glacier have been climbed from the Uttar Rishi Glacier, in the Nanda Devi Sanctuary, but have not been attempted from the Milam, from where they have difficult and dangerous approaches. On the east side lie several unclimbed 6,000ers

Nital Thaur from west-northwest. (A) West ridge. (C) South ridge. Top section of ascent and bivouac site marked. *Matija Jost*

such as Nanda Gond (6,315m), Chalab (6,160m), and Kholi (6,114m). These look less difficult, but are connected by sharp ridges with many subsidiary summits.

We wanted to acclimatize and gain more information on Hardeol, so for our first climb we decided on Ikualari. We established our first camp at 4,600m on the upper glacier and our second at 5,200m on the southwest ridge. On October 3 we reached the summit in only three hours climbing from this camp, in sunny, cold, windy weather. The only previous ascent of this peak was made in 1968 by a team from Mumbai University. We repeated their route.

A few days later Golob went home, due to ill health, while we remaining three started up the southwest ridge of Nital Thaur, directly east of base camp. There were no difficult or dangerous glaciers barring access, as with other nearby mountains, and the ridge had no seracs. It seemed a good choice for a second acclimatization ascent before tackling Hardeol. There was one previously recorded attempt; on the south ridge in 1974. We made our first bivouac at 5,400m, joined the west ridge at 5,700m, and made a second bivouac at 5,900m. We reached the top on the 10th, grading our route D (UIAA III 60°).

Ikualari from southwest. Ascent route and bivouac sites marked. Left skyline is northwest ridge, which connects with Kholi (6,114m, not pictured). Right skyline is east ridge, with (A) Pt. ca 6,060m, (B) Pt. ca 6,160m, and (C) Pt. 6,200+m. Heights estimated from summit of Ikualari. Ridge between B and C looks sharp and tricky. *Matija Jost*

At 5,300m we found old fixed rope and two pitons. The rock was so poor that we pulled both pegs out by hand. Our descent followed the west ridge at first, and then the snowy southwest face, which did not exceed 60°. Ours was probably the first ascent of the mountain.

On the 14th we cached gear on the approach to Hardeol's south face and returned to base camp for a rest. Karel didn't feel strong enough to make an attempt, so on the 16th Boris and I regained our cache and climbed an exposed gully and ramp east of the ice fall, reaching the glacier plateau beneath Hardeol at 5,300m. In late afternoon we gained the south ridge of Hardeol and bivouacked at 5,800m. From here the rock quality on the ridge looked poor, and there was very little ice on the southeast and southwest faces. Next day we attempted to climb the southwest flank of the ridge, but after 200m retreated due to the constant fall of rock and ice. We returned to the ridge, which was sheltered from objective danger, but the rock was poor, and the ridge looked desperately steep higher up. We spent another night at our previous bivouac spot and the next morning made one rappel, then reversed our dangerous approach route.

This little explored area offers many interesting objectives, but we would recommend parties think about coming pre-monsoon. Although we had good weather and much sunshine, the walls were dry and composed of terribly rotten rock. May, or possibly April, when there is more snow and ice, would be better months to climb here.

MATIJA JOST, *Slovenia*

Editor's note: The south side of Hardeol was first attempted in 1974 by an Indian-New Zealand female expedition that gave up at 5,450m due to avalanche danger. An Indo-Tibet Border Police expedition made the first ascent in 1978. They also approached up the Milam Glacier, but then climbed to above 6,500m on the ridge coming down from Tirsuli, before heading for a high col at the foot of Hardeol's northeast ridge, which they followed to the summit over a subsidiary ca 6,850m summit. In 1991 a team from the Border Security Force made the second and only other ascent, likely via the same route.

WESTERN SIKKIM

West face of Lama Lamani. (1) 2005 Bhutia-Clyma-Payne-Rai route. (2) Cohen-Swienton. (3) Hamilton-Kennedy. Unclimbed south summit out of picture to right. Paul Swienton

Lama Lamani North (5,650m), west face; Peak 5,500m; Jopuno (5,936m), west ridge, attempt. Inspired by the writing of British mountaineer Roger Payne (*AAJ 2008*), Geoff Cohen, Bob Hamilton, Dick Isherwood, Steve Kennedy, Dave Ritchie (all UK), and I (US) visited the Thangsing Valley from May 8 to 22.

We first identified an obvious line on the west face of Lama Lamani, going up to a col south of the final elegant snow arête of the north summit. We left gear in the boulders below the face, and on the 11th all except Isherwood and Ritchie, neither of whom had yet acclimatized, retrieved the gear and at 6 a.m. began climbing the face in excellent weather. Our route started below and to the right of left-trending ramps leading into a snow couloir that runs up to the col. Steve and Bob followed the highest narrow ramp tucked up against a steep rock wall, while Geoff and I traversed to a ramp below. We all then followed a blocky ridge to the right of the couloir. In the upper part we moved into the couloir and climbed out left to reach the col. To this point the difficulty had largely been Scottish II, and Steve and Bob soloed all but one pitch, while Geoff and I moved together placing runners.

At the col an impressive rock tower to the south lent a dramatic air to our perch, and we could look across at the main (south) summit, connected to the north summit by a pinnacled rock ridge. Above the col we all started up an interesting mixed ridge at about Scottish grade III, but after 100m Geoff and I decided it would be easier to traverse left and join the lower part of the final snow arête. Steve and Bob continued on the ridge to where it joined the snow arête at a level section. Overall, the 600m route was AD+.

It was noon when we all reached the summit. Afternoon cloud had already built, and we did not get a clear view to the east. We did see the impressive Peak 5,833m (sometimes mistaken for Narsing) and caught a tiny glimpse of the top of the east face of Jopuno, which seemed extremely steep. Although its unclimbed south ridge appears feasible, there seemed to be technical and time-consuming sections, and the top section, where the rock is black and reportedly less sound, is pinnacled and looks rather tricky.

We descended toward Jopuno a short way and then began rappelling the northwest face. After 120m we downclimbed on snow for 150m, then moved northeast and rappelled again. More downclimbing on softening snow got us to the last steep section, which we rappelled to the glacier. [*Editor's note: The north summit was first reached in 2005 via the northwest face to the west spur, at AD+, by Julie-Ann Clyma and Roger Payne with two friends from the Sikkim Amateur Mountaineering Association, Kunzang Bhutia and Sagar Rai. The south summit is believed to be unclimbed].*

On the 14th Bob and Dave climbed an unnamed 5,500m peak between Jopuno and Lama Lamani. They traversed steep snow and

Bob Hamilton on summit of Lama Lamani North, with Jopuno behind. Unclimbed south ridge of Jopuno faces camera, with upper west face to left. *Steve Kennedy*

ice for a couple of ropelengths to reach a snow arête on the south face, followed it for a pitch, and then climbed two short pitches up mixed grooves to the summit block, which they gained by exposed moves.

At 2:45 a.m. on the 18th, Steve, Bob, Geoff, and I left camp to repeat the west ridge of Jopuno. Above 5,450m the ridge became icy, and after two time-consuming pitches we got established on the firm brown rock mentioned by the American party that first climbed this ridge in 2008 (*AAJ 2009*). The section above was well covered in snow and, although broken, gave climbing of about Scottish III. At 11 a.m. Steve and Bob reached the foot of the looser black rock that forms the summit of the mountain; Geoff and I were a pitch behind. We had been climbing slowly, and it now appeared unlikely that we could reach the summit and descend safely before evening, so we turned around. We reversed the route by downclimbing and rappelling, regaining the tents at 5:30 p.m. Although disappointed not to have reached the top, we agreed that it had been 15 hours of very good alpine climbing in a splendid mountain setting.

Together with Tingchenkang (6,010m), Lama Lamani and Jopuno have been designated Alpine Peaks by Sikkim authorities, and it is easy to arrange permits. All three offer good, medium-grade alpine ascents and could become classics of the Eastern Himalaya. The expedition used Roger Payne's recommended agent, Barap Bhutia Namgyal, who proved invaluable, and we thank the Mount Everest Foundation and the Mountaineering Council of Scotland for their generous support.

PAUL SWIENTON, *AAC*

Jopuno, southwest face and west ridge, attempt; history and corrections. In the autumn of 2009 Julie-Ann Clyma and I were back in Western Sikkim and with Hugh Sheehan made an attempt on Jopuno. Although it became cloudy on many afternoons, we did not have a single day of precipitation. On November 7 we climbed the left side of the southwest face to gain the crest of the west ridge at the base of the black rock section. We climbed this until just below the snowy foresummit, but by this time it was windy and cloudy, and we did not have time or equipment to go farther. More than half our descent was made in the dark.

Since writing my article for *AAJ 2008* (*"Emerging from the Mists: the sublime alpine peaks of Sikkim, India"*), I have discovered that the 2001 ascent did not follow the south ridge. It appears that Kunzang Butia and Sagar Rai climbed snow on the northwest face and, if I have understood correctly, encountered loose rock but did not traverse the main ridge to reach the highest point.

I also realized that WW Graham described climbing "Jobonu" in 1883. In the 1884 *Alpine*

Jopuno from southwest. (1) West ridge (Halladay-Smith, 2008). (2) Southwest face to west ridge (Clyma-Payne-Sheehan, 2009, to high point H on west ridge). (B) Bivouac site on 2009 attempt. *Roger Payne*

Journal he writes that it was "incomparably the hardest ascent we had in the Himalaya owing to the great steepness of the glacier work." It is hard to imagine that Jopuno was climbed in 1883, but I would have thought that the west ridge would have been the line of choice in the pioneering days of alpinism. Nothing in his account fits the topography of Jopuno, and my current view is that he might have climbed the northwest glacier on Tinchenkang and mistaken it for Jopuno.

    I began to wonder if the highest point of this mountain had been reached, but after helpful correspondence with Jason Halladay and Josh Smith, who made the first ascent of the west ridge in 2008 (*AAJ 2009*), I think it fair to say that these two Americans reached the summit of this ridge, which may be the highest point of Jopuno, higher than the summit at the top of the south ridge. Halladay

Kangto from the south. The highest point is at the far end of the summit ridge. The unclimbed Kangto II (6,953m) is further south on this ridge. *Harish Kapadia*

notes that on top they were shrouded in clouds and graupel, but, from what he assumed to be the true summit, he began to follow the ridge toward the south summit. As it appeared to be the same elevation or lower than the point he was on, he turned back.

ROGER PAYNE, *Switzerland*

ARUNACHAL PRADESH

Photography of the Kangto Range. During a trek to the East Kamang district in October-November, Harish Kapadia took photos of the enigmatic high peaks straddling the Arunachal-Tibet border. These form what is generally referred to as the Kangto Range, the last high mountain group of the eastern Himalaya. (The most easterly point of the Himalaya, Namcha Barwa, lies entirely in Tibet). The peaks rise from the head of the Pachuk Valley and lie on the McMahon Line.

The highest is Kangto (7,042m), which has only been climbed once, in 1981 by Japanese from Tibet. Way to its west stands Gorichen (6,488m), while farther east lie Chomo I and II (6,878m and 6,710m) and Nyegi Kangsang (6,983m). Gorichen, with its easier access and moderate difficulties, has been climbed a few times. Kangto and Chomo I and II have never been attempted from the south; there are no passes here, so neither locals nor defense forces have any need to venture into this region. Chomo I and II have never been attempted, and Nyegi Kangsang has a checkered climbing history. It was attempted from the south by an IMF expedition, which claimed an ascent, but it was later proved they stopped a long way from the summit. The accompanying images of these rarely photographed peaks were taken from Lada Village (1,500m).

LINDSAY GRIFFIN, *Mountain INFO*

Furthest east in the group is the unclimbed Nyegi Kangsang. *Harish Kapadia*

The next peaks east of Kangto are Chomo II (left) and I. *Harish Kapadia*

Nepal

The online version of these reports frequently contains additional photos, maps, topos, and extended text. Please visit aaj.americanalpineclub.org

Helicopter usage. A helicopter whirling overhead on a flight to an expedition's base camp area is no longer a rare event brought on by a serious emergency situation. In the autumn helicopters evacuated: climbers who had failed to factor into their schedules the extra time needed for periods of bad weather and avalanches; climbers forced to take a slightly different line than planned up or down their mountain; climbers who found their inflexible time limit was up and simply had to catch their previously booked flights home; climbers who had serious, though in some cases not so serious, medical problems; a leader in a great hurry to travel from base camp to the village of a Sherpa who had a fatal accident, in order to break the tragic news to the Sherpa's wife as soon as possible; two mountaineers who got into trouble on a seldom-climbed route and had no means of getting down when the route ahead became impassable, since they had neither brought appropriate equipment nor prepared an escape route; and expedition members who just didn't want to walk when they could ride.

Next spring a prominent organizer of commercial expeditions is changing hotels. He will no longer book his groups into a friendly, comfortable hotel in central Kathmandu. Instead, he is switching to a huge, impersonal establishment far from the city center and belonging to an international chain. He explained that this is the only hotel with a helipad; his clients are wealthy, and choppers taking them close to their mountain and back is what they want.

"Don't walk when you can ride" means not being bothered to trek into base camp, or not wanting to "waste" perhaps five days' time. But in doing this, surely one loses a bit of acclimatization and a lot of local atmosphere.

Perhaps one day, high-altitude helicopters will be brought to Nepal to whisk people to Everest's summit, touch down for a few minutes while passengers take great photographs, then deliver them to a spot where they can resume a pleasant trek in the area. Will the next step in making climbs as convenient as possible be to carry people through the nerve-wracking labyrinth of Everest's Khumbu Icefall? Will this trend eventually lead to uphill and downhill tourism on the most popular mountains?

ELIZABETH HAWLEY, *AAC Honorary Member, Nepal*

HUMLA REGION
CHANGLA HIMAL

Changla (6,563m), southwest face of north-northwest ridge, then north face. Uncertain of the best line to take on unclimbed Changla, Hirofumi Kobayashi (leader), Seiya Nakasukasa, Yuta Shibayama, and Naoki Yamaguchi approached up the Chula Khola, which descends from the 5,293m Changla La on the Tibetan border north-northwest of the mountain. They made base camp at 4,700m, and then from a higher, temporary camp spent four–five days observing the southwest face of the long north-northwest ridge rising from the Changla La. Their decision was to climb directly to the crest of this ridge, then move onto the north face, ascending this to the northeast ridge.

Bad weather kept them in base camp until September 21. Without Sherpa support they made Camp 1 that day at 5,500m and, on the 22nd, started work on the mixed rock and ice face leading to the crest of the ridge. On the 26th they established Camp 2 at a 6,090m col on this ridge.

At 4 a.m. on the 27th the four left Camp 2 for a summit push. The weather was excellent, with neither cloud nor wind. Moving left, they climbed the icy north face for 300m to the crest of the northeast ridge, not far from the summit. On this section they fixed the only rope of the entire ascent. All four reached the summit at 11:40 a.m.

The return to Camp 2 was long because they decided to descend the fluted northeast ridge until it was easy to gain the glacier to the left. Then they walked southwest up the glacier and finally climbed back onto the north-northwest ridge, regaining camp at 11:30 p.m.

ELIZABETH HAWLEY, *AAC Honorary Member, Nepal*

Editor's note: The only previous attempt on this remote border mountain appears to be that made in 1998 by Tamotsu Ohnishi's 14-member expedition. They gave up on a direct approach and instead climbed the west ridge of a summit on the Nepal-Tibet border immediately to the southwest of Changla, hoping they could then follow the frontier ridge north to the main top. They reached what they refer to as Changla Southwest Peak (6,162m) but realized it would take several more days to traverse to the main summit. The highest summit in the Changla Himal is not, as might be imagined, Changla, but Kubi Kangri (6,721m), which lies much further to the south-southeast along the border, and was climbed in 2008 via the east ridge from Tibet by a seven-member Japanese team (leader Atushi Senda).

KANTI HIMAL

Kojichuwa Chuli (6,439m), attempt. Kojichuwa Chuli lies at the head of the Kojichuwa Khola above Mugu Village, and the peak was attempted with little success in 2008 and 2009 by Spanish and Japanese climbers (*AAJ 2010*). On May 16, after a six-day trek, Ken Fujikawa, Michihiro Honda, Yuta Kawahara, Satoshi Kimoto, and Ayano Suzuki established base camp at 3,600m above Mugu. Subsequently, an advanced base was placed at 4,600m, and Camp 1 at 5,100m, before the route up to the 5,625m col on the northwest ridge was fixed by Sherpas. This ridge forms the Nepal-Tibet border.

On May 24 all except Honda left advanced base and made Camp 2 on the col. They made a summit bid the next day. The ridge presented difficult crevasses and steep knife-edge sections, so the climb proved time-consuming. By 7 p.m. they had only reached a northern foresummit (height unknown). The continuation to the main top was long, steep, and sharp, so they descended.

TSUNEMICHI IKEDA, *Japanese Alpine News*

SAIPAL HIMAL

Saipal (7,030m), northeast ridge to Saipal East Humla (6,925m). In Nepal's geopolitical landscape, the West has a special place. West Nepal was one starting point of the Maoist revolution and forms a perfect example of the dramatic imbalance of economic development and tourism that exist within the country. Climbers and trekkers can be counted on the fingers of one hand, and mountaineering in this remote area has a different dimension from the popular regions of Nepal.

Ironically we nearly didn't get to the Far West; the plane was commandeered at the last minute to evacuate tourists stranded at Lukla. We finally got a flight to Simikot, headed west along the Humla

Bikrum Singh, a young Nepalese guide, enjoying the superb ambience of the upper northeast ridge of Saipal. In the middle distance the fine, triangular snow/ice pyramid is unclimbed Peak 5,638m; the more rocky peak to its left is 5,696m, also unclimbed. In the far distance lie the peaks straddling the Nepal-Tibet border. From left to right; Changla, Gorek, and Kanjiroba Himals. *Paulo Grobel*

Descending to high camp (6,400m) on northeast ridge of Saipal. Immediately behind camp a snow arête leads to the small rocky summit of Rani Himal. In the middle distance is Kairangtse, while the high bulky summit in far distance (Tibet) is Gurla Mandata (7,694m). *Paulo Grobel*

Karnali, and then south up the Kairang Khola, past Chala Village, to reach a 4,276m base camp northeast of Firnkopf (6,730m).

Saipal is little visited, and in the 12 years since the previous ascent, conditions have changed markedly. We attempted the northeast ridge, climbed on only one occasion before by two expeditions within two days of each other in October 1990 (Saipal has only five ascents, the first in October 1963 by Katsutoshi Harabayashi and Pasang Phutar Sherpa, via the south ridge). On October 29 Frank Bonhomme, Frederic Jung, and I stood atop Saipal East Humla. Despite not reaching the main summit of Saipal, only the northeast top, it was my most enjoyable expedition. We realized there is so much to discover in the West: mountains, treks, and especially the people. 2011 has been declared the Year of Tourism in Nepal. If only one percent of the tourists who went to the Annapurna or Khumbu regions could find their way west (or to other forgotten parts of Nepal), then this initiative will be successful, and our climb will have more meaning.

Saipal can be reached in six or seven days from Simikot. The northeast ridge is probably the easiest line, with no objective danger and a superb ridge traverse. It is perhaps V/AD in Himalayan grade. After a glacier approach the steepest section is the ascent of the northwest face of Rani Himal (6,382m), a small rocky summit at the start of the northeast ridge of Saipal. We hit the ridge a couple of rope lengths right of Rani Himal's top and made our final camp at 6,400m (it seems likely that with teams focused on the main summit, the top of Rani Himal has never been reached). We failed because the distance between our top camp and the summit was too long; we recommend installing another camp further along the ridge, just before it becomes narrow. However, lower virgin peaks are accessible from our base camp. Kairangtse (6,233m), Liz Himal (5,950m), and Rani Himal, all north of Saipal, would make fine objectives. Why don't you go west?

Paolo Grobel, *France*

Northeast ridge of Saipal seen during the walk to base camp from Chala Village. High point of Saipal East Humla (left), and main summit in (right) background. *Paulo Grobel*

MUKUT HIMAL
SANDACHHE GROUP

Tsartse (Tasartse, 6,343m), reconnaissance. In autumn, Peter Ackroyd, Sam McClary, and I hoped to make the first ascent of Tsartse on the east side of Hidden Valley, ca 10km northeast of Dhaulagiri. This peak is clearly visible from the Muktinath-Jomsom trail. Despite close proximity to the relatively major center of Jomsom, until recently there has been little climbing activity in the Hidden Valley. The highest peak of the Sandachhe Himal is Pk. 6,403m, followed by Tashi Kang (6,386m) and then Tsartse. Tashi Kang was first climbed in 2002 by Yasue Mogi (Japan)

Dhaulagiri and Sandachhe Group of Mukat Himal from Muktinath. *Peter Ackroyd*

Sandachhe Group from west. Tsartse is hidden behind Tashi Kang. *Peter Ackroyd*

with Gyalzen Sherpa (other members stopped 15m below). It was climbed again in 2006 by Romanian Constantin Lacatusu and two Germans, Frank Muetzner and Goetz Wiegand. They continued over the summit to make the first ascent of Pk. 6,403m (naming it Pk. Europa), and also attempted Tsartse but were foiled by poor conditions.

We decided to tie our climbing into a circumnavigation of the Dhaulagari Group, eventually crossing the French Pass (5,360m) on October 25 and descending into the Hidden Valley, where the weather remained cold and windy. We established base camp at 4,860m on the eastern edge of the valley, not far from the river. Several hundred meters north (down valley) from our camp, a drainage ran west. Climbing up it, on the 27th, we reached the site of our high camp at the edge of a glacial lake (5,540m). From this point it looks straightforward to circumnavigate the lake, climb the glacier into the high basin out of which the four major summits rise, and pick a target. While we hoped to find a more direct route to the top of Tsartse, we understood that previous attempts had focused on reaching it via a traverse of Tashi Kang.

While acclimatizing, we explored a possible exit at the north end of the valley. We learned that a French team had left the valley this way, but our sirdar concluded that it was far too steep and dangerous for laden porters. The only alternative, bar a helicopter, is over one of two 5,000m passes.

We concluded that attempting the peak would take more time and energy than we had. We worried about getting out safely, so we abandoned the climb, crossed the Dhampus Pass (5,244m), and headed out to Jomsom, wandering up Dhampus Peak (a.k.a. Tharpa, 6,012m) on the way. From the summit we could see the site of our high camp and the access to the upper glacier. Realistically, unless you're a strong party, you might want to put an additional camp in the high basin above the lake.

The road from Beni now reaches Jomsom and further north, and it won't be long until it meets the road coming south from Lo Manthang, finally connecting China and India. The Hidden Valley offers relatively quick access to moderate climbing on 6,000m peaks. Some remain unclimbed, and there are many potential new routes on the peaks flanking both sides of the valley.

JIM FRUSH, *AAC*

DAMODAR HIMAL

Yakawa Kang (6,482m), south face. At 12:50 p.m. on November 7, Sherpas Dawa Norbu (known as Ang Danu), Dawa Tshering, Tshering Tashi, and I reached the top of Yakawa Kang. It had taken 11 hours and was the result of three years' planning. It marked the 60th anniversary of the Shizuoka City Alpine Federation. We flew from Pokhara to Jomsom on October 30 and reached base camp on the Thorung La (5,416m) five days later. I didn't feel well and couldn't eat for three days. During this time, on November 4 and 5, the three Sherpas fixed rope up the south face of the mountain from 5,800m–6,300m.

Yakawa Kang from southwest showing route of ascent. Thorung La is just below the bottom of the image. *Hidenobu Tsuji*

On the 6th we all rested in base camp, and on the 7th we left at 1:50 a.m. for a summit attempt. It took two hours to climb the lower moraine slopes and then a further six to overcome the rock walls, which were steep and friable. Above, the ice was steep, taxing my calves and thighs. From the top of the fixed lines, we continued roped on easier-angled snow to the summit. From here we contacted base camp, took pictures, and then rested for 20 minutes before starting down. The batteries ran out in our headlamps, and I began to feel faint from tiredness.

Despite cold and dark conditions, various members at base camp came up to assist us in the lower section, and we finally reached the base, exhausted, at 6:30 p.m. After a day's rest we started for Jomsom, from where we returned to Kathmandu by bus, arriving on the 12th. I'm proud of my first ascent, which was achieved with the support of many people.

HIDENOBU TSUJI, *Japan*

On the upper slopes of Yakawa Kang, looking southwest over Khatang Kang (6,484m) to the distant north face of Annapurna (8,091m). *Hidenobu Tsuji*

Editor's Note: Although this mountain lies just north of the popular Annapurna Circuit trek, there was no recorded ascent prior to 2010. However, in November 2009 Shoji Sakamoto (Japan) and Pasang Kaji Sherpa reached ca 6,450m on much the same route as the first ascensionists. On their first attempt they reached ca 6,200m, just below the snow line, having fixed rope from 5,800m–6,100m, but turned back as they were late in the day. On the second attempt they fixed more rope up 50° ice to 6,250m before continuing to their high point. It was a little after 2 p.m., and they were buffeted by a strong cold wind, so they retreated.

Peaks on the ridge west of Lugula seen from the north. (A) Bhrikuti (a.k.a. Bhrikuti Shail, 6,361m). (B) Tir Hawa La (ca 6,200m). (C) Himso Himal (6,337m). (D) Shelka Kangri (6,358m). In 1952 de Hults followed the broad, rounded snow ridge falling gently north from Bhrikuti's summit to make the mountain's first ascent. *Paulo Grobel*

Bhrikuti (6,361m), north ridge and new information on first ascent. Bhrikuti is a Buddhist goddess. It is also the name of a Nepali princess, and the wife of the famous Tibetan emperor, Songsten Gampo. In addition, it is the name of a small summit in the Damodar Himal, deep in the confines of Nepal and Tibet, between Mustang and Phu. For a long time, its location and the story of the first ascent were unclear. This was partially due to there being no decent map of the area—but mainly because it was difficult to pinpoint the peak when looking from Mustang to the north. After an ascent of Bhrikuti's south side in the spring of 2005, and two traverses between Mustang and Phu, I returned again with a group in spring 2010. We reached Damodar Kunda, a group of small, sacred lakes that are wrongly marked on the HMG Finn map. We were there primarily to make a previously unexplored trek to North Mustang and the village of Samdzong. This would require us to play a few games to deal with border crossings.

Climbing Bhrikuti from the north is very easy; you can even take mules to a camp at 5,800m. Nine of us reached the summit by a route of Himalayan grade II/F. However, our climb was mainly a means of getting a glimpse into this hidden corner of the massif, in particular Lagula (6,898m) and the Tibetan side behind Chako (6,704m). In order to avoid future confusion, we have decided to name the small neighboring summits and landmarks: Himso Himal (6,337m, after the Himalayan Society); the Tir Hawa La (after Tirawa), the ca 6,200m col between Himso Himal and Bhrikuti; and the third and highest summit of this group, Shelka Kangri (6,358m), which is the Tibetan name of Michel Peissel, the French explorer and ethnologist, who has written around 20 books on his Himalayan and Tibetan expeditions.

During a previous trip to Phu, I learned an amazing story about Alfred de Hults, a passionate hunter who visited Nepal in the early 1950s. Later, thanks to de Hults's grandson Luc-Emmannuel, we were able to get in touch with Alfred and his family in Belgium. Here is what he told us.

After having searched for snow leopards deep inside the Kingdom of Lo, de Hults made his way back through the Phu valley. Not wanting to return empty handed, he used his boundless energy to climb a beautiful, snowy peak of more than 6,000m, which he named Bhrikuti. At the time he was constantly occupied with thoughts of a woman, with whom he had fallen deeply in love. He even had problems sleeping at night. This young Nepali woman possessed a radiant, almost divine beauty. But he had to keep his feelings to himself, because Bhrikuti was also the daughter of King Thribuvan.

Once back in the king's court, he told of his adventures in the mountains between Mustang and Phu, his random summit climb, and the name he gave to the mountain. The old king was no fool, well aware that his daughter had appeared particularly happy ever since Alfred returned. Far from condemning this improbable relationship, the king congratulated the young couple and offered them his blessing.

Alfred married Bhrikuti in a formal ceremony, which must have been kept discreet, because we couldn't find any record of this marriage in the royal archives. The young couple settled in India, where de Hults became a successful businessman. Later, they relocated to Belgium, where the beautiful princess converted to her husband's religion, as was the norm. They lived there happily and had several children, enjoying a humble existence.

Peaks west of Bhrikuti seen from the northeast. (A) Shelka Kangri (6,358m). (B) 6,118m pass. (C) Kumlun Himal (6,365m). (D) Unnamed (two summits: Northeast 6,378m and Southwest 6,380m. This is more a shoulder of Kumlun than a separate peak, as it appears in this photo. It was attempted from the west by Paulo Grobel, who reports the rock to be atrocious.). (E) Pt. 6,505m. (F) Belvédère d'Alfred (6,226m). (G) Pt. 6,420m (possibly climbed by a French ski team). *Paulo Grobel*

This correspondence with our new Belgian friend allowed us to lift any doubts regarding the first ascent of Bhrikuti. It had indeed taken place on April 18, 1952 via the south face by Alfred de Hults, solo. Alfred told us that he arrived at the summit at 11:25 a.m. after no great difficulty. He stayed there under sunny skies for more than half an hour, admiring the view and thinking about his distant Bhrikuti. There is only one photo, now in very poor condition, which attests to his story. In 2005 we had simply repeated Alfred's route.

Now all that remains for us to do in the Bhrikuti group is to traverse all the summits from Bhrikuti to Kumlun, or put up more difficult lines on the south side of Bhrikuti.

PAULO GROBEL, *France, translated by Todd Miller*

ANNAPURNA HIMAL

Singu Chuli (6,501m), south-southeast face to south ridge. On November 3–4 Cas van den Gevel and I climbed the south-southeast face of Singu Chuli. We reached the south ridge at 6,350m but found the crest above so heavily fluted and corniced that we deemed it too dangerous to continue to the summit.

Our base camp was placed at 4,500m on the approach to the normal route on Tharpu Chuli (5,663m) from the south-southwest. From here it took one-and-a-half days to reach the foot of the face. We climbed to the col on the ridge separating Tharpu Chuli from Pancha Chuli to the north, where we spent the night. On November 3 we followed the crest of the ridge north until it became steep and rocky. At this point we descended the east flank (one rappel at the bottom), crossed the glacier, and climbed up to the foot of Singu Chuli. Due to the middle and right side of the face having large seracs, we opted for a line on the left, very close to that climbed by Slovenians in 1995.

The same day we climbed the first 300m of face, bivouacking at 5,900m. The next day we reached the crest of the south ridge and descended to our bivouac. The route was TD/TD+ with ice up to 90°. From there it took two days to return to base camp, first southeast down the West

High point 6350M

Bivouac 5900M

The south-southeast face of Singu Chuli seen from Tharpu Chuli. The Dutch line, bivouac, and high point on south ridge are marked. The original 1957 route took the right-hand ridge. Behind and to the right are the slopes of Tarke Kang (a.k.a. Glacier Dome, 7,193m), while above and to the left is the summit of Kangsar Kang (a.k.a. Roc Noir, 7,485m) at the start of the long east ridge of Annapurna, and on the left the south face climbed by a French team in 2000. *William van Meegdenburg*

Annapurna Glacier and then via the South Annapurna Glacier.

Our original intention had been to repeat the Ghilini-MacIntyre-Porter route on the west face. However, there is some uncertainty as to the exact location of this line, and the approach across the glacier was horrendously broken. During an acclimatization ascent of Tharpu Chuli we could see that the south-southeast face presented much better conditions.

WILLIAM VAN
MEEGDENBURG, *The
Netherlands*

Meegdenburg leading the 90° exit onto the south ridge of Singu Chuli, rotten ice that was difficult to protect. *Cas van den Gevel/ William van Meegdenburg collection*

Editor's note: In October 1995 Ziga Petric and Bojan Pockar climbed the face via a line fractionally to the right of that taken by the Dutch. Toward the top they found sections of 75–80° and UIAA VI on rock. The last pitch to the crest of the south ridge was the crux (VI+ rock and vertical ice). Above, a very unstable, dangerous, and corniced crest led to the summit. Unable to reverse their ascent, they were forced to rappel directly down the face, exposed to serac fall. They named their route Perun (ED2). The Dutch noticed two sections of old fixed rope on the rock spur to their left, and a third below their exit point on the summit ridge, seemingly emerging from the rock spur. The origins of these are currently unknown. Singu Chuli was first climbed in 1957 by David Cox and Wilfred Noyce via the east ridge, but despite its current status as a "trekking peak," this mountain is ascended infrequently.

Annapurna III (7,555m), east ridge attempt. The southeast ridge of Annapurna III is a saw-tooth monolith cutting straight through the heart of a cirque of mountains so remote and difficult to access that few have seen them. The ridge is mesmerising, and the history and hearsay behind the not-so-many-attempts drip with a fabled shroud. It is a compelling challenge for the alpinist. I had researched well, gaining information from those

Singu Chuli from the south. The west face rib, first climbed by Ghilini, MacIntyre, and Porter in 1982, is seen in profile behind the unclimbed west face. Behind and left is the far right side of the south face of Annapurna. *William van Meegdenburg*

who had been before, but in April, when we first attempted to breach the south cirque, the technicalities and logistics of the approach came as a shock.

Pete Benson, Matt Helliker, and I were the climbers, accompanied by Pete's wife Laura, and cameraman Ian Burton. Helliker and I took an earlier flight to Kathmandu—on the day of the Iceland volcano eruption. Subsequent flights were grounded, separating us from the rest of the team, and vital equipment such as climbing boots and tent. The peak fee, liaison officer, flights, freight, and agent expenses had all been paid, and all were non-refundable. After much deliberation Matt

and I decided to continue with the expedition with the hope that the others would catch up.

Four days into the approach, and with still no sign of flights leaving Britain, 20 of our porters decided to quit, leaving just six to carry everything for another three days over the most technical, dangerous, and unknown ground so far. What finally stopped us was a landslide, which we have since discovered has been washed away to reveal smooth glaciated walls. Matt and I were in no doubt that if our porters

Annapurna III from southeast, showing the approximate line (and high point of 6,500m) of the 1981 Colton-Leach attempt on the southeast ridge. This is by far the highest any party has reached on this coveted line. The steep section ends well above 7,000m on the south ridge (P), from where it is still a considerable distance to the summit (S). Lower on the south ridge are (A) a subsidiary summit of ca 6,200m, and (B) a summit of ca 6,700m, both unclimbed. *Nick Bullock*

The long, snowy east ridge of Annapurna III, with the southeast pillar in profile to the left. *Nick Bullock*

attempted to cross this obstacle, one of them would die. No expedition is worth the death of a local, so we turned around while we still had all the porters to carry our belongings.

Back in Kathmandu, having invested so much time, effort, and money, and feeling that we had let down all who had supported us, Helliker and I were adamant in trying again. In this, we were boosted by our agent's generous offer to give us a vastly reduced price for the autumn. Samsung had already invested £10,000 in our first effort, and now they were prepared to contribute another £10,000 to make it happen all over again, albeit this time with the more certain, but still not guaranteed, approach by helicopter.

At the start of October Benson, Helliker, cameraman Dave Reeves, and I were this time on the same flight to Kathmandu. An Air Dynasty helicopter pilot named Pemba would fly us to base camp. Flying by helicopter is not as simple as it sounds. In fact it was very committing. Once the team was in, getting out again, if the weather turned bad, would prove extremely difficult, if not impossible. This could leave our party—which included cameraman, cook, and cook assistant—having to walk out via the unknown 5,000m technical pass that had stopped us in the spring.

After several flights along the Seti Kola Gorge, flights akin to something from a Vietnam War film, we stood in freezing cloud listening to the fading sound of the helicopter. From the air we had decided base camp should be high up the moraine toward the foot of the east ridge at ca 4,600m. Surrounded by unclimbed rock walls as big as any in Yosemite, and some of the highest mountains on the planet, we felt insignificant but extremely happy.

However, after exploring the base of the southeast ridge, we quickly realized that exfoliating rock (which rumbled regularly down the slabs at the start of the ridge) and a double serac hanging above the couloir (the only entry onto the ridge) would make an attempt suicidal. We needed a change of objective. Our back-up plan was the unclimbed six-and-a-half-kilometer-long east ridge. It was the only feasible option visible.

After several weeks, all we had to show for progress was four ascents to a snow hole at 6,000m on the crest, 1,400m above base camp. One sortie above the cave reached 6,200m, but gale force winds, experienced on all but three days, called an end to the expedition.

After an anxious wait, Pemba arrived in the helicopter, but rising cloud prevented him from leaving, and after several attempts he and his B2 Eurocopter accepted they would have to spend the night at our landing zone. The following morning was a tense time. This was the highest altitude in history that a B2 had been parked up and turned off. After the sun had been shining and warming the machine for 30 minutes, a down jacket and blanket were removed from the battery, and the rotors defrosted with boiling water. Benson and Reeves were the first to leave, but it took three more shuttles until team and equipment were evacuated, and the mountains were alone once again.

Since my return I have questioned our philosophy: Was it right to go back to Annapurna III? As one of my friends said, "Taking a chopper is not very Shipton-Tilman." The most sensible solution would have been to move on to something new, but when has climbing ever been about doing the sensible thing? The more I think about taking a helicopter to base camp, the more I think it was the correct decision (apart from not going at all). The most obvious argument I can come up with for flying is that it avoided the death of a local, and I was under no doubt that this would have happened.

Is our flight to Annapurna III any different than that made by hundreds of climbers every year to Denali, or to any of the other Alaskan ranges? Is it different than the flights made by climbers to Antarctica, Baffin, Logan, Lukla, Skardu, and Everest base camp, or a skidoo into a Canadian ice climb?

My main concern is the precedent we might be setting. In years to come will rich climbers from developed countries fly into base camps because of my decision? Did Chris Bonington stop to consider his ethics when he took a plane into the Grandes Jorasses? Did Will Gadd think twice before flying a chopper to Tengkangpoche?

One concern would be the loss of earnings by porters, but this is hardly valid, as the track to the south side of Annapurna III is certainly not a trade route; since 1981, 10 expeditions have attempted to reach this side of the mountain, and between three and five of these (there is some confusion in the available information) didn't make it.

Another argument against flying may be our selfish use of a limited resource: in using the helicopter we are delaying more important work of building bridges or flying rice to inaccessible areas, for example. However, this is no longer the case. Privately owned companies like Air Dynasty are in the business of making money by chartering helicopters.
However, try as hard as I may to justify and reason with myself, the feeling of having not taken on the full challenge is still rather overwhelming.

NICK BULLOCK, *UK*

MANASLU HIMAL

Thulagi (7,059m), attempt from the northwest. On October 25 Alexey Korochkev, Sergey Nilov (both from Moscow), and I left Kathmandu for Besisahar, with the aim of making the first ascent of Thulagi. We had little information on this mountain, the best being a report from the 2008 Japanese expedition (*AAJ 2009*). Five days after leaving Besisahar we established base camp at 3,750m on the true right bank of the Changlhi Glacier, below Phungi (6,538m). The track along the Dudh Khola had been difficult. After crossing it close to the Khasontu Khola, it took 11 hours through dense forest and complex moraine to reach base camp. There was no water at this site, and we had to carry it from the glacier.

We opted for the same line as the Japanese, a prominent snow/ice spur toward the right side of the northwest face, which we climbed on the right flank. There were large hanging seracs on either side of the spur, generally making the route objectively dangerous. We had an advanced base at 4,000m at the start of the scree; above, our route crossed broken glacier, where there was little snow, and the slope was not steep. Above 5,000m the angle increased to 45–50°, and with it came more snow. Snow depth proved the main obstacle, preventing us from reaching the crest of the spur. We climbed for two days up 50–55° slopes and ice-covered rock of M4 to gain the foot of a large rock triangle at ca 5,900m. Bypassing this buttress on the right involved difficult mixed terrain (up to M5) and ice up to 80°.

West ridge and southwest face of Manaslu (8,163m) seen from the Thulagi Plateau. This face was climbed by a large Austrian expedition in 1972, the summit reached by a certain Reinhold Messner, climbing alone. *Nikolay Bandalet*

Belarusian-Russian route up the northwest face of Manaslu shoulder to the ca 6,400m ridge. On the far side lies a large plateau—the upper Thulagi Glacier—rimmed with high peaks. *Nikolay Bandalet*

On the upper slopes the angle gradually increased. We passed the Japanese high point, and four days after leaving advanced base we reached the ridge at the top of the face (ca 6,400m). From here we descended the far side easily to a large plateau at ca 6,250m. This high-altitude plateau is the upper Thulagi glacier, which forms a sort of shoulder to the southwest of Manaslu before draining south and then west. It is rimmed by the summits of Thulagi, Peak 29 (Ngadi Chuli, 7,871m) and of course Manaslu itself.

After spending one night there, during which the temperature dropped to -25° C, we set off for the summit of Thulagi. Our ascent would follow the northeast ridge, but this now looked long and complex, and to reach it we needed to walk down the plateau some distance. These factors, together with the distance of the summit from the top of the northwest face, and the committing nature of our situation, made us abandon the attempt. From the plateau we took a further two days to descend our route to base camp.

During the ascent we had climbed above clouds, but near the base of the wall we found that a storm had raged for three days and deposited considerable amounts of snow, which made the final section of our descent highly avalanche prone. We think our route is quite possible in an alpine-style push, as long as snow conditions are good.

NIKOLAY BANDALET, *Republic of Belarus*

ROLWALING HIMAL

Peak 5,777m; Jobo LeCoultre (6,478m) northeast face to southeast ridge; Lunag I southeast top, south-
east face, Close the Door. After a flight to Lukla and a seven-day trek, including a rest day in Thame,
a four-man team established base camp south of the Lunag Group at 5,200m, close to the Lunag
Glacier. The site was superb, on grass, with running water and a nice collection of boulders. From
here they made their first acclimatization
climb together with their sirdar, for whom
it proved a novel experience. This was a
north-south traverse of Peak 5,777m,
south of the Lunag Glacier, climbed in
2009 by Stéphane Schaffter's Switzerland-
France-Nepal-Pakistan expedition (*AAJ
2010*). Several days later the four set out
to complete their acclimatization with
an attempt on Jobo LeCoultre (6,478m),
a peak on the frontier ridge southwest
of the Lunags and claimed to have been
summited by the Schaffter expedition.
The northeast face was in much drier
condition than when climbed by the Swiss
team, and the four followed the main couloir parallel to, but well left of, the 2009
route. On the first day they climbed
500m, predominately over snow, to reach
a fine bivouac site at 5,800m. The next
day 400m of gully and steep mixed climbing led to the southeast ridge, up which
they progressed to below a small "top" at
ca 6,200m, immediately before the notch
reached by the Swiss team. They made no
attempt to turn this top, as they carried no

Lunag I southeast top. Close the Door with bivouac sites
marked, the last a few meters below the summit.

suitable equipment for the route beyond, which looked really hard with huge mushrooms. Instead,
they rappelled and returned to base camp. The 800m of climbing to this point was graded III/4+.

Poor weather then confined them to base camp. This was not a bad thing, as due to the previous warm fine weather, the mixed sections on their main objective—the southeast face of unclimbed
Lunag I—had become very dry. After one aborted attempt they received a forecast promising a
week of fine weather, so set off for a light and fast ascent. At mid-day they crossed the rimaye,
and after climbing 200m found a relatively protected campsite at 5,800m. The next morning they
climbed a few hundred meters before stopped by heat and forced to shelter beneath an overhang.
As the temperature began to fall they climbed a steep pitch of F5 in a corner that avoided an easier
but objectively dangerous option. Shortly before nightfall they arrived at their second bivouac site
(6,200m). This took one hour to excavate but was nicely protected by a roof.

After a good night they climbed a series of fine pitches up a goulotte, which got them through
the narrows in the middle of the face. Finally they reached the upper flutes, where good ice gave way

Looking southwest from Jobo Rinjang at Jobo LeCoultre. (1) 2010 attempt, which stopped on the southeast ridge at ca 6,200m. (2) 2009 line claimed by French-Nepali-Swiss team (summit reached by Carrad, Haeni, Schaffter, and Vallot). *Joe Puryear*

to unstable snow. Here the climbing, though not hard, was precarious and difficult to protect. Night fell with no suitable bivouac spot in sight, so the four kept going, reaching the top of the face and a distinct summit of over 6,800m (likely ca 6,830m) on the ridge connecting Lunag I (6,895m) to Jobo Rinjang (6,778m). A strong southwesterly froze their faces as they descended a few meters north and dug tent platforms for the night.

They had hoped from this point to traverse northwest to the slightly higher main summit. Too tired the next day, they opted to descend immediately, downclimbing and making 22 rappels along the ascent route to the glacier. They named the line Close the Door (1,200m, IV/5 F5).

LINDSAY GRIFFIN,
Mountain INFO

Starting the mixed section on day two of Close the Door.

Takargo (6,771m), first official ascent. Over three days in early March, Americans David Gottlieb and Joe Puryear made the first official ascent of Takargo. They climbed a gully on the right side of the east face to reach a large glacier shelf, traversed this left, and then climbed seven ice pitches to the south summit, before following the ridge north to the main top (1,000m, TD). This long-time climbing partnership was separated last autumn during an October attempt on the South Face of Labuche Kang in Tibet, when Puryear fell unroped through a cornice. Puryear's obituary is in the In Memoriam section, and his story about the Takargo climb is a feature article, both in this Journal.

MAHALANGUR HIMAL KHUMBU SECTION

Pharilapcha (6,017m), north face, Korean Route. Hwang Gi-yong, Shin Dong-seok, and I started climbing a new line on the left side of the north face at 1 a.m. on December 13 [the prominent spur immediately left of the 2008 Polish route, Independence Day. See *AAJ 2009*]. We had hoped to find the way by moonlight, but when we reached 5,000m at 2:30 a.m., it was simply too dark, and we had to wait until 6:30 a.m. before continuing. At first the terrain was mixed, but at ca 5,200m we had to climb an eight-meter overhanging crack followed by 10m of unprotected slab, for which we took off crampons. Above, we gained the lip of a protected snowfield and settled down to bivouac for the night at 5,367m.

On the 14th we climbed moderate sections of rock and snow (5.7–5.9 and 65–85°). Toward the end,

North Face of Pharilapcha. (1) East Ridge (Bremond- Constant-Degonon-Thomas, 2006). (2) Korean Route with bivouac sites marked. (3) Independence Day (Krol- Sokolowski-Wojcik, 2008). (4) Japanese Variant (Ichimura-Nakagawa, 2007). (5) Bonfire of the Vanities (Constant- Mercader, 2003). *Yoo Hak-jae*

rockfall became prevalent, and we stopped to bivouac at 2:30 p.m. The following day Hwang, who was in the lead, showed signs of slight fatigue, though at this stage we didn't realize there was a problem. There was ice and mixed terrain to 85°, but placing screws was almost impossible; we resorted to protecting ourselves with rock features protruding from the snow, and snow bollards.

On the 16th, after a bivouac at 5,863m, I took over the lead in order to speed things up. At ca 5,900m, after climbing through mixed ground at 60°, we came to a steep 25m crack. We left our sacks at the base and carried only cameras. Although the crack was merely 5.9, it was loose, and we had to climb it carefully, making sure the rope didn't snag on precariously balanced rock. Above, we experienced dangerous rock fall, but climbed the intervening ground to the summit of Pharilapcha East without too much effort [the east summit is almost as high as the main or west top]. We took summit shots with Everest in the distance. Hwang was elated, showing no visible signs of distress. We descended to our sacks and then traversed to the east ridge, which we downclimbed to 5,735m, where we bivouacked. Although Hwang had not felt right since day two, when he started to suffer stomach pains, his condition had not deteriorated. Neither had he complained of any major discomfort. We simply had no idea that there was something seriously wrong.

The following morning, in the initial stages of our rappel descent, Hwang suddenly collapsed and died. Shin Dong-seok and I continued down, arriving at Machermo in the Gokyo Valley at 5 p.m. Four days later, with help from Sherpas, we retrieved Hwang's body and transported it to Kathmandu for cremation. (Hwang was with me on the successful 1997 Gasherbrum IV west face expedition and had recently made a special trip to Seoul to suggest we made a pure alpine-style ascent together.)

We named the line the Korean Route. There were 1,200m of climbing, in which no pegs or bolts were placed. We rated it VI 5.9 A3 M5 WI5+. We climbed in alpine style and left only slings and carabiners during our descent.

Yoo Hak-jae, *Corean Alpine Club, translated by Peter Jensen-Choi*

Kyajo Ri (6,186m), rapid (non-calendar) winter ascent, and alternative approach. In early December Dawa Steven, Nanga Dorje, and Pemba Tenzing inaugurated a new approach to the Kyajo Glacier, and made a rapid, quasi-winter ascent of Kyajo Ri's standard route on the southwest ridge. The normal approach is via Mende and the valley of Kyajo Drangka, but the three Sherpas began from Khumjung village, leaving at 8 a.m. on the 5th. Working first west, then north, they crossed the Gongla Danda at the Gongla La. They descended the far side into a hidden valley, skirting the steep rocky flanks of Khumbila on a faint but safe path. At one point it is necessary to descend a steep ice gully, or exposed rocks on the outside. (The team used the gully on the approach, but on their return climbed the rock. If using porters, this section would need to be fixed.) On the far side of the valley they slanted up loose scree on the right side of the headwall to enter a second, hidden valley, where they pitched camp north of a small lake. Waking at 3 a.m. on the 6th, they took just an hour to cross the headwall of the second valley and reach the Kyajo Glacier. From there they quickly gained the col at the foot of the southwest ridge of Kyajo Ri and climbed it unroped until ca 200m below the summit. They then fixed 180m of rope up a 50° slope of hard, blue ice above. When their rope ran out, they were fortunate to find a 70m rope, left by a previous expedition, that led to the summit. All three stood on top at noon, having made the ascent from Khumjung in just 28 hours. Normally, an acclimatized team would take around five days. They enjoyed sunny days and calm winds. Ice conditions were hard and solid, and the snow quite firm. This led to a very quick and safe climb of the mountain.

DAWA STEVEN *and* ANG TSHERING SHERPA, *Nepal*

North face of Cholatse seen from Lobuche East. (1) French Route (Bad-aroux-Batoux-Challamel-Mora-Robach, 1995). The dotted line shows the Korean variations during the first winter ascent (Park Jung-hun-Chai Kang-sik, 2005). (2) 2010 Russian Route. To the left is Pk. 6,367m on the ridge north-west of Tawoche. *Joel Kauffman*

Cholatse (6,440m) north face, calendar winter ascent, Russian Route. Galya Cibitoke, Alexander Gukov, Sergei Kondrashkin, Viktor Koval, and Valery Shamalo from St. Petersburg arrived in Kathmandu at the end of February and from there reached the north side of Cholatse via a trek over the Chola Pass. Their goal was the large rock buttress right of the 1995 French Route. During the second week of March, five days into the first attempt, the very strong female alpinist, Cibitoke, lost consciousness. She had to be brought round by artificial respiration and an injection of dexamethasone. The team retreated to base camp.

Despite Cibitoke recovering quickly, and eager for another attempt, her teammates felt it best for her to descend to lower altitudes, and Kondrashkin accompanied her. Later, they realized the probable cause of her sickness was carbon monoxide poisoning from a faulty Jet-Boil stove.

On March 14, after only one day's rest at base camp, Gukov, Koval, and Shamalo started back up the route but with a change of plan. The first foray had showed that the upper, partially overhanging pillar would need much aid, a portaledge, and capsule style. The team had not brought a ledge and wanted to climb in alpine style, so they followed a slanting line up left, bypassing the overhanging pillar to reach the upper section of the French Route. The initial pitches followed snow and ice runnels to a complex rock section, which the three crossed on aid. Above, the climbing was a mixture of free (with ice tools) and aid.

They made their first bivouac at the top of pitch 11, the second on pitch 14, third on pitch 18, fourth on pitch 20, fifth on pitch 23 (above which they joined the French Route), sixth on pitch 28, seventh on pitch 33, and on the eighth day, their 37th pitch took them to the summit. Most bivouacs were of the "sitting" variety, but the weather was generally stable throughout, with temperatures down to -20°C. On a couple of days it snowed

Approximately 24 pitches up the Russian Route on Cholatsé, before the junction with the French Route. *Supplied by Anna Piunova, mountain.ru*

in the afternoon, causing spindrift avalanches. On those occasions they stopped early for the night. The Russians found no trace of previous passage until they joined the French Route, where they discovered a piton. Difficulties were Russian 6B, VI+ A2 80°, and the height of the route just over 1,600m (2,030m of climbing). They reached the summit at 2 p.m. on March 20, just within the calendar winter season.

After spending the night on a snowfield, below and southwest of the summit, they descended the southwest ridge. This proved difficult, as they had only a vague idea of the line. They ended up on the southwest face and had to make a few rappels, another bivouac, and then a tricky descent of the lower icefall and glacier before they reached level ground and were able to take off their harnesses for the first time in 10 days. For the last two of these days they had nothing to eat, so the descent to Gokyo Valley proved harder than expected. They reached base camp on the 24th.

From material provided by ANNA PIUNOVA, *mountain.ru*

Lobuje East (6,119m), southwest face, Night Terror. On October 29, Jared Vilhauer and I started up what we believe to be a previously unclimbed ice line on the southwest face of Lobuje East. We'd spotted it while making day hikes toward the Cho La (pass). Ice in the back of a prominent weakness caught our attention.

We woke at midnight and were soon ascending a moraine that gave out onto scree-covered ice, which we climbed to gain recently revealed, glacier-polished bedrock. Jared drew the first pitch, which earned the nickname "sparky." After pounding in a Lost Arrow and a stopper, he locked off on a left tool torqued in a crack, and reached high with the right. The right tool raked and bounced off a ledge covered in a veneer of ice and loose rocks; at the same time his feet skated off the polish and showered me with sparks. This was the first M7 pitch and a great warm-up.

Above, glacial slopes rose at 50–60°. We climbed simultaneously up runnels, running out

Southwest face of Lobuje East. Night Terror climbs the obvious rectilinear ice plastered into the back of the right-facing granite diedre. It then slants right to gain the crest of the northwest ridge. *Joel Kauffman*

Jared Vilhauer climbs a long, delicate pitch of WI5+ on Night Terror. *Joel Kauffman*

of ice screws on three occasions and having to set belays. Making a rightward rising traverse, we covered ca 300m before arriving at the base of the weakness. I took the mixed entry pitch, which was characterized by great stemming on relatively good granite with sufficient protection. The next pitch was steep WI5+ with a chandelier of stalactites. It was delicate; Jared avoided placing screws in the hollow curtain.

A few steps of moderate ice gave way to steep mixed climbing on marginal rock. In order to protect the M5 crux, I had to use tied-off stubby ice screws and a Camalot 4. Above, a nine-meter-wide snow couloir gave a good opportunity to stop for a second brew. We made two liters of water and a liter of soup while watching the sun set. We were now about six hours behind schedule.

Jared continued on snow and AI3; I followed when the rope came tight. We dead-ended just below the ridge and traversed three short pitches to the right. It turned midnight while Jared was leading 65m of AI4 in runnels on the upper west face; we had already begun nodding off at belays. When Jared handed over the lead two hours later, we both thought it was no more than 40m to the ridge. I climbed 20m of AI4 before entering a 20m horizontal tunnel under a cornice. At the end I dug a snow bollard and draped the ropes over it before climbing onto the ridge. The crest rose as far as I could see; the snow was like sand inside an hourglass, only lighter.

After 2½ hours I reached a flat spot on the ridge and dug a hole. I sat on my pack and put Jared on a hip belay. This was the first flat spot since leaving our high camp 27 hours earlier. From here it was a short distance over similar snow to the true summit. It was 4:30 a.m. and pitch black as we snapped one photo before simul-climbing along the ridge and down the normal route. We named the line Night Terror (VI AI4 M7 WI5+ 85°).

JOEL KAUFFMAN, *AAC*

Lhotse (8,516m), west flank of north ridge. The idea of a route up Lhotse from the South Col had been floating in the air for a long time. The north ridge is a logical line, but what about the pinnacles on the crest? What about climbing lower, along the west flank, along the rocky ledges that run toward the couloir of the Normal Route? For many years I had looked at this variant as a possible means of completing an Everest–Lhotse traverse. I'd tried it with Simone Moro. In spring 2010 I was back again with Simone, and together we reached Camp 3 (7,300m) on the Lhotse Face. Then the situation became complicated and put me under great psychological pressure. A Russian on the expedition died; our client refused to continue with the ascent; Simone fell ill; the wind was strong, and

Lhotse west face from Western Cwm. (1) Standard Everest route to (SC) South Col. (2) Normal Route on Lhotse (west face couloir). (3) Urubko route on west flank of north ridge. *Denis Urubko*

Lhotse from the South Col, showing Urubko's route across west face. *Denis Urubko*

the rocks of the ridge looked sinister. And I could not forget my friend Sergey Samoilov, who died in 2009. [*Editor's note: Samoilov and Urubko climbed new routes in alpine style on Broad Peak in 2005 and Manaslu in 2006. He died in the spring of 2009 during a Kazakh expedition attempting the Everest-Lhotse traverse.*] On May 15 when I reached the South Col alone and pitched my tent at 7,900m, all these negative thoughts were in my mind.

At dawn on the 16th I decided to go down, but having passed the Geneva Spur I realized I was not doing the right thing. I sat in the wind, thinking for several minutes. There was a real chance to do it, and I had to make an attempt. I climbed back up to the col.

At 6:10 a.m. I started up the moderate 400m névé slope above the col. At its top I only climbed 50m up the loose rocky ridge before leaving the crest and traversing equally loose rocky ground on the right. Above 8,100m the slope gradually steepened, and I climbed several sections of UIAA II and III. I moved up to a snow-covered ledge and followed it around the first pinnacle. Further on I reached a chimney. I wasn't keen on this, as I didn't know what the ground above would be like or whether I could reverse it. So I continued in the same line with no height gain. The climbing wasn't difficult, but it was delicate and dangerous. Little slabs fell away toward the Western Cwm, and below these the ground appeared even steeper. It reminded me of the tiled roofs in Europe. Then I began to gain height, climbing up to the ridge below the second pinnacle.

Ahead of me now I could see the couloir that forms the upper section of the Normal Route. But I couldn't cross the slabs and was forced to lower myself five or six meters down a chimney to a good ledge. From there I could make a rising traverse through the slabs, and after a few hundred meters I could "slip" into the couloir. This was just below the narrows at an altitude of 8,300m.

The rest of the route is well known; the difficulties were slopes of névé with no fixed rope, as the gear had either been buried by recent snowfall or ripped out by the wind. At 11:30 a.m. I stepped onto the summit, having completed, in my opinion, a logical and interesting route [Urubko was the first to summit Lhotse that season]. During the ascent the weather has been clear, and the wind no stronger than 50km/hour.

I descended the Normal Route as far as Camp 2 (6,400m), where I spent the night. I had no desire to wander about in the Khumbu Icefall during evening. The next morning I slipped out at 5 a.m., and three hours later had reached base camp.

DENIS URUBKO, *Central Sport Club of Kazakhstan Army, translated by Luca Calvi*

Melanphulan (6,573m), north face, correction. In *AAJ 2010* we reported an ascent of the north face of Melanphulan by Kozub, Michalek, and Starek. The three Polish climbers reported that they stopped just below the cornice on the summit ridge, not far from the highest point of the mountain (aaj. americanalpineclub.org/melanphulan-6573m-north-face-not-to-summit).

After an interview between wspinanie.pl, the largest Polish climbing website, and Wojciech Kurtyka, doubts were raised on the high point reached. A team of eminent Polish mountaineers made a careful analysis of the ascent and photos, after which the three climbers were forced to conclude that they had not reached the main ridge; they had stopped on a snow ridge ca 50m below the summit crest. They now realize they were confused by darkness and tiredness, the latter due to having already climbed non-stop for more than 30 hours. Their high point is more or less the same as that achieved by Kurtyka and Erhard Loretan during an attempt in 2000. These two highly experienced alpinists rated their ascent to that point at TD+. Although the two lines are not quite identical, the Polish analysts do not feel there should be any difference in standard. The detailed analysis has been published at wspinanie.pl/serwis/201012/04-Malanphulan-komisja.php.

LINDSAY GRIFFIN, *Mountain INFO, from information provided by Wojciech Słowakiewicz, wspinanie.pl, and Wojtek Kozub, Polish Mountaineering Association.*

Tsuro Ri (ca 6,100m), north face attempt. While walking back from Island Peak I saw what I thought was a series of ice runnels on the northern flank of Tsuro Ri, the shoulder on the northwest ridge of Ama Dablam, and decided I had to try them. I believe every mountaineer has demons that try to stop him pursuing his or her dreams, and I had to fight against my own before starting up this virgin face of Tsuro Ri. Andrea di Donata and I attempted a line right in the middle of the face. The route was midway between the righthand ridge (climbed in 2001 by Cartwright and Cross as the opening part of their complete ascent of Ama Dablam's northwest ridge), and the Japanese route on the northwest face. We took food for five days, a gaz stove, and three canisters. Earlier on the trip I'd lost a rucksack containing my bivouac sack, so a lodge keeper gave me a blue plastic bag that I could slip inside of.

The alarm woke us at 2 a.m. It took four hours to reach the lower slopes, which were ca 400m high and 45–50°. The snow was often knee-deep, and only when the angle steepened to 60° did we start using front points. On the first few pitches, which I led, axes bounced against the rock beneath, crampons scratched the face.

Daniele Nardi high on the north face of Tsuro Ri. *Daniele Nardi collection*

Ice screws went in only a few centimeters. I climbed for more than 50m—more than the length of our rope—without placing any real protection. Andrea understood, unclipping from the belay and moving up. Normally, the second would climb with the heavier sack, but this situation was different, and we had to share the same fate.

The game of balance lasted almost 250m, blunting our axes while we overcame ice sheets up to 85°. We reached the steepest part of the face and dug into the snow slope below it, excavating a snow cave for our first bivouac.

The alarm rang at 6 a.m., but we didn't need it; Vasco Rossi, AC/DC, Dire Straits, Heroes del Silencio, they had all been roaring in our ears to quell the shivering due to cold. We moved up, and from time to time succeeded in placing a piton, which allowed us to feel a little more comfortable. We had hoped for a snow ramp leading through the upper wall to the summit ridge, but reality shattered our hopes. When I watched Andrea fight for an hour on a traverse where ice gave way to powder snow, I understood that things were clearly going wrong. At the foot of the face we expected good ice and found only a thin layer of snow. Why had we expected it to be better higher up? Above lay a vertical rock wall covered with powder. Andrea reversed delicately, took out a couple of Friends and gasped, "Dan, careful, hold me." He slowly returned to the belay, and at 5 p.m. we rappelled to our previous bivouac. The next morning we continued to rappel the route.

If I had completed this line I would have called it Human Rights 1945. The United Nations was created in 1945, and I thought it might be good that every time someone looked at the line they would think of human rights. The first right is "all are free and equal."

Find more information in Italian on danielenardi.wordpress.com.

DANIELE NARDI, *Italy, translated by Luca Calvi*

Ama Dablam (left) and Tsuro Ri. (1) North ridge. (2) Stane Belak-Srauf Memorial Route. (3) Goettler-Hiraide exit. (4) Italian attempt on north face of Tsuro Ri. (B) marks the bivouac sites. *Daniele Nardi*

Ama Dablam, northwest face to north ridge, and accident. In early November, David Goettler (German) and Kazuya Hiraide (Japanese), both experienced and talented climbers, found themselves in a very tight spot when they attempted to ascend Ama Dablam by their own variation of an unusual route up the northwest face to the north ridge. They climbed alpine style with a minimal amount of gear.

[*Editor's note: Goettler and Hiraide more or less followed the line of the Stane Belak-Srauf Memorial Route (Furlan-Humar, 1996) on the northwest face, making bivouacs at 5,877m and a reported 6,358m. Above their second bivouac, where the original route breaks right and climbs directly to the summit, the pair slanted up left to the crest of the north ridge.*]

On the 6th they gained the north ridge at ca 6,450m and then continued up the crest for 50m, until at 10:15 a.m. a snow avalanche hit them and carried them down 10m. Snow conditions on the ridge made it impossible to go higher. Snow on the east face was very unstable; on the north face it was like sugar.

They started down the north ridge, but at ca 6,350m encountered cornices and seracs. It seemed impossible to descend any farther, and they did not have the equipment to rappel the face. They could neither retreat nor advance. "We were trapped," said Goettler.

They bivouacked at a small col on the ridge and phoned their Kathmandu agent, asking him to send a helicopter. That night they became concerned that a chopper might not be able to reach them, because a strong wind was blowing from the west. Luckily, however, the wind dropped the next morning. Above and below their bivouac were high seracs, and Hiraide fixed a rope to the top of the lower serac using a snow stake. The pair decided that Goettler would be taken off first, and all the gear, including tent, food, fuel, the two ropes, medical kit, and phone, would be left with Hiraide.

At 9 a.m. a helicopter approached from the east in a light breeze, and circled around them before touching down on top of the lower serac. Goettler was airlifted to the nearby village of Chukkung.

Hiraide now waited atop the serac for his turn. Soon the helicopter reappeared from the east and tried to hover ca 30cm above him. Instinct told Hiraide it was dangerous to attempt to get on board, and as he hesitated, the helicopter slid slowly onto the northeast face "with a bang and a roar." Black smoke billowed out, and there was a strong smell of oil. (Hiraide did not actually see the chopper's rotor touch the serac because he was crouching in the snow.) The crew, pilot Sabin Basnet and engineer Purna Awale, were killed.

Hiraide now re-pitched the tent and waited. On the following morning he was successfully plucked off the mountain. At 7 a.m. he heard another helicopter's engine, and as it approached, he gestured to the pilot that the top of the serac was a danger to the rotor; the pilot flew several circles to check conditions, and informed Hiraide that he could not pick him up from that point. The pilot signaled to Hiraide that he should try to descend 50m to a flatter spot. Hiraide did this using one of the ropes, and at 7:15 was evacuated, with all the gear, to Lukla.

ELIZABETH HAWLEY, *AAC Honorary Member, Nepal*

Kyashar (6,770m), south pillar, attempt. On October 22, after a three-day trek from Lukla, Tony Stone and I arrived at Tangnag (4,300m), a collection of tea houses that has grown over the years due to the popularity of nearby Mera Peak. We made base camp here and then set about acclimatizing on Mera. Tony suffered from the altitude at high camp and decided to descend while I continued to the south summit.

We had planned to reach the upper south pillar of Kyashar via the mixed ground directly below, left of the large rock wall above Tangnag. This was the way taken by Czech parties that reached the start of the upper pillar in 2001 and 2008 (*AAJ 2009*). However, this autumn there was no trace of the ice the Czechs had used, just blank granite and rubble-strewn ledges. Instead, we decided to find a line through the rock wall that forms the base of the ridge.

We left Tangnag at 6:45 a.m. on November 3 and scrambled up to the start of the main climbing at 4,890m. Dirty slabs, steep grass, rock steps, and an exit gully led to three long and very loose pitches of British HVS, the last being particularly bold. Broken ground, followed by a 200m rightward-trending fault line,

Andy Houseman at the start of Kyashar's South Pillar at 4,890m, soloing the easy slabs. Kusum Kanguru behind. *Tony Stone*

Kyashar from the Hinku Valley to the southwest. (1) West ridge (Broderik-Frank-Normand, 2003; the team moved left at ca 6,400m and reached the summit via the west face). (2) Southwest face, Ramro Chaina (Doudlebsky-Holecek, 2005; the climbers stopped on joining the west ridge). (3) South Pillar attempt (Doudlebsky-Holecek, 2008). (4) South Pillar attempt (Houseman-Stone, 2010). *Andy Houseman*

led to the final rock band and snow slopes at 5,500m, where we bivouacked. Next day we climbed a small glacier to reach the snow ridge leading to the upper pillar. Unfortunately, Tony was still struggling to acclimatize and did not feel up to continuing, so we bailed at 5,700m, 100m below the start of the upper pillar. We descended by down-climbing and five rappels and were back in Tangnag at 3 p.m.

We organized our expedition through Loben Expeditions (lobenexpeditions.com). They provide a first-class and personal service, and we would recommend them highly to anyone planning a trip to the Himalaya, trekking or climbing. We are also grateful to the financial support provided by the BMC and Alpine Club Climbing Fund.

Andy Houseman, *UK, Alpine Club*

Mahalangur Himal Makalu-Barun Section

Makalu, partial new route, southwest face and west pillar. A large expedition from Ukraine, using fixed rope but no bottled oxygen and no high-altitude Sherpa support, climbed new ground on the left side of Makalu's southwest face. Led by Mstislav Gorbenko, the team divided into three groups to work on the route in shifts of five–seven days. While one group was pushing out the fixed ropes, the other two would carry loads to high camps. Each group had two–three days of rest in base camp after its working shift on the face.

Base camp at the Hillary site (4,850m) was established on April 7, and advanced base (5,850m) two days later. Above, the line of ascent can be divided into three sections. Up to Camp 2 at 6,600m the team followed the 1975 Slovenian Route. At this point the Slovenians had slanted right on a rocky rib toward the center of the face, whereas the Ukrainians now worked up left through snow fields and mixed ground, placing Camp 3 on April 21 at 7,000m. Camp 4 (7,500m), close to the crest of the west pillar, was established on the 30th. From here to the summit they followed the 1971 French route.

The main technical challenge lay on the new ground between Camps 2 and 4. The rock above 6,600m was slabby, polished, and generally offered little in the way of protection. There were no ledges suitable for camping except the tiny shelf used for Camp 3. The average standard of this section was UIAA IV–V, with one pitch of A1/2. Only one bolt was placed, and this at the site of Camp 3. The crux of the French Route is a 30m rock wall of A1/2 at 7,700m.

On May 1, having reached 7,600m on the crest of the pillar, the climbers were forced down by high winds (up to 140 km/hour), which confined everyone to base camp for 11 days. When they eventually managed to get back onto the face, they were forced to re-establish most of the high camps. One tent was blown out at advanced base; Camp 1 was partially destroyed; Camp 3 was partially destroyed; and Camp 4 completely destroyed.

On May 17 Camp 5 was established above the pillar crux at 7,750m, after which three teams made summit attempts. Only one got a suitable weather window. Sergey Bublik, Vladimir Roshko, and Dmitry Venslavovsky reached the top on May 23, after a total of 3,000m of rope had been fixed from 6,000–7,800m.

Arriving on the summit in the dark, not wanting to reverse their route, and finding that climbers from other expeditions had reached the top via the Normal Route from the north, the three Ukrainians chose to follow tracks down toward the

The new Ukrainian Route on the southwest face of Makalu. The left skyline is the French (West) Ridge. Camps marked are ABC (5,700m), Camp 1 (6,200m), Camp 2 (6,600m), Camp 3 (7,000m), Camp 4 (7,500m), and Camp 5 (7,770m). *Supplied by Anna Piunova, mountain.ru*

Makalu La, reaching at tent at 7,700m with a lot of assistance from Marty Schmidt from New Zealand. Schmidt was alone and had placed the tent for a night's rest prior to a summit bid the following day. He had to climb through the night to 8,100m to assist the third and final Ukrainian down to his tent but was then able to turn around, climb back up, and reach the top by 3 p.m. on the 24th.

The French (west) pillar has still received few ascents. On the last, in 2004, American Jay Sieger and Ukrainian Vladimir Terzyul reached the summit but were killed on the descent. Sieger's body was discovered at 8,300m by two Kazakhs on the same expedition, but Terzyul, who had climbed 13 of the 8,000m peaks, some by new routes, was never found. During their summit push Bublik, Roshko, and Venslavovsky found equipment belonging to Terzyul at Camp 5 and passed Sieger's body on their way to the top.

ANNA PIUNOVA, *mountain.ru*

OMI KANGRI HIMAL

Pabuk Kang (a.k.a. Yangma, 6,244m) southwest ridge. Far East Nepal is best known for being crowned by the Kanchenjunga massif. Between there and Makalu the Himalayan crest makes an uncommon drop in altitude. Perhaps that is why climbers have not given peaks west of the Ghunsa Valley much attention. However, there are plenty of interesting summits between 5,500m and 6,500m.

Pabuk Kang seen from the Marson La, a distance of almost 20km to the south. The first ascent followed the snow ridge immediately left of the rocky face. *Tim Macartney-Snape*

In 2003, while trekking in the Yangma valley, I saw a number of peaks worthy of a small expedition and vowed to return. In October, accompanied by some of the members from my first foray to the Himalaya (Dunagiri in 1978), I got a permit to climb a peak near the head of the Pabuk Valley, which lies above the Bhotia village of Yangma. This village is remarkable in that it lies on a sunlit south-facing slope at 4,200m and is one of the, if not the, highest permanently settled village in Nepal. Yangma people trade over the 5,746m Ghan La at the head of the valley. They are closer to a Tibetan roadhead than one in Nepal by at least one week's walk.

It was a late monsoon, so rather than fly, Ken Baldwin, Dave Barton, Colin Cameron, John Finnegan, Theo Hooy, Stacy Rodger, Keith Scott, and I took a bus from the Terai up to the roadhead town of Taplejung, a journey none of us cares ever to repeat. We reached our base camp after eight days of walking. It took a couple of days' exploration to decide which was our peak—the locals had no idea. We opted for the most prominent peak at the head of the valley and found a friendly south-facing base camp site, with bountiful clear water and unknown access to our favored route on the peak, the southwest ridge.

It was heartening to see that these valleys still held healthy-looking herds of blue sheep, frequent sightings of which gave us the vain hope that we might spy a snow leopard. Our lack of stealth meant all we saw were tracks in the snow. Luckily, access to our preferred route proved both interesting and relatively straightforward. After meandering across, down, and then up the sides of old ablation valleys, we followed the bed of a long-retreated glacier on clean, high-friction slabs, which were just low angled enough to allow walking to a safe but spectacularly situated site for advance base. This provided a good view of our objective. From here we climbed onto a glacier and up to a short rock step, on which we fixed a rope before retreating to base camp in the face of an upcoming storm. This produced a foot of snow: the only significant fall of the trip.

When the weather cleared, we returned to see if we could make the climb. We established camp under a short headwall leading to a low point on our chosen ridge. On November 5 we left this camp at 4 a.m. The going was fast on firm snow, and by daylight we found ourselves faced with a choice of climbing a rocky tower that looked like a stack of shattered blocks, or making a traverse around the obstacle. I opted for the traverse and was treated to spicy climbing on overlapping iced-up slabs. Unfortunately my ropemate Dave and I had the best of it, as Ken, Keith, Theo, and Colin, who followed, found the going more precarious due to decreased ice. They were slowed to the point where they only made it a short distance past the start of the ridge proper before wisely deciding to call off a summit bid.

Back on the ridge we found conditions to be perfect, but as this was Dave's first time at altitude, we thought it prudent to remain roped, so we simul-climbed, placing the odd snow picket very firmly. We were blessed with a crystal-clear autumn day. There was hardly a murmur of a breeze, and the vista in all directions presented peak after peak in fine detail, particularly to the west, where we could see Everest's Kangshung face, the east face of Lhotse, Chomo Lonzo, and Makalu.

By 1:30 p.m. we stood as close to the corniced summit as we dared. To our north a broad brown valley dropped to a shimmering plain, and beyond it rose a group of peaks dangling stranded névé and glaciers: the Nyonni Ri Group (6,730m), explored by the 1935 Everest Expedition. Closer scrutiny revealed roads scarring the Tibetan landscape, the first time I've ever seen any roads from atop a Himalayan peak.

We were back down to the saddle, and the others, at 4 p.m. Deciding not to retrace the traverse, we made the short climb up to the summit of the sub-peak and rappelled down the teetering tower as darkness enveloped us. We all made it back safely to base camp the next day to find that John's condition had worsened. He was the only member of the climbing team not to acclimatize, and eventually he had to be evacuated by helicopter.

TIM MACARTNEY-SNAPE, *Australia*

JANAK HIMAL

Janak, East Summit, south face attempt. A six-member team from Aoyamagakuin University Alpine Club tried to climb the virgin East Summit of Janak (7,041m) via the route on the right side of the south face, attempted in 2005 by Slovenians Miha Habjan and Andrej Stremfelj. Ages of the members ranged from 20–66, the latter that of the leader, Tsugio Iwai. Unlike the Slovenian duo, the team operated in heavyweight style, using climbing Sherpas and fixed rope.

On September 29 they established base camp at

Janak from the upper Broken Glacier to the southeast. The route attempted by the Japanese on the south face is marked. The left skyline, leading directly to the 7,041m main summit, is the southwest pillar, climbed in 2006 by Andrej Stremfelj and Rok Zalokar, to make the first ascent of the mountain. *Lindsay Griffin*

5,200m on the Broken Glacier, then made two advanced camps, at 5,400m and 5,850m. On October 10 Masayuki Murakami and a Sherpa bivouacked high on the south face at 6,650m. The next day they started for the summit but gave up at 6,700m.

HIROSHI HAGIWARA, *Chief Editor ROCK and SNOW, Japan*

China

The online version of these reports frequently contains additional photos, maps, topos, and extended text. Please visit aaj.americanalpineclub.org

Xinjiang

Venus peak from south. (S) Summit. (E) Southeast ridge. (B) Bivouac and (C) Peak 5,980m. The Italians climbed far flank of ridge to reach crest at point close to bivouac. (Inset) Southeast ridge of Venus . In the distance Shaksgam River valley rises southeast toward peaks of Indian Karakoram. *Hervé Barmasse*

Unclimbed northeast face of Gasherbrum I (8,068m) from Urdok Glacier. *Hervé Barmasse*

Karakoram, Venus Peak (6,279m), southeast ridge. In June and July Daniele Bernasconi, Mario Panzeri, and I traveled to the Shaksgam Valley to attempt an alpine-style ascent of Gasherbrum I. Unfortunately, due to the inefficiency of the agency that organized our logistics, it took 45 days to reach base camp. We then had only seven days before returning home, not enough time to make an attempt. However, during the approach we made the first ascent of the 6,279m peak [Polish 1:80,000 Satellite Map] north of the entrance to the South Skyang Lungpa Glacier, which flows east to the Shaksgam River.

Northwest from Venus Peak. (A) Broad Peak South (7,731m). (B) Broad Peak Main (8,047m; southeast ridge is unclimbed). (C) Broad Peak foresummit (Rocky Summit, 8,028m). (D) Broad Peak Central (8,016m). (E) South Kharut (6,934m). *Hervé Barmasse*

South from Venus Peak. (A) Urdok Kangri Peaks (7,137m, 7,136m, and 7,250m). (B) Gasherbrum I (8,068m). (C) Gasherbrum II East (7,772m). (D) Gasherbrum II (8,035m). (E) Gasherbrum III (7,952m). (F) Gasherbrum IV (7,925m). Peak in middle distance below (A) is one of South Nakpo massif. *Hervé Barmasse*

It was a beautiful but difficult adventure. We climbed the southeast ridge on July 10-11. It comprised numerous rock towers, with demanding mixed pitches, cornices, and sections of deep, dangerous snow. However, there was a fantastic panorama of the Gasherbrums, Broad Peak, and K2. The elevation gain was 2,150m; we climbed the upper 800m from our bivouac in eight hours, then descended a different route to avoid a second bivouac on the mountain. The grade was ED, and we named the peak Venus, after the planet that shone brightly each morning above the summit.

HERVÉ BARMASSE, *Italy*

North Buttress of Sulamar (Khanjaylak II), showing Fowler-Ramsden line. *Bruce Normand*

Ramsden on Sulamar's summit ridge after climbing north buttress. *Mick Fowler*

Tien Shan, Xuelian Range, Sulamar (5,380m), north buttress. From mid-August to mid-September Mike Morrison, Paul Ramsden, Rob Smith, and I visited the north side of the Xuelian Range. This area had been visited twice before by mountaineering trips, both led by Bruce Normand; it is where Bruce, Jed Brown, and Kyle Dempster climbed their 2010 Piolets d'Or-awarded route on Xuelian West. We operated as two independent teams, with Morrison and Smith exploring side valleys off the Muzart Glacier, while Ramsden and I descended the rarely traveled Xiate Trail to explore the mountains beyond the snout of the Muzart Glacier.

Our original aim was to ascend the Muzart Glacier to the col at its head and attempt Xuelian East. However, heavy snowfall during the acclimatization period made glacier travel overly exciting. Both Paul and I fell completely into crevasses: a first for both of us in over 30 years of mountaineering. Deciding that the long approach to the head of the Muzart Glacier would prove too time-consuming and dangerous with so much fresh snow, we decided to retrace part of the walk-in and strike up an unknown valley to the foot of the north side of Sulamar.

This peak was first climbed in 2008 by Normand and Guy McKinnon, who refer to it as Khanjaylak II. Approaching from the south, they climbed the northeast slopes that rise from the col between Khanjaylak I (5,424m) and II (*AAJ 2009*).

It was with some relief that we eventually discovered we had chosen the correct valley and could reach our objective, the prominent 1,600m north buttress. We took a full day to walk to the foot of the face from our base camp by the Muzart on the Xiate Trail. From there we climbed for just over two days up steep ice and mixed terrain, at TD+, to gain a fine snow ridge leading back left to the summit. Our bivouacs on the face were sitting/hanging.

We descended the previously unclimbed south ridge and regained base camp in a six-day round trip. All four of us felt the area to be one of the most beautiful in which we had climbed.

MICK FOWLER, *UK, Alpine Club*

QINGHAI - QILIAN MOUNTAINS

Peak 4,722m; Peak 4,880m; Gradiska (5,254m), southwest face. Located on the Qinghai-Ganshou border in central China, the Qilian (locally, the "Heavenly Mountains") run northwest for some 800km from the town of Xining. The main range is split between northwestern and southeastern sections, though a separate sub-group to the west of the southeastern section includes the highest peak, Kangze'gyai (ca 5,800m, see AAJ 2010). The highest peak in the main range is Qilian Shan (Qilianin, 5,547m), situated in the northwestern sector. From late July to early August Oh Young-hoon's 14-member Korean Youth Expedition planned to climb Gradiska (5,254m), the highest peak in the southeastern group. This peak has only been open to foreign mountaineers since 2000, and the first ascent is believed to have been made by Japanese in 2004. Information is hard to find, but the mountain is rarely visited and only the southwest face has been climbed.

The group established base camp at 4,100m, after a four-hour drive from Xining to Menwuan (3,600m), followed by three or four hours of walking. They placed Camp 1 at 4,600m, from where moraine led to 400m-high summit slopes up to 55°.

Most other mountains in the region are unclimbed and the expedition made first ascents of Peaks 4,722m and 4,880m.

CHRISTINE PAE, *Director Korean Alpine Federation, and* LINDSAY GRIFFIN, *Mountain INFO*

SICHUAN

New regulations. Beginning January 1, 2011, new Chinese regulations make it financially much harder for small parties to attempt virgin peaks in Sichuan. Climbers will face up to five or six times the cost compared with 2010, with the rise in royalties more acute for lower-altitude peaks. Even for previously climbed peaks, individuals pay more than double 2010 prices.

For peaks above 7,000m the fee in 2011 is 2,800 Yuan

Foreshortened image of Xiaqiangla's 400m northeast face. Peaks 2 and 3 on north ridge are marked. (1) Matsushima-Sato Route. (2) Upper section of descent on north ridge. (3) North ridge, attempted by Kato and Yoshimura over Peak 3. *Chiharu Yoshimura*

per person. In reality, as there is only one peak of this height in the Province, this figure applies to parties attempting new lines or repeating established routes on Minya Konka (7,556m), which has seen several ascents since 1932.

Attempting an unclimbed peak between 6,000m and 7,000m costs 25,000–45,000 Yuan per expedition. If the mountain has been climbed, this drops to 1,800 Yuan per person (or a total of 15,000 for an expedition of 10 or more). At the time of writing, the criteria that define the sliding scale for expeditions remain unclear.

For peaks between 5,500 and 6,000m, the equivalent royalties are 20,000–35,000 for an expedition attempting an unclimbed peak and 1,000 per person for a climbed peak (9,000 for a team of 10 or more). Compare this with 2010 prices, when an expedition to an unclimbed peak was charged 9,000 Yuan.

For peaks from 3,500m to 5,500m, the cost is 15,000–30,000 per team for an unclimbed peak, 500 per person for a previously climbed summit (no expedition price quoted).

Those wanting simply to rock or ice climb pay 500 Yuan each, while everyone is required to contribute a 200-Yuan environment protection fee. When climbing within a national park, local entrance and environmental fees are additional.

Staff fees increase less drastically. A Liaison Officer (officially mandatory when climbing on a mountain above 3,500m) costs 680 Yuan a day. This price includes wages, equipment, and insurance. Assistant L.O.s and interpreters cost 580, cooks 480, and other staff 300 Yuan. If a high-altitude porter is employed, the cost is 880 per day. On top of this each member of the Chinese staff needs a food allowance of 120 per day. It also seems likely that climbers will have to pay a service charge of five percent on the overall expenses incurred during their expedition.

LINDSAY GRIFFIN, *Mountain INFO, with assistance from Tamotsu Nakamura and Jiyue Zhang*

DAXUE SHAN

Dangling Range, Xiaqiangla (5,470m), northeast face. After my first ascent in 2007 of Bawangshan (5,551m) in the Qonglai Shan (AAJ 2008), I wondered what my next target should be. It didn't take long to find a mountain that fit my criteria: unclimbed, prominent, beautiful, and with easy access.

Xiaqiangla is an outstanding peak in the northern Daxue Shan, west of Danba and the Dadu

Xiaqiangla from northeast. Summit to right apparently unspecified on maps, though another off-picture to right is marked as 5,240m. North ridge attempt climbed from broad snowy col between the two mountains. Peaks 2 and 3 on north ridge are marked. *Chiharu Yoshimura*

Tatsienlu Massif from west. (A) Yipingfeng (First Peak). (B) Erpingfeng (Second Peak). (C) Sanpingfeng (Third Peak). (D) Szepingfeng (Shehaizishan, Fourth Peak). (E) Wupingfeng (Fifth Peak). (F) Haopingling (5,864m, PLA Map). (G) Tshungpingling (Baihaizishan, White Lake Peak, 5,924m PLA Map). (H) Tshien-pingling (5,612m, PLA Map). Lamo-she (6,070m) is off-picture to right. *Tamotsu Nakamura, captions by Pedro Detjen*

River. Only Kiyoshi Kawajiri, Tom Nakamura, and Tadao Shintani had accessed these mountains before. [Nakamura's photo of Xiaqiangla appeared in *AAJ 2009*.] The peak was alluring not only because it was a fine unclimbed pyramid, but also due to the surrounding area, the so-called Valley of Beauty, where unique local Tibetan culture features fine and historic art, literature, and

Part of Tatsienlu Massif seen from west-northwest in November 2008. (A) Erpingfeng (ca 5,850m). (B) Sanpingfeng (ca 5,910m). (C) Shehaizi Shan or Szepingfeng (5,878m, PLA Map). (D) Wupingfeng (5,672m, PLA Map). 2010 Chinese route marked. 1996 route starts left of lower rock barrier, then moves right to broad snow crest of west ridge. Names Erpingfeng, Sanpingfeng, etc. mean "Second Peak," "Third Peak," etc., numbered from north, names given by cartographer Eduard Imhof and explorer, Arnold Heim, both Swiss, who surveyed range in 1930. *Tamotsu Nakamura*

architecture, including stone towers that are typical of the Dadu River Basin.

Our expedition took place from April 24-May 9 and comprised Mitsuru Kato, Hiroshi Matsushima, Ken Sato, and me, all from the JAC. We first drove from Chengdu to Dang Ling (3,300m), via Danbu, and set up base camp on the shores of Da Haizi at 4,350m, after an eight-hour walk to the west-southwest. After reconnaissance we placed an advanced base at 5,020m and attempted two routes: the northeast face and the north ridge. The former would involve climbing a snow couloir leading toward the north ridge and then striking up left on a steep rock wall leading directly to the summit. The route up the north ridge would start from the north col and also be steep, with rocky gendarmes resembling a dinosaur's back. It would feature a subsidiary summit (Peak 3) and a smaller rock pyramid (Peak 2) before rising to the main summit.

On May 2 we started from advanced base at 6 a.m. Matsushima and Sato climbed the northeast face and reached the main summit at 2:40 p.m. Mixed/rock climbing in the upper section was III-IV, and their GPS gave an altitude of 5,497m. Kato and I got as far as Peak 3 on the north ridge but had to give up at that point due to lack of time. Our parties regrouped at the col between Peaks 2 and 3, then descended the couloir together, reaching advanced base at 8:40 p.m.

Tom Nakamura notes that it is now impossible to ignore the serious environmental destruction to the Dadu River region caused by accelerated West China Development projects. A huge dam is under construction near Luding.

CHIHARU YOSHIMURA, *Japanese Alpine Club, translated by Tom Nakamura*

Tatsienlu Massif, Wupingfeng (5,672m), west face direct. From a base camp below the glacier on the west side of the mountain, Gu Jie, Liu Yang, and Peng Xiaolong made the likely second ascent of Peak 5,672m on the Chinese PLA Map, via the west face direct. The trio made a single-push ascent and descent, leaving base camp at 4 a.m. on July 24, reaching the summit at 5:20 p.m. the same day, and returning to base at 2 a.m. on the 25th. It took two hours to reach the left side of the glacier, where they climbed through the steep snout via 60m of 60° ice. They then followed the gently angled glacier to the foot of the west face, where after crossing the bergschrund, Peng led the first four pitches, Liu the next six, and Gu the final three to the summit. Difficulties were AI3+ 70°.

The Tatsienlu (Lamo-she) Massif lies immediately southeast of the town of Kangding. It is a compact range with all the main peaks situated on a ridge running north-south and ca 10km in length. Wupingfeng, at 29°58'56.32" N, 102°03'02.16" E, was first climbed in October 1996 by Fred Beckey's expedition. (Beckey had reconnoitered the area in 1993, while other members of his expedition were climbing the massif's highest peak, Lamo-she.) John Chilton, Jia Condon, and Rich Prohaska climbed the lower west face and moved right onto the moderately angled west ridge, which they followed to the summit. Meanwhile, Mark Carter and Steve Must climbed the corniced north ridge. They referred to the summit by a local name, Snake Lake Peak (*AAJ 1998*). However, Snake Lake Peak is Shehaizishan (5,878m on the PLA Map), which lies immediately north. *She* means "snake" and *haizi* means "lake." This was also climbed by the 1996 Beckey expedition, via the northwest ridge. Beckey's team then moved into the next valley north and climbed Sanpingfeng (ca 5,910m) via the north ridge. All three peaks were likely unrepeated until 2010. The highest peak in the massif, Lamo-she (6,070m), toward the southern end of the chain, was climbed by Americans in 1993 (*AAJ 1994*).

Yan Dongdong, *China, with historical information from Pedro Detjen, Germany, and Tamotsu Nakamura, Japan*

Ruiche Gongga from southwest. Korean route marked. In 2008 French made second ascent of this small peak northwest of Jiazi by climbing to col on right and following southeast ridge to top. *Supplied by Peter Jensen-Choi*

Minya Konka Range, Ruiche Gongga (5,928m), south-southwest face. A 23-member expedition, led by Kim Kyu-tae and sponsored by the GyeongBuk Alpine Federation, left Korea on July 22 and arrived at base camp (4,200m), on the west side of the range, on the 27th. At 2:30 p.m. on August 11 seven members reached the summit by a new route on the south-southwest face. This was the third ascent of the mountain (AAJ 2009). The following day another two climbers summited. The successful members were Ahn Sang-hun, Bae Chang-su, Baek Jong-deuk, Gwon Gyeong-yeon, Jang Heon-mu, Lee Myeong-hee, Mo Young-man, Oh Sang-go, and Park Jae-seok. The ascent was made in semi-alpine style, but no grade or specific route details have been disclosed. The team evacuated base camp on the 18th.

Peter Jensen-Choi, *Corean Alpine Club*

Minya Konka Range, Reddomain (6,112m), second ascent, first ski descent via west ridge. Jimmy Chin, Giulia Monego, Kasha Rigby, and I established base camp on September 29, 2009, at 4,500m and the following day scoped a new access to the west ridge from the north. On October 4 we walked up moraine and climbed steep snow to the west ridge. After a section of loose rock and delicate steps,

Reddomain from northwest, showing line of ascent and ski descent in 2009. *Photo supplied by Tamotsu Nakamura*

we reached the hanging glacier at 5,200m, where we set up camp.

On the 5th we climbed mixed snow and rock on the crest to reach a snow gully, where we joined the route of the first ascensionists, who arrived at this point from the south [Japanese Norisuke Ogawa, Hiroyuki Takahashi, and Yuji Tashiro, who in 1999 fixed ropes and placed two camps on the west ridge, reporting dangerous cornices and slopes up to 70° a little below the summit]. From that point it was a long walk on snow, navigating through crevasses, while keeping our distance from the crest. Due to unstable weather from the south, which brought strong wind and poor visibility, the climb was tough and slow. We expected to find wind-packed snow, but it was surprisingly soft.

The top appeared to be split by a huge fracture, dividing it into two summits. Visibility wasn't good enough to see which was the higher, but the difference seemed insignificant. We assumed the one we reached was the top and put on our skis. We were able to ski all the way to the junction with the original route at ca 5,400m. Keeping skis on, we rappeled for 10m, then skied to the rocky section directly above camp. We took off skis, made one full-length rappel, downclimbed a section, and resumed skiing to our camp.

Next day we climbed back onto the west ridge and skied the snowy talus we'd ascended. The visibility was good and the snow soft at the outset, though it became heavy and wet toward the end. The snow line was at ca 4,800m, from where we walked down to base camp. Next day we were back in Kangding.

INGRID BACKSTROM, *provided by Tamotsu Nakamura, Japanese Alpine News*

Minya Konka Range, Dogonomba (5,960m), first and second ascents. In late autumn 2008 Aidan Loehr made the first ascent, solo, of Dogonomba, which lies on the main ridge immediately south of Reddomain. Loehr had been guiding an American Alpine Institute team on Dogonomba's east ridge. They were unsuccessful, but after the group departed he went to the other side of the mountain and climbed the west ridge. The lower section, reaching the ridge itself, proved quite difficult, with exposed 4th class climbing. Once he reached snow and ice, the route became more reasonable. Slopes of 30-40° led to the summit ridge, where he was forced to traverse 60° slopes of poor snow, below the corniced crest. He gained the tiny summit in high winds. The only previously recorded attempt on this peak was made by another AAI party in 1995.

Donogomba from west, showing line of 2010 New Zealand ascent. 2008 American route is thought to be similar. *Yvonne Pfluger*

This ascent was unknown to Tim Church (New Zealand) and Yvonne Pfluger (Austrian living in NZ), when they visited the range in May 2010. Heavy snow cover delayed access, and they first attempted 5,928m Ruiche Gongga from the north, getting within 300m of the summit. This left only a week for an attempt on Dogonomba. Spotting an obvious route up the west ridge, they established an advanced base at 4,400m among moraine debris and scrubby vegetation in a side valley south of the ridge.

The lower ridge appeared difficult, with extensive broken rock, but they spotted a snow gully rising from near the head of the side valley to easier ground on the upper, glaciated part of the ridge. They made a 12½-hour roundtrip reconnaissance from advanced base, stashing gear at a proposed high camp (5,300m) and climbing some distance up the ridge above. Next day they carried a second load to high camp and stayed the night. The following morning they made their summit bid, retracing their steps up the ridge and continuing on heavily loaded 30-40° slopes to a broad low subsummit. The ridge between the subsummit and main summit proved technical, with loose rock, a knife-edge, an exposed ridge of bullet-proof ice, and the 50-60° summit pyramid. Only Church completed the final pitch, as the weather rapidly deteriorated to snowfall and high winds. White-out conditions accompanied the return to high camp, where they spent the night before descending to base camp next day. They note that south of their summit, between it and Daddomain (6,380m), stands the unclimbed Peak 5,962m, possibly called Sequinomba.

LINDSAY GRIFFIN, *Mountain INFO, from material provided by Tamotsu Nakamura and Yvonne Pfluger*

Minya Konka Range, Edgar (6,618m), east face, The Rose of No-Man's Land. The previously untouched east face and upper south ridge of Edgar rises 2,500m and features an objectively threatened approach couloir. The smaller southeast face to the left was where Americans Jonny Copp and Micah Dash, with film maker Wade Johnson, were killed by an avalanche in 2009. American Kyle Dempster and Scot Bruce Normand climbed the ice-plastered east face and south ridge in an eight-day round trip, with sustained difficulties of M6 and WI5 on the east face. For details see Normand's feature article in this Journal.

QONGLAI MOUNTAINS – SIGUNIANG NATIONAL PARK

Abi (5,694m), west face and southwest ridge, Shivering (not to summit). Abi has been climbed several times from the southeast and southwest but had not been attempted from the west until July 2009, when He Lang and I tried from the Jiesigou Valley. The peak lies between the north end of the Shuangqiao Valley and the northeast branch of the Jiesigou, the valley immediately west of the Shuangqiao. We reached 5,500m on the southwest ridge, near the point where the rock met ice. However, it was around 2:20 p.m., cold, and we weren't prepared for a bivouac on the glacier, so we retreated. That night our tent at 5,100m was destroyed by ice falling from the glacier tongue, so we had to bivouac after all. It rained all night, and we shivered in wet sleeping bags.

Abi from the west, with line Shivering. *Yan Dongdong*

In August 2010 Li Lan, Zhao Xingzheng, and I returned, hoping to complete the route. On the 16th we took a van from Rilong to the point where the Jiesigou splits, spent a night in the village there, and next day hired a tractor to take us to the end of the mud road. From here we trekked to 4,900m, where we camped below the rocky ridge rising to the glacier.

On the 18th we left at 6:10 a.m. and before 8:30 a.m. had reached the site of the previous year's camp at 5,100m. From there we climbed a full pitch of rock and one and a half pitches on ice, to gain the glacier. We only had one 50m half rope, so Li tied onto the end and Zhao a few meters above her. Every pitch was less than 45m, and because it was misty all day, Zhao and I could barely see each other when the rope was run out.

We climbed the glacier to the start of the ice face rising to the southwest ridge. Two and a half pitches led to the crest, where rock met ice. I led another pitch up broken slate to gain more ice. After one pitch of ice climbing we were able to walk for about two ropelengths to the junction of the southwest, southeast, and north ridges, a point we assumed must be the summit. It was 6:00 p.m., so we just took a few photos and started our descent. It was only later, when I checked the map, that I found the ridge junction was at 5,650m. If the mist had cleared, we would have seen the true summit just 100m to the north.

It had been dark for some time when we reached 5,300m and realized we had no hope of finding the right spot to rappel the glacier tongue. (The wrong spot would lead to overhanging terrain.) We had one down jacket between us and no stove but decided to bivouac. We spent two hours digging into a snow/ice crest with our axes, until there was nearly enough space for us to cram inside, with feet out in the open. We ate little, shivered a lot, and I threw up twice on Li's down jacket. We regained our camp at 3:00 p.m. on the 19th and slept for 17 hours.

The tent leaked in continuous rain, and there was more shivering in wet sleeping bags. The obvious name for our route was Shivering, though of course we really didn't finish it to the summit. The part we completed was 800m, IV 5.7 AI3 M2.

YAN DONGDONG, *China*

Jianshanzi (5,472m), southwest face. Briefly noted in the 2010 AAJ (p. 84), Jianshanzi (Jianzi Peak) was climbed solo in 2005. The ascent was by Wang Bing, who climbed the southwest face Septem-

Niuxin Shan from north, showing Japanese route on southeast face. *Hiroo Kameda*

ber 28-29, 2005. This mountain lies halfway up the Shuangqiao, immediately west of this valley at 31° 08'39.67" N, 102° 44'39.29" E. It is south of Hunter's Peak (Lieren Feng, 5,360m) and connected to it by a ridge. There was no known ascent of the mountain prior to 2005.

YAN DONGDONG, *China*

Niuxin Shan (4,942m), southeast face. Kazuyoshi Uematsu led a three-man team that made the first ascent of the southeast face of Niuxin Shan (Ox Heart mountain), the biggest rock wall on this outstanding peak above the east bank of the Shuangqiao Valley. In 2002 a five-man Japanese team led by Naoki Ohuchi attempted this mountain from the west. Three members reached easy ground after having climbed difficulties up to 5.10c. They left some pitches fixed and returned to base camp. Subsequently, heavy snowfall prevented a return to the route. The peak was climbed in 2004 by Anne and John Arran, via the north face and west ridge (AAJ 2005), attempts to reach the southeast face being foiled by impenetrable rhododendron.

We established base camp on September 11 at 4,300m in the valley and made a reconnaissance of the face. The following day Makoto Hashimoto and I left at 7 a.m. for our attempt. The leader climbed with a four-kilo sack, while the second carried seven kilos, including bivouac gear.

After an initial pitch of 5.7, we lost much time attempting our proposed second pitch, before retreating and climbing another, rather exciting line at 5.10a R. We now left sacks and climbed two enjoyable pitches (5.10b and 5.8), then rappelled 100m to collect the sacks. After a re-ascent, Hashimoto led a short pitch of 5.6 to a small bivouac site, where we spent an uncomfortable night sitting, Hashimoto with a bad headache from altitude.

Next day was fine, and after four pitches from 5.6 to 5.9 we reached the summit ridge, which was sharp and exposed. The climbing above was not difficult (three pitches of 5.6-5.7) but was often run out and a little loose. By 10 a.m. we were at the highest point. Ten rappels got us back down the wall by 2 p.m., and we returned to base camp, elated, that afternoon.

HIROO KAMEDA, *Mountaineering Federation of Yamanshi Prefecture, translated by Tamotsu Nakamura*

Seerdengpu (5,592m), northeast ridge, Headwaters; Peak 5,086m, near miss. On September 13, after two earlier attempts, Chad Kellogg and I reached the summit of previously unclimbed Seerdengpu, the high point above the heads of the Changping and Shuangqiao valleys. The north and west faces above the Shuangqiao are 1,500m granite walls, and remarkably accessible. One can take a public bus along a paved road to within a couple of hours walk of the base. The more remote south and east faces above the Changping are 1,200m high and provide a combination of big walls and alpine mixed terrain. Chad and I had made a reconnaissance of this peak in 2008, after our ascent of Siguniang (AAJ 2009).

Seedengpu has been translated as "Barbarian," "Yeti," or "Savage Peak." Its northern aspect distinctly resembles the head of a savage, and our original plan was to climb the unmistakable 1,400m nose. This compelling line has attracted around a dozen expeditions over the last decade, and when we entered the park we learned that three teams were attempting it during August and September. The first of these—Japanese—had been rescued after sustaining injuries from rockfall, one week prior to our arrival.

Our itinerary called for acclimatizing in the adjacent Changping Valley until mid-September, and we promptly set to work establishing an advanced base camp at the head of the valley under the east face of Seerdengpu. As we did so, our liaison officer informed us that a Polish team had reached the base of the north face. The abandoned Japanese tent was still visible at

North Face of Seerdengpu above Shuangqiao Valley, showing route of first ascent (mostly hidden). The nose, unsuccessfully attempted by several teams, divides shadow and sunlight. (inset) East face of Seerdengpu showing line of first ascent, Headwaters. *Dylan Johnson*

one-third height on the nose. Storms arrived during the first week of September and deposited the first autumn snowfall. This new snow, and crowds on the north face, encouraged us to remain focused on the mixed terrain of the east side.

On our first attempt we found solid granite climbing, free at 5.10 for the first 250m. At nightfall, we rapped back to our high camp, left a line fixed over the crux slabs, and set the alarms for a pre-dawn start. The skies deteriorated throughout the night, and by 4 a.m. 30cm of snow had fallen.

Four days later we returned in marginal weather, and as we gained the northeast ridge proper, Chad took the lead and was pleasantly surprised to find straightforward passage in a hidden gully, offering 300m of snow and mixed climbing up to M5.

At 5,200m the gully terminated at a small col, above which a series of complex gendarmes guarded the upper mountain. In the waning daylight, I led up a steep gendarme, dry-tooling a thin crack. While trying to clear snow and find some gear, my tool ripped and sent me hurling backwards for my first real alpine whipper. A bit shaken up, discouraged, and without bivouac

Chad Kellogg on summit day of Seerdengpu. Below, Changping Valley flows east, before bending sharply south in front of large distant peak, Siguniang (6,250m). In 2008 Johnson and Kellogg climbed right skyline of this peak. *Dylan Johnson*

Peak 5,086m and almost-completed line up northwest arête. *Dylan Johnson*

gear, we decided to rap and try the following day. Again we awoke to new snow, so we cached food and fuel and headed down the slippery talus to base camp.

After we spent a rest day, my wife Jenna called in a splitter forecast, so we set off at 1:30 p.m. for the 25km of swamp and talus leading to the base of the route. We agreed that we didn't want to risk getting stopped by a sudden storm again, and thought the best strategy would simply be to begin climbing as soon as we reached the base. We started up the route at 11:30 p.m., and with the 5.10 slabs running with snow melt, I was forced to do interesting A2 by headlamp. We had left a line fixed over a section of the second pitch, but, nervous about the rope's integrity after the last storm, I free-climbed most of the wet and snowy pitch "protected" by a Ropeman.

Reaching our previous high point at dawn, we traversed left beneath the gendarmes, completing four 5.10 C2 horizontal pitches to arrive at simul-climbing terrain on the upper mountain. The weather was holding, and we climbed the last 300m to the summit ridge in a single pitch. The ridge offered spectacular cornice walking and easy mixed climbing, with giant raptors flying below. At 2:30 p.m. we reached the top and enjoyed unmatched views of the entire range. For the first time I was able to mentally organize the complex topography of the Quonglai Mountains; it was my third summit in this area, but Chad's seventh.

The descent went relatively smoothly. The traverses were difficult to reverse, but we sorted them with a few pendulums and sideways raps. Our lead line suffered two debilitating core shots, and during the final, overhanging rap our tag line became hopelessly stuck behind a flake, and we had to leave it behind. We arrived at high camp at 11:30 p.m. after 34 hours on the go. We named the 1,000m route Headwaters, after its obvious position in the hydrology of the region, a gesture to the Yeti himself, and as an acknowledgment of the alarming glacial recession taking place—a major threat to the extensive, crowded Chinese lowlands downriver.

A few days later, with John Dickey along, we nearly made the first ascent of a stunning granite spire of 5,086m, which is on the southern rim of the upper Changping, southeast of Potala Shan. In the dark, after 600m of absolutely classic free climbing (5.10) up the northwest ridge, I had to turn back 25m from the summit when faced with a steep, unprotectable arête and no bolt kit. During the descent we destroyed our only remaining lead line. On our return to Rilong we found members of the Polish team on the nose had also been hit by rockfall and were in a

Chengdu hospital. They had been replaced by a group from China.

We extend our sincere thanks to the American Alpine Club, Mugs Stump, and Lyman Spitzer grant programs for their generous support. For us these exploratory trips to Asia would not be possible without the financial support of these programs. The expedition was also supported by the Four Sisters Film project; keep your eyes out for its impressive work.

DYLAN JOHNSON, *AAC*

Peak 5,086m, south face, attempt. On October 7 and 8 Chinese climbers Gong Xiaorui, He Chuan, and Wu Peng attempted the south face of Peak 5,086m, a granite shark's fin nearly climbed from the opposite side a month earlier by Americans Dickey, Johnson, and Kellogg via the northwest ridge [see previous report]. The Chinese approached from the Shuangqiao, climbed seven and a half pitches the first day, bivouacked, and climbed a further two and a half pitches on the second. Although they believed they had completed the major difficulties, they were still some distance from the summit; concerned about timev, they retreated. To their high point at 4,910m, they had climbed 520m (310m vertical gain) at V 5.10b A0. They estimate another 250m of climbing (180m of vertical gain) to the summit.

YAN DONGDONG, *China*

Daogou West (5,422m), northeast couloir and north ridge. On October 23 and 24, 2008, Chinese mountaineers Chen Hui, Gu Qizhi, and Peng Xiaolong made the second known ascent of Daogou West, via a new route up the northeast couloir and north ridge, with a bivouac halfway up the couloir. The team approached from the upper Changping Valley and sited base camp immediately below the face.

Kester Brown and Vaughn Thomas made the only previous ascent of this summit, climbing the south face from the Shuangqiao Valley in September 2006 (*AAJ 2007*).

Looking southwest towards Daogou (5,465m, left) and Daogou West (5,422m) from north side of upper Changping Valley. 2008 Chinese route is marked. Daogou was climbed from far side by an American team in 2005, while an Australian-New Zealand pair climbed Daogou West from far side in 2006. *Jeremy Thornley collection*

YAN DONGDONG, *China*

Tibet

The online version of these reports frequently contains additional photos, maps, topos, and extended text. Please visit aaj.americanalpineclub.org

NYANCHEN TANGLHA WEST

Langbu Qu (valley), five ascents. In late autumn 2009, Yan Dongdong from China joined Guy McKinnon (New Zealand) and me for a three-man attempt on attractive 6,000+m summits accessed from the Langbu Qu, the third valley system west of Nyanchen Tanglha Main (7,162m). At the time

Sir Duk (left) and Chorten Garpo seen from the summit of Pt. 6,382m to the west. The arrow marks the snow couloir, which was climbed by the 2009 team directly to the upper slopes and summit; they descended the left skyline. The 2000 team, with the mountains in much snowier condition, climbed the ridge to the right. On Chorten Garpo the 2000 team climbed the right skyline ridge, then descended part of the left skyline before heading down the West Face; the 2009 team climbed slopes behind the right skyline, up and down. *Bruce Normand*

we were unaware of previous visits to this group of peaks, despite their ready accessibility. The mountains lie just north of the largest village in the area, Yangbajain, on the old northern Lhasa to Shigatse road. Subsequently we found that a small team of Austrians had climbed from the same valley in 2000.

From October 27–November 9 we summited five peaks. Four of these presented only moderate difficulties with 40–50° snow climbing in parts; the fifth, and also the highest in the group, was rather more serious and required a rope, the placement of gear, and two rappels during the descent. Our summits (heights taken from the Mi Desheng map, or by altimeter) were Pt. 6,382m and Pt. 6,286m at the head of the valley, Pt. 6,120m (altimeter reading) above the west bank, Pt. 6,380m (altimeter) above the east bank of the valley, and to its north-west, Pt. 6,614m.

In September 2000, Austrians Erich Gatt, Christian Haas, and Hans-Jorg Pfaundler climbed three peaks here in much snowier conditions than we found. Above the east bank of the valley, and from southeast to northwest:

Another view of Sir Duk, this time from Chorten Garpo to the southeast. *Bruce Normand*

Looking west-northwest at (A) Pt. 6,516m (unclimbed), (B) Pt. 6,382m, and (C) possibly Pt. 6,263m (unclimbed) on Mi Desheng Chinese Map. The route to 6,382m followed the obvious broad snow plateau on the right and then up the steep summit snow slope in shadow. *Bruce Normand*

Pt. 6,256m (GPS), which they named Yarlung Ri; Pt. 6,415m (GPS but the same summit as our Pt. 6,380m), which they named Chorten Garpo (Tibetan for White Pagoda); and Pt. 6,614m, named Sir Duk (Golden Dragon). Our ascents of Chorten Garpo and Sir Duk differed from those made in 2000. On Chorten Garpo the Austrians climbed the south ridge and then descended the northwest ridge and west face; we climbed the southeast face up and down. On Sir Duk the Austrians climbed the south ridge, moving left towards its top and finishing up the northwest ridge; we climbed the south-southwest face direct and descended via the northwest ridge.

The immediate region still contains many apparently unclimbed peaks in the low- to mid-6000m height range. The most appealing would seem to be the shapely Pt. 6,516m, which would be accessed most readily from the next valley west of the Langbu Qu.

BRUCE NORMAND, *Beijing, China*

Pt. 6,120m from the east. The 2009 ascent followed snow slopes on left, then took the gentle south ridge to summit. *Bruce Normand*

Pt. 6,286m (right) seen from southeast. The Chinese-Kiwi-Scottish trio first tried the pointed rocky peak to the left from behind the south-facing rock ridge but failed due to snow overlaying slabs. They then moved right and climbed the long east ridge (right skyline) of 6,286m. From the summit they climbed directly down the ice slope facing the camera. *Bruce Normand*

Dongxung, southeast ridge. Dongxung is the most northerly of a cluster of peaks, several more than 6,000m, that lie a short distance south of the town of Yangbajain (Yangpachen). These peaks lie south of, but close to, the southwestern end of the Nyanchen Tanglha. Only one is known to have

been climbed previously: the highest, Beu-tse (6,270m, *AAJ 2004*). Li Lan and I visited the area from May 7–12 with hopes to climb two or three peaks. We approached from the valley southeast of Maruguo village, camping the night of the 8th on the glacier at ca 5,700m. Because of our rapid altitude gain, we decided to rest on the 9th, during which time I spent two hours walking to the base of Dongxung to check out the southeast ridge.

Li Lan on the southeast ridge of Dongxung. Yan Dongdong

Thinking the ridge was short, we didn't leave camp until 9:20 a.m. on the 10th. It proved longer—or we were slower—than we thought. We reached the start of the rocky ridge at 11:30 a.m., and then either followed the crest or the left flank, not reaching the summit until 4:40 p.m. My watch read 6,095m. We regained camp at 10:10 p.m., one hour after dark.

We slept late on the 11th. It was misty and snowing a little, but we decided to stay for another night, hoping to attempt the north ridge of Beu-tse. However, the following day was also misty, and we'd now run out of toilet paper, not to mention motivation. We trekked out to Maruguo and hired motorcycles to reach the main road near Yangbajain. We named our route The Present after a Chinese pop song we both love. The grade is III/IV 5.5 M2 35° snow.

YAN DONGDONG, *China*

CENTRAL TIBET

Noijin Kangsang (7,206m), first quasi-winter ascent, south-southwest spur and south ridge. Noijin Kangsang lies immediately north of the Gyantse-Lhasa road at 28.9° N, 90.1° E. At least five routes have been climbed: the west ridge (Japanese, 1999); southwest ridge (Tibetan Mountaineering Association, 1986); south-southwest spur and south ridge (Japanese, 1995); south ridge (Japanese, 1992); and east ridge (Japanese, 2000). Approaching the south-southwest spur is really easy: you get off the bus at 4,950m and start climbing. I tried this route with a Tsinghua University Student team in 2007 and reached 7,130m. When I decided to climb a non-technical 7,000er in December, to know what it's like to climb at high altitude in winter (and in preparation for a future attempt on Minya Konka), Noijin Kangsang was the obvious choice.

Li Lan and I needed decent acclimatization. We left Lhasa on December 2 and camped by the road at 4,950m. The next day we went up onto the south-southwest spur, found a flat snowy spot at 6,050m partially protected from the wind, and camped for the night. We returned to the road and hitch-hiked to Lhasa the next day, leaving our tent and equipment behind.

Dongxung, showing the line of ascent on the southeast ridge. *Yan Dongdong*

We came back on the 6th and regained our camp at 6,050m that night. We set off in the dark at 8 a.m. on the 7th, taking a stove and sleeping bag but no tent. We wore harnesses and carried 10m of rope but never used it, as the snow was sufficiently hard to rule out crevasse danger. The only steep part of the route lies between 6,200m and 6,400m, where the crest rises to 40° before joining

The south-southwest spur of Noijin Kangsang is the left skyline. The visible high point is ca 6,400m. *Yan Dongdong*

the south and southeast ridges. After following the south ridge for a while, we traversed right to take the shortest path. By 4:20 p.m. we had reached 6,900m, crossed a covered crevasse, and could see the summit in the distance. However, we were also breathing hard, and the snow had become softer; our feet often sank to the ankle. The crevasse did not offer protection from the wind, but nearby we dug beneath a layer of hard snow and constructed a shelter within an hour. It proved to be the highest and most comfortable bivouac I've ever had.

At our 6,050m camp my watch had stopped recording temperature, meaning it was below -10°C. Up here I estimate it could have been below -30°C at night. However, inside the snow hole it was dry, calm, and actually not so cold.

We left at 8:20 the next morning. I reached the summit at 1:20 p.m. and Li at around 3 p.m. Although the wind was westerly, and we mostly stayed east of the south ridge, it was still windy all the way. After passing the 7,130m col, the route became more exposed to wind, and it was hard to stay on my feet.

Li Lan on the south-southwest spur of Noijin Kangsang. The view south passes over Kuluxung (6,674m) to the distant Himalayan peaks on the Bhutan border. *Yan Dongdong*

Bivouac at 6,900m on Noijin Kangsang. Yan Dongdong

The temperature on the summit might have been -20°C; the wind was wild, and high tufts of cloud occasionally dimmed the sun. I could not expose my nose and lips for more than half a minute before they went numb.

We returned to our shelter, melted some snow for a drink, and then started down at 4:30 p.m. We reached the top of the south-southwest spur at sundown, then down-climbed the spur in the dark. Li Lan later told me that one of her crampons came loose in the middle of the steep section, but being on a few centimeters of hard snow over ice, she was afraid to stop and fix it, so she just continued down with it dangling. She reached the 6,050m camp at around 11 p.m. We then ate, slept till noon, continued down, and hitchhiked back to Lhasa.

YAN DONGDONG, *China*

Winter ascents, definitions for Tibet, China, and Nepal. The official definition of a winter ascent in China and Tibet seemed to have been resolved with the January 2005 ascent of Shishapangma by Piotr Morawski and Simone Moro. They were issued a certificate from the CTMA (China Tibet Mountaineering Association) stating they had made the peak's first winter ascent. This came shortly after the late Jean-Christophe Lafaille claimed a winter ascent of the same peak on December 11, 2004; the Frenchman cited Nepal's regulations.

In Nepal the official winter season runs from December 1 to February 15, dates that contrast significantly with the accepted Northern Hemisphere calendar winter that spans from December 21 to March 20. Most climbers, and particularly those in the vanguard of serious Himalayan winter mountaineering, disagree with Nepal's rules. Prior to 2004, all winter ascents of 8,000m peaks had been done after December 21. Krzysztof Wielicki, a veteran of seven Himalayan winter expeditions, explained the Nepal Ministry of Tourism's logic for setting the date at December 1: this was to be the day when an expedition arrived at Base Camp. The arbitrarily designated departure date of February 15 may have been set because Sherpas needed a rest period before starting work in the pre-monsoon season. In Nepal there can be a world of difference between the first week in December, when it is not unusual to find conditions similar to late October, and the end of the same month, when the jet stream has lowered and snow has fallen.

LINDSAY GRIFFIN, *Mountain INFO*

Laos

The online version of these reports frequently contains additional photos, maps, topos, and extended text. Please visit aaj.americanalpineclub.org

PHA TANG MOUNTAINS

Typical scenery in the Pha Tang mountains. *Jens Richter*

White Tower, Deeper than the Day. In January–February 2008 I spent eight days during a two-week period putting up, and then trying to redpoint, a new route on an unclimbed tower at Na Pha Daeng. I eventually managed to climb the whole of the crux pitch to a point just four meters from the belay, where on relatively easy ground a handhold snapped and I fell. Out of time, I had to leave, but I was not happy with the situation. So, in December 2009, while on a climbing trip to Thailand, I returned with Philip Flaming for just three days to finish it.

The route lies on what we called the White Tower, 20km along the road north of Vang Vieng. Four years ago Vang Vieng was a quiet village, but in the intervening time it has evolved into an ugly tourist resort. The tower is easily reached via a trail across rice fields, and to its right are good sport routes on the "red walls" (Pha Daeng means red walls) put up by the German, Volker Schöffel.

The route has eight pitches, the first five from 6a+ to 6c+. Pitch six is 7a+, and pitch seven is 7c. The crux is the eighth and final pitch on the overhanging

On the overhanging headwall pitch of Deeper than the Day. *Jens Richter*

White Tower with Deeper than the Day. *Jens Richter*

Watch where you put your hands. Pitch seven of Deeper than the Day.
Jens Richter

headwall, but the highlight is undoubtedly the fourth. Here, you climb up a smooth wall to a hole, where you enter a cave and climb most of a ropelength inside the rock before emerging onto the front face again. On one of my earlier attempts I got bitten by a huge green snake, which was lying on the edge right where you stick your hand out of the cave. It jumped into the air and sidled away in the jungle below. I've never seen anything like this before. And in the big cave above pitch four we found ancient drawings on the walls.

After a long period on the incredible headwall, I finally got it at 8b. We have named the 220m route Deeper than the Day. Natural gear and some bolts were placed for protection, and we equipped the belays for rappel. It is a beautiful climb, and as far as I know the hardest multi-pitch route in Asia. For more information on Laos visit laos-climbing.com.

JENS RICHTER, *Germany*

Kyle Dempster during the first ascent of the east face of Mt. Edgar in Sichuan, China [p. 34].   *Bruce Normand*

AMERICAN ALPINE CLUB GRANTS

The American Alpine Club provides resources for climbers and explorers to attempt new challenges, conduct scientific research, and conserve mountain environments. The AAC awards more than $80,000 annually, although the size and number of awards vary from year to year. For more information on all the

Madaleine Sorkin on Women at Work, Proboscis, Canada. *Emily Stifler*

grant programs, please visit americanalpineclub.org. The information below about 2010 grant recipients and objectives was accurate at the time of the grant; in some cases, recipients may have decided to attempt other objectives. Expeditions labeled with an asterisk (*) are reported in this *Journal*.

LYMAN SPITZER CUTTING-EDGE AWARDS

Cory Richards
North face of Chamlang (7,319m), Nepal
$4,000

Freddie Wilkinson
South face of Nuptse (7,800m), Nepal
$3,000

Dylan Johnson
Seerdengpu (5,592m) north buttress, Sichuan Province, China*
$2,000

Lorna Illingworth
Free ascent of the Mt. Proboscis Original Route, Canada*
$1,500

Renan Ozturk
Tooth Traverse, Ruth Gorge, Alaska*
$1,500

MCNEILL-NOTT AWARDS

Clint Helander
Revelation Mountains, Alaska
$2,000

Nate Farr
North ridge of Mt. Ambition, Coast Mountains, Canada*
$1,500

Mike Ybarra
Singu Chuli (6,501m), Annapurna Sanctuary, Nepal
$1,500

MOUNTAIN FELLOWSHIPS (FALL 2009)

Blake Herrington (23)
Ambition, Stikine, Alaska
$900

Roberto Gonzales-Pita (21) and Greg Mionske (21)
Cordon Granito, Chile.
$800 each

Bryan Friedrichs (24)
The Tusk, Hidden Range, Alaska
$700

Ryan Huetter (25)
Cajon de los Arenales, Argentina
$400

MOUNTAIN FELLOWSHIPS (SPRING 2010)

Josh Garrison (25)
Pirate Valley, Argentina*
$700

Graham Zimmerman (24)
North face of Chamlang, Nepal
$700

Michael Royer (25)
Djangart region, Tien Shan, Kyrgyzstan*
$700

Blake Herrington (24)
Cerro Pollone, Argentina*
$500

Hayden Kennedy (20)
West face of North Howser Tower, Canada
$500

Sam Schabacker (24)
Fitz Roy's North Pillar, Argentina
$500

ZACK MARTIN BREAKING BARRIERS GRANT

Jonathan Mingle
Passive heating-cooking home, and first ski descent of Sultan Lango (19,117')
$1,800

NIKWAX ALPINE BELLWEATHER GRANT

Kevin McManigal
Glacial change, as compared to the 1910 Royal Geographic Society expedition, Turgun Mountains, Mongolia
$2,000

Ann Piersall
Glaciation and indigenous perspectives on climate change, At-Bashy Range, Tien Shan, Kyrgyzstan
$1,000

RESEARCH GRANTS

Adam Clark
Northwest Montana Summer Glacial Run-off Study
$1,000

Pete Clark
New River Gorge Climber Impact Study
$1,000

Jessica Lundin
Updated Mass Balance Measurements of Blue Glacier, Mt. Olympus, Washington
$700

Justin Stroup
Building a Climate Connection: Quelccaya Ice Cap, the Peruvian Andes—a link between Northern and Southern Hemispheres
$700

Kevin McManigal
Glacial Retreat and Impacts on Water Security, Bhutan
$700

Matthew Sanborn
Implications for Understanding High Altitude Cerebral Edema
$700

Teresa Chuang
Photography in the Sierra Nevada: Documenting Climate Change
$700

Zach Guy
The Influence of Terrain Parameters on Spatial Patterns of Snow in Steep Couloirs
$700

Ann Piersall
Glaciation and Local Perspectives in the At-Bashy Range, Kyrgyzstan
$400

Jeffrey Hallo
Visitors' and mountain guides' perceptions of bio-physical change at Mount Rainier National Park
$400

Nathan Furman
The Role of Environmental Conditions on Decisions to Ski in Avalanche Terrain
$400

Nicholas Kanaan
Prevention of Altitude Illness with Non-steroidal Anti-inflammatory Study
$400

Noah Reid
Integrating Phylogeography and Macroecology in the Study of Alpine Insect Communities
$400

Alexandra Urza
Investigating the Implications of Climate Change for the Timing and Composition of Post-disturbance Plant Reestablishment in Glacier National Park, Montana
$400

Edward Chang
8,000-meter Peak Effects on Humans
$100

BOOK REVIEWS

EDITED BY DAVID STEVENSON

Desert Towers: Fat Cat Summits and Kitty Litter Rock. **Steve "Crusher" Bartlett. Sharp End Publishing, 2010. Color photos. Hardcover. $49.95.**

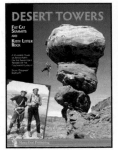

As climbers craving a fix, we accept almost any writing if we cannot get to the rock. A few sexy pictures and a few words about grunting up 5.hard, and we set literary standards aside. We lap up writing we would not accept in another genre. Let there be a story about rock or ice, with a picture or two, and our critical facilities get tossed aside.

But once in a long time something is published that not only gives us our fix when the weather keeps us indoors, but actually has literary or historical or visual merit. Think of the writing of W.H. Murray in *Mountaineering in Scotland*. The history in books like Chris Jones' *Climbing in North America* or Doug Scott's *Big Wall Climbing* or Roper's *Camp 4*. Or the visual appeal of your favorite coffee table climbing porn. Then think about how wonderful a book would be that combines all three merits—well-written, visually stunning, and bringing to life the climbing history of a uniquely important region. Crusher Bartlett's *Desert Towers* comes as close to that ideal as any climbing book I can think of.

Its 350 pages cover the history of desert tower climbing in the Southwest, from John Otto's ladder of steel pipes leading to the summit of Independence Monument in 1911 to today's 5.13 free climbs. In addition to Bartlett's own narrative, *Desert Towers* is graced with stories by 27 desert rats ranging from Raffi Beydan's "Shiprock Finale" (originally published in 1940 in *Trail and Timberline*, the Colorado Mountain Club's journal) to Jason Haas's "Free Cottontail" (an account of the 2009 first free ascent of West Side Story, written for *Desert Towers*). Included are some classic desert stories, including Chuck Pratt's "The View From Dead Horse Point." But Bartlett has also unearthed a few new gems—stories as good as or better than the famous tales. Other than his omission of anything by my favorite desert writer, Dave Insley, I have nothing but praise for these selections.

The history doesn't end there. More than reprinting some existing stories and retelling others in his own words, Bartlett has interviewed desert climbers from all eras. We meet them as real people, hearing their tales as if at a campfire or a pub.

A final word on history: The issue of banned climbing on Navajo lands figures prominently. But in addition to the usual complaints by climbers, *Desert Towers* devotes five pages to the Navajo perspective. Those five pages alone are worth the price of the book. They should be required reading for every climber who visits the desert.

Desert Towers is full of stunning images. The book is big (9" x 12"), and many photographs are given a full page or even two pages. While we have come to expect "historical" photos to include amateurish head and butt shots, in this case the author has dug up photos that are of real historical interest while at the same time being strong images.

Finally, the writing: Given that *Desert Towers* is fundamentally a history of one specific area, it could easily have been boring. That it is interesting and entertaining from the first word to the last is a tribute both to Bartlett's own writing ability and to his skill at weaving together the tales of others.

> *Consider how difficult it must be to write anything fresh about landscape near the end of a 350-page volume in which you and others have described that landscape a hundred times already. We wandered through an immense, colorful maze. Above was hard blue sky, porcelain brittle. The sun, already fierce, slowly ascended its grand arc over the distant La Sal Mountains. To left and right, cliffs and buttresses were daubed with impasto stripes of chocolate, cinnamon, marzipan, vanilla, and coffee. We wandered under flying saucers, balanced on immense spindly pillars. We were in Van Gogh's head, looking out at his demons.*

No doubt *Desert Towers* leaves out something important or gets a date or a name wrong. Someone more familiar with the history of climbing on the Colorado Plateau may spot errors that escaped me. But no history is either complete or completely accurate. I suspect this one comes closer to those ideals than any other. It is entertaining, informative, and beautiful. It contributes meaningfully to the historical record. And it even comes close to explaining how seemingly sane men and women could convince themselves that groveling up a filthy, desperately dangerous curtain of mud for five days, at the rate of 60 or 80 feet per day, is worth doing. Not just once, but over and over again. This is a truly magical book.

DAVID HARRIS

The Last Man on the Mountain: The Death of an American Adventurer on K2. **Jennifer Jordan. W. W. Norton, 2010. 302 pages. Black & white photos. Hardcover. $26.95.**

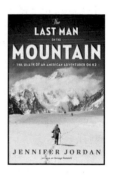

Dudley Wolfe, who died high on K2 during the 1939 American expedition, has been neglected and patronized. He has been portrayed as clumsy and overweight, an aristocrat invited to the mountain because of his wealth. While his sturdiness on the peak has evoked admiration, it has often been accompanied by the charge that he was virtually hauled up by the exceptionally strong leader, Fritz Wiessner. But this is only a partial view. Jennifer Jordan has provided the fullest portrait yet of Dudley Wolfe; we are in her debt for this account.

Dudley Wolfe emerges from her book as a gentle and generous man—and unfulfilled. In World War I, "While other men were shooting themselves in the foot or leg to get out of combat, Dudley volunteered for some of the worst duty possible." After the war he returned to Harvard, became a skilled yachtsman, and started to climb. He married athletic and wealthy Alice Damrosch, who seemed the perfect match. But there was something unsettled in Dudley, and he sought to end the marriage before he accepted Wiessner's invitation to K2.

On the mountain, his performance belied his weak reputation, and even his detractors liked him. Except for Wiessner, he was the only American to climb high, where he stayed in good health and spirits for many weeks. Finally the altitude caught up with him. He died alone in his tent at nearly 25,000 feet. His remains were eventually swept down to the base of the mountain, where Jennifer Jordan found them in 2002.

The descriptions of Wolfe are the best thing in Jordan's book. Her account of the climb itself is questionable. The recriminations over this expedition were bitter and reverberate to this day, even after the death of all the participants. Almost everyone has been blamed for the bitter outcome, in which Wolfe and three Sherpas died. But beside the picture of Wolfe, Jordan has not much to add to this sad story. She relates the climb vividly, and the book is extremely readable, but the readability comes at a price. She rarely tells us where her dramatizations come from. Her Preface says that she uses "direct quotes, which I gathered from journals, letters, books, and witnesses," and italicized conjectured speech and thoughts. One can't quarrel with the italics, but other quotations are infrequently documented, rarely supported by a footnote. There are unquoted passages such as: "Tony [Cromwell] strutted about, officiously checking his clipboard...." Strutting, officiously—says who?

At times Jordan's grasp of mountaineering history and practices seems uncertain. Some errors are minor, but it is unsettling to read of climbers rappelling each other down a cliff. And does she think that Bill House led his famous chimney, in 1938, without a rope? (He even placed pitons.) Jordan describes this alleged achievement as a "free ascent," but one wonders how she defines the term. Earlier she writes of a climb being done "'free'—without protective gear anchoring them to the rock."

In view of the continuing rancor over this expedition, it is unfortunate that Jordan's text nowhere engages its most significant predecessor: *K2, The 1939 Tragedy*, by Kauffman and Putnam (1992). She lists it in her bibliography and has Putnam on her interview list, but her only references to the authors omit even their names. That book, which is far better documented than Jordan's, springs from a disillusionment with Wiessner, about whom the authors had planned a biography, and a corresponding resurrection of the reputation of Jack Durrance. Durrance had long been blamed for stripping the mountain of its supplies, with fatal consequences. Relying heavily upon Durrance's recently revealed diaries, Kauffman and Putnam place the blame elsewhere, partly upon Wiessner himself. But if they are critical of Wiessner, Jordan is much more so. She acknowledges his prodigious climbing skills. Otherwise she sees him as an autocratic womanizer who wants the summit so that he can be famous and marry a wealthy widow. To be sure, there are no American heroes in Jordan's book, except Wolfe. Durrance comes off badly, too. Apart from his selfless ministrations to an ill teammate, he is depicted as childish and self-absorbed and, like Wiessner, turning scant thought to Wolfe once he had been given up for lost.

Durrance's role is puzzling. He had the strongest record of anyone but Wiessner yet felt repudiated by him from their first shipboard contact on the way to India. Kauffman and Putnam state that the two men had never met before, but Jordan points to an earlier training weekend in the Shawangunks. She argues that Wiessner was keen to have Durrance on K2, even if disappointed by the withdrawal of the strong Bestor Robinson. In any case, the two men become estranged, though less during the expedition than in its apparently endless aftermath. Durrance was forever scarred; one of the saddest parts of the book is the account of his later years.

The 1939 disaster is less mysterious than controversial. We know a lot more about what happened to Wolfe and the heroic Sherpas who tried to save him than we do about Mallory and Irvine on Everest, or Boardman and Tasker on the same peak years later. What is uncertain about K2 in 1939 is less what was done than why. Why was Wolfe left at Camp VII after so many days at altitude? Why did Cromwell (apparently) order that lower camps be stripped? Why did so many of the party leave base camp before everyone was accounted for? And why did Durrance withhold his diary for so many years?

There is one tantalizing conjecture: What if, on that fateful July 19, Wiessner had turned right onto the ice instead of left onto the rocks? The route he rejected became the regular one. Wiessner and Pasang Lama would almost surely have made the top, which would have been an astonishing achievement at a time when no other 8,000-meter peak had been climbed. Then they would have escorted Wolfe down to base camp, and we would not still be arguing about what happened and why. Wiessner thought the ice route, now known as the Bottleneck, to be dangerous. He was right: A serac collapse there in 2008 led to many more fatalities than were incurred in 1939. But he might well have reached the summit.

We may never have a truly definitive account of this fateful climb. Jordan's is certainly not it. But the book paints a comprehensive and endearing picture of Dudley Wolfe, a picture long overdue.

STEVEN JERVIS

One Mountain Thousand Summits, The Untold Story of Tragedy and True Heroism on K2. Freddie Wilkinson. New American Library, 2010. 342 pages. Hardcover. $24.95.

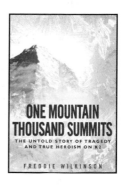

If you're a reader of this journal, you know that K2 has some of the most storied literature in the canon of mountaineering. So why would anyone write another book on K2? Is there anything new to be told? We certainly don't need another pompous rehashing full of self-aggrandizement. Let me say right away, then, that this is a fantastic book. Freddie Wilkinson takes on an audacious objective and creates a truly engaging work. This book is in the top five of books written about K2, and is the best book I've seen about the current state of 8,000m climbing. That Wilkinson is a world class climber and conscientious working reporter adds tremendously. When he writes about hypoxia, exposure, knots, and cold fingers, he knows the ropes.

On the surface this book is about one of the deadliest events in Himalayan climbing. On August 1, 2008, more than three dozen climbers from 13 different countries left high camp for the summit. By the end of the next day 11 had perished. The author deciphers the tragic developments with the precision of an investigative detective. I can only imagine the volume of notes Wilkinson had to take, and I envision him trying to fit an oversized white board into his tiny New England cabin.

The tragic events of August 2, 2008, played out in living rooms around the world in almost real time, as satellite calls were made and web pages updated. There was a frenzy of Internet-driven media attention that ended up in major magazines and networks around the globe. Unfortunately, and predictably, no one could see the whole picture or know all the details. It's like when you're climbing in the dark and your world is only the jumping shadows in your headlamp's beam. Piecing together disparate reports from hasty reporting and foggy recollections is the author's greatest challenge. This quest consumed him for more than a year, as he pored through documentation and visited the survivors in order to ferret out what really happened.

The narrative includes captivating, sweaty-palm-inducing descriptions of serac falls, open bivouacs, black toes, and the angst of personal loss. But this book is much more than that. Wilkinson takes the sharp end and honestly, truthfully, and accurately describes the complex relationships between professional climbers, amateurs, clients, high-altitude porters, and climbing Sherpas. Beside the dynamics of current-era climbing expeditions, we also learn a diverse set of facts from Korean history to the workings of the Nepali school system to cognitive science.

These are not distracting but lend credence, context, and depth to the discussion at hand.

But primarily this is a story that delves deeply into the hubris, ethics, and racism that is consuming modern mountaineering. One of the thorniest questions is, what is a hero? Who were the heroes of that tragic event—were there any true heroes at all? As Wilkinson states, history is written by the white guys with the sat phones and the blogs.

Like a good climbing route, this book is honest, fearless, passionate, relentless, direct, and fully captivating.

CHARLEY MACE

Fail Falling. Royal Robbins. California: Pink Mountain Press, 2010. 190 pages. Paperback. $19.95.

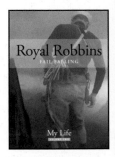

Royal Robbins is writing his life story, and what a story it is. The whole project will stretch over eight chronologically ordered volumes. This one goes from 1950 to 1957; in that time Robbins becomes a legit climber. He starts with top-roping and small boulders, but by 1957 he's putting up the Northwest Face route on Half Dome. Along the way there's stirring climbing, life as a high school dropout in a fatherless household, car crashes, and Los Angeles in the blazing fifties.

The title of Volume Two is *Fail Falling*, which is not just a bold approach to climbing, but Robbins' credo. It means trusting yourself to succeed. He explains that "attitude makes all the difference between success and failure." His life story certainly demonstrates the benefit of grit and enthusiasm (along with really good balance). The book's many photos give you a lot of ropes tied around waists, trailing straight and clean through space, the only protection the gleam in the climber's eye. And these are first ascents done in sneakers—you'll see them wearing Chuck Taylors, not my first choice for the Steck-Salathé, but that's how Robbins did it. And with his introductions of fellow climbers from the era, a community comes alive.

Fail Falling is best in its extended descriptions of memorable climbs like the Northwest Face. Robbins can craft a narrative with depth of character and uncertainty of outcome. We can then sit back while his memory returns to the rock he consumed with ferocious skill. Robbins has the spotlight throughout but is generous in praise for the many people who helped him succeed. He makes it clear that his early climbing was enabled by a social structure that's no longer influential in American climbing: the climbing club. Robbins got his start with the Rock Climbing Section of the Sierra Club, which offered tutelage to beginners, guidance to youths, and organized outings for all. His subsequent prominence as an environmentalist-climber—he advanced the clean-climbing movement in word with *Basic Rockcraft* and in deed with the Nutcracker—likely owes much to this provenance. Robbins' evolution embodies John Muir's dream that the Sierra Club outings would take urban citizens into the wild and inspire them to take the wild under their protection back in the city. In *Fail Falling* the virtuous cycle from wild experience to environmental ethics spans the era of Yosemite's Golden Age.

Fail Falling brings to mind the old paradox, "Great men make history. History makes great men." Should we praise the individual for achieving in the circumstances, or recognize the circumstances that elevated the individual? The fifties and sixties combined the technological revolution of nylon ropes and lighter gear with an unprecedented expansion of disposable income and inexpensive transportation. *Fail Falling* shows that Robbins' generation and the Baby Boomers right behind it were in the right place at the right time to scoop what the circumstances gifted them and get credit for doing it. *Fail Falling* also shows a few heroic men and women grasping their moment and blowing through the limits that restrain the rest of us. Robbins is such a hero.

Fail Falling shares a remarkable story. Robbins' early days run on the jet fuel of enthusiasm, and these pages reveal a unique spirit to his life that can possess and inspire the willing reader.

JEFF MCCARTHY

Climbing—Philosophy for Everyone: Because It's There. **Stephen E. Schmid, ed. Foreword by Hans Florine. Wiley-Blackwell, 2010. 256 pages. Paperback. $19.95**

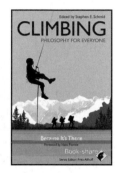

Eric Shipton once said "climbing is a form of philosophy," or something like that. His philosophy was a wooly mix of Emersonian transcendentalism and nature worship—pretty much what most of us subscribe to. But you'll not find any of it in this collection of 17 essays by contemporary professional philosophers—nor by the writer-climbers mimicking their style. In his introduction editor Stephen F. Schmid, a devotee of Ayn Rand, whose Objectivism is hardly everyone's idea of philosophy, declares that his goal is to pose "intriguing questions that make philosophy interesting and exceptionally so when applied to the activity of climbing." But most of the questions raised cover familiar ground: the justification of risk, the pursuit of virtue or character, and thumb-sucking on ethics. This may have been no bad thing had the philosophical perspective yielded originality. But there is too little of that. I felt as if I'd landed in the same old climbers' bar, thrashing the same old conversations about reasons *why?*, the same natter on bolting, trad vs sport, only this time with guys with a compulsion to stick Wittgenstein, Hegel, John Stuart Mill, Locke, Aristotle into their shop talk. I give Schmid high marks for intellectual audacity. His attempt to shoehorn the ideas of great philosophers into a sporting activity that requires no self-knowledge—the lack of which may improve performance (action at its purest)—is riskier than climbing the Eiger wearing flipflops.

The few creditable pieces in this collection make their point without belaboring ties to the philosopher pantheon. "From Route Finding to Redpointing: Climbing Culture as a Gift Economy," by Debora Halbert, is a fine discussion of the value created by new routes and how they are unique objects—never mind that gift economy is an old idea in anthropology and not philosophy. Another piece I liked looked at the climber's access to his or her inner mental states and the unreliability of remembered impressions. Stephen M. Downes in "Are You Experienced?" references psychological experiments that illuminate how we are not as we seem to ourselves. "Consider another familiar predicament: you reach the anchors of a route and while clipping in declare 'That felt easy.' Everyone watching, including your nervous belayer, witnessed a desperate by-the-skin-of-your-teeth, wobbler of an ascent. Were you experiencing what it feels like for a climb to feel easy?" He warns us to be aware of the unreliability of our impressions and to get feedback from others and, further, that "failure to remember can easily be understood as a failure to access an inner state." This trait, he surmises, explains the wide prevalence of inaccurate reporting of first ascents and of post-accident narratives.

In "Why Climb?" analytic philosopher Joe Fitschen explores evolutionary explanations of the question that never dies. He warns against a teleological approach, i.e., that climbing serves a purpose, fits a grand design, and by his whimsical approach to the material, he cautions us not to take the climbing-philosophy connection too seriously. In "Jokers on the Mountain: In Defense of Gratuitous Risk," Heidi Howkins Lockwood does a good job making distinctions between ineliminable types of risk and elective risk-taking in climbing. Society puts climbers in the position of justifying risk as if it were their primary pursuit, when in fact risk is not an end in itself.

The essay that is most genuinely philosophical and yet bears down with immense authority on a vital climbing issue is William Ramsey's "Hold Manufacturing: Why You May Be Wrong About What's Right." This is a tour de force of the modern analytic methods applied to a problem in practical ethics: lucid, candid, reasoned with a fine razor. Here is the gist of the matter: "The reason hold manufacturing still occurs in the preparation of many routes despite its widespread condemnation is because the condemnation itself is not properly justified." He then goes through arguments pro and con with careful and consistent reasoning and, half a dozen pages later, winds up with an analysis that suggests that at least in some circumstances, which he explores in detail, manufacturing can be philosophically defensible.

I was surprised that there is no mention of the one philosopher of note who was also a magnificent climber, Arne Naess, and of the omission of Nietzsche, a big influence (for good and bad) on the climbing zeitgeist of the 20th century (case in point: überman Dougal Haston). Nor of later philosophies that speak to climbing: e.g., the limit or edge philosophy of men like Jaspers and Heidegger, Bataille, and Foucault. Instead, the chief authorities, who get mentioned every sixth page, are not philosophers at all, but Tejada-Flores and his "Games Climbers Play" and Frost and Chouinard, with their famous 1974 testament on clean climbing. So Lito, Tom, Yvon, how do you feel about being caught in this kind of company? Proud? Embarrassed? Indifferent?

JOHN THACKRAY

***Ron Fawcett Rock Athlete*. Ron Fawcett, with Ed Douglas. Vertebrate Publishing, 2010. 256 pages. Color photographs. Hardcover. £20.00.**

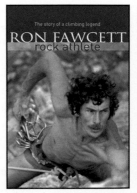

Strawberries, Lord of the Flies, The Cad. These routes are synonymous with bold standard-pushing and with Ron Fawcett in the 1970s and early 80s. In this autobiography, Fawcett depicts his beginnings as a cad making the first ascent of England's Mulatto Wall to his years working in the entertainment industry. Along the way, Fawcett pioneered the life of a professional climber.

"I just wanted to find the edge I'd felt that I'd lost," Fawcett writes in the opening chapter, "A Century of Extremes." Fawcett planned to climb 100 extreme routes in a day. After a lifetime on the rock, his lost edge was still sharp somewhere inside him, and his ability remained strong through an epically long day, as he ascended 3,957 feet and traveled 12 miles on foot between crags. "For almost twenty years I'd spent every waking moment either climbing or thinking about it.... I'd given pretty much everything I had to the sport. What did I have left?" He lived and breathed climbing, an obsession that comes with its costs. His lifestyle contributed to breaking his marriage. When his wife moved away from the outdoors, toward dinner parties, theater, "situations that were not my natural habitat," Fawcett couldn't move with her. "She was becoming connected to a world that filled me with dread." These difficulties are what transformed him into the *Rock Athlete*.

For the filming of *Rock Athlete*, a movie watched by millions on BBC, Fawcett walked away with a new pair of EBs and the paltry sum of 80 pounds. His life as the star of the landmark documentary was not an easy one. He put himself in dangerous positions not just for himself but for his livelihood. He felt at odds with his role. More than that was the shy man's ego in the public view. While climbing Lord of the Flies for the film, Fawcett uttered, "C'mon arms, do your stuff." The phrase was heard at pubs across the world, and climbers emulated Fawcett with their talk of "crozzly pockets" and other Fawcett-speak. "I felt deeply self-conscious at the best of times, and found generating media interest embarrassing," he writes about his film life. Fawcett's life in the public eye seemed more out of necessity than desire. "I felt confident in my own ability, but putting myself on a pedestal made me uncomfortable. I had too thin a skin for the flak it drew." Fawcett loved the climbing, though, and the experiences. It wasn't about the job or the fame but about the experiences and the friends.

The absurdity of his climbing life, of traveling across the globe to meet fellow climbers, comes out in his dry wit. At Camp VI on the Nose, John Long and Fawcett dangled their feet off the ledge. The pair climbed the route in a speedy day and a half, stopping to rest for the night on the ledge, where they stuffed themselves with hard-boiled eggs. In a wild attempt to stave off dehydration, Long added salt to their water. "A lot of salt," Fawcett emphasizes. Early in his climbing life, young friends of Fawcett's rappelled off the ends of their ropes. The first broke his legs. The second broke his wrists. The pair struggled to a nearby farm, where the fellow with the broken wrists knocked on the door with his head. With subtle humor Fawcett describes the climbing life and takes a bit of the edge off the danger and stress of his lifestyle.

Fawcett's life on the rocks was a remarkable one. Later he shifted toward running. "When you've been very good at something, when it's been the purpose of your whole existence, it feels odd carrying it on at a lower standard." Fawcett's move toward running was a way to fight off depression, to numb his mind. After his daughter's mother left him, running became the only time when he could forget his pain. Ultimately, both climbing and running provided a deeper fulfillment in his life. "But through it all I needed that sense of space and freedom to be myself, and that's as true now as it was then," he reflects. Fawcett's autobiography depicts a man in constant search of space and freedom. As much as he finds them, he continues to search for more. His constant search made him a great climber and, more than that, a great man.

JAMES LUCAS

The Sunny Top of California: Sierra Nevada Poems and a Story. Norman Schaefer. La Alameda Press, 2010. 120 pages. Paperback. $14.00.

The Sunny Top of California
SIERRA NEVADA POEMS & A STORY
Norman Schaefer

> *A poem is like a Chinese fortune cookie: surprise and insight,*
> *wrapped inside a small mystery.*
> *The joyous hardship of climbing a peak*
> *For a clear far view*

Climbing poems are so rare—odd, even—that it helps, it's reassuring, when a poet like Norman Schaefer has chalk under his fingernails and real gobies from firing V4s. You gain some trust when his shoulders are sore from dropping his pack at timberline: this guy speaks our language. The edge of each line may be ragged, but its knot is tight:

> *Blue lakes with golden trout,*
> *Meadows and all their flowers,*
> *Granite that won't break*
> *When you pull down hard.*

A century and a half is all that white guys have been tromping the Sierra. Mountaineers who write down words about it are just a blink to the melting glaciers. The Paiutes before us spoke only in footpath and sweat lodge, and before them there's nothing but mute, powerful scratchings, storied into soft volcanic rock near the Happy Boulders. Puzzled, we retreat to our own time of words, brief as Schaefer's "paper-thin silver crescent" rising barely before dawn.

Within our span here, already Jack Kerouac and Gary Snyder climbing Matterhorn Peak together in the fifties—that's a third of the way back to our white kin's 49er dawn in the Sierra. Yet I can't shake their influence (happy not to, really), and I notice that Schaefer can't either. Thanks to the Beats we sound more like T'ang Dynasty Zen Lunatics dancing over ragged cliffs than we do like Paiutes or even the crag rats in our own lineage like John Muir:

> *I lift a cup of tea to the alpenglow*
> *and clear autumn morning,*
> *alone, happy,*
> *thirty miles from a road.*

That's "shack simple" in the words of the Beat poet Lew Welch. To catch its mood, where the simplest things become poignant, it helps to be emptied of action-figure busyness and filled instead with a receptive stillness, as you are after climbing, after exhausting yourself on terrain. Poems are quick hits, a distilled essence. You'd think they would get more popular in a distractible, sound-bite age. But no, nowadays poets mostly talk to other poets:

> *Awareness blossoms everywhere*
> *This lake knows I'm here.*
> *I thought I heard a voice on Diamond Mesa:*
> *"Forget yourself and you're free."*

Tune in, I urge you. It will be illuminating. A slim volume in the pack, poetry is Light & Fast. Best of all, take these poems back to from where they came. Read them up high, in the alpine zone. Sure to produce shouts of joy.

DOUG ROBINSON

Unexpected: Thirty Years Of Patagonia Catalog Photography. **Jane Sievert and Jennifer Ridgeway, eds. Patagonia Books, 2010. 213 pages. Hardcover. $49.00.**

The photographs collected here are beautiful and inspiring.

We all know in our cynical little hearts that these photographs have some dark connection to advertising, *branding*, marketing, and all that stuff about which I know nothing and will not address further, except to say that the Patagonia catalogs have long been portraying a lifestyle, and the stuff they sell by association would be, in their view, good stuff to acquire in pursuit of that lifestyle. Everyone gets it.

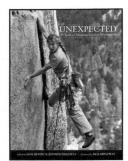

What the book makes clear, in its essays and in the photos themselves, is that the best criterion for getting into the catalog is that the editors will know *it* when they see *it*. Founding photo editor Jennifer Ridgeway's essay, "Capture a Patagoniac," ends with the famous dictum, "What we really want (well, what Yvon really wants) is Dr. Hunter S. Thompson dressed in a Pataloha Fish and Tits shirt, cigarette holder in mouth, and a visor down over his eyes, shooting pool with Ted Kennedy." (This essay is described as "classic" in the book itself; I concur.) The statement, of course, is just a stance; none of the photos really aspire to this. They do aspire to Yvon's other dictum, "real people doing real things." The only false step here for me is when that "law" appears to be broken, which isn't often: for instance, the photo of a glamorous blonde woman leaning against a 1957 Beaver, applying lipstick. *Please*.

There are occasions when, if you think about it too much, the photograph feels posed (*posing, as we all know, is evil*). But usually the photograph is so good you either aren't conscious of the probability of its having been posed, or you just don't care. Take the famous cover shot of Lynn Hill hanging off the jug on Insomnia. Okay, it's a fine photograph … but wait a minute, Ridgeway happened to be right there to take it, and how many times had Hill done the route? That's one in which my cynical brain interferes with my aesthetic appreciation. I would much rather see Steve House's summit photo of Vince Anderson after doing the Rupal Face—you *know* that sucker wasn't rehearsed. And that was a Patagonia catalog photo that's not in the book. Perhaps my appreciation of it depends too much on its outside-the-frame context—something I just happen to know.

To repeat: The photographs are beautiful and inspiring. Many have acquired iconic stature and exist in my memory apart from the occasion of my first seeing them in a catalog. With the book not in front of me, I wondered how many of the hundred I could describe. I named five off the top of my head that I love:

> • *The opening overleaf of the dusty car in the pampas on the way to the Fitz Roy massif (although I was wrong in remembering it as a Funhog photo; it's a Barbara Rowell shot).*
> • *Roman Dial's shot of a smiling Carl Tobin, nose bloodied, ferrying his bike across some raging current.*
> • *John Sherman's beer-swilling free-solo in flip-flops, which I've always been a fool for, though everyone knows he was clipped in. That's not, and never was, the point.*
> • *Meredith Wiltsie, head in hands, car broke down, child playing with a hammer. Been there, done that.*
> • *Chouinard himself on ice in full Sco'ish conditions. (My memory was wrong again: it's a Chouinard photo of Doug Tompkins.)*

See what I mean? You probably don't have the book in front of you now, either, but you know you've seen several of those shots before.

In addition to Jennifer Ridgeway's classic essay, all the writing is up to speed. I liked the interview with John Russell, whose images had registered with me in the past but not his name (probably because he's not a climber). And it's always good to hear from John Sherman, though one doesn't know whether to be happy or sad that he seems to still be living in his van. Cory Richards' short essay, "Perspective," is an absolutely first-rate rendering of the artist's long road.

Looking at the photos, I discovered surprising aspects of my own tastes: liked a lot of the kid photos, didn't care too much for animal shots, liked the ocean and surfing shots, (though I almost never go there and don't surf). Despite a longstanding admiration for the work of Greg Epperson and Cory Richards, the climbing shots didn't do as much for me as I thought they might.

Everyone with a pulse will have their favorites; if at least two big handfuls of these photos don't work for you, there's probably not much hope: try a blood transfusion or at least get up off that couch.

DAVID STEVENSON

Grasping for Heaven: Interviews with North American Mountaineers. **Frederic Hartemann and Robert Hauptman. Foreword by Jan Reynolds. McFarland & Company, Inc., 2010. 224 pages. Paperback. $35.00.**

This book transcribes conversations with 16 climbers and three historians, almost all North American and Himalayan mountaineers. The conversations are interesting because the persons being interviewed are accomplished and articulate and because Hauptman, who conducts the interviews, is generally very well informed, that is, well read in mountaineering history, and this keeps the discussions at a reasonably sophisticated level.

I like the book best when we hear from folks who have until now more or less slipped under my radar: Charlotte Fox—I love her takes on Jon Krakauer and on Sandy Pitman—the late Christine Boskoff, and Carlos Buehler, for example.

Likewise, I very much enjoyed the inclusion of Elizabeth Hawley, Maurice Isserman, and Audrey Salkeld (who together raise questions about the *mountaineer* and *North American* in the subtitle). Although Hawley is the subject of a recent book by Bernadette McDonald (who is flatteringly mentioned enough times to deserve her own interview), she is not someone whose own voice has been widely heard until recently.

Isserman comes across as particularly wise, reminding me to return to his excellent Himalayan history, *Fallen Giants*, co-authored with Stewart Weaver. Discussing why so many Himalayan peaks were first climbed in the 1950s instead of the 1930s he observes that "mountaineers were willing to assume greater levels of risk than were previously thought appropriate…. What's a poor decision for one generation of climbers has proven to be within the spectrum of acceptable risk for later generations."

The average age of the interviewees is 63; thus the lens is mostly retrospective. Furthermore, quite of few of these subjects have written books of their own or had books written about them or both. Perhaps the *mountaineer* in the subtitle is a tip-off to some kind of generational divide: who thinks of themselves as *mountaineers* today? I doubt that Steve House does, but then he's not included here. In fact, I was surprised (maybe a little *alarmed*) when Hauptman admitted that he hadn't heard of House and Vince Anderson's Rupal Face climb. I suppose this speaks to the book's generally historical, rather than contemporary, perspective.

Question: What do these have in common: Mount Si, James Tabor, Nanga Parbat, Willi Unsoeld, Grand Jorasses, Les Droites?

Answer: They're all misspelled in the book. It seems doubtful to me that Hauptman himself does not know the correct spelling of these, so, can we no longer get an editor or proof-reader who knows or will learn these things? I fear this situation will only worsen in the future.

Many of the subjects are, well, the *usual subjects*, climbers who have been in the spotlight (our somewhat dim spotlight, anyway) for a long time: Roskelley, Ridgeway, Houston, Wick-wire. These are, of course, some of the most interesting and storied fellows in our pantheon, but we know their stories, don't we? There is perhaps a hint of diplomacy or perspective from them here that may have been absent when we last heard from them. Like any good book, one of the effects of this one is to remind the reader to return to some of these subjects' earlier works, and, my quibbles aside, I expect to return to this book in the future as well.

DAVID STEVENSON

Pilgrims of the Vertical: Yosemite Rock Climbers and Nature at Risk. **Joseph E Taylor III. Harvard University Press, 2010. 384 pages. Hardcover. $29.95.**

Taylor's unique book stems from an earlier article that has evolved to 276 pages, with another 72 of notes. *Pilgrims* is intended as both a detailed climbing history and an environmental essay. We traverse a myriad of anecdotes and details as climbing mutates from Victorian beginnings through bucolic Sierra Club stewardship to the extreme sacred practices of our current vanguard. Few have worked this hard to write the Ameri-can Climbing Story. The text is strongest and most interesting as a stan-dard history, specifically up to about 1960. Bringing us to the current day, the second half is more ambitious and apparently difficult for Taylor to resolve. He is a bit of a climber but more an environmental historian. Accordingly, Taylor is trying for much more than climbing history.

He sketches how climbing has mirrored the general social forces of each era. In recent decades top participants—think Robbins or Harding—have helped foster a seldom-questioned image of climbing as rebellious but also elitist. The story behind this essentially Romantic image presents many serious issues. Taylor holds all accountable in a sympathetic and humor-ous near-polemic, while warning of climbing's heavy use of the natural world—the pinning out of cracks, climbers' trails, uncontrolled camps, chalk on everything, crowds abounding.

Taylor loves to point out how in the Sierra Club days climbing was vigorously heterosocial, but when the new assumption of risk reached serious extreme, women were whisked out of "harm's way" in a Byronic runaway toward chimerical icons on high. Taylor then shifts gears from his rigorous, friendly perspective on our early years to a more skeptical gaze at modern climbers, which may be more emotional on his part. His sympathy ends; he smells a rat.

According to Taylor, climbers began to feel that authentic experience is based on the proposi-tion that only risk and suffering bring genuine "passage," and that passage is the point. Risk and suf-fering become an ideal, rather than a ubiquitous but temporary part of growing up and of the cycle the individual takes in his society everywhere. He admits having bought into such rites of passage as a youth, and even today they retain "latently powerful" influences on him. He assures us, however, that these fallacious ideals are easily "unmasked" once one understands what props them up: "false promises, elitist privilege, and a sense of entitlement." And here is where the real fight begins, with Taylor's deconstruction and dismissal of the Romantic heritage of risk—a heritage that is especially integral to the conventional narrative of climbing today. Perception of risk, often curiously flawed when one examines actuarial tables, is a subject dear to the hearts of many climbers. Taylor makes some excellent criticisms, but in the end his analysis is unconvincing.

His claims regarding the environmental costs of climbing are not established or convincing, either. They read more as stipulated bulwarks dramatized for his arguments. For the reader the damage and depletion remains apocryphal. All the bolt holes and pin scars in Yosemite occupy less volume than a dozen copies of his hardback. Trails worn down by climbers' access, lichen scraped off walls, and dirt dug from cracks are all renewable and represent less biomass than a hundred yards of landscaped highway median.

In the final sentences all Taylor can offer is that sustainability and balance in future climbing might be reached by "restrained" use, which would be "respectable," and we would thereby "grow up." Concluding, he affirms that risk culture is an illusion, and that our ideal-ization of the Wild, with the elite individual center-pieced within it, is a deeply flawed vision. It's an end-of-days outlook. As a history, however, *Pilgrims of the Vertical* is one of our best. *[Editor's note: an AAJ editor who has read this book found it to be riddled with historical errors.]*

PETER HAAN

In Memoriam

In Memoriam

Edited by Cameron M. Burns

Ross Bronson, 1946–2010

We now-graying mountaineers remember well the climbing days with our Ross Bronson of yore: confident, skilled, and ever of good humor. Ross came into climbing more than 40 years ago, before almost anyone I queried can remember. Hiram Connell recalls that in 1966 Ross and his friend Bob Seymour were already active in their club's climbing group. There is no Boston climber active today who predates him. Throughout the 1970s he grew into an important rope leader, an active member of the Appalachian Mountain Club Mountaineering Committee, and one of the established New England climbing clan. Competent on rock, snow,

Ross Bronson. *Bill Atkinson*

and ice, Ross ventured as far away as the Teton and Wind River Ranges and the Bugaboos in British Columbia. Every Club climbing program beginner of that decade will remember Ross as a competent mentor and instructor. Over a span of 25 years some 2,500 trainees felt the jolting heft of the 125-pound "bucket" that Ross fashioned for us in 1968.

Ross was a generous, smart, and diffident guy, who managed an independent and productive life from hard physical effort, an honest business sense, and the employment of his climbing expertise as a safe and skillful tree surgeon; over the years he took down a half-a-dozen major monsters in my yard alone.

He sacrificed much during his years as the caregiver for his aging parents, after whose passing Ross became the long-time companion and chauffeur to an elderly friend and neighbor. Climbing, and its community, has lent sharpness and meaning to many an otherwise unfocussed life—many more lives saved than were shortened by it. Ross was one of those rescued, at least for a while. So sad that he drifted away from the heights so early, for I think they might have sustained him longer than they did, maybe long enough ultimately to have saved him from his demons.

Bill Atkinson

Rich Jack, 1948–2010

In 1987 I was the rock-climbing director of a Boy Scout Ranch outside of Fort Collins. I needed to hire a couple of climbers to set up top-ropes, so I put up a notice at the climbing store and met with a tall, blond guy the next day.

"And what qualifies you to set up top-ropes?" I asked.

Rich Jack smiled and gave me his AAC climbing resume, which consisted of 25 to 30 big walls. I hired him on the spot. As I was to find out, Rich was not only an expert big-wall and rock climber, but a

Rich Jack. *CJ Joplin*

balls-out skier, pedal-to-the-metal mountain biker, and ultra-competent ice climber. His wacky sense of humor and buoyant spirit inspired me, as well as the scouts. I can still hear the laugh he'd give when he got in a tense situation—whoooooaahhhhh.

A native of Minnesota, Rich climbed extensively in Yosemite in the 1970s. He and Lou Dawson did their first El Capitan route, the Dihedral Wall, in 1973. The hardest thing they did together was the second ascent of the Hallucinogen Wall in the Black Canyon of the Gunnison River in 1981. At the time it was the hardest aid climb in the Black, and had such a scary aura that no one wanted to repeat it. Rich was always proud of being part of the duo that took some of the foreboding away by doing the second ascent. Another of his accomplishments was a first ascent, the Dawson-Jack Route on the Diamond on the east face of Longs Peak in Rocky Mountain National Park, in the summer of 1975.

His adventurous spirit took him to the Canadian Rockies to ice climb, to Moab to mountain bike, and to Crested Butte and Aspen to ski. Professionally, he was a highly respected critical-care nurse and supervisor in the Intensive Care Unit at Boulder Community Hospital for over 20 years. His skills saved countless lives and his compassion comforted patients and families coping with end-of-life issues.

Due to medical issues, he retired from climbing and turned his energy and drive to long-distance motorcycle riding. Always hardcore at whatever he did, he completed two trips from Boulder to Alaska and crossed the Arctic Circle on both the Dempster and Dalton Highways. He'd ride in snow, sleet, and hail, always in full-on motorcycle safety regalia.

Around this time, he met and married the love of his life, C.J. Joplin. He was as happy as I had ever seen him, was looking forward to retirement, and was dreaming of riding his bike to the southern tip of South America. His dream was cut short when a deer jumped in front of his motorcycle, throwing him off his bike into the path of an on-coming truck.

This summer friends and family will be trekking into Chasm Lake near Longs Peak to scatter his ashes. Vaya con Dios, mi hermano.

SALLY MOSER

CHRISTIAN WILLIAM PRUCHNIC, 1968–2010

Chris Pruchnic died on November 20 as the result of an accident while climbing the All Mixed Up route on Thatchtop Mountain, in Rocky Mountain National Park.

A graduate of Franklin and Marshall College, Pennsylvania (where he was born), Chris received his master's degree in archaeology from Denver University. His love of travel and interest in exploring other cultures took him on adventures touching all seven continents. He used his degree in archaeology to learn about history and cultures wherever he traveled, whether under the ocean or high in the mountains.

Christian Pruchnic. *Barry Reese*

It was through his work as an archaeologist that Chris came by the name by which many in the climbing community knew him: Haliku, Zuni for bighorn sheep. Chris earned the nickname through his fearlessness and love of climbing. Many of us are familiar with the Haliku pictogram that Chris used as the logo for his company, Haliku Adventures.

Chris participated in and led a number of expeditions to remote locations to attempt classic high-altitude peaks. A list of his climbing exploits can be found on summitpost.org/ users/haliku/16437.

Chris described himself as mountain climber, ultrarunner, scuba instructor, world traveler, and student of life. To us he was a partner, son, brother, friend, teacher, and colleague. Chris was known and loved for his indomitable spirit, incredible generosity, genuine caring, impressive talent, and dedication in all that he applied himself to. Chris was never known to give anything less than his best effort, be it a personal accomplishment or assisting others. For example, in October 2010 he ran his first 100-mile race, the Boulder 100, and finished in eighth place.

Chris joined the AAC in 2003 and became Colorado's Front Range Chair in 2008. Professionally, he was Manager of Disaster Preparedness and Risk Management at Qwest, and was an Advanced Open Water Instructor with Denver Divers. His interests extended well beyond these official roles. He volunteered at many events including the AAC's Exit Strategies conference, cooking at the Teton Climbers' Ranch for Iranian exchange participants, organizing trips to Ouray, and co-organizing the Lumpy Ridge trail repair in October. He could be found at many AAC events promoting new memberships.

Chris embodied the concept of life-long learning and never passed up an opportunity for new experiences or relationships. He lived as he encouraged others to: "Get out and explore the world!" He took every opportunity to share his enthusiasm, experiences, and knowledge with those around him. He was an active participant in online communities, where he is remembered for his unfailing good humor and willingness to offer assistance wherever he could. He shared many of his stories on his blog, halikuadventures.wordpress.com.

Never without plans, Chris would have gone to Romania later in November, would have participated in the Iranian-American Alpine Club exchange in Iran in June, and would have been with his family and friends on Kilimanjaro in October. Among his future plans was Annapurna IV; a possible return to Denali, which he summited in 2009; travel in South America to improve his Spanish and climb more extensively in Ecuador and neighboring countries; and a possible move overseas. Whatever the future was to bring, we can be sure that Chris would have filled it with adventure.

Chris was unforgettable; his indomitable spirit will live on in all those whose he touched and enriched by his presence. He will be missed forever and remembered by so many. Thank you, Chris, for being you and for touching our lives in the many ways you did, for your enthusiasm, love and unfailing support.

Chris is survived by his parents Dr. William F. and Carol Ann (Urbas) Pruchnic; brother, Timothy F.; and me, his partner.

CAROLYN M. WALLACE

JOSEPH NICHOLI PURYEAR, 1973–2010

On October 27, 2010, while unroped on a ridgecrest low on unclimbed Labuche Kang in Tibet, Joe Puryear broke through a cornice and fell 700 feet to the glacier below. Joe was one of the authentic talents of the American climbing community, an inspiration to friends and strangers alike, and he lived an extraordinary life of pure devotion to all that he loved. He was only 37 years old.

Joe Puryear. *David Gottlieb*

Joe was raised on a winery in Washington's Yakima Valley. His parents, Gail and Shirley Puryear, are a remarkable couple who provided a supportive atmosphere that would allow Joe's many talents to flourish. Joe was very close to his family, including his sister Tash and her husband, Ben Summit. In his youth Joe became an expert carpenter, an all-around farmhand, and a professional vintner. In his teenage years he also began to take a keen interest in the mountains. This started with skiing and progressed to climbing after his parents took him up Mt. Adams when he was 15. Throughout his life, Joe had a devious and eccentric sense of humor. He loved puzzles, games, and most of all, pushing people's buttons, but it was always good natured. Unsurprisingly, he took a math degree from the University of Washington, though he knew he would never work in that field. He was a problem solver by nature and endlessly curious, traits that would drive him toward mountain climbing as a full-time pursuit.

Joe and I met in 1994 when we were just starting into the world of alpinism, and we formed a fast friendship that proved enduring and immoveable. We were young and highly motivated, with similar goals, abilities, and attitudes. Above all we were like brothers, and we became nearly inseparable, spending the next decade climbing almost exclusively together, with productive results. We worked together for four seasons at Mt. Rainier as climbing rangers, spending all of our off-work days climbing classic routes in the North Cascades. We climbed peaks in Patagonia, big walls in Yosemite, and used Aconcagua to learn about altitude. But our signature venue was the Alaska Range, where we climbed together for nine consecutive seasons. We spent a month making a rare ascent of Denali's full south buttress, an experience that cemented our partnership. We made many progressively harder ascents in Alaska, culminating with Denali's Cassin Ridge in 2000, and a year later, the Infinite Spur on Mount Foraker; these were our finest achievements together. Six years earlier, we had sat wide-eyed at a slideshow of the Infinite Spur's second ascent, given by Jim Nelson in Seattle. It was far from our ability at the time; in retrospect, it made sense that this route would become the zenith of our partnership. In the ensuing years, as our climbing goals diversified, they also began to diverge. Regrettably, we climbed together less often, but we remained everlasting friends.

In his 20s Joe had been an introvert and somewhat lacking in confidence; this was the only thing that really held him back at the time. But in the last ten years he truly blossomed. I think the primary catalyst occurred in 2001, when he met Michelle O'Neil, who was close friends with my future wife. Joe and Michelle fell in love and were married in 2004 on the Pika Glacier in the Alaska Range. They settled in Leavenworth, Washington, where their home became a social hub for climbers and friends. Joe lamented having what he felt was a lack of marketable skills; this discontent drove him to teach himself graphic design. The first result was his beautiful select guidebook to the Alaska Range, *Alaska Climbing*, published by Supertopo. His skills in graphic design and photography, and his obvious creativity, soon landed him a job as Sherpa Adventure Gear's chief photographer and editor of their product catalog.

Meanwhile, as a climber Joe began to excel. He developed full confidence and became a solid rope gun on both rock and ice. It wasn't long before he turned his attention to the massive peaks of China, Tibet, and Nepal. He made seven expeditions to Asia in seven years, exploring remote valleys and logging many significant first ascents. In China he and Chad Kellogg made the first ascents of Mt. Daogou, the Angry Wife, and Lara Shan. In Nepal he and David Gottlieb made the first ascents of Kang Nachugo, Jobo Rinjang, and Takargo, all just over 6,700 meters. Joe formed a close connection with many Nepalis, and he reveled in the exploratory nature of his climbing. He and Kellogg also did a major first ascent on Kichatna Spire in Alaska. In between these adventures, on only a handful of trips, Joe also managed to climb over 70 desert towers in Utah, Colorado, and Arizona. His drive was unquenchable.

Joe's final adventure was on an unclimbed 7,000-meter massif in a desolate, remote corner of Tibet. Such a setting and undertaking, in the company of a dear and trusted friend, David Gottlieb, was a reflection of all that Joe valued in the experience of alpinism.

Joe's death has cut deeply into our community of friends. I am at a loss to summarize in words the remarkable life he lived or the gifted person that he was. I can only say that my friendship with him, forged in the limitless potential of our youth, was of the sort that may never again be replicated in my life. For that opportunity, but most of all for Joe himself, I am forever grateful.

Goodbye, brother.

MARK WESTMAN

LORNA REAM, 1930–2010

In the fall of 1965, I was a restless 17-year old growing up in Spokane, Washington, and trying to find my place in a tribe of outdoor people known as the Spokane Mountaineers. They had a chalet halfway to the summit of nearby Mt. Spokane, and one Saturday night in the late fall I barged into this Mountaineers Chalet unannounced with a couple of rowdy friends in tow. There at the door was a tall, slender, vivacious woman who introduced herself as Lorna Ream. Lorna immediately took charge of us boys, made sure we ate a proper dinner, stayed away from beer, gave us a place to lay our bags, and made us feel welcome. My first impression of Lorna as a take-charge lady never waned until her passing in 2010.

Lorna Ream. *Rich Landers*

In 1959 Lorna joined the Spokane Mountaineers at the suggestion of her husband, Joel. From that time onward, while raising her two children, she became very active as a climber, scaling dozens of the peaks in the western United States and British Columbia. A few of peaks she managed to climb while raising her family were Baker, Shuksan, Glacier, Bonanza, Stuart, Rainier, St. Helens, Adams, Hood, Shasta, Middle Sister, Borah, Trout Mountain, the Grand Teton, Athabasca, and the first ascent of Mt. Cooper in British Columbia, in 1962.

Few people loomed larger in the history of the Spokane Mountaineers than Lorna Ream. Beside her considerable climbing skills, Lorna was the organizer and leader of all types of events and committees in the group from the early sixties until her death. On weekends she provided climbing instruction and leadership. More importantly, Lorna was politically active as a leader in the community, offering behind-the-scenes guidance on many of our area's conservation and wildlife issues.

One of the most important projects of our region was the proposed Spokane River Centennial Trail. Long before the Centennial Trail became a reality, Lorna Ream helped lay the groundwork while working at the Spokane County Engineering Department. When the trail was finally constructed, it immediately became one of our area's most beloved accomplishments. Another dream was a trail from the Spokane Valley over the local mountains to a huge cluster of climbing rocks called Big Rock. Lorna worked tirelessly providing leadership and devotion to the Dream Trail Committee, which led to the purchase of this important climbing and hiking area. For anything that required action involving trail building, climbing, and wilderness issues, Lorna found the time. She inspired not just with her voice, but with her pocketbook too.

Lorna Ream's dedication to wilderness was unwavering, and she walked her talk. She changed our landscape for the better. I will miss her great enthusiasm, her laugh, and her happy smile.

Excelsior Lorna!

CHRIS KOPCZYNSKI

DOUGLAS CRAIG ZIMMERMAN, 1957–2010

Doug Zimmerman. *Robert Plucenik*

Whether in the mountains, working on his farmhouse, or enjoying a short hike, Doug Zimmerman was most at home in the outdoors, where he found peace and beauty. On a sunny day in June 2010, Doug died suddenly while running through a park alongside the Connecticut River, apparently of a malignant arrhythmia.

Doug was a mountaineer in the truest sense. His unyielding spirit for adventure, humor, strength, and determination made him a wonderful traveling companion and the best of climbing partners.

Doug's climbing career spanned four decades, with ascents and climbing adventures throughout the U.S., Canada, Peru, and Alaska. He was an uncomplicated man and a traditional climber. His pleasures were simple and his needs were few. He endured hardship with quiet calm and determination.

Doug loved to tell stories, especially of one particular adventure in the Canadian Rockies. He, Doug Bonoff and I spent nearly five days sitting out a storm on the Dome of Mt. Robson. Where others might have made hasty decisions to climb on or retreat, Doug understood the risks and exercised calm patience. Doug loved to say that it was the longest stay on Mt. Robson not resulting in a rescue.

Doug was a calm, levelheaded leader. He understood his limits and climbed competently and confidently within them. He was not a bold climber. His plan was to climb late into life, to become an old climber.

Doug's wife Bet supported his climbing wholeheartedly. When she met Kenneth Henderson at an AAC black-tie event, she asked why he was always so well-dressed when climbing, as evidenced by old photos on display. Ken responded by saying, "My dear, you just never know who you'll run into while in the mountains." Doug clearly never heeded Ken's philosophy of attire. For Doug, fashion was irrelevant. In his pack, a moth-eaten army green wool sweater, Dachshtein mittens, and a crampon-slashed pair of wind pants could always be found. On ice routes he continued to carry his wooden alpine hammer well past its usefulness. On our last climb together, at Pinnacle Gully on Mt. Washington this past March, a single Chouinard ice screw still dangled from his harness. Dulled and weathered, the screw was perhaps a connection to adventures past and those he thought lay ahead.

As I reflect back on the many adventures that others and I shared with Doug, I pay tribute to a friend who gave me some of the best days of my life. For this I thank Doug. Those who knew Doug and had the privilege of climbing with him will miss him forever.

Notes: Doug graduated from Eastern Connecticut State University in 1980 with a degree in Environmental Earth Science; he had been the co-president of the school's Outing Club. His career in public service spanned 27 years with the Connecticut Department of Environmental Protection, where he helped clean up countless polluted sites. In addition to rock and ice climbing and mountaineering, Doug was a runner, completing six marathons. He was also a regular blood donor, giving more than 65 units of blood during his life. He was a tissue donor, which he referred to as "the gift that keeps on giving." Perhaps another person will be able to walk a trail or climb a mountain thanks to Doug's gift of muscle and bone.

Donations in Doug's honor can be made to the American Alpine Club or to the Founders of Environmental Earth Science Fund, Eastern Connecticut State University, Foundation, 83 Windham St., Willimantic, CT 06226. More about Doug's life and loss can be found at cragman.com.

ROBERT PLUCENIK

NECROLOGY

Ross Bronson
Jake Farmer
Ralph Fickel
Rich Jack
Heidi Kloos
David P. Pearson
Dr. John K. Prentice

Chris Pruchnic
Joseph Puryear
Lorna Ream
Spencer Swanger
Tommy S Taylor
Roe D. Watson
Douglas Craig Zimmerman

CLUB ACTIVITIES

EDITED BY FREDERICK O. JOHNSON

Alaska Section. Our Section celebrated the summer of 2010 by commencing construction of the new hut on the edge of the Snowbird Glacier. Located in the Hatcher Pass area of the Talkeetna Mountains, the original hut was purchased by the Alaska Section in 2005 from a private party. This hut has been an important haven for hikers, climbers, and backcountry skiers in an area known for unpredictable weather. The original structure is now over 30 years old and has experienced a partial collapse from heavy snow load.

Harry Hunt, James Brady and "Hut Mistress" Cindi Squire have led the charge by actively fundraising for the last four years to fund the new hut construction. Rim Architects of Anchorage donated time and effort to design the new 18' by 18' building. The design utilizes the onsite natural granite boulders for a gabion foundation and features south facing windows providing panoramic views over the Snowbird Glacier and collecting solar heat during winter months.

An August 14 fundraising event at the Alaska Rock Gym celebrated the launch of the summer's construction efforts. A pig roast, locally brewed Moose's Tooth Beer, live music provided by "Back Acres," a continuous slide show, and gym climbing rounded out the event. The next day several thousand pounds of building materials were helicoptered into the new hut site. Working weekends and a few five- to seven-day stretches, a host of volunteers made the four-hour trek into the site and donated several hundred man-hours of labor. Prior to the season's first snowfall the new hut was weather-tight, insulated, sparsely furnished, and had an operable oil-heat stove. Progress and photos are available on the AAC Web site and snowbirdhut.com. A formal hut dedication and pig roast is planned for August 2011. All members are invited to join in.

HARRY HUNT AND JAMES BRADY, *CO-CHAIRS*

Sierra Nevada Section. The Sierra Nevada Section was pleased to welcome over 130 new members, bringing total membership to over 800. The annual "Climbmunity" gatherings continued to be popular and well attended. The first was our January ice climbing weekend in Cold Stream Canyon near Truckee. Because of the record late snowfall, the Sierra summer climbing season did not begin in earnest until late June with the Donner Summit Climb-munity, which was followed by the Tuolumne Meadows Climb-munity in August. Both these events afforded our members not only great rock climbing, but also fine camaraderie with group camping, barbeques, parties, and raffles.

The AAC's Craggin Classic made its first foray to California the last weekend of August at Donner Summit. The Section worked closely with the AAC in Golden in organizing and promoting the event, which included a day of cragging, free clinics, dinner, and a slideshow by Tommy Caldwell. Despite the unseasonably cold and windy weather, the event had a large and lively turnout of over 100 attendees for the dinner/slideshow.

In September the Section organized and hosted the Pinecrest Climbmunity after taking over these responsibilities from Royal and Liz Robbins and Tom Frost who had done so for many years. Members and friends enjoyed cragging at Gianelli Edges and a wonderful party at the Robbins' cabin. In early November the Section held its inaugural Castle Rock Climbmunity at Castle Rock State Park in the hills above Saratoga, which consisted of a day of cragging and bouldering, followed by a fun party generously hosted by Sarah and Fred Glover at their nearby home.

The Section continued to sponsor the year-round free climber's coffee, held every Sunday morning in Yosemite with the Climbing Rangers, where members interact with other climbers and spread the good word about the AAC. Further, Section member and AAC Yosemite Committee Chair Linda McMillan continued to lead the free Saturday evening slideshow series in Yosemite as part of the climber's interpretive program, which generates further goodwill and exposure for the AAC.

On the conservation front, in September our members again represented the AAC at the Yosemite Facelift clean-up week organized by the Yosemite Climbers Association. The Section underwrote commemorative AAC/Facelift bandanas that were given away to all the Facelift volunteers.

The year ended with our Holiday Dinner, highlighted by AAC past president Jim Donini, who presented an outstanding slideshow of his four-decade long career pioneering hard alpine climbing and first ascents in Patagonia, Alaska, and the Karakoram. We had a record turnout for the event, due in no small part to Jim's prolific postings on Supertopo.

TOM BURCH, *Chair*

Southwest Section. We had three events in 2010, finishing strongly with a successful winter dinner after a climbing day in April at Malibu and a bit of climbing in Palos Verdes. On April 17 six climbers met at Malibu Creek State Park and hiked to the Power Wall. The Wall sits right above a stream with a variety of climbs and a diversity of pocketed terrain with some overhanging bits. Other climbers were already on the Wall but were happy to share the routes. We did some enjoyable sports climbing, sharing the camaraderie and lovely setting. After the climbing, several of us adjourned to Ted Vaill's house for a potluck dinner. The group enjoyed good food, more camaraderie, and to finish the day some of Ted's interesting videos of Tibet and trekking to Everest through Nepal. Thanks to Ted for hosting us and to Mary Tomkins for her excellent help.

On November 7 Brian Cox hosted a visit to a "secret" climbing spot in Rancho Palos Verdes near his home. There were a few fun super-short top ropes and assorted boulders right on the ocean. Ted Vaill, Jim Pinter-Lucke, and Mike and Mary Tomkins joined Brian for a pleasant seaside afternoon which was topped off by a beautiful sunset. Thanks, Brian!

The Section held its first holiday dinner in many years on December 5. It was a resounding success with 55 attendees with new, old, and prospective members. While the food and drinks were good, the two highlights were the considerable camaraderie and Phil Power's presentation and slideshow. Thank you all for coming and helping to contribute to the dinner's warm atmosphere. Special thanks to Tony Yeary for helping with the planning and to Phil for speaking at our dinner.

JIM PINTER-LUCKE, *Chair*

Northern Rockies Section. The Northern Rockies Section started out the year with its 2nd annual Sun Valley Dinner on January 7 at The Cellars Pub. Jamie Laidlaw, a Hans Sari Grant Recipient, presented a show of his most recent exploratory trip to Western Nepal. It was a fascinating story, more about exploration than skiing, but there now is the potential to open up some new territory for future exploration. There were about 20 people present including local Sun Valley area members Dick Dorworth, David Stelling, Bob Rosso, Greg Wilson, Clark Gerhardt, Marc Hanselman, Tim Ball, Wolf Riehle, Wick Warrick and AAC Board Member Doug Colwell. During brief technical difficulties, resident Aussie, Tim Ball, entertained the crowd with sheep jokes. A good night was had by all, members were pleased with the Club coming to them, and plans were made for another dinner in the future.

On March 10 the AAC sponsored a film event in Salt Lake City at Brewvies Cinema: The Continuum Project, with members receiving a discount. *The Continuum Project* follows some of the world's best climbing talent around the globe to document bold new routes and daring repeats on ice, rock, and in the alpine.

Rockreation, a Salt Lake City area climbing gym, generously offered a discount on Wednesday nights to AAC members which extended for the entire year.

In mid-July the Section sponsored Piolets d'Or winners Kyle Dempster and Bruce Normand, who presented a unique slideshow on their Lyman-Spitzer Grant supported climb in China's Middle Kingdom. Dempster, Normand, and Jed Brown made the first ascent of Xuelian West (6,422m). The three men completed an alpine-style ascent of the 2,650-meter north face during a five-day round trip. The show, taking place at Black Diamond's retail store, played to a packed house. Both Kyle ("younger rope gun") and Bruce ("the professor") brought their own distinct styles to the show, making for a great evening.

At the end of July members in Salt Lake City gathered downtown for a movie night to see fellow Club member Conrad Anker in the Wildest Dream Imax film. Club members received a discount on their tickets and enjoyed a little pre-movie banter at a local restaurant prior to the show. No Kendal Mint Cakes were harmed during the attending of this event.

BRIAN CABE, *CHAIR*

Wyoming Section. The Section was active in 2010 as it continued to spread the word about the value of the AAC as an important climber's resource and to attract new members. We have found that climbers in Wyoming are young and have no money to pay annual dues. Yet they want to belong to established conservation and climbing organizations like the AAC. Several small fundraisers were held, but had minimal attendance and no income. The Section made a strong appearance in July during the 17th annual International Climbers Festival in Lander. The southforkice.com Mountain Hardware Monster Tent was used as the AAC booth. Climbers gathered in awe of the tent and to find out what the AAC was all about. Refreshments were provided, and we had a free raffle for AAC goodies. The climbers could learn about the Global Rescue Program and the advantages for joining the Club. Over 100 AAC informational brochures were handed out, but few, if any, membership applications received. The Section plans to be even more involved in Club membership drives in 2011. If you are new to the climbing community in Wyoming, please contact us (donfoote@southforkice.com) so we can assist you. Climb safe and enjoy Wyoming's outdoor adventures.

DON FOOTE, *CHAIR*

Great Lakes Section. In January the first Ice Pit Festival was held in Green Bay, Wisconsin, where 110-foot vertical walls provided an almost instant pump for 100 new climbers. The Section staffed a booth and participated in a membership drive and raffle.

In February one of the country's oldest ice festivals took place in Munising, Michigan, on the southern shores of Lake Superior. Mild temperatures greeted a record 481 participants at this year's Michigan Ice Fest. Climbers visited from 11 states and Canada, with one from California traveling the farthest. Days were spent at clinics, demos, and exploring climbs at Pictured Rocks National Lakeshore. After hard days of climbing, participants were treated to slideshows featuring Barry Blanchard, Ben Clark, and Raphael Slawinski.

In the fall the Section hosted CLIMB UP! in Marquette, Michigan. This four-day event was organized for our members to gather, climb, socialize, and celebrate another year of adventure. On September 30 the film *180 Degrees South* played to a packed house of Midwest climbers at Northern Michigan University. On October 1 Mark Wilford presented *Climbing: A Forty-year Perspective,* which offered the audience a whirlwind tour of many classic climbing areas around the world featuring some of Mark's biggest adventures. On October 2 the crew headed to the local crag, the AAA Wall, for climbing and camping. The climbers were greeted with steel-gray skies and freezing cold rain. Nevertheless, the climbers participated in slack lining, a crate stacking competition, aid climbing, and lively campfire discussions. Fortunately, the skies cleared later and everyone hopped on routes to finish the day. At the AAC BBQ party, brats (a Midwest staple) were grilled and a great opportunity provided for climbers to socialize and network. The first edition of the *Marquette County Rock Climbing Guide* was released at the party. Half of the group stayed to work projects and demo shoes on the AAA Wall while the others ventured off to the Secret Crag to develop a new route.

BILL THOMPSON, *CHAIR*

New England Section. On March 20 the New England Section held its 14th annual Formal Dinner at the elegant Henderson House in Weston, Mass. Walt Hampton displayed his photographs *Where Awe Dwells: Journeys in the Great Ranges.* Our guest speaker was Glenn Denney, who treated us to a brilliant presentation entitled *Yosemite in the Sixties.* Among the notables in attendance were past AAC Presidents Mark Richey and Jed Williamson and board members Bruce Franks and John Kascenska. New Hampshire hardmen Steve Arsenault and Paul Boissioneault joined in the festivities along with John Reppy, who traveled from New York. Bill Atkinson, our former Chair, also attended, and I thank him once again for all his help this past year as I transition into the role of Chair.

In June the annual summer BBQ was held at Teresa and Mark Richey's new home in Madison, New Hampshire. Prior to the party Bill Atkinson, Susan Clark, Rick Merritt, and Marvin Wright seconded me in a conga line up Beginner's Route on Whitehorse Ledge near North Conway. Despite the heat wave the expedition managed three pitches before bailing for a cold pint. Rick Merritt skillfully manned the BBQ grill, a task not fit for the faint of heart with Teresa and Mark providing a meadow full of lamb chops. Karen Bates and Joe Terrevechia, Janet Bergman, and Freddie Wilkinson were among others joining us.

Our Fall BBQ in October was held at my lair at Albany, New Hampshire. Despite the cold weather we had a crew of about 30 who partied well into the night with the likes of D. Byer, Paul Boissineault (aka Base), Steve and Joan Arsenault, and New England ice hardman, Doug Millen.

November marked our second annual "It Ain't Over 'Til It's Over" meet in Connecticut hosted by Chad Hussey. The cold forecast held back a few, but those of us who went were rewarded with warm rock and sun and spent the day enjoying the phenomenal rock that Ragged Mountain offers. Chad and AMGA guides Bob Clark, Jeff Lea, and Kevin Johnson showed their crag off to us for a great day.

We lost long-time member and friend Doug Zimmerman in June. Doug often attended our annual dinner along with good friend and climbing partner Dale Janic. Also, Ross Bronson passed away after an accident in his home just before the close of the year. He was another staple at our dinners and BBQs and will be missed.

NANCY SAVICKAS, *CHAIR*

New York Section. In 2010 the New York Section of the American Alpine Club continued its upward trajectory as new records were set in terms of membership count and number and variety of events, both indoors and outdoors. Starting with the latter, our Annual Outings to the Adirondacks draw sell-out crowds each and every January and June. Our favorite winter haunt is Adirondack Rock and River, in close proximity to the High Peaks Area near Lake Placid, and our early summer home for almost three decades is the historic Ausable Club in Keene Valley. Meanwhile we enjoyed slide presentations in the New York City area by Olaf Soot, Jeff Blumenfeld, Michael Lederer, and Mike Barker. In addition there were book signings by Majka Burhardt on Ethiopia, Graham Bowley on K-2, and Jennifer Jordan on the Dudley Wolfe/Fritz Wiessner K-2 mystery and controversy. We also partnered with the Nepal Mission to the UN to celebrate the launch of Nepal Tourism's 2011 year. Additionally we were invited to the grand opening in June of David Breashears' *Rivers of Ice* exhibit at the Asia Society and Conrad Anker's film on the mystery of Mallory and Irvine's disappearance. And, for the fourth consecutive year, we volunteered guides for the Rubin Museum's very popular program, *Peak Experience*, a simulated climb of Everest and sleepover for kids 11–14 years old inside the Museum.

Our Annual Dinner, a mid-November black-tie benefit now in its 31st consecutive year at New York's Union Club, undoubtedly attracts the most attention, out-of-town guests, and press coverage. Last year we undertook one of our most ambitious programs. We celebrated the 25th Anniversary of the First Completion of the Seven Summits by Dick Bass, a long-time friend. It was also his 80th birthday. Besides Dick, presenters included some old friends and climbing partners including Dave Breashears and Phil Ershler. "Bo" Parfet, one of the many younger followers of Dick's historic accomplishment, completed the line-up. We also feted another significant birthday, that of Vic Benes, who had recently celebrated his 80th atop Forbidden Peak in the Cascades with partner Ron Bixby. At the other end of the age spectrum was guest Jordan Romero, who at 17 has only Vinson to climb to become the youngest Seven Summiteer of all time. Among the many attendees were seven successful Seven Summiteers from the Section who were presented with special plaques marking their achievement as well as Charles Irion, the author of the Seven Summits Murder Mystery Series.

None of the above would have been possible without the help of a large cadre of dedicated volunteers including Andrea Salerno, Howard Sebold, Jon Light, Mike Barker, Michael Lederer, Kaitlin Herlihy, Martin Torresquintero, Vic Benes, our previously mentioned slideshow presenters, and others.

A special thank you goes to our new webmaster, Conor Moran , who has created an instructive, attractive and very popular blog where members can post trip reports and photos, and where news of upcoming events are frequently posted and updated. If you want to know what's happening in busy New York, look for a partner or whatever, log on to nysaac.blogspot.com.

PHIL ERARD, *CHAIR*

Blue Ridge Section. In 2010 the Blue Ridge Section continued to meet at the Rhodeside Tavern in Rosslyn, Virginia. In April four members—Daniel Ressler, Hunt Prothro, Rob Borokantics, and Simon Carr—presented an overview of Sierra climbing, ranging from cragging in Tuolumne to routes on remote backcountry peaks such as the Incredible Hulk. In July, with the ACC Golden office, we helped organize a talk by Freddie Wilkinson to publicize his book, *A Thousand Summits Shining*, on the 2008 K2 tragedy. We also held our "Not-so-black-tie" annual dinner in December at the home of Jeanette Helfrich, a previous Section Chair. Section members also participated in Access Fund Adopt-A-Crag events at Carderock and Great Falls, and have continued to work with the National Park Service to preserve climbing opportunities at these and other nearby national parks.

SIMON CARR, *CHAIR*

Southern Appalachian Section. The primary objective for the new Southern Appalachian Section was to establish itself as relevant to AAC members as well as to the broader climbing community across the southern Appalachian mountains. Our membership continued to grow, fueling a expanded offering of Section events. In early April the Section welcomed the spring rock climbing season at the Moore Weekend with the AAC, held at the home of Susan and Jeff Hanks in Oak Ridge, North Carolina. We climbed at Moore's Wall and Pilot Mountain on a beautiful spring Saturday, enjoyed drinks and dinner that evening courtesy of Susan and Jeff, camped out in the Hanks' backyard Saturday night, rose early on Sunday for a robust country breakfast, and then headed out for another beautiful day of climbing. Adding to the AAC camaraderie were visiting members of the Blue Ridge Section.

A superb example of increased emphasis on locally produced AAC events were the self-rescue classes taught in June and July in Brevard, North Carolina, by AAC partner Fox Mountain Guides and Climbing School. These classes were offered free to AAC members. Class pricing for non-AAC members was set to encourage participants to join the AAC rather than pay class tuition. Attendees came away with new or enhanced self rescue skills; the AAC gained new members. Our thanks to Adam Fox and AAC Ambassador Karsten Delap for their contributions.

As a follow-up to the success of the AAC Wilderness First Aid class delivered in 2009 in the Raleigh/Durham area, two classes were offered to AAC members in March and October. Instructor Danny McCracken delivered the classes to Red Cross WFA certification standards with significant customization to focus upon climbing accident first response.

Building on a strong tradition, the 6th Annual Eastern North Carolina AAC Get-Together was held on November 6 in Wake Forest. Thirty members and their guests gathered at the home of Brigitte Weston and Keith Nangle to discuss over food and drink how the AAC community could help.

people achieve climbing goals. The speaker was Dr. Amer Adam, who presented slides from his 2010 expedition to Mt. Everest.

I would like to thank all of the AAC staff for their support for our Section. In 2011 we will focus on recruitment of additional AAC Ambassadors, an increased focus on alpine conservation issues in the Appalachian range, and the continuing effort to build a strong AAC community across our region.

DAVID THOENEN, *CHAIR*

Deep South Section. Our Section is plugging along with three AAC Ambassadors in place: Jay Love (Athens, Georgia), Frank Nederhand (Atlanta), and Gray Ruhl (Tampa).

We have been attracting new members and establishing a presence in the Deep South by having ongoing events throughout the year. Our most important event is the upcoming CBEE Expedition to Peru's Cordillera Blanca to test air quality, with Frank Nederhand, Chadwick Hagan, and Ellen Lapham as co-leaders. For more information, contact chagan@gmail.com or go to www.americanalpineclub.org/p/cbee2011.

CHADWICK HAGAN, *CHAIR*

INDEX

Compiled by Ralph Ferrara and Eve Tallman

Mountains are listed by their official names. Ranges and geographic locations are also indexed. Unnamed peaks (eg. Peak 2,340) are listed under P. Abbreviations are used for some states and countries and for the following: Article: art.; Cordillera: C.; Mountains: Mts.; National Park: Nat'l Park; Obituary: obit. Most personnel are listed for major articles. Expedition leaders and persons supplying information in Climbs and Expeditions are also cited here. Indexed photographs are listed in bold type. Reviewed books are listed alphabetically under Book Reviews.

A

Aartun, Bjorn-Eivind *art.* 70-6, 110
Abi (Siguniang, China) 348-**9**
Abu, P. (Kyrgyzstan) 240-1
Acevedo, Elvis 174
Aconcagua (Argentina-Chile) 172
Acopan Tepui (Venezuela) **159-60**
Adankasima Tepui (Venezuela) **158**-9
Adyrtor Mts. (Kyrgyzstan) 252-3
Afghanistan 256-68
Agamemnon (Antarctica) 202-**3**
Ak Alakha (Russia) 226-**7**
Ak Alakha Rg. (Russia) 226-7
Al Hamra Tower East (Oman) **206**
Ala Archa (Kyrgyzstan) 234-5
Ala Daglar (Turkey) 204-5
Alaska (US) *art.* 70-6; 106-124
Alaska Range (AK) *art.* 70-6; 107-9
Allen, Mark 113-4
Altai (Russia) 226-7
Alvarenga, Ana 163
Ama Dablam (Nepal) **334**-5
Andes (Argentina-Chile) 171-88
Angegoq Tower (Greenland) *art.* 24-33
Angnikitsoq (Greenland) *art.* 24-33
Annapurna Himal (Nepal) 319-23
Annapurna III (Nepal) **321**-3, **322**
Ansilita 4 (Argentina) 171
Antarctic Peninsula 196-203
Antarctica 189-203
Anthamatten, Simon 178
Anvers Island (Antarctica) 197-202
Arfi, Thomas 302-3
Argentina 171-87
Arken (Greenland) 145-**8**
Arnold, Dani 178
Artesonraju (Peru) 164

Arunachal Pradesh (India) 311
Asa (Sichuan Province, China) *art.* 77-87, **81**
Ashagonge (Sichuan, China) *art.* 77-87, **82**
Asiaq Tower (Greenland) *art.* 24-33
Asperity Mtn. (Coast Mts., CAN) **129**, 130
At Bashi Rg. (Kyrgyzstan) 241-4
Atkinson, Bill 377
Auer, Hansjörg 219-20
Augusta, Mt. (St. Elias Range, CAN) 125-7, **126**
Awful P. (Chugach, AK) 116

B

Backstrom, Ingrid 347
Baendelberg (Greenland) 145-8, **147**
Baffin Island (CAN) 138-9
Baig, Samina 271
Balchen, Mt. (AK) **107**-9
Baltoro Muztagh (Pakistan) 272-4
Banck, Mt. (Antarctica) 202-3
Bandalet, Nikolay 323-4
Baranov, Sergy 196-7
Barma Kangri (Ladakh, India) 291-2
Barmasse, Hervé 340-1
Baroness (Greenland) 155-7, **156**
Bass, Malcolm *art.* 58-69; 303
Baush-ul (Pakistan) 275-**6**
Baylyan Bashi, P. (Kyrgyzstan) 234-**5**
Beartooth Mtns. (MT) 98-9
Benign P. (Chugach, AK) 116-**7**
Benowitz, Jeff Apple 109
Beyer, Jim 120
Beyyt Kashka-Suu Valley (Kyrgyzstan) 243-4
Bhagirathi III (Garhwal, India) 302-3
Bhrikuti (Nepal) **318**-9
Bhushan, Bharat 305
Big Rock Candy Mtn. (India) 285-**7**
Bizot, Henry 171

Blammanen (Norway) **219-20**
Blyth, Jim 202-3
Bodhona (Tajikistan) 230-2, **231**
Bohin, Sébastian 189
Bolivia 168-70
Bongonzhong (Sichuan Province,
    China) *art.* 77-87
Book Reviews
    *Climbing—Philosophy for Everyone: Because It's
        There* edited by Stephen E. Schmid 369-70
    *Desert Towers: Fat Cat Summits and Kitty Litter
        Rock* by Steve "Crusher" Bartlett 364-5
    Fail Falling by Royal Robbins 368-9
    *Grasping for Heaven: Interviews with North
        American Mountaineers* by Frederic
        Hartemann and Robert Hauptman 374-5
    *The Last Man on the Mountain: The Death of an
        American Adventurer on K2* by Jennifer Jordan
        365-7
    *One Mountain Thousand Summits, The Untold
        Story of Tragedy and True Heroism on K2* by
        Freddie Wilkinson 367-8
    *Pilgrims of the Vertical: Yosemite Rock Climbers
        and Nature at Risk* by Joseph E Taylor III. 375-6
    Ron Fawcett Rock Athlete by Ron Fawcett, with Ed
        Douglas 370-1
    *The Sunny Top of California: Sierra Nevada Poems
        and a Story* by Norman Schaefer 371-2
    *Unexpected: Thirty Years Of Patagonia Catalog
        Photography* edited by Jane Sievert and Jennifer
        Ridgeway 372-4
Booth Island (Antarctica) 202-3
Boyd, Andrew 131-2
Bradley, Mt. (AK) 113-5, **114**
Branscomb (Antarctica) 189-**90**
Brazil 163
Broad P. (Pakistan) 269, 272
Bronson, Ross *obit.* 377
Brooks Range (AK) 106-7
Buchanan Hills (Antarctica) 195-6
Bugaboos (CAN) 134-5
Buil, Cecilia 279-80
Bullock, Nick 321-3
Burdekin, Matthew 144-5
Burns, Cameron 377-83

C
California (US) *art.* 43-8; 90-7
Camp Peak (Greenland) 155-**7**
Canada *art.* 16-23; 125-39
Canadian Rockies (CAN) 136-8
Canary Islands (Spain) 212-13
Cape Farewell (Greenland) 151-7
Cape Farewell Region (Greenland) *art.* 24-33

Cappadocia (Turkey) 204-5
Carrascal, Sergio Ramírez 164-7
Cassin Ridge (Denali, AK) *art.* 70-6
Central Peak (Sichuan Province,
    China) *art.* 77-87
Chacraraju (Peru) 167
Chad 215-8
Chalten Massif (Argentina-Chile) 178-87
Chamberlain, Tom 167
Chamberlin, Mt. (CA) 96-**7**
Changla (Nepal) 312-3
Changla Himal (Nepal) 312-13
Charakusa Valley (Pakistan) 277-84
Charles Pk. (Antarctica) 191-6, **192**
Chashkin Sar (Pakistan) 271
Chaukhi Mts. (Georgia) 228-30, **229**
Chiche P. (Pakistan) **269-71**
Chief's Head (CO) 102
Chile 171-88
Chimbote (Chile) **173**
Chin, Jimmy 215-8, 347
China *art.* 34-42, 77-87, 340-53;
    winter ascent definition 358
Cholatse (Nepal) **328-9**
Cholon (Pakistan) **275-6**
Chomo II (Arunachal Pradesh, India) **311**
Chorten Garpo "P. 6,380m" (Tibet) 354-5
Chugach Mts. (AK) 116-7
Church, Mt. (Ruth Gorge, AK) 116
Church, Tim 347-8
Cirque d' Umq (Oman) 208
Cirque of the Unclimbables (CAN) 127-8
Clark, Gordon 189-90
Cloos (Antarctica) 197-20**3**, **199**
Coast Mts. (AK) 122-4
Coast Mts. (CAN) 128-31
Cochamó (Chile) 175-6
Cocker, Mike 298
Coffield, Dana 189, 196-7
Colchuck Balanced Rock (WA) 88-9
College Glacier (AK) 109
Colorado (US) 102-4
Copp, Jonny 35, 127, 186, 348
Cordillera Blanca (Peru) 164-6
Cordillera Central (Peru) 167-8
Cordillera Huayhuash (Peru) 166-7
Cordillera Quimsa Cruz (Bolivia) 170
Cordillera Real (Bolivia) 168-9
Côrtes, Ralf 163
Criscitiello, Alison 292
Cromwell, Mt. (CAN) 136

D

Dagestan (Russia) 228
Dallmeyer (Antarctica) 197-202, **200**
Damodar Himal (Nepal) 317-9
Dana Plateau (CA) 96-**7**
Dangchezhengla (Sichuan Province,
     China) *art.* 77-87, **80**
Dangling Range (China) 344-6
Daogou Qonglai Mts. (China) **353**
Daogou West Qonglai Mts. (China) **353**
Dash, Micah 35, 186, 348
Dashkevich, Sergey 234-5
Dauru (Garhwal, India) 301-**2**
Dawa P. (Ladakh, India) 285-7, **286**
Daxue Shan (China) 344-8
De la Silla (Patagonia, Argentina) 186-7
Delaite Island (Antarctica) 196-7
Delta Rg. (AK) 109
Demaria (Antarctica) 202-3
Dempster, Kyle *art.* 34-42; 348
Denali (AK) *art.* 70-6; 110
Denali NAT'L PARK (AK) 70-6; 110-1
Denis, Sophie 165, 168
Desmochada (Patagonia, Argentina) 178, **185**-7
Detjen, Pedro 346
Devil's Thumb (Coast Mts., AK) 122-4, **123**
Ditto, Ben *art.* 24-33; 140
Djangart Rg. (Kyrgyzstan) 250-2
Dogonomba (China) 347-**8**
Dolence, Mt. (Antarctica) 191-6, **192**
Dome P. (Miyar Valley, India) 296-**7**
Dongdong, Yan 346, 348-50, 353-8
Dongxung (Tibet) 356, **357**
Drum, Mt. (AK) 118
DuBois, Justin 101
Dusic, Matjaz 178
Dzhirnagaktu Valley (Kyrgyzstan)
     5-7; *map* 246
Dzo Jongo (Ladakh, India) 289-**90**

E

Echo Tower (Fisher Towers, UT) 98-9
Edgar, Mt.(China) *art.* **34**-42; 348
Egger, Torre 178
Ekdant (Garhwal, India) 303-5, **304**
El Capitan (Yosemite, CA) *art.* 43-8; 90-1
Elias, Simon 275-6
Elías, Simón 166-7
Ellsworth Mts. (Antarctica) 189-96

Elson, Nick 130
Emma Island (Antarctica) 196-7, 202-3
Endeavor, Mt. (Coast Mts., CAN) 128-9
Endicott Mts. (AK) 106-7
Ennedi Desert (Chad) 215-8
Erydag Northwest (Russia) 228
Estorach, Francesc 275-6
Executive Committee Rg. (Antarctica) 196
Eye Tooth (Ruth Gorge, AK) 115-6

F

Fainberg, Fernando 173
False P. (Kyrgyzstan) 238-40
False Shackleton (Antarctica) 197-203, **198**
Faniskiy Gory (Tajikistan) 230-2
Faraday, Mt. (Antarctica) 197
Farol West (Pakistan) **277**-9
Farr, Nate 128-9
Fava, Gabriel 171-2
Favresse, Nicolas *art.* 24-33; 90-1, 140, 184
Favresse, Olivier *art.* 24-33; 140
Figg, Paul *art.* 58-69; 303
Finkelstein, Josh 96-7
Fiorenza, Luciano 175
Fisher Towers (UT) 98-9
Fitz Roy, Cerro (Patagonia,
     Argentina) 178, **182**-4, 186-7
Foraker, Mt. (AK) *art.* **70**-6; **110**
Fourth Needle (Whitney Crest, CA) 95, **95**
Fowler, Mick 342-3
Français, Mt. (Antarctica) 202-3
Free Tibet (Kyrgyzstan) 240-1
Frush, Jim 315-6
Fujikawa, Ken 313

G

Gagner, Paul 98-9
Gal, Maria 248-9
Gangotri (Garhwal, India) *art.* 58-69; 302-3
Ganzi Prefecture (Sichuan
     Province, China) *art.* 77-87
García, Cheo 158-9
Garhwal (India) 301-7
Garhwal Himal, India *art.* 58-69
Garibotti, Rolando 178
Gasherbrum I (Pakistan/China) 269, **273**-4, **340**
Gasherbrum II (Pakistan) 269, 272-3
Gasherbrum V 269, 274
Gateway Peaks (Antarctica) 191-6

Geisler, Chris 178
Genyen (Sichuan Province,
    China) *art.* 77-87, **78, 86**
Georgia 228-30
Ghujerag Mts. (Pakistan) 271
Gietl, Simon 148-9
Gildea, Damien 189-97
Glowacz, Stefan 159, 161
Goettler, David 334-5
Golob, Urban 306-7
González, Pablo David 174
Goodman, Pat 101-2
Gorbenko, Mstislav 336-7
Göschl, Gerfried 273-4
Gottlieb, David *art.* 49-57; 326
Gradiska (Qilian Mts., China) 343
Greenland art. 24-33; 140-57
Gregson, Jim 145-8
Griffin, Lindsay 148-9, 207-8, 223-4,
    257-8, 271-4, 302-3, 311,
    325-6, 332, 343-4, 348, 358
Griffith, Jonathan 178
Grobel, Paolo 313-4, 318-9
Grosvenor, T. (Riwuqie Feng,
    China) *art.* 34-42, **35, 36**
Grundtvigskirchen (Greenland) 148-**9**
Guillaumet, Aguja (Patagonia, Argentina) 178
Guiupponi, Luca 204-5
Gukov, Alexander 328-9
Gulmatonga Valley (India) 293
Guyana 161-3

H
Haan, Peter 375-6
Haden, Jimmy 96-7
Hagiwara, Hiroshi 116, 339
Haidri, Karrar 269
Hajar, Western (Oman) 207
Hak-Jae, Yoo 326-7
Halewood, Alan 263-4
Haley, Colin *art.* 70-6; 110, 122-4, 178
Half Dome (Greenland) **154**-5
Hand of Fatima (Mali) 214
Hardeol (Garhwal, India) **306**-7
Hari (Sichuan Province, China) *art.* 77-87, **81**
Harlin, John III 12
Harris, David 364-5
Harris, Mt. (Antarctica) 202-3
Hassal Hidn Pillar (Oman) **208**-11

Hasson, Max 88-9
Hawley, Elizabeth 312-13, 334-5
Hayden Spire (CO) 102
Hayes Rg. (AK) 107-9
Hayes, Mt. (AK) 107-9, **108**
Helen, Mt. (WY) 101
Helicopters 12, 312
Helling, Ruediger 159-60
Henspeter, Mark 119-20
Heritage Rg. (Antarctica) 191-6
Hermelnbjerg (Greenland) 151-3, **152-3**
Herrington, Blake 103, 128-9, 180
Herron, Punta 178
Hill, Florian 168-9
Himachal Pradesh (India) 294-301
Hindu Kush (Afghanistan) 257-62
Hiraide, Kazuya 334-5
Hoegh, Mt. (Antarctica) 202-3
Hoinkes (Antarctica) 191-6, **192**
Hokanson, Ryan 107-9
Holsten, Jens 88-9; 178
Hombori Mts. (Mali) 214
Honnold, Alex *art.* 43-8; 215-8
Hooker, Mt. (WY) 101-2
Horn, The (Paul Stern Land, Greenland) **145**-8
Horobin, Chris 287-9
Houlding, Leo 90-91
Houseman, Andy 335-6
Hovgaard Island (Antarctica) 202-3
Howard, Stuart 120-1
Howard-Bury, P. (Kyrgyzstan) 250-2, **251**
Howse P. (CAN) 137
Huaguruncho (Peru) **167**
Huantsàn Chico "Nevado
    Quillujirca" (Peru) 165-**6**
Huantsan North (Peru) **165**
Huantsan West (Peru) 165
Huetter, Ryan 176-7
Hui, Chen 353
Humla Region (Nepal) 312-14
Hyung-il, Kim 274

I
Iannilli, Roberto 165-6
Ibsti Kangri (Ladakh, India) **289**-90
Ikeda, Tsunemichi 313
Ikualari (Garhwal, India) 306-**7**
Ilgner, Arno 105
Illimani (Bolivia) **168**-9

Illumination, P. (Kyrgyzstan) **250**-2
Impossible Wall (Upernavik,
    Greenland) *art.* 24-33, **26, 28, 31**
India *art.* 58-69; 285-311
Inglis, Peter 121-2
Internacional, P. (Argentina) **175**
Iñurrategi, Alberto 272
Inverleith (Antarctica) 197-202, **201**
Ivanov, Vjacheslav 283-4
Iwai, Tsugio 339

J
Jabal Awi (Oman) 208-11
Jabal Kawr-Kawr Tower (Oman) 208-11, **210**
Jabal Yiti (Oman) 208-11, **209**
Jabet P. (Antarctica) 196-202
Jack, Rich *obit.* 377-8
Janak (Nepal) **339**
Janak Himal (Nepal) 339
Javakishvili (Georgia) 228-**30**
Jefferies Glacier (AK) 120-1
Jenkins, Mark 98-9
Jensen-Choi, Peter 346
Jervis, Steven 365-7
Jianshanzi "Jianzi P." (China) 349-50
Jianzi P. (China) *see* Jianshanzi
Jie, Gu 346
Jiwa Nala (India) 298
Jobo LeCoultre (Nepal) 325-**6**
Johnson, Dylan 115, 350-3
Johnson, Frederick O. 384-9
Johnston, Dylan 134-5
Jopuno (Sikkim, India) 308-11, **310**
Jost, Matija 306-7

K
K7 West (Pakistan) 277-84, **278, 280, 283-4**
Kameda, Hiroo 350
Kangju Kangri (Ladakh, India) **291**-2
Kangsaimathung (Ladakh, India) 285-7
Kangto (Arunachal Pradesh, India) **310**, 311
Kanti Himal (Nepal) 313
Kapadia, Harish 285, 293
Karakoram (Pakistan/China) 271-4, 340-3
Kartik (Garhwal, India) **303**-5
Karyshkyr, P. (Kyrgyzstan) 238-**40**
Kauffman, Joel 329-31
Kautz, Markus 187
Kazakhstan 232-3
Kelley, John 116-7

Kellogg, Chad 134-5, 350-3
Kensu Valley (Kyrgyzstan) 241-3; *map*243
Ketil Pyramid (Greenland) 157
Khan Tengri (Kyrgyzstan) 253-5
Kings Canyon NAT'L PARK (CA) 92-3
Kinnaur (India) 298-9
Kizilin Baci (Turkey) **204**-5
Kleslo, Michal 226-7
Klonfar, Martin 154-5
Kobayashi, Hirofumi 312-3
Koh-e-Ak Su Rg. (Afghanistan) 265-8
Koh-e-Atram 265-8, **267**
Koh-e-Baffa (Afghanistan) 258-61, **260**
Koh-e-Beefy (Afghanistan) **258**
Koh-e-Forot Zorman (Afghanistan) 258-61, **259**
Koh-e-Grivel (Afghanistan) 261-2
Koh-e-Hoppa (Afghanistan) 258-61, **259**
Koh-e-Ikiv East (Afghanistan) **265**-8
Koh-e-Ikiv West (Afghanistan) **265**-8
Koh-e-Iskander (Afghanistan) 263-**4**
Koh-e-Khar (Afghanistan) 263-**4**
Koh-e-Se Zeboi (Afghanistan) 265-8, **267**
Koh-e-Ski (Afghanistan) 261-2
Koh-e-SuzAnna (Afghanistan) 261-2
Koh-I-Baba Mts. (Afghanistan) 256-7
Koh-I-Baba Towers (Afghanistan) **256**-7
Kojichuwa Chuli (Nepal) 313
Kok-e-Wawel (Afghanistan) **265**-8
Kokshaal-too (Kyrgyzstan) 245*51
Koltunov, Oleg 283-4
Kongsberg, P. (Kyrgyzstan) 252-**3**
Kopczynski, Chris 381-2
Kruk, Jason 137-8, 178
Kuipers, Daniel 258-61
Kusum Kanguru **335**
Kvaloya Island (Norway) 219-20
Kyajo Ri (Nepal) 328
Kyashar (Nepal) 335-**6**
Kyrgyzstan 234-54
Kyu-tae, Kim 346

L
Ladakh (India) 285-92
Lama Lamani North (Sikkim, India) **308**-9
Langbu Qu (Tibet) 354-5
Laos 359-60
Larcher, Rolando 204-5
Laurel Knob (NC) 105
Lavigne, Joshua 137

Lavrinenko, Alexander 230-1
Le Petit Cheval (WA) 88-**9**
Leach, Sam 240-1
Leary, Sean *art.* 43-8
Lemaire Island (Antarctica) 196-7, 202-3
Lhotse (Nepal) **331**-2
Libecki, Mike 162-3, 256-7
Liberty Cap (Yosemite, CA) 91-**2**
Lim, David 252-3
Linder P. (Antarctica) 191-6
Lingsarmo "Pinnacle P. (India) 292-**3**
Litang Plateau (Sichuan Province,
    China) *art.* 77-87
Little Pamir (Afghanistan) 261-2
Littlejohn, Pat 212-3, 241-3
Lobuje East (Nepal) 329-31, **330**
Loehr, Aidan 347-8
Logan Mts. St. Elias Range (CAN) 127-8
Logan, Ben 243-4
Logan, Mt. (CAN) *art.* **16**-23; **125**-7
Long's Peak (CO) 103-**4**
Lopez, Camilo 296-7
Lorencic, Boris 306-7
Lucas, James 370-1
Lunag I (Nepal) **325**-6
Lyskamm (Antarctica) 191-6, **193**

M

Macartney-Snape, Tim 337-9
MacDonald, Mt. (Selkirk Mts., CAN) 132-4, **133**
Mace, Charley 367-8
Mackay, Sean 142-3
Madge, Suzy 261-2
Magro, Whit 186-7
Mahalangur Himal (Nepal) 326-37
Maiktoli (Garhwal, India) **305**
Majulah (Kyrgyzstan) **252**-3
Makalu (Nepal) 336-**7**
Makara(Sichuan Province, China) *art.* 77-87
Mali 214
Maluck, Kai 149-50
Manaslu (Nepal) 323-**4**
Manaslu Himal (Nepal) 323-4
Manon Dos (Peru) **168**
Mantok II (AK) 111
Marecek, Lukas 222
Margherita's Peak (Pakistan) **277**-9
Marie Byrd Land (Antarctica) 196
Mariposa, Valle 176-7

Markert P. (Pakistan) 269-71, **270**
Marrosu, Marco 208-11
Masherbrum Rg. (Pakistan) 275-6
Matin, Mt. (Antarctica) 197-202, **199**
Mawal Needle (Oman) 208-**11**
Maxirain, Alexander 231-2
McCarthy, Jeff 368-9
McCormick, Matt 281-2
McNamara, Chris 88-9
Melanphulan (Nepal) 332
Menitove, Ari 92-3
Menthosa (Pangi Valley, India) 294-**5**
Mermoz (Patagonia, Argentina) 178
Micheilsen, Marian 258-61
Miller, Bruce 103-4
Milne Land (Greenland) 148-9
Minya Konka Range (China) *art.* 34-42; 346-8
Mituraju (Peru) **166**-7
Miyamoto, Taki 101-2
Miyar Valley (India) 296-7
Montana (US) 98-9
Moorhead, Colin 130-31
Moose's Tooth (Ruth Gorge, AK) 112-3
Morangma 161-3, **162**
Morel Tower (Greenland) *art.* 24-33
Moretti, Bruno 294
Moro, Simone 269, 272-3, 331, 358
Moser, Sally 377-8
Moyano (Patagonia) 187
Mucci, John 91-2
Mukut Himal (Nepal) 315-6
Muni, Divyesh 289-90
Mur Samir (Kyrgyzstan) 238-41, **239**
Muryshev, Andrey 296
Mustabbes Valley (Kyrgyzstan) 241-3; *map* 243

N

Nakamura, Tamotsu *art.* 77-87;
    343-4, 346-8, 350
Nanda Khat (Garhwal, India) **305**
Nanga Parbat Rg. (Pakistan) 269-71
Nantina Point (Chugach, AK) 116, **117**
Nardi, Daniele 277-9, 332-3
Navarro North, P. (Andes, Argentina-Chile) **174**
Nemari Left (Rolwaling Himal,
    Nepal) *art.* 49-57, **51**
Nepal *art.* 49-57
Nepal 312-39; *winter ascent definition* 358
Nettle, Dave 96
Nevada (US) 98-9

Nicholson, Ian 88-9
Night Butterfly (Kyrgyzstan) **245**-7
Nilo P. (Pakistan) 269-71, **270**
Nilsson, Henrik 151-3
Nital Thaur (Garhwal, India) **306** 7
Niuxin Shan (China) **350**
Noble P. (Antarctica 196-7
Noijin Kangsang (Tibet) 356-8, **357**
Nordeide, Hege 225
Normand, Bruce *art.* 34-42; 348, 354-5
North Carolina (US) 105
North Howser Tower (CAN) **134**-5
Norway 219-25
Noshaq (Hindu Kush, Afghanistan) 257-8
Nyanchen Tanglha West (Tibet) 354-5
Nyegi Kangsang (Arunachal Pradesh, India) **311**
Nygren, Mt. (Antarctica) 197-202, **200**

O

Obra Valley (Garhwal, India) 301-2
Okada, Yasushi *art.* 16-23; 125
Oki, Masato 291-2
Oman 206-11
Omi Kangri Himal (Nepal) 337-9
Oshairak Valley (Kyrgyzstan) 243-4
Owerko, Tomasz 244-7
Ozturk, Renan 112-3; 215-8

P

P. 1,295m (Milne Land, Greenland) 148-9, **150**
P. 1,494m. (Antarctica) 195-6
P. 10,020' (AK) 111
P. 2 (Ladakh, India) 285-7, **286**
P. 2,240m (Brooks Rg., AK) 106-7
P. 2,280m (Ummannaq Region, Greenland) 144-5
P. 4,300m (Kyrgyzstan) 234-**5**
P. 4,530m (Oshairak Valley, Kyrgyzstan) 243-**4, 245**
P. 4,772m (Qilian Mts., China) 343
P. 4,880m (Qilian Mts., China) 343
P. 5,086m (Qonglai Mts., China) 350-3, **352**
P. 5,445m (Jiwa Valley, India) **298**
P. 5,480m (Garhwal, India) 301-**2**
P. 5,500m (Sikkim, India) 308-9
P. 5,600m. (Sichuan Province, China) *art.* 77-87, **83**
P. 5,625m (Uchjilga Valley, Afghanistan) 265-8, **267**

P. 5,687m. (Sichuan Province, China) *art.* 77-87, **81**
P. 5,777m (Rowaling Himal, Nepal) 325-6
P. 5,780m (India) **293**
P. 5,784m. (Sichuan Province, China) *art.* 77-87, **81**
P. 5,838m. (Sichuan Province, China) *art.* 77-87, **81**
P. 5,850m (Ladakh, India) 287-9, **288**
P. 5,851m. (Sichuan Province, China) *art.* 77-87, **83**
P. 5,860m (Pangi Valley, India) 294-**5**
P. 5,873m. (Sichuan Province, China) *art.* 77-87, **78, 85**
P. 5,912m. (Sichuan Province, China) *art.* 77-87, **84**
P. 5,926m (Shafat Glacier, India) **293**
P. 5,965m. (Sichuan Province, China) *art.* 77-87, **86**
P. 5,995m (Ladakh, India) 287-9, **288**
P. 5312m (Djangart Rg., Kyrgyzstan) **250**-2
P. 6,120m (Langbu Qu, Tibet) 354-**5**
P. 6,286m (Langbu Qu, Tibet) 354-**5**
P. 6,380m (Tibet) *see*Chorten Garpo
P. 6,382m (Langbu Qu, Tibet) 354-**5**
P. 6,614m (Tibet) *see* Sir Duk
P. 8,692' (Coast Mts., CAN) 128-9
P. James (Miyar Valley, India) 296-**7**
P.10,510' (Wrangell Mts., AK) 120
P.2,220m. North (AK) **106**
P.2,220m. South (AK) **106**
P.7,400' (Ruth Gorge, AK) 116
P.7,679' (Wrangell Mts., AK) 120-**1**
P.8,100' (Delta Rg., AK) 109
P.8,329' (Wrangell Mts., AK) 120
Pabuk Kang "Yangma" (Nepal) 337-9, **338**
Pae, Christine 274, 343
Paine Group (Patagonia) 188
Paine, North Tower 188
Pakistan 269-84
Palo Plantado, Cerro (Chile) **174**
Pamiagdluk Island (Greenland) 155-7
Pamir (Afghanistan) 261-8
Pamir-i-Wakhan (Afghanistan) 263-4
Pangi Valley (India) 294-6
Pangong Rg. (India) 291-2; *map* 292
Pantoja, Holmes 172
Panwali Dwar (Garhwal, India) **305**
Parada, Francisco 188

Parandas (Tajikistan) 230-**2**
Patagonia (Argentina-Chile) 178-88
Pathan Brakk (Pakistan) **281**-2
Patterson, Mt. (CAN) **136**-7
Paul Stern Land (Greenland) 145-8
Payne, Roger 309-11
Peary, Mt. (Antarctica) 197-202, **198, 202**
Pedra do Elefante (Brazil) **163**
Pellissier, Manu 125-7
Pennings, Mike 96-7
Peru 164-7
Peterson, Erik 107
Pfluger, Yvonne 348
Pharilapcha (Nepal) 326-**7**
Phillips, Everett 170
Phillips, Jonathan 301-2
Piergiorgio, Cerro (Patagonia, Argentina) 178
Pinnacle P. (India) *see* Lingsarmo
Pirita, Valle 176-**7**
Pitelka, Michal 178
Piunova, Anna 228, 230-2, 253-5, 328-9, 336-7
Pizem, Rob 92-3
Plucenik, Robert 382-3
Polaco North, P. (Argentina) 171-**2**
Pollone East, Cerro 180-82, **181**
Pollone, Cerro (Patagonia, Argentina) **179**-80
Powers,Phil 14-5
Prism (Sequoia NAT'L PARK, CA) 93-**4**
Prittie, Willi 118
Proboscis, Mt. (CAN) 127-8
Pruchnic, Christian William *obit.* 378-9
Puryear, Joe *art.* 49-57; 326; *obit* 371-89

Q
Qaersorssuaq Island (Greenland) 140-2
Qali-i-Hurst (Afghanistan) 258-61; *map*260
Qaqqardivaq Emanuela
   (Greenland) 149-50, **151**
Qaqqardivaq Kohler (Greenland) 149-50, **152**
Qilian Mts. (China) 343
Qinghai (China) 343
Qonglai Mts. (China) 348-53
Quemados, Los **212**-3
Quvnerit Island (Greenland) *art.* 24-33; 157

R
Raffetseder, Gerda 175
Ramada Rg. (Argentina) 171-2
Ramparts (CAN) 136

Ramsden, Paul 342-3
Ranglana (Garhwal, India) 301-**2**
Ratouis, Emmanuel 207-8
Rau, Alejandro Bonilla 175-6
Rauch, Robert 168-9
Raven P. (Kyrgyzstan) 244-**7, 246**
Ravier, Christian 206
Rawlinson, Grant 252-3
Ream, Lorna *obit.* 381-2
Red Rocks (NV) 98-9
Red Wall (Upernavik, Greenland)
   art. 24-33, **26, 28**
Reddomain (China) **347**
Renland (Greenland) 148-9
Richards, Cory 269, 272-3
Richardson, Simon 228-30
Richter, Jens 159-60, 214, 359-60
Robinson, Doug 371-2
Robson, MT (CAN) 136, **137-8**
Rock Creek Canyon (MT) 99-**100**
Rock Horse (Kyrgyzstan) 244-**7**
Rocky Mountain NAT'L PARK (CO) 102-4
Rojas P. (Antarctica) 196-7, 202-3
Rolwaling Himal (Nepal) *art.* 49-57
Romsdal (Norway) 223-5
Ronge Island (Antarctica) 197
Roraima, Monte (Venezuela) **161**
Rosa, Monte (Bolivia) 170
Rossman West (Antarctica) 191-6, **194**
Rossman, Mt. (Antarctica) 191-6, **193, 195**
Rousseau, Louis 273-4
Rowaling Himal (Nepal) 325-6
Royer, Mike 250-2
Ruck, Andy 285-7
Ruddy, Dana 136
Ruiche Gonga (China) **346**
Rundtinden (Norway) **221**-2
Rungofarka (India) **293**
Russell, Adam 238-40
Russia 226-8
Russian Tent (Altai, Russia) **226**-7
Ruth Gorge (AK) 112-6
Rutherford, Kate 182-4

S
Sable Pinnacle (Antarctica) 197
Saether, Sindre 223-4
Saipal (Nepal) 313-4, **315**
Saipal Himal (Nepal) 313-4
Sandachhe Group (Nepal) 315-**6**

Sanders, Olly 140-2
Sanderson's Hope (Greenland) **140**-2
Saturno (Bolivia) **170**
Saunders, Victor 191-6
Scanu, Marcelo 172, 175
Schaefer, Mikey 178, 182-4
Schweizerland (Greenland) 149-50
Scott, Mt. (Antarctica) 202-3
Seerdengpu (China) 350-3, **351**
Selkirk Mts. (CAN) 131-4
Senf, Thomas 178
Sentinel P. (India) **298**
Sequoia NAT'L PARK (CA) 93-4
Serkhe Khollu (Bolivia) **169**
Shackleton, Mt. (Antarctica) 197-202, **198**
Shalmuki P. (Pakistan) 269-71, **270**
Shaluli Shan (Sichuan Province,
       China) *art.* 77-87, *map* 77
Sharratt, Dave 101-2
Shepherd, Doug 99-100
Shepton Spire (Greenland) *art.* 24-33, **32**
Shepton, Bob *art.* 24-33; 157
Sherpa, Ang Tshering 328
Shimsal Region (Pakistan) 271
Shinn (Antarctica) 190
Shiva (India) **295-6**
Shiva Shankar West (India) **294**
Sichuan Province (China) *art.* 34-42,
       77-87; 343-53; *regulations* 343-4
Sidley, Mt. (Antarctica) 196
Siegrist, Stefan 178
Sierra Nevada (CA) 92-7
Siguniang Nat'l. Park (China) 348-53
Sikkim (India) 308-11
Simon, Eli 185-6
Singekang Valley (India) 300-1
Singu Chuli (Nepal) 319-**20, 321**
Sir Duk "P. 6,614m" (Langbu Qu, Tibet) **354**-5
Siula Grande (Peru) 167
Skiing: Antarctica 196-7, 202-3;
       Hindu Kush (Afghanistan) 261-2;
       Reddomain (China) 347
Slawinski, Raphael 136-7
Slowakiewicz, Wojciech 332
Smith, Zack 112-3
Snaght Kang (India) **300**-1
Snider P. (AK) 119-**20**
Snow Leopard P. (India) 298
Snowcock P. (India) 298
Sognefjord (Norway) 225
Sokolov, Gleb 253-5

Sorkin, Madaleine 127-8
Sortehul Fjord (Upernavik,
       Greenland) *art.* 24-33
Spirit Mtn. (MT) 99-**100**
Spiti Valley (India) 300-1
Squamish Chief (CAN) 130-31
St. Elias Range (CAN) *art.* 16-23; 125-7
St. Elias, Mt. (AK) 121-2
Stanhardt, Aguja (Patagonia, Argentina) 178
Stanhope, Will 131-2
Steven, Dawa 328
Stevenson, David 372-5
Stewart Valley (Baffin Island, CAN) 138-9
Suiricocha (Peru) **168**
Sulamar (China) **342**-3
Suri Tondo (Mali) 214
Sutherland, P. (Kyrgyzstan) 250-2, **251**
Svihalek, Jiri 221-2
Svobodnaya Korea (Kyrgyzstan) **234**-5
Swienton, Paul 308-9
Swinburne, David 120-1
Synnott, Mark 215-8

T
Taban Bogdo Rg. (Russia) 226-7
Tahab Canyon (Oman) 207
Tajikistan 230-2
Takargo (Nepal) *art.* **49**-57, **56**; 326
Talgar (Kazakhstan) 232-**3**
Talgar, South (Kazakhstan) 232-**3**
Tangle Ridge (CAN) 136
Tapley, Pete 101
Tasartse (Nepal) *see* Tsartse
Tasermiut Fjord (Greenland) 151-5
Tatsienlu Massif (China) **345**, 346
Tehipite Dome (CA) 92-**3**
Teixeira, Daniela 303-5
Tengri Tag (Kyrgyzstan) 253-5
Thackray, John 369-70
Thanglasgo Valley (India) 285-9
Thau, Brandon 93-4
Thulagi (Nepal) 323-**4**
Tibet 354-7
Tien Shan (China) 342-3
Tien Shan (Kazakhstan/Kyrgyzstan) 232-44
Tininnertuup III (Greenland) 151-3
Titan (Fisher Towers, UT) **98**-9
Tofel, Bartek 265-8
Toman, Jim 180-2
Torolok (Kyrgyzstan) 240-**1**, **239**
Torre Norte (Pataongia) *see* Paine, North Tower

Torre, Cerro (Patagonia, Argentina) 178
Torssukatak Fjord (Greenland) *art.* **24**-33; 157
Torugart-too (Kyrgyzstan) 235-41
Tribulation P. (India) 298
Troll Wall (Norway) 223-4
Tromso Region (Norway) 219-22
Tronador, Cerro (Argentina) **175**
Tsartse "Tasartse" (Nepal) 315-6
Tscherrig, Kaus 191-6
Tsuji, Hidenobu 317
Tsuro Ri (Nepal) 332-3, **334**
Turkey 204-5
Turner, Mike "Twid" 138-9
Turret (Selkirk Mts., CAN) **131**-2

U

Uchjilga Valley (Afghanistan) 265-8; *map 266*
Uematsu, Kazuyoshi 350
Ulrich, Thomas 148-9
Umanaq Island (Greenland) 140-2
Ummannaq Mtn. (Greenland) **142**-3
Ummannaq Region (Greenland) 142-5
Union Glacier (Antarctica) 191-6; *map 191*
United States 88-124
Upernavik (Greenland) 140-2; *map 141*
Upernavik Region (Greenland) *art.* 24-33
Upper Granite Creek (AK) 120-1
Urubko, Denis 232-3, 269, 272-3, 331-2
Utah (US) 98-9

V

Vallunaraju (Peru) **164**
Van Meegdenburg, William 319-20
Vasuki Parbat (India) *art.* 58-69, **59, 66**; 303
Venezuela 158-61
Venus P. (China) **340**-1
Vernyi, P. (Kyrgyzstan) **248**-9
Vicunita (Peru) **168**
Vidal, Sílvia 298-9
Vilhauer, Jared 115-6, 329-31
Villanueva, Sean *art.* 24-33; 90-1, 140, 178, 184
Vinkeldal (Greenland) 145-8, **147**
Vinson (Antarctica) 189-90
Vinson Massif (Antarctica) 189-90

W

Wadi el Hemia (Oman) 207
Wadi Surwayh (Oman) 208
Wadi Tiwi (Oman) 207-8
Wakhan Corridor (Afghanistan) 257-8; *map258*

Wallace, Carolyn M. 378-9
Walsh, Eamonn 136
Walsh, Jon 131-4, 137-8
Walter, Christian 269-71
Washington (US) 88-9
Waterloo (Antarctica) 191-6
Weeding, Mark 235-8
Weidner, Chris 103-4
Welshman's P. (Baffin Island, CAN) 138-9
Westman, Mark 379-81
Wharton, Josh 127, 186-7
White Tower (Laos) 359-**60**
Whitney Crest (CA) 95
Wickens, Phil 197-202
Wiencke Island (Antarctica) 202-3
Wiik, Odd-Roar 219
Wilkinson, Freddie 112-3
Wilson, Mt. (Red Rocks, NV) 98-9, 98
Windsor, Jeremy 300-1
Wrangell-St. Elias NAT'L PARK (AK) 118-22
Wright, Christopher 111
Wupingfeng (China) **345**, 346
Wynne-Jones, Dave 197-202
Wyoming (US) 101-102

X

Xiangqiuqieke (Sichuan Province,
    China) *art.* 77-87, **79**
Xiaqiangla (China) **344**-6
Xinjiang (China) 340-3
Xuelian Rg. (China) 342-3

Y

Yakawa Kang (Nepal) **317**
Yangma (Nepal) *see* Pabuk Kang
Yangmolong (Sichuan Province,
    China) *art.* 77-87, **80**
Yerupaja Grande (Peru) 166-7
Yokoyama, Katsutaka *art.* 16-23; 125
Yosemite Valley (CA) *art.* 43-8; 90-2

Z

Zailiskiy Alatau (Kazakhstan) 232-3
Zanskar (India) 292-3
Zeravshin Rg. (Tajikistan) 230-2
Zeugswetter, Bernd 95
Zhang, Jiyue 343-4
Zimmerman, Douglas Craig obit. 382-3

INTERNATIONAL GRADE COMPARISON CHART

To download the complete "American Alpine Journal International Grade Comparison Chart," including alpine and ice grades, go to: aaj.americanalpineclub.org

This chart is designed to be used with the *American Alpine Journal* to help decipher the difficulty ratings given to climbs.

Seriousness Rating:

These often modify the technical grades when protection is difficult.

R: Poor protection with potential for a long fall and some injury.

X: A fall would likely result in serious injury or death.

YDS	UIAA	FR	AUS	SAX	CIS	SCA	BRA	UK	
5.2	II	1	10	II	III	3			D
5.3	III	2	11	III	III+	3+			
5.4	IV-/IV	3	12		IV-	4			VD
5.5	IV+		13		IV	4+			S
5.6	V-	4	14		IV+	5-		4a	HS
5.7	V / V+		15	VIIa		5		4b	VS
5.8	V+ / VI-	5a	16	VIIb	V-	5+	4 / 4+	4c	HVS
5.9	VI- / VI	5b	17	VIIc		6-	5 / 5+	5a	E1
5.10a	VI / VI+	5c	18	VIIIa	V	6	6a	5b	
5.10b		6a							
5.10c	VII-	6a+	19	VIIIb		6+	6b		E2
5.10d	VII	6b	20	VIIIc	V+	7-	6c		E3
5.11a	VII+	6b+		IXa			7a	5c	
5.11b		6c	21	IXb		7	7b		
5.11c	VIII-	6c+	22	IXc	VI-	7+	7b		E4
5.11d	VIII	7a	23				7c	6a	
5.12a	VIII+	7a+	24			8-	8a		E5
5.12b		7b	25	Xa	VI	8	8b		
5.12c	IX-	7b+	26	Xb			8c		
5.12d	IX	7c	27			8+	9a	6b	E6
5.13a		7c+	28	Xc			9b		
5.13b	IX+	8a	29			9-	9c		
5.13c	X-	8a+	30			9	10a	6c	E7
5.13d	X	8b	31	XIa	VI+		10b		
5.14a		8b+	32	XIb			10c	7a	E8
5.14b	X+	8c	33						
5.14c	XI-	8c+		XIc		9+		7b	E9
5.14d	XI	9a							

YDS=Yosemite Decimal System; UIAA=Union Internationale des Associations D'Alpinisme; Fr=France/Sport; Aus=Australia; Sax=Saxony; CIS=Commonwealth of Independent States/Russia; Sca=Scandinavia; Bra=Brazil.